MAKING THE LIBERAL MEDIA

MAKING THE LIBERAL MEDIA

HOW CONSERVATIVES BUILT A
MOVEMENT AGAINST THE PRESS

A. J. BAUER

Columbia University Press
New York

Columbia University Press
Publishers Since 1893
New York   Chichester, West Sussex
cup.columbia.edu
Copyright © 2026 Columbia University Press
All rights reserved

Library of Congress Cataloging-in-Publication Data
Names: Bauer, A. J. (Andrew Joseph), 1984– author
Title: Making the liberal media : how conservatives built a movement against the press / A. J. Bauer.
Description: New York : Columbia University Press, [2026] | Includes bibliographical references and index.
Identifiers: LCCN 2025031981 (print) | LCCN 2025031982 (ebook) | ISBN 9780231218351 hardcover | ISBN 9780231218368 trade paperback | ISBN 9780231562201 ebook
Subjects: LCSH: Press and politics—United States—History—20th century | Fairness doctrine (Broadcasting)—United States—History—20th century | Conservatism—United States—History—20th century | United States—Politics and government—20th century
Classification: LCC PN4888.P6 B385 2026 (print) | LCC PN4888.P6 (ebook)
LC record available at https://lccn.loc.gov/2025031981
LC ebook record available at https://lccn.loc.gov/2025031982

Cover design: Noah Arlow
Cover image: Shutterstock (paint)

Portions of chapter 1 were initially published in *Radical History Review*.
A. J. Bauer, "Propaganda in the Guise of News: Fulton Lewis Jr. and the Origins of the Fairness Doctrine," *Radical History Review* 141 (2021): 7–29.

GPSR Authorized Representative: Easy Access System Europe, Mustamäe tee 50, 10621 Tallinn, Estonia, gpsr.requests@easproject.com

FOR MARIA

CONTENTS

INTRODUCTION 1

1. THE FAIRNESS DOCTRINE AND ITS SUBTEXTS 22

2. THE PROGRESSIVE ORIGINS OF CONSERVATIVE PRESS CRITICISM 44

3. CULTIVATING A CONSERVATIVE CRITICAL DISPOSITION TOWARD THE PRESS 66

4. BEYOND BUCKLEY 93

5. LIBERAL MEDIA GOES MAINSTREAM 119

6. CONSERVATIVE PRESS CRITICISM AND THE NEW RIGHT 141

7. THE END OF FAIRNESS 161

CONCLUSION 182

Acknowledgments 197
Notes 201
Selected Bibliography 255
Index 267

MAKING THE LIBERAL MEDIA

INTRODUCTION

On January 20, 2025, Donald J. Trump was sworn in for a second term as US president. Among the dignitaries in the Capitol Rotunda, in a section commonly reserved for government officials and family members, sat a row of some of the richest men in the world: Mark Zuckerberg, Jeff Bezos, and Elon Musk.

Four years earlier, when Trump supporters scrawled "MURDER THE MEDIA" on a US Capitol door during a failed attempt at preventing the certification of Joe Biden's 2020 presidential election, they likely had at least two of those men in mind. Zuckerberg, founding CEO of Meta (Facebook, Instagram, WhatsApp) had imposed guardrails on his social media sites to mitigate the sorts of hate speech and misinformation that were widely (if dubiously) credited with helping Trump win the White House in 2016. Bezos, founding CEO of Amazon and owner of *The Washington Post*, had positioned his paper diametrically against Trump during his first term under the slogan "Democracy Dies in Darkness."

But by 2024 the media headwinds had shifted demonstrably rightward. Musk bought Twitter in 2022, rebranding it X and lifting the platform's previous bans on Trump and various other right-wing agitators. Following Trump's 2024 election victory, Zuckerberg named Trump supporter and Ultimate Fighting Championship CEO Dana White to Meta's board and shuttered the company's fact checking unit—clear signals that Meta was ready to "Make America Great Again." Bezos stopped *The*

Washington Post from endorsing Democrat Kamala Harris in 2024. And in February 2025 he announced that the *Post*'s Opinion Page would be adopting a new editorial stance oriented around supporting and defending "personal liberties and free markets."[1] Reacting to the newly emergent right-wing mainstream media environment, The New York Times Pitchbot, a social media parody account joked: "The Washington Post and LA Times editorial pages have gone full MAGA, MSNBC has purged all of its anti-Trump anchors, and Twitter is owned by a literal Nazi. Here's why liberal media bias is still a problem."[2]

Critics of conservatism have long suggested that the "liberal media" claim represents little more than an attempt to "work the refs" in the conservative movement's favor or serves as "flak" designed to discipline the mainstream news media against growing too critical of capitalism or US imperialism.[3] Such metaphors overlook the long-standing and entrenched conflict between the modern conservative movement and the press, and how that conflict has shaped the lived reality of conservatives at the grassroots. *Making the Liberal Media* shows how that conflict emerged. As we will see, from the modern conservative movement's earliest formations in the late 1940s to Trump's authoritarian return to power in 2025, belief in structural liberal media bias has played a central and constitutive role in the formation of modern conservative identity and movement strategy. It has also profoundly altered our media culture, giving rise to a distinct right-wing media sector that is actively competing with professional journalism over the cultural authority to tell the "true" story of public life.[4]

TAKING CONSERVATIVE PRESS CRITICISM SERIOUSLY

In the years since Trump took (then lost, then regained) power, historians of conservatism have struggled to situate him. Writing in *The New York Times Magazine* not long after Trump's first presidential inauguration in 2017, historian Rick Perlstein described how the prevailing historical narrative of the modern conservative movement had failed to anticipate Trump. That narrative, which Perlstein himself has documented over the course of four volumes, often begins in 1955 with William F. Buckley Jr.'s founding of the *National Review* and culminates with the Reagan

Revolution in 1980.⁵ It is an ascension narrative wherein a small but committed group of conservative activists built movement infrastructure to roll back the New Deal and ultimately wrest control over the Republican Party. Those activists promoted a new "fusionist" conservatism, which blended traditionalist beliefs about religion and social hierarchy with neoliberal economic theory and militant anticommunism. They also engaged in a vigorous form of respectability politics, seeking mainstream approval by tempering illiberal and racist rhetoric and distancing themselves from so-called fringe groups like the John Birch Society and from more avowed white supremacists, from Citizens Councils in the South to the Ku Klux Klan and White Power movements more nationally. In defining their object of study, historians of modern conservatism have largely reinforced the mainstream/fringe distinction that enabled the movement itself to gain momentum.⁶ To correct this oversight, Perlstein called for increased attention to "conservative history's political surrealists and intellectual embarrassments, its con artists and tribunes of white rage."⁷

As a corrective, historians have rightly turned their focus on the losers of internecine movement conflicts, whose ideas and power persisted at the margins—most notably paleoconservative figures like Pat Buchanan, whose failed runs for the presidency in 1992, 1996, and 2000 were vital precursors to Trump's xenophobic campaign strategies in 2016, 2020, and 2024.⁸ New works on the John Birch Society have rightly pointed to the group's long and enduring role in cultivating conspiracist thinking among the conservative grassroots—pushing back on an earlier conventional wisdom that their influence had waned following Buckley's famed denunciation of group leader Robert Welch in 1962.⁹ John Huntington has even challenged the validity of the mainstream/fringe distinction itself, pointing to deep interconnectivity between the movement's paragons of respectability and its ideological extremists, artfully demonstrating how modern conservatism as we know it was produced in dialogue between the two. "The reality was that ideological, tactical, and organizational overlaps blurred the line dividing the far right from the conservative mainstream," Huntington writes. "The difference between the radicals and the respectables was one of degree, not kind."¹⁰

Making the Liberal Media emphasizes yet another vital throughline connecting radicals and respectables, a persistent aspect of modern conservatism shared by William F. Buckley and Donald J. Trump alike—antipathy toward the mainstream press. Despite its seeming coherence, modern conservatism has long been plagued by deep contradictions and internal conflicts.[11] Its main themes and policy imperatives have always been historically contingent, emerging dialectically between the defense of traditional social hierarchies and advocacy for laissez-faire capitalism (which at times threatens those hierarchies), between authoritarian and libertarian impulses, between nationalist and internationalist visions, between elitist and populist vernaculars.[12] Conservatives have often avoided these internal tensions by defining themselves and their beliefs against an external enemy—as we will see, for instance, the modern conservative movement was anticommunist before it was "conservative." There has been no foil for the modern conservative movement as enduring and productive as the "liberal media."[13]

In her great book on the "first generation" of modern conservative media activists, Nicole Hemmer follows a circle of figures orbiting Buckley, depicting them as the movement's "architects." She contends that these activists are the authors of the "liberal media" claim. "The consequences of their leadership were profound. First and foremost: media activists crafted and popularized the idea of liberal media bias," Hemmer writes. "We have grown so used to this claim that it is hard to comprehend just how radical an idea it was in the 1940s and 1950s. After all, this was an era when institutional neutrality was considered the special genius of the American system."[14] While it is true, as Hemmer writes, that there was a great fixation among prominent Cold War–era intellectuals with promoting liberalism as a "vital center," to be defended at all costs against communists on the left and "pseudo-conservatives" on the right, that vision never adequately described political reality.[15]

As it happens, the idea of structural media bias was hardly a radical idea by the late 1940s. Although initially relegated to left corners of the labor movement and muckrakers like George Seldes, the idea that the press was biased against the New Deal and in favor of the interests of big business became increasingly mainstream throughout the 1940s—thanks to the progressive media reform movement, whose history has been well documented by Victor Pickard.[16] Indeed, Buckley and his colleagues were less architects than reverse engineers—they obsessed over the effective organizing tactics of communists and liberals alike and set about building conservative corollaries. The American Conservative Union, for example, was explicitly modeled after Americans for Democratic Action, a prominent liberal advocacy group founded in 1947. Even the *National Review* was designed as a peer of liberal ideas magazines like *The Nation* and *New Republic*. As we will see, the modern conservative movement has also been profoundly shaped by ex-leftists whose personal politics drifted to the right.[17] These converts brought tactical and practical political lessons with them as they shifted rightward—including notions of structural media bias.

When we narrate the modern conservative movement as a coherent, tight-knit network of activists who authored their own destiny and reshaped US political culture, we give them more credit and historical agency than they are due. Modern conservatism emerged out of conflict with its left and liberal counterparts—not only in opposition but also through tactical borrowing and conceptual appropriation. The conservative movement capitalized on the affordances of regulations and rhetorical tactics that were authored and implemented by their political foes. Likewise, the liberal media was not self-consciously "crafted" by conservative media activists. It was a by-product of real and entrenched political conflict between the modern conservative movement and the press. That conflict drove conservative tendencies toward media criticism and toward building a robust alternative media system. Such media activism became both a practical concern for conservatives seeking to expand their reach and popularity and an animating vision that helped the movement smooth over internal disputes. As internecine ideological conflicts arose, threatening to sow disunity, mutual hostility toward the mainstream press held conservatism together.

The liberal media has no single author. As a discourse, it is both concentrated and diffuse—structuring common sense while evading attempts at determining linear causality. The liberal media as we know it today is better understood as having accrued over time. It is the result of thousands, perhaps millions, of claims and counterclaims—allegations of bias, of fellow traveling, of conspiracy, of bad faith, of culture warfare, of epistemological crisis.[18] Documenting such a sprawling and amorphous object has required more than a decade of research. This book draws on primary source material—correspondence, unpublished manuscripts, ephemera— housed at more than twenty archives around the United States, from the Ronald Reagan Presidential Library in California to the National Archives and Records Administration in Maryland, from the L. Tom Perry Special Collections at Brigham Young University in Utah to a privately held collection in Birmingham, Alabama. It is based on extensive periodical research with more than three dozen movement and mainstream media outlets spanning the 1930s through the 1980s. Given the sheer volume of conservative press criticism and the near-constant (and ongoing) conflict between the modern conservative movement and mainstream press outlets, however, no examination of the liberal media can ever be truly exhaustive.

Rather than attempting to document all instances of the liberal media claim, this book focuses on how conservatives came to believe that the media was biased against them. It narrates the key figures, organizations, and conflicts, whose combined efforts resulted in a distinctly conservative critical disposition toward the press. Unlike countless works—left, right, and academic—that aim to prove or disprove the existence of the liberal media, this book is agnostic as to whether structural media bias exists, either for or against liberalism.[19] Not only is there no objective or impartial means of definitively answering that question, attempting to answer it only perpetuates the discourse that gives the liberal media claim its power.[20] It does not matter, for this book's purposes, whether structural media bias empirically exists—as a claim and discourse, the liberal media has been profoundly influential both within and beyond the modern conservative movement. I show how the *idea* of liberal media bias has been more historically consequential than any given instance of putatively biased reporting.

There is a critical strain of left and liberal writing about conservative media that engages from a "paranoid position."[21] This tendency—which was popularized by progressive media reformers in the 1940s—focuses on the unspoken or underlying motivations of conservative media activists and somewhat ironically mirrors common conspiratorial interpretive strategies on the right. Books like David Brock's *The Republican Noise Machine* (2004) and Jen Senko's *The Brainwashing of My Dad* (2021), exemplars of this genre, focus on "secret" memos and other internal movement communications to reify what Hillary Rodham Clinton once called a "vast right-wing conspiracy" against liberalism and its leading public figures. These and similar works assume that their audience is unaware of the robust conservative movement and media infrastructure that surrounds us, plain as day.[22] They suggest that if we only knew that the liberal media claim was a billionaire plot, we would reject it and the right-wing media who have emerged to promulgate it—turn off talk radio and Fox News or at least consume them with a generous dash of salt. The historical record suggests otherwise.

In researching the origins and historical development of conservative press criticism in the United States, I was repeatedly struck not by the secret machinations of activists and billionaires (although I found plenty of that too) but by how transparently conservatives wrote about the epistemological stakes of their political projects. The history of modern conservatism is replete with metacommentary about the disconnect between the world as depicted in journalistic accounts of the news of the day and the putative realities of the free market and supposed inevitabilities of social hierarchy on the lines of race, gender, sexuality, and class. Conservatives in the 1930s and 1940s knew they were losing the battle over how to comprehend the world and the news through which regular people come to know it. With varying degrees of pessimism and optimism, they openly and publicly theorized how to win over public opinion to their interpretation of reality. They funded and built organizations and media outlets to realize this vision.

Interestingly, the tendency—among progressive media critics and professional investigative journalists—toward exposing the funding models and motivations beneath the surface of those conservative projects *itself* stoked conflicts that created the conditions of possibility for realizing the vision of conservative media activists. Unlike paranoid accounts that ascribe almost superhuman agency to conservative movement figures and funders, I read conservative media activists as fundamentally opportunistic—taking advantage of political, regulatory, and discursive interventions that they did not create and never fully controlled. Conservative media activists may have made the liberal media, but they did not make it as they pleased.

This book shows how conflict with the press has been a central and constitutive element of conservative identity and movement mobilization from the very beginning. The idea of liberal media bias is the most tangible, even ubiquitous, result of this decades-long conflict. I am by no means claiming that other factors—conflicts, ideas, psychological dispositions—have not *also* played pivotal, even deterministic, roles in the formation of modern conservatism.[23] The conservative movement has waged many ideological and policy battles in its eighty-plus years of existence. Its earliest formations were largely focused on protecting the class interests of wealthy businessmen who opposed federal investment in social welfare programs, organized labor, and Keynesian economics. Race, and defense of white supremacy, has also been a driving motivation of the modern conservative movement from its outset.[24] The movement's search for respectability coincided with the rise in public prominence of the civil rights movement, which forced conservatives to navigate rapidly shifting popular understandings of race and cultural norms surrounding the expression of anti-Black racism.[25] Carefully calibrated conservative racial politics, known as the "Southern Strategy," ultimately effected party realignment and enabled the movement's capture of the Republican Party.[26] Its calculated embrace of colorblind racial rhetoric to defend the imperatives of white supremacy have given rise to significant support within certain Latino and Asian American contexts.[27] Modern conservatism's rise can also be attributed to its defenses of gender and sexual hierarchies, particularly from the 1960s onward as second-wave feminism and queer liberation movements elevated critiques of patriarchy, compulsory heterosexuality, and the gender binary.[28] Despite, or perhaps because of, its defense of gender hierarchy, the modern conservative movement has long attracted white women as leaders and organizers.[29]

What distinguishes conservatism's battle against the press from these other political identitarian factors is that it is embedded in every other discrete policy and ideological struggle. Part of conservatism's opposition to the civil rights movement and its defense of white supremacy involved criticizing media coverage of that movement and its impacts on broader racial discourse. Anticommunism may have been the ideological tie that bound Cuban exiles to modern conservatism, but their alliance was forged through acts of media activism.[30] Modern conservatism's abstract opposition to equal gender rights was exemplified in Phyllis Schlafly's successful crusade against the Equal Rights Amendment, which often took the form of complaints to the Federal Communications Commission (FCC) designed to force antifeminist narratives into mainstream news coverage. Conservative support of laissez-faire capitalism and hawkish military interventions against communism served as a foundation for Accuracy in Media's decades of complaints that the press was biased against US business and military interests. So, while conservatism is not reducible to its conflict with the press, that conflict imbues and lends structure to all other conflicts. In this way, the liberal media claim is foundational to modern conservatism—not enough to explain how it works in full, but a factor in every battle against its many enemies.

Since its earliest iterations, the modern conservative movement has attributed the unpopularity of its political ideals to a rift between the reality of daily occurrences and conditions and the reported news of the day. In each generation, conservatism is redefined anew in dialogue between the ideologies devised and curated by movement intellectuals and commentators and the current events that frame those ideologies' implementation and capacity for explanation. In historicizing the conservative critical disposition toward the press, *Making the Liberal Media* illuminates a vital mechanism in the reproduction of conservatism as a political identity whose breadth otherwise defies neat social categorization or ideological definition. It suggests that conservatives come to identify with one another in part based upon shared assumptions about the press's unwillingness or inability to adequately convey lived reality.

THE ORIGINS OF THE LIBERAL MEDIA

Before the liberal media, there was the *reactionary* media—a common sense within the United States in the 1930s and 1940s that newspapers and, increasingly, radio stations were skewing their news coverage and commentary toward the political right. This concept of structural right-wing media bias resulted from a historical confluence of distinct, if intersecting, lines of scholarly inquiry, press criticism, and political imperatives. In the years following World War I, progressive journalists, scholars, and educators in the United States became concerned at the ability of propagandists to manipulate public sentiments. This anxiety, which historians have called "propaganda consciousness," spurred new theories of democracy, public opinion, and media effects. Debates over these theories, which coincided with the development of commercial radio and later television, proved foundational to the burgeoning academic discipline of mass communication.[31] They also laid the political, cultural, and regulatory foundations that would give rise to a distinctly conservative critical disposition toward the press.

In the 1940s liberal and left media critics diagnosed a "newspaper crisis" in the United States resulting from a decades-long trend within the industry toward the concentration of ownership and reduction of intracity competition. The number of newspapers in the United States peaked in the first decade of the twentieth century and has declined ever since—2,600 dailies were published in 1909, only 1,998 in 1940.[32] During roughly that same period the average number of newspapers per city dwindled from 4 to 2.6.[33] Those fewer newspapers were increasingly owned by chains (as opposed to being owned locally). In 1900 the nine newspaper chains in operation owned only 1 percent of all daily newspapers. By 1940 the number of chains had grown to fifty-six, and their newspapers accounted for 15.7 percent of all daily newspapers in the United States, which meant that nearly a quarter of all newspaper readers received their daily news from a chain.[34] All told, more people were getting their news from fewer sources owned and controlled by fewer people, and the public was beginning to notice—in part due to the efforts of watchdogs like leftist media critic George Seldes and media reformers like ACLU attorney Morris L. Ernst, whose 1946 book *The First Freedom* proved highly influential among media reform-minded liberals.[35]

Growing liberal distrust of the mainstream press in the 1940s was also a reaction against the newspaper industry for its opposition to various social reform projects that constituted the New Deal in the 1930s. During his presidency, Franklin Roosevelt was fond of claiming that "85 percent" of newspapers opposed his administration. While historians have since shown that number to be hyperbolic, newspaper studies conducted during his administration did find some evidence of antagonism. The belief that the press was against him influenced, and was used to justify, the Roosevelt administration's reliance upon radio as the cornerstone of its media strategy, often remembered in the form of the president's famed "fireside chats." Roosevelt's success utilizing the broadcast medium was based on both his skill as an orator and the favorable treatment extended by radio networks. The FCC was founded in 1934 and, to curry favor as a hedge against federal intervention in the broadcast industry, the networks donated airtime for presidential speeches and, with some notable exceptions, tended to air programs supportive of New Deal efforts.[36]

By the mid-1940s common sense in the United States held that print media tended toward conservatism and a reactionary stance against the New Deal, while radio tended to be a safer media environment for more liberal commentators, ideas, and interpretations of daily events. However, by the late 1940s a series of high-profile firings of liberal radio commentators stoked fears of total right-wing domination of the media. These conditions led to a series of regulatory efforts under the Roosevelt administration, including a Justice Department investigation into the Associated Press, which led to a Supreme Court decision extending antitrust provisions to the newspaper industry, and the FCC scrutinizing whether newspapers should be allowed to own radio stations.[37] They also resulted in efforts by liberal intellectuals to reform journalism as a profession, chief among them the Commission on Freedom of the Press, also known as the Hutchins Commission, an endeavor launched in 1942 and led by University of Chicago chancellor Robert M. Hutchins. The commission outlined new social responsibilities to which it called upon press owners and managers to adhere. In addition to advocating for more accurate and objective reporting of the news, the report appealed to the "fairness" of owners, imploring them to admit their political biases and actively counterbalance them.[38] As we will see in chapter 1, this progressive media reform era culminated with the FCC issuing its Fairness Doctrine in 1949. The Fairness Doctrine required all broadcast licensees to dedicate airtime to the discussion of issues of public concern and in a way that granted the public a "reasonable opportunity to hear different opposing positions."[39]

While progressives strove for fairness and balance in hopes that media regulations might ensure some modicum of liberal perspectives over the airwaves and in the mainstream press, the forebearers of the modern conservative movement (often labeled the Old Right by historians) were cultivating a propaganda consciousness of their own. In the fall of 1937, as an influential group of progressives were forming the Institute for Propaganda Analysis to combat commercial and fascist propaganda both at home and abroad, the *American Mercury* magazine was busy exposing the propaganda techniques used by the Roosevelt administration to promote the New Deal.[40] Then under the ownership of conservative Paul Palmer, the *Mercury* was an influential platform for antilabor, anti–New Deal commentary. Its writers often waxed philosophical, lamenting the epistemological headwinds facing conservatives in an era when leftists and liberals were aligned in a popular front.[41] In an essay titled "The United Afront," published alongside the *Mercury*'s propaganda analysis in 1937, Ernest Boyd wrote, "In a world half-mad with fear and hatred, in which all intellectual, spiritual, and esthetic values are being destroyed, our ears are deafened by the discordant cries and the irreconcilable claims of sects, parties, races, and nations, whose zealots and their cowed devotees profess to be in possession of absolute Truth and Justice and demand that the world recognize the special superiority thereby conferred onto them."[42]

Albert Jay Nock, a dour but influential right-libertarian who had a monthly column in the *Mercury*, praised Boyd's assessment of the epistemological perils of modernity and linked Roosevelt's liberal reforms with the looming specter of totalitarianism in Europe. Totalitarianism, according to Nock, capitalized not only on the slippage of meaning attendant with modernity but upon flaws inherent to human nature itself: "Without exception the human being has always found it easier to feel than to act, and both much easier than to think."[43] Nock believed that only a privileged few are endowed with the capacity for contemplative thought. A year earlier, writing in the *Atlantic Monthly*, he had named these privileged few "the Remnant." An assemblage of right-thinking individuals whose ears are not attuned to techniques of mass persuasion, the Remnant, in Nock's view, was ultimately responsible for the salvation of the masses, which on their own were fundamentally incapable of rational discernment.[44] Nock's assessment was emblematic of a broader pessimism among conservative opponents of the New Deal who struggled to win over public opinion to belief in free markets and limited government. In their 1948 self-help book *How to Be Popular, Though Conservative*, Fred G. Clark and Richard Stanton Rimanoczy wrote, "As a conservative, you must constantly bear in mind that your arguments are psychologically handicapped by the very nature of man. You are selling economic morality which in the long run is essentially in the public good. But you are competing with economic immorality (in plain English, *looting*) which in the short run offers an escape from economic reality."[45] In short: New Deal-era conservatives saw social welfare liberalism not merely as bad policy but as an epistemological threat—an attack on the public's ability to know and comprehend the world.

Faced with the stubborn unpopularity of their interpretation of reality, businessmen and other opponents of the New Deal focused their energies on supporting neoliberal intellectuals and economic education initiatives designed to build credibility for their worldview within the academy and among the public.[46] They also began targeting the press. In 1938 the antilabor Constitutional Educational League launched a newsletter called *Headlines, and What's Behind Them*. Edited by Joseph P. Kamp, *Headlines* is perhaps the first instance of modern conservative press criticism. Composed of several pages of news commentary and briefs designed to add right-anticommunist context to news developments pertaining to labor unions and New Deal agencies, Kamp positioned *Headlines* as a corrective to "an avalanche of Red and Communist publications." Its slogan, "All the Facts That Should Be Printed," was a nod and implied corrective to *The New York Times*'s "All the News That's Fit to Print." Kamp's stated mission was to "acquaint the public with the *true facts* behind the many stories in the news these days which have Communist implications."[47] These Old Right initiatives laid the groundwork for the postwar conservative movement by giving it its animating purpose—building the educational, media, and journalistic infrastructure to make their ideological worldview seem like empirical reality.

The Second Red Scare, more commonly known as McCarthyism, was a crucial bridge between the Old Right and new, as we will see in chapter 2. The mid-to-late 1940s saw the emergence of new right-anticommunist periodicals like *Human Events* and *Plain Talk*. As the US government shifted away from its wartime alliance with the Soviet Union and into the Cold War, these journals helped draw left anti-Stalinist writers and critics rightward—and structural media criticism followed. Fear of Soviet infiltration resulted in a proliferation of anticommunist research organizations, often employing former FBI agents. One such group, American Business Consultants, kept extensive records on wide swaths of liberal and left intellectuals, educators, and journalists. They published a newsletter, *Counterattack*, that in the late 1940s engaged in the sort of guilt by association, red-baiting, and character assassination that would become the hallmarks of Senator Joseph McCarthy's infamous hearings in the early 1950s.

In 1950 American Business Consultants published *Red Channels*, a radio and television industry blacklist, which quoted FBI Director J. Edgar Hoover's 1947 warning to Congress that the Communist Party had "departed from depending upon the printed word as its medium of propaganda and has taken to the air. Its members and sympathizers have not only infiltrated the airwaves but they are now persistently seeking radio channels."[48] The McCarthy era had a devastating impact on the left in the United States, destroying the conditions of possibility of the Popular Front and effectively salting the earth to inhibit future left–liberal collaboration. It also relegated many leading left media critics, including most notably George Seldes, to the margins of public life. By raising suspicion that liberal and progressive media professionals may be, wittingly or unwittingly, spreading Soviet propaganda, McCarthy-era right-anticommunist media activism laid a foundation of general distrust of mainstream media upon which the modern conservative movement was built.

The 1950s saw a rapid growth of media activist initiatives on the right, although not yet united under the label "conservatism." Anticommunist evangelical broadcasters like Carl McIntire and Billy James Hargis fused fundamentalist Christianity with a defense of capitalism, but their prejudiced and wildly conspiratorial claims limited their appeal. While somewhat idiosyncratic and uncoordinated, these "ultra" conservatives (self-identified as "superpatriots") proved a useful foil against which modern conservative respectability politics were defined.[49] That project began in 1951 when Texas oilman H. L. Hunt bankrolled Facts Forum. Like many conservatives in the 1940s, Hunt was concerned by the overwhelming popular support for progressive taxation and governmental regulation of the economy. He initially suggested rebranding *conservatism* as *constructivism*, a term he believed to have an inherently positive meaning.

But, as chapter 3 will show, Hunt was also concerned with changing the "strangely warped minds" who supported social democracy at home and abroad. He proposed Facts Forum as a nonpartisan organization "whose membership may comprise sincere and open-minded members of all political parties or adherents to any philosophy of government so long as they dedicate themselves to securing, listing and using facts." Doing so, according to Hunt, required securing, "impartial presentation of all the news through all news channels concerning issues of public interest." Hunt framed this ideal impartiality as beset on both sides by political ideologues, and he tasked Facts Forum with advocating for the public's entitlement "to the facts on both sides of all issues," noting that it "cannot be pacified with the part and kind of news which Left Wing workers or Right Side partisans are willing to let them have."⁵⁰

Initially a loosely coordinated series of discussion groups where participants were encouraged to debate "both sides" of issues of public concern, Facts Forum was quickly adapted into radio and television programming with national reach. These programs, nominally balanced but rhetorically slanted to favor conservative perspectives over liberal ones, were freely available as educational programming to any broadcaster looking to fulfill the FCC's newly issued Fairness Doctrine requirement. When Ben Bagdikian, then an investigative reporter at *The Providence Journal-Bulletin*, published an exposé of Facts Forum as a right-wing front at the end of 1953, it sparked an ongoing conflict between the conservative movement and the press, giving rise to mutual distrust. By 1954 Facts Forum was playing defense against what its supporters perceived as an unrelentingly hostile press. In its final two years of existence, Facts Forum appealed to a conservative audience that felt underserved and even targeted by mainstream media outlets. It platformed conservative activists who would soon play crucial roles in building the modern conservative movement, including professor and writer Medford Evans (later a John Birch Society organizer) and even a young William F. Buckley Jr.

Buckley is often depicted as a founder of modern conservatism, and not without reason. In 1955 he and William Rusher founded the *National Review*, a magazine that served as the movement's central mouthpiece for much of the mid- to late twentieth century. Inspired by Nock's concept of the Remnant—although reinterpreting it as a vanguard charged with forging a conservatism with wider appeal—Buckley positioned the *National Review* and the modern conservative movement itself as an underdog pushing back against liberal hegemony. "*National Review* is out of place, in the sense that the United Nations and the League of Women Voters and *The New York Times* and Henry Steele Commager are in place," Buckley wrote in the magazine's mission statement in the fall of 1955. "It is out of place because, in its maturity, literate America rejected conservatism in favor of radical social experimentation."⁵¹ Hemmer has argued that Buckley, along with Rusher, book publisher Henry Regnery, and radio commentator Clarence Manion, represented a "first generation" of postwar conservative media activists.⁵² The group surrounding these men played a particularly consequential role in the Republican Party's decision to run Arizona senator and conservative darling Barry Goldwater as its presidential nominee in 1964, and in crafting a respectable conservatism that eventually found its standard-bearer in Ronald Reagan. This group also built the initial infrastructure of the modern conservative movement, from the American Conservative Union to Young Americans for Freedom.

But, as chapter 4 will show, understanding the origins of the liberal media claim also requires attending to less reputable wings of modern conservatism—groups and figures relegated to the "fringe" by Buckley and established movement groups. In 1958, two years after the fall of Facts Forum, businessman Robert Welch founded the John Birch Society. Modeled after communist vanguard groups, the Birchers were militantly opposed to both the Soviet Union and the civil rights movement—believing the two were in cahoots. They contended that communists had subverted most mainstream institutions, from the United Nations to the US Supreme Court, from universities to the press. As Welch wrote in his *Blue Book* explaining the group's mission, "With the metropolitan press and big circulation general periodicals not only largely denied to us, but in many cases either consciously or blindly promoting the Communist line, we need to use every feasible channel to get more of the truth over to more of the American people."[53]

The Birchers established anticommunist lending libraries, promoted avowedly conservative periodicals and radio commentators, and organized letter-writing campaigns to ensure that politicians and newspaper editors would feel the pressure of their conservative constituents and readers. By the early 1960s the Birchers and other anticommunist groups like the Minutemen militias and Fred Schwarz's Christian Anti-Communism Crusade had attracted considerable press scrutiny for their outlandish conspiratorial claims.[54] Crackdowns on right-wing radio broadcasters during the Kennedy and Johnson administrations stoked conservative animosity against the FCC.[55] Supporters of those targeted conservative groups and broadcasters interpreted such scrutiny as evidence to justify their belief that mainstream media was structurally biased against them.[56]

Concerned that elites and the public at large would associate these so-called fringe groups with modern conservatism more broadly, Buckley sought to relegate them to his movement's margins. In 1962 he denounced Robert Welch in the pages of *National Review*.[57] Less publicly, Buckley also insisted on excluding John Birch Society leaders from participating in movement-affiliated groups. Marginalizing the Birchers was literally the first order of business for the American Conservative Union, after electing leaders and approving bylaws in late 1964.[58] While Buckley succeeded at helping to stigmatize the group among conservative elites and the public more broadly, it persists to this day. From the "fringe," the John Birch Society has played a crucial role in fostering a conservative critical disposition toward the press at the grassroots—engaging in concerted campaigns against CBS News and regularly publishing criticism of other media outlets both in nationally circulating magazines like *American Opinion* and *Review of the News* and by way of syndication in hyperlocal right-anticommunist newspapers.

Initially cultivated among ideologically driven conservative activists, the liberal media claim gained popular salience in the late 1950s and early 1960s as the civil rights movement seized mainstream media attention.[59] The notion of an elite cabal of leftists controlling media to serve their personal and political ends had always relied upon old antisemitic logics.[60] But as television news cameras documented the nonviolent civil disobedience of Black freedom protestors alongside white police and vigilante violence, the liberal media claim became a cover for a new formation of white identity politics. White audiences, initially in the US South and Sunbelt and later in so-called ethnic enclaves in Northern cities like Philadelphia, Boston, and Brooklyn, bristled at the gap between the spectacular violence against Black protestors on television and the subtler forms of white supremacy within their own largely segregated communities.[61] While mainline conservatives like Buckley and "fringe" groups like the Birchers navigated the politics of white supremacy differently, both depicted the mainstream news media as overly sympathetic to Black freedom protestors. This narrative grew in salience throughout the 1960s as antiwar, Black Power, second-wave feminist, and queer liberation movements pushed for revolutionary changes in US society and political culture. By the late 1960s the Nixon administration amplified the perception that the "Big 3" television networks (CBS, NBC, ABC) were not merely covering but *promoting* these movements. Vice President Spiro Agnew famously denounced the networks in a November 1969 speech, helping cement the "liberal media" as a foil against Nixon's "great silent majority."[62]

The 1970s saw a new institutionalization of the liberal media claim both by and beyond the modern conservative movement, as we will see in chapter 5. Accuracy in Media (AIM), a watchdog group founded in 1969, began documenting "liberal bias" in mainstream news outlets. Initially framing their work as impartial, AIM participated in a broader reassessment of professional journalism. Due to a confluence of factors—ranging from television coverage of the Vietnam War to newspaper reporting on Watergate—scholars began diagnosing a burgeoning "credibility crisis" facing working journalists. Major public opinion polling operations, like Pew and Gallup, started assessing public "trust in journalism" in the 1970s. The National News Council (1973–1984) was formed to serve as an independent ombudsperson. In 1985 major newspaper companies, the American Society of Newspaper Editors, and the Associated Press Managing Editors Association sponsored surveys of public attitudes regarding the press. Their concern was heightened by a series of press controversies in the early 1980s, including the journalistic fabrications of *Washington Post* reporter Janet Cooke and Gen. William C. Westmoreland's libel lawsuit against CBS News—both of which were highly publicized by AIM. While the surveys produced conflicting results, longitudinal studies show a persistent decline in public trust in mass media—especially among self-identified conservatives—throughout the latter quarter of the twentieth century and—now—well into the twenty-first.[63]

AIM's activism—news releases, letters to editors, FCC complaints, and shareholder resolutions—helped make media bias an explicit conservative movement cause. As we will see chapter 6, this dovetailed with a broader shift in movement strategy in the 1970s, pushed by activists like Lee Edwards, Phyllis Schlafly, Paul Weyrich, and Richard Viguerie. Self-branded as the "New Right," these activists used direct mail to target cross-pressured voters, mobilizing them to support conservatism more broadly by appealing to their interests in distinct issues. Media bias became one among many such single-issue campaigns, which included opposition to abortion and the Equal Rights Amendment, antipathy toward desegregation busing and the end of US control over the Panama Canal, and support for religious liberties and easier access to firearms. New Right advocacy often involved drawing strong contrasts with mainstream reporting of these and other pet issues.

Several book-length efforts also contributed to increasing perceptions of liberal media bias—including Edith Efron's *The News Twisters* (1971) and Kevin Phillips's *Mediacracy* (1975). The latter, which posited the rise of a postindustrial liberal knowledge elite, couched long-standing conservative fears of press and broadcast bias in the language of cutting-edge social science. Phillips contended that the primary political conflict of his time was evident in the competing worldviews of putatively liberal media producers and presumably conservative, white, middle-class media consumers.[64] By 1980, when Ronald Reagan's election to the presidency solidified the modern conservative movement as an entrenched force in US political culture, the idea of structural liberal media bias was no longer a fringe or conspiratorial belief. It was increasingly an object of study, analysis, and debate. In 1981 political sociologists S. Robert Lichter and Stanley Rothman published a highly influential study in *Public Opinion* titled "Media and Business Elites." Based on interviews with print and broadcast journalists working at national outlets, they identified the "media elite" as overwhelmingly white, male, highly educated, and Democratic in their voting habits. A book-length expansion of their findings, *The Media Elite: America's New Powerbrokers*, was published in 1986, prompting conservative acclaim and, perhaps more importantly, prolonged scholarly engagement.[65]

It was amid this climate of uncertainty over journalistic credibility and scholarly debate over the existence of structural press bias and a liberal media elite that Reagan-appointed FCC chair Mark S. Fowler pushed to end the Fairness Doctrine. While conservatives disagreed as to the doctrine's tactical utility, as we will see in chapter 7, it was ultimately rescinded in 1987. For nearly forty years, the policy had mandated balanced coverage of politically controversial issues over the airwaves. During those same years, the modern conservative movement had cultivated a critical disposition toward that nominally "balanced" press, leveraging belief in liberal media bias to expand their base of support to the level of national electoral viability. Those same supporters would soon become the audience base for a newly commercially viable form of conservative media—talk radio.

In 1988, a year after the end of the Fairness Doctrine, Sacramento-based radio host Rush Limbaugh took his conservative talk show national—revitalizing the AM radio business, and reconfiguring US political culture.[66] Limbaugh's show represented a proof of concept that right-wing partisan media could be profitable. The key—learned the hard way in the early 1990s by failed conservative television pioneer Paul Weyrich—was to convey conservative ideology in an entertaining way. Employing tabloid style, with a tongue-in-cheek nod to Fairness Doctrine–era journalistic propriety, Rupert Murdoch and Roger Ailes launched Fox News Channel in 1996 under the slogan "Fair and Balanced."[67] By the early aughts Fox was boasting the highest ratings in cable news, paving the way for further right imitators like Newsmax TV and One America News Network and an entire online ecosystem of conservative news outlets by the 2010s.[68] We turn to these developments in this book's conclusion.

For most of its history, conservative media functioned as a means toward the end of advancing the ideological and political interests of the modern conservative movement and, increasingly from the 1980s onward, the Republican Party. As late as 2008, when Kathleen Hall Jamieson and Joseph Cappella published their pathbreaking book *Echo Chamber* on the "conservative media establishment," it was still possible to imagine outlets like Rush Limbaugh, Fox News, and *The Wall Street Journal* opinion page as committed to doing the conservative movement's "fusionist" bidding.[69] By 2016, when Donald Trump leveraged the support of Limbaugh, Fox, and online outlets like *Breitbart* to seize the reins of the Republican Party, it became clear that the modern conservative movement had lost control of its creation. A movement that had spent the better part of a century cultivating a critical disposition toward the mainstream press was eclipsed by commercial outlets founded to capitalize on disaffected conservative audiences.

While movement media outlets like *National Review* persist, they now compete in an attention economy with commercial outlets like Fox who are more focused on maintaining market share than on enforcing ideological purity or conservative respectability. Profitability has enabled the contemporary right-wing media sector to grow into a source of political power all its own, resulting in asymmetrical political polarization and right-wing radicalization.[70] This book offers a prehistory of our contemporary profit-driven conservative news culture.[71] It tracks the rise of the liberal media claim as a driving force behind conservative demand for alternatives to mainstream sources of news and commentary. It shows how hostility toward the press became a core element of conservative identity, informing the conservative movement's long-standing and ongoing drive toward media ownership, innovation, and activism.

1

THE FAIRNESS DOCTRINE AND ITS SUBTEXTS

"**N**ow don't believe what you read in the newspapers, we're not pirates."

Rev. Carl McIntire's voice beamed across the Eastern Seaboard from a 140-foot converted World War II minesweeper. Deposed by the Presbyterian Church in 1935 for opposing "modernism" within the faith, McIntire had long courted controversy as an outspoken proponent of fundamentalist Christian theology and right-wing politics. The ship, which McIntire variously called *Columbus* and *Radio Free America*, was equipped with a ten-thousand-watt transmitter and had spent nearly a month anchored three miles off the coast of Cape May, New Jersey. On September 19, 1973, McIntire sailed it twelve miles out to sea to inveigh against "the unelected bureaucrats in Washington" who months earlier had stripped him of his broadcast license, forcing him to shutter his Media, Pennsylvania–based station, WXUR. "We are here on the high seas telling the American people of the realization that they have lost free speech, the free exercise of religion on television and radio," McIntire intoned, his voice muffled by static and interference. "We're way out in international waters where we don't need a license, and where we are free to talk like a preacher ought to be able to talk every day of the year on the radio in the United States."[1]

McIntire did, indeed, need a license. The FCC had been regulating radio transmissions, including for ships at sea flying under the American flag, since the late 1920s, back when it was called the Federal Radio Commission. The agency was authorized to regulate the airwaves according to the "public interest, convenience, or necessity," which included ensuring orderly transmission through licensing and electromagnetic spectrum allocation.² McIntire's illegal broadcast at 692 kilocycles, nearly the same wavelength as the station he was forced to shutter, was aimed at reaching listeners in his biggest markets—Philadelphia and the northern Virginia suburbs of Washington, DC.³ But it interfered with the signal of WHLW, a radio station located in Lakewood, New Jersey. While McIntire's engineers worked to reconfigure his broadcast equipment to avoid such interference, a federal judge signed an injunction forbidding his return to the air.⁴

McIntire had purchased WXUR in 1965 when no station in the Philadelphia area would sell him airtime for his thirty-minute daily radio show, the *Twentieth Century Reformation Hour*. As historian Heather Hendershot has shown, McIntire not only used the program to settle religious doctrinal scores but also to oppose the civil rights movement and to promote draconian countersubversive measures domestically as well as hawkish military interventions against communists abroad.⁵ By the late-1960s, the *Twentieth Century Reformation Hour* was aired on as many as six-hundred radio stations around the United States, reaching an audience of millions who reportedly answered McIntire's calls for donations to the tune of $3 million per year.⁶ While radio commentators like McIntire were free to speak their minds politically, different rules applied to station owners, who were subjected to licensure by the FCC. In 1949 the FCC issued a requirement that broadcast licensees dedicate airtime to the discussion of issues of public concern and that they do so in a way that granted the public a "reasonable opportunity to hear different opposing positions."⁷ McIntire purchased WXUR with no such intention and quickly ran afoul of this policy, known as the Fairness Doctrine.

When the station's license came up for renewal in 1966, it was contested by a coalition of nineteen liberal political and religious organizations who accused McIntire of airing programs that were "one-sided from a political and religious standpoint." Groups including the Anti-Defamation League, the Catholic Community Relations Council, the American Baptist Convention, and the Pennsylvania Labor Federation accused McIntire of airing "highly racist, anti-Semitic, anti-Negro, anti-civil rights and anti-Roman Catholic" programming while refusing to air alternative perspectives or accommodate requests for equal time.[8] The FCC ultimately revoked McIntire's broadcast license in 1970—making him the only broadcaster to lose his license due to Fairness Doctrine violations. McIntire managed to keep WXUR running into 1973 as he appealed the ruling, but the US Court of Appeals ultimately sided with the FCC. The highly public battle over WXUR, punctuated by McIntire's brief stint as a radio pirate, cost the reverend his station and caused more than one hundred other stations to drop his *Twentieth Century Reformation Hour*. But it also briefly made McIntire a cause célèbre on the right, reigniting debate over federal broadcast policy, and amplifying long-standing right-wing complaints that the Fairness Doctrine was being used to discriminate against conservative broadcasters.[9]

While the Fairness Doctrine was not expressly designed to target right-wing broadcasters like McIntire, the policy was rooted in the epistemological and political theoretical assumptions of the progressive media reform movement, whose history has been well-chronicled by Victor Pickard. That movement advanced what Pickard calls a "social democratic" interpretation of media, which included "an expansive view of the First Amendment, one that protected the audience's 'positive' right *to* information as much as broadcasters' and publishers' 'negative' rights protecting their speech and property *from* government intervention."[10] Progressive media reformers unwittingly influenced the modern conservative critical disposition toward the press in two important ways. First, as we will see in chapter 2, they developed structural modes of analyzing and criticizing the press, enabling vernacular conceptions of "media bias" that were later adopted and adapted by media activists on the right. Second, by insisting that media producers prioritize an abstract "public interest" over their own individual commercial or ideological interests, progressive media reformers rendered "bias" as a problem in need of professional and regulatory redress. As this chapter will show, in the 1940s progressive media reformers succeeded in making bias a primary hermeneutic of federal broadcast regulation—a key lens for determining when broadcasters ran afoul of the public interest. Fairness and balance became the prevailing remedies as well as the basis for later conservative movement initiatives to contest "liberal media" hegemony.

Even if, on its face, the Fairness Doctrine advanced high-minded aims—fair administration of scarce broadcast frequencies, a novel and more democratic interpretation of the First Amendment, a media culture characterized by the impartial conveyance of factual information, and rational-critical debate regarding matters of public disagreement—the political climate out of which the policy emerged imbued it with certain subtexts. As the United States transitioned out of a wartime political economy and culture and into a cold war with the Soviet Union, long-standing debates concerning the role of government in society were rekindled by conservative activists. As this chapter shows, abstract defenses of the "public interest" by progressive media reformers often alluded to or referenced a more tangible concern—right-wing propaganda. In particular, the 1948 FCC hearings that resulted in the Fairness Doctrine coincided with and drew upon a highly publicized battle between conservative radio commentator Fulton Lewis Jr. and the consumer cooperatives movement over the mechanics of federal tax policy. For progressive media reformers, Lewis epitomized the "bias" problem they hoped to mitigate through federally mandated balance. But by framing Lewis, and right-wing broadcasters like him, as a problem in need of regulation, they unwittingly laid the foundation for postwar conservative press criticism and media activism.[11]

THE SPECTER OF REACTION

In the spring of 1948, at the request of the National Association of Broadcasters, the FCC held hearings to consider whether owners of radio stations had the right to broadcast editorials supporting causes of their choosing.[12] The question stemmed from a 1941 ruling in which the FCC determined it had the power to refuse to renew the broadcast licenses of station owners who editorialized over the air. Explaining the rationale for its decision, the FCC wrote, "Radio can serve as an instrument of democracy only when devoted to the communication of information and the exchange of ideas fairly and objectively presented." It ruled that in order for a station to meet its statutory requirement to serve the public interest, it was obliged to present "all sides of important public questions, fairly, objectively and without bias."[13]

What became known as the Mayflower Doctrine was an important regulatory achievement for progressive media reformers, and especially for James Lawrence Fly, a New Deal stalwart who Franklin Roosevelt appointed to chair the FCC in 1939. Roosevelt was most interested in strengthening the FCC's regulatory might toward stanching increasing newspaper ownership of radio stations, which he saw as an encroachment of right-wing propaganda into the still-young and liberal-leaning broadcast medium. But FCC hearings on newspaper ownership from 1941 to 1944 did not result in meaningful reforms.[14] The Mayflower decision, on the other hand, imposed the possibility of real sanction on any station owner too cavalier in expressing their personal political views over the air.

While the Mayflower decision had based its prohibition of editorials on a technical argument about the scarcity of radio frequencies—fearing that if stations reflected the partisan leanings of their owners, then opportunities for dissent would be limited by the broadcast spectrum itself—by 1948 technological innovation had reduced the salience of this rationale. As such, the hearings to reconsider the Mayflower Doctrine amounted to a dispute over the proper subject of the First Amendment. Representatives for the three largest radio networks (CBS, NBC, and ABC) testified that the prohibition on broadcast editorials impinged upon their freedom of expression. Rev. Carl McIntire, who would later lose his broadcast license by ignoring federal balance imperatives, agreed that the First Amendment protected the rights of broadcasters to editorialize. But he also suggested that editorial transparency was the only viable solution to the problem of bias. "Stations usually have an opinion, whether they express them or not, and ofttimes and in subjective ways affect the program of the station," he testified before the FCC in March 1948. "It will be conducive to a more healthy attitude on the part of the public to know a station's position."[15] Progressive media reformers, chief among them former FCC Chairman Fly, preferred balance to mere transparency, arguing that the First Amendment implied a "freedom to hear all points of view"—reframing the freedom of speech as a freedom to listen.[16]

Yet it was clear that Fly and his allies—labor unions, progressive associations, Catholics, and other supporters of media reform who flooded the commission with letters opposing the repeal of Mayflower—were more interested in hearing *less* of certain points of view.[17] This point was raised on the first day of the hearings by Frank Stanton, testifying in his capacity as president of CBS: "Aside from arguments based on scarcity, the only argument against the right of stations to editorialize which I have heard is based upon a supposition as to the content of editorials which radio stations would broadcast."[18] Stanton cited articles published in *The Nation* and *New Republic*, both expressing concern that allowing station owners to editorialize over the air would result in the spreading of "reactionary propaganda."[19] Stanton continued, "What the Mayflower decision comes down to is a distrust of the owners and managers of American radio stations, and indirectly a distrust of the American people themselves. Radio executives, it is implied, would abuse the right to voice their opinions, and their listeners would follow blindly or uncritically."[20]

Judging by the public outcry against overturning Mayflower, however, by the late 1940s listeners were far less willing than Stanton to trust one another. Fears concerning radio's power to influence the masses were reflected in hundreds of letters and postcards received by the FCC in response to its request for public commentary on the question of broadcast editorials. While most of these letter writers exhibited liberal or progressive ideological perspectives, several right anticommunists also expressed concerns that, as a result of overturning Mayflower, "this country could easily be turned both atheistic and Communistic."[21] Nevertheless, it was not the fear of communist subversion but the specter of reactionary propaganda that loomed largest in Mayflower supporters' minds. One way this fear manifested was in the common sentiment that radio networks were systematically removing liberal broadcasters from the air. As a concerned citizen from Los Angeles wrote, "The liberals of this country do not, at present, have any reason to feel that the broadcasting companies or the networks are at all interested in preserving their fair names nor in giving their views a fair share of radio time."[22] This anxiety concerning network bias against liberal commentators preceded the reconsideration of Mayflower and is evident in complaint letters received by the FCC in the years leading up to the hearings.

In early 1944 Mutual radio network fired Sam Balter, in what he claimed was retribution for "attacks I had made upon pro-Fascist elements in this country, particularly Colonel Robert McCormick of the *Chicago*

Tribune."²³ In addition to owning the *Tribune*, McCormick, a stalwart of the Old Right and outspoken critic of the New Deal, owned WGN, a Mutual-affiliated radio station that exerted considerable sway over the network's board of directors—effectively making McCormick one of Balter's bosses. Balter alerted his audience to this fact in his final broadcast, beseeching them to write to the FCC to protest his firing. And respond they did: then US vice president Henry A. Wallace sent a letter to FCC Chairman Fly directly to inquire into Balter's claims, writing: "Undoubtedly one of the most prominent issues in the future will be the problem of keeping the channels of information open and pure."²⁴ Secretary of the Interior Harold Ickes, a leading proponent of progressive media reform within the Roosevelt administration, and members of the Democratic National Committee also wrote to express their concern, as did hundreds of listeners.²⁵

Robert B. Lacy, a listener from California, lamented that Balter "was one of the FEW radio commentators who dared speak in behalf of the [Roosevelt] Administration." But for Lacy, and others, the silencing of liberal broadcasters also highlighted the growing influence of right-wing news commentators; he continued: "This while such as Fulton Lewis continues to spew political propaganda in the guise of news."²⁶ From the vice president down to everyday listeners, the response to the Balter firing revealed a liberal common sense of the mid-1940s: broadcast purity required the presence of liberal commentators, while right-wing commentators were viewed as pollutants, mere vehicles for propaganda as opposed to news.

FULTON LEWIS JR. VERSUS THE COOPERATIVES

Fulton Lewis Jr. was born into a prominent Washington, DC, family and married into elite Republican Party circles.²⁷ He cut his teeth working as a reporter, first for the *Washington Herald* and then for the Hearst-owned Universal News Service, where he began writing a column. By 1937 he had switched mediums, serving primarily as a nightly news commentator on national affairs with Mutual Broadcasting System. While Lewis was a leader within the broadcast journalism industry, cofounding the Radio

Correspondents' Association and leading a successful effort to reserve galleries in the House and Senate for radio reporters covering Congress, his pro-business tirades against the New Deal quickly earned him notoriety in liberal and progressive corners.[28] Beginning in 1942 Lewis became a regular target of progressive press critic George Seldes, who accused him of propagandizing for the National Association of Manufacturers and other business-led campaigns to promote "free enterprise" ideology.[29] Such was Lewis's status within what Seldes regarded as a vast "native fascist" press conspiracy that Seldes devoted an entire book chapter to exposing Lewis.[30]

Radio listeners had their suspicions about Lewis even earlier than did Seldes. The FCC had been receiving listener complaints about Lewis since at least the summer of 1939 and received them in such volume throughout the 1940s that, whereas complaints about individual broadcasters were typically filed under the network or station that aired them, entire complaint folders were devoted to Lewis alone. In what appears to be the first such complaint letter, a listener in San Francisco wrote of Lewis: "He is such a bitter critic of President Roosevelt that he went to the length some time ago of ridiculing governmental action in rounding up Nazi spies.... I believe Mr. Lewis should be better identified. Who is behind him?"[31]

Questions concerning Lewis's backers, both financial and ideological, roiled steadily as his popularity and audience grew throughout the 1940s and just so happened to boil over in 1947, the year leading up to the Mayflower hearings. On February 20, Lewis devoted his evening broadcast to the issue of federal tax policy concerning consumer cooperatives—he accused them of exploiting a loophole, avoiding income tax by claiming nonprofit status despite effectively using earnings as capital for investments benefiting the cooperative's commercial interests.[32] "This is a very controversial subject and without a doubt this discussion of it over this microphone tonight is going to set off some verbal fireworks in some quarters," Lewis admitted in his first of seven broadcasts aimed at exposing the alleged misdeeds of cooperatives. "But it will just have to set them off, because here is a question of a new and highly threatening form of super big business which already has reached the point at which it is doing a twelve billion dollar a year volume here in the United States by the exploitation of special privileges which Congress never for a moment intended to be used as they are being used."[33] In subsequent broadcasts, which ran for a week into early March 1947, Lewis repeatedly framed his opposition to the tax loophole as opposition to special government privileges for private business: "Frankly, as far as I am concerned, I can see no reason why the Federal Government should be nurturing any form of Big Business or any form of little business, so far as that's concerned, by granting it special exemptions from income taxes and regular business has to pay."[34]

Lewis's critiques largely advanced the interests of the National Tax Equality Association (NTEA), a group founded in 1943 by midwestern businessmen and devoted to reducing tax burdens on private corporations.[35] The NTEA targeted consumer cooperatives from its outset and had been nurturing Lewis's own interest in the issue since as early as 1944, when an operations manager at the Derby Oil Company of Wichita, Kansas, connected Lewis with the group's then secretary and later vice president, Vernon Scott.[36] By 1946 Lewis was in regular correspondence with NTEA president Ben McCabe and with Ross Murphy, who routinely sent Lewis NTEA memoranda, position papers, and talking points throughout Lewis's battles with the cooperatives in 1947 and 1948.[37] Indeed, while the exact nature of the NTEA–Lewis collaboration is rendered opaque by the archive, there is little doubt that their efforts were coordinated—Lewis gave the NTEA advance notice of his February 1947 broadcasts, and the NTEA's president sent a "highly confidential" letter to NTEA members two days before Lewis's first program aired, suggesting that they tune in. "Mr. Lewis has conducted, as is his custom, exhaustive research on this question and these broadcasts on his regular radio program are an important development in the fight for tax equality," McCabe promised, failing to mention that the NTEA itself was Lewis's primary source of information on the issue.[38]

Not surprisingly, Lewis's broadcasts raised the ire of the cooperative movement, which lambasted Lewis in its many newspapers and newsletters, often focusing on his ties to the NTEA and his prior work with the National Association of Manufacturers (NAM) as a "paid propagandist"—glossing over the fact that the NTEA and the NAM actually disagreed on the issue of cooperative taxation.[39] In response to the growing controversy, and in accordance with demands for equal time under the auspices of the Mayflower Doctrine, the Mutual network chose to balance Lewis's commentary with a three-part rebuttal by liberal commentator Arthur Gaeth.[40] In his first broadcast Gaeth fact-checked Lewis, criticizing his reliance on the "definitely partisan" NTEA as a source of authority and noting that Congress had already investigated the claims made by the NTEA and belabored by Lewis. Gaeth's second and third broadcasts were, respectively, interviews with Karl D. Loos of the National Council of Farmer Cooperatives and W. G. Wysor of the Southern States Cooperative. While the Loos interview focused on the minutia of cooperative finances and the federal tax code, the Wysor interview was aimed at rejecting Lewis's criticisms and undermining his credibility. Wysor revealed that Lewis was himself a member of the Southern States Cooperative, and that Lewis's receipt of a sixty-one-dollar patronage refund made him a hypocrite. Further, Wysor implied that it was *Lewis* who might be guilty of tax evasion. "Is it not a fact that under the Bureau of Internal Revenue's regulations, the $61 patronage refund was taxable income to Mr. Lewis?" Gaeth asked. To which Wysor replied: "Certainly it was taxable income. If he did not report this income in his income tax return it is an appropriate subject for audit by the Bureau of Internal Revenue."[41]

The Gaeth broadcasts were only the first return salvo in what became a months-long public relations and legal battle between Lewis and the Southern States Cooperative, culminating in a vote by the co-op's board to revoke the broadcaster's membership in October 1947, which itself provoked a lawsuit by Lewis.[42] They also resulted in a Mayflower complaint from none other than the NTEA, which, despite privately feeding Lewis the bulk of his research materials on cooperatives, publicly distanced itself from the broadcaster in order to directly counter Gaeth. "Fulton Lewis, Jr., while accurate on facts, suggests taxing retained income of cooperatives only. He doesn't represent the viewpoint of business which seeks taxation of all cooperative profits," NTEA president Ben McCabe wrote in a telegram requesting equal time from Mutual. "Arthur Gaeth's program is replete with misinformation and cannot be allowed to go unchallenged."[43] While the NTEA was ultimately allowed to respond by participating in a forum program with cooperative supporters, including Loos, private correspondence between Lewis's office and Ross Murphy continued apace as the NTEA continued to provide Lewis with strategy and talking points.

The legal dispute between Lewis and Southern States kept the issue of cooperatives, as well as Lewis's reputation for mixing his reporting with generous advocacy of the interests of businessmen, in the public eye well into 1948. Indeed, on March 2, 1948, the second day of the FCC hearings in Washington, DC, considering overturning Mayflower, Lewis was in Chicago for a WGN-hosted debate with Jerry Voorhis, executive secretary of the Cooperative League of the USA, addressing the question "Are Cooperatives Unfair Competition to Other Types of Business?"[44] While Lewis fixated on his battle against the cooperatives, which he would later call "the most intense conflict of my career," progressives were busy exploiting his heightened public profile to paint him as a poster boy for retaining Mayflower.[45]

A PROBLEM EMBODIED

The framing of Lewis as a problem in need of federal regulatory solution proceeded on two fronts: one public, the other bureaucratic. The effort to turn public opinion against Lewis and other reactionary radio commentators was spearheaded by the Voice of Freedom Committee (VOF), a group founded in New York by Dorothy Parker one week after Lewis aired his initial series against the cooperatives, in early March 1947. With a stated mission of maintaining radio as a "democratic instrument of the people," the VOF consisted of loosely organized groups of liberal "monitors" who would listen to the programs of radio commentators and write letters to both the networks and the FCC.[46] VOF monitors were urged to listen to one "good" commentator, such as liberals Algernon Black or Don Hollenbeck, and one "bad" commentator, such as conservatives Lewis, Gabriel Heatter or H. V. Kaltenborn, each day and to write one letter each week to "commend or protest."[47] While the VOF targeted several reactionary commentators, Lewis was often depicted as among the most odious. One anecdote, conveyed in the first issue of the group's newsletter, went so far as to imply that Lewis's program possessed the power to provoke spontaneous domestic abuse: "A Listening Post member requested a new assignment in place of Fulton Lewis, as he was on just when her husband came home from work and hungry, and the program threw him into a frenzy."[48]

The VOF shared a tendency, common among progressive media critics of the era, to treat political disagreement as the result, as opposed to the cause, of propaganda—attributable more to the "harmful air" spewed by reactionary broadcasters than to earnest differences of opinion.[49] "Don't fool yourself that people do not believe what the reactionary commentators feed them," an anonymous writer warned in the group's first newsletter. "To many Americans—too many Americans—the words of a Winchell, Lewis, Heatter are the gospel truth. They sound authentic, so how can there be any possible doubt? You can let the program makers know there is doubt."[50] Even your well-meaning, presumably liberal neighbors, the newsletter's tone implied, might be coaxed into reaction not by the salience of Lewis's ideas but by the sincerity of his voice. The VOF also articulated a materialist analysis of reactionary propaganda's origins: "Isn't there a similarity throughout all the various rantings of Winchell, or Gabriel Heatter, or Fulton Lewis, Jr., or H. V. Kaltenborn? Don't they all sound as though they were all heading in the same direction, pulled by the same unseen string? Well, they are. The same group pays the bills in all cases—the same clique that now dominates our foreign policy."[51]

At the same moment that the VOF was pleading with supporters to listen with their "eyes open," ignoring their presumably more affect-susceptible ears, it was closely monitoring the FCC's motions toward revoking Mayflower. In its December 1947 newsletter, on a page adjoining a letter calling for a boycott of Golden West Coffee for sponsoring the Fulton Lewis Jr. program, the VOF urged its readers to write the FCC in anticipation of the upcoming Mayflower hearings, expressing their opposition to any change in the policy: "Although the spirit and letter of the law have long been violated, especially by the networks, it is VOF's belief that revocation of the decree will only encourage that much more editorializing by the present offenders."[52]

As the VOF was rallying the public against Lewis and other reactionary broadcasters, it was simultaneously confronting their influence bureaucratically. In October 1947 the VOF formally requested an opportunity to testify before the FCC during its upcoming Mayflower hearings and, failing to receive an initial reply, wrote again in November.[53] Their request was ultimately granted, and VOF counsel Stanley Faulkner testified on March 2, 1948, the second day of the hearings. While the VOF was unabashed in its liberalism within the pages of its own newsletter, it struck a decidedly more neutral tone while testifying before the FCC. In his testimony, Faulkner elided his group's ideological basis, describing it as simply "representing citizens who are interested in preserving freedom of expression over the air for and by the people." Rather than framing his group in explicit opposition to voices of "reaction," Faulkner described the group's opposition to editorials as being rooted in a concern that their "emotion" might "create passion or extend prejudice." Indeed, when asked point-blank, "Aren't you really urging that the reason why the broadcasters should not be permitted to express an opinion is because they have a particular kind of opinion?" Faulkner answered "no" and reaffirmed his group's opposition to *any* broadcaster's attempts to "invade our homes with his opinion."[54]

Faulkner's assertion that the VOF was merely interested in a general freedom of expression and universally opposed to the invasion of political opinion into the home was undermined by the group's explicit advocacy of "good" liberal commentators and vociferous opposition to "bad" reactionary commentators. His ability to nevertheless testify as to his group's ideological neutrality underscored the extent to which the interests of social liberalism had been superimposed as the boundaries of the public sphere itself, at least for the purposes of federal regulation. VOF equated right-wing speech with subjectivity, histrionics, and irrationality, maintaining a liberal tradition that dated back to the origins of radio as a medium and modern conceptions of public opinion during the interwar years. According to this ideology, the interests of the people were assumed to be concomitant with a liberal social welfare agenda as epitomized by the New Deal. Any speech that roused popular support against that agenda was thought to be, at best, irrationally influenced by emotionalism or, at worst, paid for explicitly by nefarious interests (corporate or communist). The specter of propaganda of either variety masked a deeper liberal fear of conflict, a fear that political disagreement would undermine the legitimacy of liberal governance.

THE BALANCE IMPERATIVE AND ITS CONTRADICTIONS

Somewhat ironically, while Mayflower was both an expression of this liberal ideology and an enforcement of the idealized public sphere upon which it was based, its focus on content and requirement of balance exacerbated the problem its proponents hoped it would solve—anticipating conflicts that would later dog the Fairness Doctrine. Lewis's battle with the cooperatives serves as a case in point. While Lewis was indeed disingenuous as to his degree of collaboration with the NTEA, it is difficult in hindsight to read his critique of cooperatives as overly emotional, let alone superlatively controversial. While he did, in his second broadcast, engage in what might be considered dog-whistle red-baiting—he suggested that the cooperative movement had ties to the Congress of Industrial Organizations and described a speech by cooperative supporter Murray D. Lincoln as "an outright attack on the profit system in business and industry," accusing him of saying that "the profit system must be abolished"—Lewis's broadcasts were primarily composed of the minutiae of cooperative financing and the federal tax code: hardly the stuff of demagoguery.[55]

Furthermore, Lewis's remarks, however irrational or false they must have seemed to cooperative supporters at the time, were immediately countered by Gaeth, who himself invited two leaders of the cooperative movement to directly refute Lewis's allegations—to say nothing of the many gallons of ink spilled contesting Lewis's charges within the cooperative and progressive press. Indeed, the perspectives of both sides of the cooperatives debate were aired and printed ad nauseam in the spring and summer months of 1947, with allegations growing more, not less, heated as equal time was continuously requested and, to varying degrees, granted. By August, stoked primarily by Wysor's allegations of hypocrisy and the Southern States Cooperative's move to expel Lewis from membership for his public criticism of the cooperative movement, Lewis aired a vigorous denunciation of the Southern States Cooperative that nevertheless defended cooperatives in general as "admirable and excellent institutions," so long as they did not take advantage of what Lewis saw as a tax loophole. Despite this nuance over the air, the NTEA circulated a pamphlet containing a transcript of Lewis's August 14 broadcast under the much more provocative title, "Fulton Lewis Jr. (A co-op member) EXPOSES Co-Op Tyranny over Members."[56]

Whether or not equal time encouraged tit-for-tat politics, ratcheting up rhetoric with each response, Mayflower had made objectivity and balance a bureaucratic imperative of the state, making Lewis's repeated editorial provocations, his "bias," a problem in constant need of redress.

Indeed, after Lewis's August broadcasts against Southern States, Wysor once again petitioned Mutual for equal time, arguing that Lewis had "attacked me personally and used the broadcast facilities available to him to publicize his prejudiced version of a personal feud." Appealing to the formalistic language of the Mayflower Doctrine, Wysor chided, "The public interest is not served when radio facilities are given or sold to anyone who uses them for the broadcasting of innuendo and for misinforming and misleading the public." Never mind that Wysor had himself engaged in innuendo over the Mutual network during his appearance on Gaeth's third co-op broadcast, when he suggested that Lewis might be committing tax evasion. Mutual news director Milton Burgh rejected Wysor's request under the banner of objectivity: "The matter reported by Mr. Lewis is simply a straight-forward account of the operations of the organization that has been taken, for the most part, word for word from the official records of the Southern States Cooperative. In doing so, Mr. Lewis has exercised the right of a reporter to state the news." Burgh offered to correct any "errors of fact" that Wysor could point to in Lewis's report but declined to offer equal time under the justification that Lewis was not guilty of "misrepresentation." Instead, Wysor reiterated his demand for equal time and forwarded the matter to the FCC for consideration.[57]

Wysor's informal Mayflower complaint happened to coincide with the commission's reconsideration of the doctrine, which was announced five days before Mutual rejected Wysor's request for equal time. While the initial doctrine was limited to editorials expressing the personal opinions of station *owners*, the commission tasked its hearings with "determining whether any editorialization is consistent with the licensee's obligation to operate in the public interest; and, if so, whether any limitations or conditions for the expression of the licensee's subjective opinions are advisable or necessary to insure the maintenance of a system in which all sides of controversial issues are to be afforded a fair and equal opportunity for the presentation of their particular viewpoints."[58] To answer these queries, the FCC invited testimony from a wide array of interested parties ranging from an alphabet soup of media industry groups (chief among them the National Association of Broadcasters) to other interest groups with stakes in the central civil libertarian and social justice issues of the day: from the American Civil Liberties Union, National Association for the Advancement of Colored People, and Progressive Citizens of America on the left, to the American Legion and the National Committee to Uphold Constitutional Government on the right. While the FCC went out of its way to accommodate broadcasters regarding scheduling and making space for industry voices, as historian Victor Pickard has noted, the invited testimony "seemed to over represent critics, activists, and media reformers."[59]

In addition to overrepresenting explicit proponents of liberal media reform, the FCC saw fit to invite testimony from both the National Council of Farmer Cooperatives and the Cooperative League of the USA—both of which were especially concerned with protecting equal time due to their ongoing dispute with Lewis. That the commission was aware of the conflict and seemed inclined to channel it toward the end of retaining Mayflower is further indicated by their reply to Wysor's equal time complaint against Lewis. In acknowledging receipt of Wysor's correspondence with Mutual, FCC secretary T. J. Slowie extended an unsolicited invitation to testify on the matter of broadcast editorials: "The Commission is desirous of hearing testimony at this hearing from persons and organizations interested in the problem. If, therefore, either you or your organization wish to testify at the hearing or to submit written comments concerning the matter, we should appreciate being advised at your earliest convenience."[60] While no representative of either Southern States or the National Council of Farm Cooperatives testified at the hearings, Angus MacDonald of the National Farmers Union used his time before the FCC to defend the interests of both.

Drawing heavily on the example of Lewis's crusade against the cooperatives, MacDonald accused the FCC of failing to fulfill its obligation to serve the public interest by continuing to license Mutual-affiliated stations that he suggested were broadcasting rightward biased content without offering equal time to left labor or farm groups. "Day in and day out Mr. Lewis assails farmer cooperatives over the air," MacDonald testified. "He has refused frequent requests to allow cooperative speakers to use his time on the air. Mutual Broadcasting System has assured us that it has no control over Mr. Lewis in this refusal to allow both sides of the question to be heard. Letters of protest to the Federal Communications Commission have brought no action." MacDonald explained that his constituents' treatment by Lewis was "what farm people fear may happen" if the FCC lifted its ban on broadcast editorials: "Granting that Lewis is not the owner of the Mutual network or even a radio station, as far as I know, is this the kind of treatment cooperatives and farm organizations can expect if the Mayflower decision is dropped, with no balancing requirement that equal time be given for the presentation of controversial issues?"[61] If the FCC could not maintain balance for a commentator with only fifteen minutes of airtime per day, MacDonald suggested, it was unlikely to achieve any semblance of balance if station owners themselves were granted the right to editorialize at will.

Testifying on behalf of the UAW-CIO International Radio Committee, Norman Matthews echoed MacDonald's testimony. He noted that broadcasters tended to air disclaimers after labor-friendly commentators, distancing the station from their views. "We notice, as I pointed out to you gentlemen, that when Fulton Lewis or people of his description go on the air, it must be the opinion of the radio station operator, otherwise he would make the same comments on the statement of Fulton Lewis." Station owners, Matthews suggested, were already editorializing by proxy by failing to explicitly distance themselves from Lewis's commentary. He urged the commissioners to ensure proper labeling of editorials, giving station managers an affirmative obligation to state whether each viewpoint was or was not shared by the station.[62]

Cooperative leaders had more draconian measures in mind. Accepting the FCC's invitation to testify, the Cooperative League of the USA sent the director of its Washington office, John Carson, to frame the attack on cooperatives as an attack on the very "public interest" the FCC was charged to protect. In his testimony, Carson explicitly compared the anti-cooperative forces to the Ku Klux Klan.[63] Whether as an active conspirator or mere dupe to "more irresponsible propagandists," Carson depicted Fulton Lewis as representative of a bigger problem facing broadcasting. A former editor himself, Carson admitted that "it is impossible to keep editorial influence out of the news pages" but worried that allowing outright editorialization would inevitably benefit moneyed interests who could better afford to "buy" presumably unscrupulous commentators like Lewis than could the hapless victims of their "slander." Carson went so far as to suggest that the FCC establish a tribunal where complaints against specific commentators might be adjudicated and where "judgment in two or three cases of irresponsibility, or of dis-service to the public interest, might result in the public banishing the guilty person from the air."[64]

After a full year of confrontation with Lewis, Carson's testimony suggests that by the spring of 1948, cooperative leaders yearned for an escape from what must have seemed like an endless cycle of equal time requests, rejections, and appeals required to advance their interests under Mayflower. In seeking redress from the FCC, they ultimately sought a reprieve from politics itself—some way of reducing the impact of reactionary commentators whose dissent undermined what liberals preferred to imagine as a natural consensus around the beneficence of cooperative business practices. Frustrated by the inability of balance to achieve the liberal outcomes they assumed a rational-critical public sphere would necessarily yield, cooperative leaders sought more explicit barriers to entry and the exclusion of any commentator who failed to affirm their assumptions about the liberal nature of the public interest. This more explicit opposition to reactionary speech over the air and the outright embrace of more repressive approaches to mitigating that speech placed the testimony of cooperative leaders in tension with the deliberately neutral tone struck by other liberals at the hearings, such as the VOF and former FCC commissioner James Fly.

As Mayflower's author, Fly well understood the importance of maintaining the appearance of content neutrality, characteristic of the FCC's initial decision on editorials—which avoided any appearance of cracking down on reactionary broadcasters by abstracting the problem into a generalized concern with the public interest. While the Second Red Scare was not yet in full swing, liberals were already sensitive to the threat of being accused of fellow traveling, which explicitly targeting right-wing commentators surely would have yielded. In 1941, the same year the FCC issued its Mayflower decision, it was embroiled in a scandal over hiring Goodwin Watson as its chief broadcast analyst. Watson, a professor at Columbia University's Teacher's College, was publicly accused of communist sympathies by Martin Dies, the Texas congressman whose House Un-American

Activities Committee was a vital precursor to McCarthyism. Fly defended Watson, but his efforts to protect FCC staff from congressional red-baiting were ultimately unsuccessful. By 1943 Congress voted to deny the FCC funding for the salaries of Watson and two other staff members with ties to alleged "subversive organizations," effectively forcing the FCC to let them go.[65] The increasing salience, throughout the 1940s, of red-baiting as a tactic to silence critics of right-wing speech surely informed more ideologically neutral liberal approaches to solving the problem of reactionary commentators.

The Mayflower Doctrine was also part and parcel of a broader agenda of the Fly FCC, which was primarily concerned with inhibiting monopolistic conditions within the broadcast industry. The problem of broadcast monopoly, however, was inextricable from the political outcome that the Fly FCC presumed such a monopoly would yield—that is, the commissioners' concern with monopoly resulted from the same materialist assumptions that underlay progressive press criticism of the era. Such critics understood media monopoly as necessarily benefiting reactionary forces. Indeed, Fly's anti-monopolistic instincts were among the reasons why FDR selected Fly to lead the FCC in the first place. As former Roosevelt adviser Thomas Corcoran later recalled, the president was "very concerned that the press, ganged-up as it was against him, shouldn't be able to control his access to the people and other Democrats and people of his own political views through the radio and later the television. I think he probably hoped as a matter of policy that this kind of monopolistic [behavior] wouldn't be allowed. Now, of course, you want to remember you can't go any further than the statute lets you go."[66] By conceptually equating monopoly with reactionary hegemony but focusing on the former, the Fly FCC employed a content-neutral approach that Roosevelt thought would necessarily advance liberal political ends within the statutory bounds of the Communications Act of 1934, which had charged the commission with serving the public interest.

Thus abstracted, the problem of protecting the public interest against monopolistic tendencies within the broadcast industry set the discursive parameters of the Mayflower hearings themselves, allowing them to appear as a debate over the proper subject of the First

Amendment—between the right of broadcasters to speak and the right of audiences to listen—as opposed to an explicit referendum on the problem of right-wing radio bias. Nevertheless, the testimony against Lewis points to the real political stakes underlying the liberal advocacy of a right to listen, evidence that media reform efforts, while no doubt earnestly rooted in abstract civil libertarian principles, were catalyzed by partisan fears and repressive urges. This tension between a liberal ideological commitment to neutrality and the realpolitik of the New Deal era was embedded in the resulting Fairness Doctrine and its reception in the decades to come. While formally impartial—the policy simply required broadcasters to discuss issues of public concern, enabling broadcast editorials while mandating balance between opposing positions—vestiges of its partisan stakes lingered on in the modern conservative movement's antipathy toward and appropriation of the policy.

Conservative anxiety regarding the Fairness Doctrine accelerated in the 1960s, alongside Carl McIntire's escalating feud with the FCC. McIntire first came under scrutiny by federal authorities in 1963. Officials with the United States Information Agency complained that his shortwave radio broadcasts, which carried his screeds against the "one-world government" of the United Nations, were being confused for official US governmental communications.[67] That same year, Chicago-based journalists Donald Janson (*New York Times*) and Bernard Eismann (CBS) published *The Far Right*, a book that mapped a growing constellation of right-wing anticommunists in the United States and their various media and activist initiatives. In it, Janson and Eismann credited McIntire with having brought the Australian physician Dr. Fred Schwarz, and his Christian Anti-Communism Crusade, to the United States, describing Schwarz as among the most successful figures in the "professional anticommunist trade." It also revealed that Attorney General Robert Kennedy and United Auto Workers president Walter Reuther had identified right-wing extremism as a problem as early as 1961, and that the latter had prepared a "twenty-four-page blueprint for action against the extremists."[68] The so-called Reuther Memo advised the Kennedy administration to use the Internal Revenue Service and FCC to mitigate right-wing propaganda. Reuther wrote, "Certainly, there is sufficient public information indicating possible tax violations in this area and possible violations of FCC policies to justify the most complete check on these various means of financing the radical right."[69]

The Reuther Memo revelations and increasing FCC scrutiny of McIntire's broadcast initiatives played into long-standing right-wing fears of communist subversion within the federal government and of a more generalized conspiracy to stifle conservatism.[70] McIntire and fellow right-wing evangelical broadcaster Rev. Billy James Hargis each seized on the memo to raise funds and reinforce the ongoing sense of persecution among their audiences.[71] So did the conservative movement periodical *Human Events*. "What the liberals really fear, of course, is neither 'neo-fascists' nor 'crackpots'—as they have tried to label conservatives—but the possibility this genuine grass-roots patriotism will effectively come into play at the polls," *Human Events* cautioned its readers regarding the Reuther Memo in June 1963. "This would spell an end to America's long rule of liberalism."[72] At a moment of genuine right-wing ascendance—conservative darling Senator Barry Goldwater would claim the Republican Party presidential nomination in 1964—conservatives were fixated on their putative repression in large part due to the federal imperative to safeguard the airwaves against bias.

As this chapter has shown, the Fairness Doctrine's nominal neutrality obfuscated the regulation's real political stakes. The FCC's balance imperative made bias a fundamental hermeneutic of federal broadcast regulation at a historical moment when the modern conservative movement was gearing up to contest the prevailing New Deal consensus. Faced with a federal prohibition on openly promoting conservative interpretations of daily events on radio without also offering liberal rebuttals, the Fairness Doctrine effectively forced conservative media activists into subterfuge—as we will see in the cases of both Facts Forum and Accuracy in Media—in order to advance their political ideology over the air. The disconnect between conservative claims of impartiality and allegations of ideological bias would become a central contention of journalistic coverage of modern conservative movement initiatives. The regulatory and discursive expectation of "fairness and balance" became central not only to journalistic exposés of the Right, but to right-wing complaints about the unacknowledged ideological biases of mainstream journalists as well. The Fairness Doctrine thus fundamentally structured the modern conservative movement's contentious relationship with mainstream journalism and the critical disposition toward the press that emerged.

2

THE PROGRESSIVE ORIGINS OF CONSERVATIVE PRESS CRITICISM

"I believe the great weakness of the First Amendment in operation in America comes from the fact that we have this terrific concentration of power over the minds of the people."

Morris L. Ernst, then general counsel of the American Civil Liberties Union (ACLU), was among the slew of media reformers who urged the Federal Communications Commission to maintain its ban on broadcast editorials during the 1948 Mayflower hearings, discussed at length in the preceding chapter. A proponent of the so-called marketplace theory of freedom of expression, which posits that the truth will ultimately prevail amid competing ideas, Ernst favored a media system that promoted viewpoint diversity. His testimony decried dwindling local ownership of print and broadcast media. Anticipating Vice President Spiro Agnew's famous 1969 speech denouncing the liberal bias of network television news, Ernst also lamented that the country's information "pipelines are held in the main by a few people living on the Eastern Seaboard and in the main in a big city known as Manhattan."[1]

Agnew, as we will see in chapter 5, was part of a Nixon administration known for its combative relationship with the press.[2] The late 1960s and early 1970s are often depicted as an origin of widespread conservative complaints of liberal media bias.[3] Contemporary progressive media critics have foregrounded the weaponization of press criticism by conservative activists during the Nixon era, often depicting the practice in conspiratorial terms.[4] But Nixon-era conservatives did not merely appropriate the progressive rhetoric of liberal media reformers like Ernst.[5] They benefited from twenty years of conservative movement building, much of it centered on cultivating a critical disposition toward the mainstream press. They also benefited from the political migration of anticommunist socialists and liberals who brought structural approaches to media criticism with them on their rightward journeys.

Ernst's own political trajectory illustrates this shifting political and discursive terrain. Born in 1888 to German Jewish immigrant parents in Alabama, Ernst was raised in New York City where he earned a law degree in 1912 and became partner of a distinguished firm by 1915. By the mid-1920s he had joined with ACLU cofounder Roger Baldwin on a series of progressive initiatives, including the American Fund for Public Service, or the Garland Fund, a major benefactor of socialist, Popular Front, and civil rights organizing in the 1920s and 1930s. Ernst further bolstered his progressive credentials as general counsel of the ACLU from 1929 to 1954, a tenure that earned him a reputation as a staunch opponent of government censorship and obscenity law.[6] He also litigated landmark cases in support of birth control access, was a vocal critic of racial segregation and police brutality, and served on the national legal advisory boards of the NAACP and President Harry Truman's Committee on Civil Rights.

Despite his many associations with radicals (or perhaps because of them), Ernst was an ardent anticommunist.[7] In 1940, in response to the Nazi–Soviet pact, Ernst drafted a resolution prohibiting the ACLU from hiring or electing to its board "a member of any political organization which supports totalitarian dictatorship in any country, or who by his public declarations indicates his support of such a principle."[8] Ernst also spearheaded a subsequent effort to purge longtime ACLU board member and renowned communist Elizabeth Gurley Flynn.[9] And while it would not become publicly known until after Ernst's death in 1977, he corresponded regularly with FBI director J. Edgar Hoover from the 1940s through the 1960s—sharing sensitive ACLU information and offering Hoover advice for how best to respond to the bureau's liberal critics.[10] Ernst also penned liberal apologia for the bureau. He even sent his 1950 *Reader's Digest* essay, "Why I No Longer Fear the FBI," to the bureau for surreptitious vetting.[11]

While Ernst's anticommunism, not to mention his collusion with the FBI, might seem to contradict his otherwise dogged support of such First Amendment principles as freedom of speech, assembly, and petition, his opposition to totalitarianism was constitutive of his otherwise radical civil libertarianism. For example, in his 1946 book *The First Freedom*, Ernst argued that concentration of media ownership and the resulting monopolistic conditions in the radio, film, and newspaper industries were stifling freedom of thought. He called for federal regulations to ensure a diversity of perspectives over the air and in the press. While the book amounted to a critique of corporate capitalism run amok in the US media industry, Ernst framed his case against a backdrop of looming totalitarianism abroad. He wrote in the book's forward, "The peace of the world depends on human understanding and human understanding depends on the free flow, throughout the planet, of movies, radio and the printed word." Ernst noted, "Russia and many other nations still under dictatorship are not in agreement with us on this our basic way of life." He continued, "Regimentation of thought satisfies the dictator and relieves the masses from the need of any decisions or critical judgments. But until ideas can roam our earth without restraint, there is slight chance for peace in the world."[12] For Ernst, the freedom of thought he held dear was contingent on the prior elimination of totalitarian forms of governance, which he equated communism. His anticommunism might be best understood, then, as a means toward the end of liberal pluralism.

As historian Victor Pickard has noted, *The First Freedom* was "considered a primer for the postwar media reform movement."[13] That movement, composed of grassroots organizers as well as progressive policymakers and litigators active in the mid- to late 1940s, advocated for a media system that was answerable to and in service of a social democratic vision of the public interest. This included antitrust and public service regulations on broadcast media as well as social responsibility standards for professional journalists. The postwar media reform movement produced the "high modern" journalism conditions that, as we saw in chapter 1 and as we will continue to see in chapters ahead, marginalized conservative reporters and commentators and alienated their audiences.

Among the media reform movement's thought leaders, Ernst helped develop a structural approach to media criticism. Structural media criticism is about more than simply disagreeing with one outlet's reporting on a particular issue. It alleges systematic bias, often attributed to structural factors like political economy (who controls the means of media production, and how commercial imperatives shape the news) and regulatory climate (who is *allowed* to own media, how much they are allowed to own, and what they are allowed to do with it). Typically, such media criticism associates structural factors with political ideological bias: for instance, many progressives in the 1930s and 1940s felt that the high costs of newspaper and radio station ownership inevitably skewed coverage in favor of capitalism and the political interests of the moneyed elite. While ultimately popularized by civil libertarians like Ernst, this mode of critique was initially developed and cultivated in the left corners of the labor movement and by progressive muckrakers like Upton Sinclair and George Seldes. As this chapter will show, Seldes' confrontational mode of press criticism would be embraced in the late 1940s by right-anticommunist antecedents of the modern conservative movement, who summarily red-baited Seldes to the margins of public life during the Second Red Scare.

A civil libertarian, Ernst found himself in the late 1940s politically aligned with progressives, even (unwittingly) with communists. By the 1970s, Ernst would join the board of Accuracy in Media, a conservative press watchdog with deep anticommunist roots that, as we will see in subsequent chapters, played an outsized role in promoting the idea of liberal media bias. As Daniel Oppenheimer has shown, there is a long tradition of left-wingers shifting rightward; among them are Whittaker Chambers, James Burnham, Ronald Reagan, Norman Podhoretz, David Horowitz, and Christopher Hitchens.[14] What's interesting about Ernst is that his core political interests and positions were fundamentally unchanged between the 1940s and the 1970s: he remained devoutly anticommunist and maintained an almost single-minded focus on the necessity of viewpoint diversity in mass media. What changed, I contend, is the broader discursive and political terrain around him.

That's not to say that the rightward drift of structural press criticism from the late 1940s to the early 1950s didn't also benefit from left-wing defectors. Eugene Lyons, who would turn George Seldes's critical methods against him in 1947, spent the early to mid-1940s writing for left-wing anti-Stalinist publications like *The New Leader*—which itself helped popularize structural understandings of media bias on the left—only to serve as a contributing editor to William F. Buckley's *National Review* by the late 1950s. Lyons's shift to the right was enabled by a burgeoning right-anticommunist movement infrastructure, under development in the late 1940s. From small-circulation periodicals like *Human Events* and *Plain Talk* to private research initiatives like American Business Consultants (publishers of the infamous radio and television industry blacklist *Red Channels*), by 1950 the forebearers of the modern conservative movement had adopted and weaponized structural media criticism, a key component of what we now call McCarthyism.

This chapter foregrounds a largely forgotten battle between Eugene Lyons and George Seldes in 1947 that pitted structural press criticism against itself. The conflict illuminates tectonic political shifts, of which Seldes and Lyons themselves were only vaguely aware, that in hindsight help explain the modern conservative movement's early investment in structural media criticism as an effective political tactic. The divergent paths of Lyons and Seldes after the incident are indicative of a broader discursive and infrastructural shift—the end of popular front liberalism and the launch of modern conservatism—that would ultimately give rise to the "liberal media," not to mention Ernst's political realignment.

"THE PRESENT COMMERCIAL PRESS IS OUR ENEMY"

If Ernst was among the leading popularizers of structural approaches to press criticism, George Seldes was the genre's most prolific innovator. Seldes began his career working as a newspaper reporter for the Pittsburgh *Leader* in 1909, a year he later remembered as "the peak of the great muckraking era" of US journalism. Inspired by the press criticism of Will Irwin and Upton Sinclair, whose *The Brass Check* (1920) was perhaps the first book-length exposé of the US newspaper industry, Seldes began a second career as a press critic after resigning from *The Chicago Tribune* in 1928. In 1929 he published his first book, *You Can't Print That!*, which documented the news suppression and censorship he had experienced while working as a foreign correspondent covering European affairs for the *Tribune* during the decade following World War I. The *Tribune* was owned by Robert McCormick, a staunch anticommunist and leading press baron of the Old Right who went on to oppose the New Deal and US military involvement in World War II. Seldes saw his experience under McCormick as emblematic of a broader trend in US journalism—newspapers tended to be owned by wealthy men with deep connections to industry and resistance to the concerns of labor.[15] These affinities, Seldes believed, resulted in structural biases against working-class interests that skewed public opinion toward the right.

In the spring of 1940 Seldes was presented with an opportunity to push back against this right-wing press bias. Seldes's neighbor Bruce Minton suggested cofounding a newsletter that would enable Seldes to circulate his press criticism, as well as news that had been suppressed by other outlets, among working-class readers. Minton had written for the liberal magazine *New Republic* and had also been an editor of *New Masses*, an important organ of the popular front era that was closely aligned with the Communist Party USA, of which Minton was a low-key member. The party had approached Minton about establishing the newsletter to serve as a "front."[16] The goal was to circulate the Communist Party line beyond its membership and to have a backup publication in case their newspaper, *The Daily Worker*, was shut down by the US federal government. Unaware of this ulterior motive, Seldes agreed to edit the newsletter, which they named *In Fact*. Minton provided $3,000 in start-up costs, secretly sourced from Communist Party coffers.[17]

Leveraging Minton's connections within AFL and CIO union locals in New York, *In Fact* launched in May 1940 with six thousand rank-and-file subscribers. Subscriptions grew steadily, providing enough cash flow to repay the Communist Party in full by the end of its first year, and for the newsletter to run independently and without advertising thereafter. That first year also saw tensions emerge between Seldes and Minton as the latter attempted to implement a communist editorial line and the former bristled. "I was in an awkward position," Minton later recalled in a written confession. "I was responsible for the contents of *In Fact* to the Party, and yet I was unable to control the contents and unable to influence Mr. Seldes. The notion that he would be a 'front,' inactive and passive, was a complete illusion; the hope that Mr. Seldes could be persuaded by communist ideas or by me equally preposterous."[18] The newsletter's runaway success was attributed to Seldes's personal popularity and to the publication's unwillingness to simply toe the line, making the prospects of a party takeover untenable. While Minton would step aside in the spring of 1941, effectively ending *In Fact*'s direct if clandestine affiliation with the Communist Party, his subsequent expulsion from the party in 1946 would expose Seldes to considerable red-baiting.

In the meantime, *In Fact* thrived as the first mass audience newsletter devoted to press criticism. Its circulation soon outpaced the leading liberal outlets of the era, including *New Republic* and *The Nation*, peaking in 1947 with 176,000 subscribers, a third of whom were union members.[19] Seldes regularly called out mainstream US newspapers and wire services for what he viewed as antilabor, antisemitic, and racist content. For instance, in the newsletter's first issue, Seldes attacked the Associated Press for using courtesy titles like *Mr.* or *Mrs.* when referring to white people but not when referring to Black people. "The Associated Press prides itself on Olympian honesty—because it is a non-profit cooperative," Seldes wrote. "But the non-profiteering cooperators are the owners of the press, not the newspapermen who work for it; it is a phony co-op of bosses, most of whom are anti-labor and some, Ku Kluxers."[20] That Seldes, in challenging the AP's reputation for impartiality, focused on the news cooperative's ownership structure speaks to the materialist basis of his approach to media criticism. For Seldes, right-wing bias in the press was most often a by-product of the commercial media system itself—newspaper owners sought to cultivate positive relationships with industry leaders, who funded their efforts through advertisements, which sought out mass (presumably white) audiences to purchase their goods. When political economic factors weren't directly implicated—as with the not-for-profit Associated Press—Seldes sought answers through, at times conspiratorial, class analysis.

"What is the most powerful force in America today?" Seldes asked in his 1942 self-published book, *The Facts Are . . . A Guide to Falsehoods and Propaganda in the Press*. "Answer: public opinion. What makes public opinion? Answer: the main force is the press. Can you trust the press?" Seldes's answer was that "98 percent (or perhaps 99½ percent)" of major newspapers and magazines in the United States could not be trusted due to their corporate ownership and their reliance on advertising revenue, which aligned them with the commercial and political interests of "Big Business."[21] This collusion, according to Seldes, manifested in what topics received coverage (and which did not), impacting the public's ability to know and act upon its own interests. "It seems to me that everyone who is intelligent enough to read is intelligent enough to know what to do when the truth, hitherto hidden, has suddenly been brought into the light of day," Seldes wrote.[22]

Truth, for Seldes, corresponded with class consciousness. He lamented that union members accounted for a minority of the overall US labor force and blamed antiunion sentiments on a press beholden to the special interests of capital. Seldes saw cultivating a critical disposition toward the mainstream press as a crucial first step toward raising awareness among US workers of their shared interests as a class. Seldes cited a *Forbes* magazine poll indicating that 27 percent of Americans were "already skeptical of the standard press, doubtful to its honesty, suspicious of the news it serves, and therefore by implication, ready to join in a movement for a non-commercial, fair and honest press." Seldes saw *In Fact* as a tool for heightening the contradictions between the interests of newspaper owners and those of their working-class audiences. He wrote: "Our first objective should be the creation of the consciousness of the power of a future free press, the realization that the present commercial press is our enemy, and that we have the power to change all that."[23]

Seldes's most famous crusade, against Big Tobacco, exemplified this project of shedding light on how profit-seeking newspapers materially harmed their readers. On January 13, 1941, *In Fact* reported on the growing scientific evidence of negative health effects related to tobacco use, including a groundbreaking study by Johns Hopkins University biologist Dr. Raymond Pearl that found a significant correlation between smoking and shortened lifespans.[24] While the Associated Press picked up the story, Seldes nevertheless felt it was being suppressed by major newspapers. He published a follow-up excoriating the "venality of the press as regards tobacco—an industry which pays the press $50,000,000 a year." When Dr. Pearl publicly disputed allegations that newspapers were suppressing the report, Seldes attacked him too. "Dr. Pearl was asked to name two or three newspapers, outside of country dailies and country weeklies (which are not subsidized by tobacco advertising) which ran his story," Seldes wrote. "He refused to answer." Seldes contended that the only papers to pick up the story were smaller outlets who did not receive advertising money from major tobacco companies. He concluded: "The newspapers, *Editor & Publisher, Saturday Evening Post,* all say that advertising has nothing to do with editorial policy. The facts are: 1) The cigarette companies spend up to $50,000,000 a year. 2) News inimical to tobacco is not published, 3) 99% of the American press suppresses government fraud orders against advertisers."[25] During its decade of existence, *In Fact* ran dozens of stories warning readers of the negative health impacts of tobacco use, emphasizing how enormously profitable it was for newspapers to downplay those harms.

DOMESTIC FASCIST CONSPIRACY

In Fact also routinely reported on the financial dealings of US corporations with fascist regimes abroad, news Seldes felt was being similarly suppressed by newspaper owners who did not want to upset their corporate benefactors.[26] He was especially critical of Henry Ford, drawing attention to the automaker's antisemitism and support for the Nazi regime in Germany, and exposing Ford's antiworker tactics at his own factories and antipathy toward the labor movement more broadly. "Automobiles and cigarettes are the two biggest advertisers in the world," Seldes reminded his readers. "The press knows who supplies both its bread and its butter."[27] But the press, according to Seldes, was not only extending favorable coverage to industries with dubious ideological and ethical commitments—it was complicit in a broader effort to bring European-style fascism to the United States.

Seldes was particularly concerned by the political and propaganda initiatives of the National Association of Manufacturers (NAM), which he referred to as the "center of American fascism."[28] As historian Kim Phillips-Fein has written, NAM was founded in the late nineteenth century by businessmen who wanted to join forces against organized labor. The group played an important role in mobilizing opposition to President Franklin Roosevelt and his New Deal. Its leaders, including chemical manufacturer Lammot du Pont and General Motors CEO Alfred P. Sloan, funded educational initiatives designed to promote free market capitalism by championing neoliberal economic theory, a key ideological component of what would become the modern conservative movement.[29] NAM also invested heavily in media designed to promote the political and economic interests of industry: billboard and newspaper advertisements, radio and film productions, even an antilabor newspaper comic called *Uncle Abner Says*. NAM provided funding to college professors whose research affirmed the virtues of the free market and even paid *New York Herald Tribune* syndicated columnist George Sokolsky $1,000 per month to write sympathetic commentaries.[30] Seldes depicted these early conservative movement building efforts as a campaign to "poison the minds of the American people." He wrote, "Of course, the organization calls it 'enlightenment' or the spreading of the doctrine of 'free enterprise,' but it is nevertheless propaganda, since it is aimed to insure the private profits of the few, as against the general welfare of the many."[31]

The increasing prevalence of NAM propaganda corresponded with the emergence of a small but influential early modern conservative print culture in the 1930s and 1940s. *American Mercury*, founded by H. L. Mencken and George Jean Nathan in 1924, spent its first decade as a venue for literary nonfiction and satire, publishing many leading writers of the era. While it had long promoted a centrist conservatism, what Menken called "an educated Toryism—the true Disraelian brand," the *Mercury* took a sharp rightward turn in 1935 when publisher Alfred A. Knopf sold it to Lawrence Spivak, who had previously served as the magazine's business manager, and Paul Palmer, formerly of Joseph Pulitzer's *New York World*. Under Palmer's editorship (1935–1939), the *Mercury* adopted a strong anti-Roosevelt and anti–New Deal editorial line.[32] Meanwhile, another storied early twentieth century US magazine, *Scribner's*, was undergoing a rightward shift of its own. In 1939 the magazine folded before merging with the pictorial magazine *Commentator*. The newly launched *Scribner's Commentator*, under the editorship of George T. Eggleston, promoted an isolationist editorial line that featured sympathetic coverage of fascist regimes abroad. Both the *Mercury* and *Scribner's Commentator* regularly published early forms of conservative press criticism targeting British and American propaganda efforts against Nazi Germany and revealing putative communist bias within nominally conservative US newspapers and magazines.[33] With two leading US magazines turning against the New Deal and toward isolationism in the face of growing fascism abroad, Seldes sounded the alarm of what he saw as growing, coordinated, and radical right-wing press.

According to Seldes, the centerpiece of this domestic fascist press conspiracy was *Reader's Digest*—the largest circulation magazine in the United States. Founded in 1920, its publisher, DeWitt Wallace, was a staunch anticommunist who regularly used his magazine to amplify conservative commentary that had been published in smaller venues.[34] In April 1945, for instance, *Reader's Digest* published a twenty-page abridged version of Friedrich Hayek's 1944 book *The Road to Serfdom*, an important work of neoliberal theory that remains a key primary text for modern conservatives.[35] Seldes's first exposé of *Reader's Digest* came in November 1942, when the magazine hired former *Mercury* publisher Paul Palmer as an editor. Seldes wrote that Palmer had "introduced American Fascism to the *Mercury* during his editorship" before passing the reins to the journalist Eugene Lyons, who, Seldes wrote, continued Palmer's legacy of printing "reactionary propaganda." Both men, according to Seldes, conspired with *Reader's Digest* publisher Wallace—publishing pro-fascist articles in otherwise reputable publications so that Wallace could then amplify them to his millions of readers.[36]

If Palmer's hiring confirmed, for Seldes, a conspiratorial collaboration between the *Mercury* and the *Digest*, Wallace's decision to hire Eggleston in May 1946 added then-defunct *Scribner's Commentator* to the domestic fascist publishing nexus.[37] In June 1946 Seldes alerted his readers to a report produced by the US Army for use by the Nuremberg prosecution of Nazi war criminals, which in part alleged that German diplomat Heribert von Strempel had given between $10,000 and $15,000 to Eggleston and Douglas Stewart while the two were running *Scribner's Commentator*.[38] Despite the fact that the allegations did not directly involve *Reader's Digest*—except insofar as the von Strempel testimony noted that Eggleston and Douglas wanted to form a magazine "like *Reader's Digest*"—Seldes used the *Digest's* recent hiring of Eggleston to treat the revelation as evidence of its collaboration with the Nazi regime. When in September of that year the US Justice Department recommended indicting Eggleston on perjury charges relating to the von Strempel allegations, Seldes was quick to take credit and to accuse *Reader's Digest* of hushing the case. Seldes later called the scoop "one of our most important news stories in our six years of publishing."[39] Much to Seldes' chagrin, the Justice Department ultimately decided against charging Eggleston, which *In Fact* characteristically chalked up to pressure exerted by *Reader's Digest* itself.[40]

Seldes's penchant for conflating a wide array of right-wing politics with "fascism," for depicting interpersonal associations as evidence of nefarious conspiracy, and for focusing on domestic connections to foreign powers with totalitarian ideologies almost perfectly mirrors the rhetorical tactics we have since come to associate with the Second Red Scare or McCarthyism. While Seldes's materialist approach to structural press criticism inspired the progressive media reform movement of the 1940s, it also raised the ire of his many targets. This included anticommunists on the left, who felt that *In Fact* hewed too closely to the Communist line and employed combative tactics commonly associated with the party's vigorous enforcement of its ideological orthodoxies.

"HAVE YOU DONE YOUR RED-BAITING FOR TODAY?"

Perhaps Seldes's most avid critic on the left was *The New Leader*. Founded in 1924 by figures associated with the Socialist Party of America, *The New Leader* was a leading outlet for liberal and progressive anticommunists by the 1940s. It was also a key incubator of anticommunist journalists, most notably Ralph de Toledano and Eugene Lyons, who would shift rightward and join the ranks of the modern conservative movement by the 1950s. *New Leader* published its first full-length critique of George Seldes in 1941. Written by future conservative de Toledano, the article included then-unsubstantiated allegations that the Communist Party had founded *In Fact* as a front, "trading on the rather bedraggled reputation of George Seldes, ex-champion of an honest press."[41] *New Leader* hit Seldes again in 1944, republishing an article by James A. Wechsler that had first appeared in *The Guild Reporter*, the official organ of the American Newspaper Guild. "Brother Seldes invariably pictures himself as the lone independent thinker of our time, nature's noblest crusader against fraud and suppression," Wechsler wrote. "But the same George Seldes has been demonstrating a nimbleness which matches that of any wage-slave inhabiting the darkest pastures of the newspaper field. Mr. Seldes speaks (and apparently thinks) as the Communist Party, a ruthless and exacting boss, does."[42]

The *New Leader*'s criticisms of Seldes were part and parcel of its more general focus on the "problems of the press," as evidenced by the magazine's devotion of considerable space to news media criticism throughout the 1940s. This media critical emphasis seems to have begun in earnest as early as 1942, after the magazine published a series of articles by Ferdinand Lundberg criticizing the left-leaning daily newspaper *PM*.[43] That same summer *The New Leader* experimented with a short-lived column titled "Slants in the News," which consisted of a series of news briefs containing some metacommentary about biased newspapers but mostly news items that were presumably omitted from mainstream news coverage of the preceding week.[44] Between 1942 and 1947, in addition to publishing two critiques of *In Fact*, *The New Leader* at various points singled out *Life* magazine, *Atlantic Monthly*, and the *Nation*, among others, all for their supposedly sympathetic coverage of the Soviet Union or of groups *The New Leader* identified as communist fronts.[45]

By 1946 *The New Leader* supplemented its occasional critiques of various left-leaning and liberal newspapers and magazines with more structural critiques of the US press system writ large. It invited Oswald Garrison Villard to write a series of articles considering the systematic failings of the daily press. Villard's 1944 book, *The Disappearing Daily*, raised awareness of the so-called newspaper crisis resulting from a decades-long trend toward the concentration of ownership and, like Ernst's *First Freedom*, inspired the era's progressive media reformers.[46] In *New Leader*, Villard lamented the emergence of what he called the "conservative press," a phenomenon he attributed less to the ideological machinations of owners than to market forces, which drove daily newspapers to pander to the lowest common denominator of public opinion in order to maintain the high circulation necessary to turn a steady profit. He found this tendency in "liberal and conservative dailies" alike, writing: "Taking the conservative group as a whole, there is the familiar hostility to any change in the status quo, the same suspicion of any new economic or social ideals and of anything foreign, and the same trend toward nationalism and imperialism which has distinguished our reactionary dailies in the past and is now reinforced by the bitterness, disappointments and losses due to the Second World War."[47] Villard's criticism was reflective of the emerging consensus among progressives and liberals over the course of the 1940s, which resulted in serious efforts to reform journalism as a profession and to more closely regulate it as an industry.

While *The New Leader* contributed to the growing popular consensus that the daily press was an increasingly conservative or reactionary force, offering an anticommunist iteration of the materialist press criticism initially popularized by George Seldes, it was also invested in legitimizing red-baiting as a viable critical tool in its struggle to combat communist propaganda. By the late 1940s the magazine was running in-house ads proclaiming, "Have You Done Your Red-Baiting for Today?"[48] Perhaps not surprisingly, regular Seldes target and future *National Review* editor Eugene Lyons was an especially vocal proponent of the tactic. In 1945 Lyons took to the pages of *New Leader* to red-bait Seldes—juxtaposing his critical coverage of the Soviet Union in the 1920s with his more favorable coverage in the 1940s, suggesting that Seldes had sold out to Moscow. Lyons wrote, "If, by his current definition, I am a Fascist, then Comrade Seldes, in his previous incarnation, was a super-duper-Fascist."[49]

By playfully turning Seldes's own tactics against him, Lyons illuminated a key parallel between his red-baiting and Seldes's penchant for associating his opponents with fascism. While Lyons did not appreciate this tactic when aimed at him, he clearly relished wielding it. In a "Defense of Red-Baiting," published in a 1946 issue of *New Leader*, Lyons criticized *Fortune* magazine for its pejorative use of the term "professional Red-baiters," which Lyons found needlessly stigmatizing. For Lyons, red-baiting was merely an act of transparency or proper labeling, an attempt to uncover the communist motivations and sympathies behind nominally liberal writers, broadcasters, and advocates. Lyons took particular offense at the implication that red-baiters materially benefited from their craft: "The implication is that Red-baiting is a remunerative crime; that Red-baiters are loaded with gold by someone somewhere. Only the victims of the smear know how much easier it is for namby-pamby 'neutrals' on the Soviet issue, not to mention outright fellow travelers, to get a hearing in the press and on the radio."[50]

In playing the victim, Lyons implied a general press bias against anticommunists. He also reinforced the materialist explanation for that bias that undergirded *The New Leader*'s criticisms against both Seldes and the mainstream press he criticized. If Seldes's parallel thinking with the

Communist Party suggested he was under their employ, Lyons's complaint of poverty was meant to convey the independence of thought behind his red-baiting. Driving home this point, the former *American Mercury* editor wrote: "The one advantage we Red-baiters enjoy is the professional domain is easier access to *The New Leader*, but that alas does not seriously affect our income tax brackets."[51] Of course, as Lyons very well knew, career opportunities for red-baiters were at that very moment proliferating. Just three months after his ode to red-baiting was published in *The New Leader*, Lyons red-baited Seldes again in the new, right anticommunist journal *Plain Talk*. Disenchanted socialists like Lyons and de Toledano would bring structural media criticism and its associated rhetorical tactics with them on their steady march rightward.[52]

COUNTERATTACK

By 1947, as the progressive media reform movement was in high gear, stoking public concern with right-wing bias in the press and over the air, right anticommunists were quietly building their own alternative press and research operations designed to counteract their political enemies. If early conservative press criticism, in outlets like *American Mercury* and *Scribner's Commentator*, involved sporadic exposés of New Deal public relations efforts or critiques of the wartime propaganda campaigns of the United States and its allies, this new, right anticommunist infrastructure would adopt more structural modes of media criticism initially popularized by their opponents on the left. In 1944 right-anticommunist journalists Frank Hanighen and Felix Morley founded *Human Events*, which would become an important early organ of the modern conservative movement. The newsletter was funded by a group of midwestern businessmen and activists formerly affiliated with the anti-interventionist America First Committee, including both Old Right press baron Robert McCormick and William H. Regnery, whose son Henry would launch a highly influential conservative publishing company in 1947. As historian Nicole Hemmer has shown, *Human Events* was initially less concerned with liberal press bias than with the exclusion of isolationist and anti–New Deal points of view from mainstream news outlets.[53]

But other right-anticommunist media initiatives of the era, especially those funded by wealthy textile importer and future John Birch Society leadership council member Alfred Kohlberg, were more directly engaged in countering progressive press criticism by adopting its tactics. Kohlberg's business connections in China made him sympathetic to Chiang Kai-shek's Nationalists and fearful of the ascendance of the Chinese Communist Party. He was particularly concerned with how China was covered by the US press, which he regularly accused of pro-communist bias.[54] In 1946 Kohlberg decided to fund two initiatives designed to counteract this bias while promoting a more confrontational approach against communism. He provided $25,000 in start-up funds to the Russian-born anticommunist journalist Isaac Don Levine to launch *Plain Talk*, a magazine that would specialize in "factual exposés" aimed at convincing policymakers and other elites of the communist threat, both abroad and domestically. He also gave $25,000 to a small group of ex-FBI agents to build a private anticommunist research organization, which Kohlberg described as "a sort of Unamerican Activities Committee or FBI file system for the use of the magazine and for others interested."[55] While the latter would ultimately spin off under the name American Business Consultants, launching its own anticommunist newsletter, *Counterattack*, in 1947, the two initiatives actively collaborated as *Plain Talk* began planning its first issues.

In October 1946, one month after Seldes alleged a domestic fascist press conspiracy with *Reader's Digest* at its center, Kohlberg's anticommunist researchers approached Levine with a list of twenty-five possible subjects to be exposed by *Plain Talk*. According to an internal memorandum, drafted by American Business Consultants cofounder Ted "T. C." Kirkpatrick, Levine was uninterested: "His only request was . . . for information regarding *In Fact*. His proposal dealt principally with securing information identifying George Seldes with the Communist Party."[56] The ex-FBI agents had already produced a twenty-three-page confidential report on Seldes's alleged subversive activities, drawn from public records and other documents they had gathered while researching the *In Fact* publisher's many radical associations.[57] Missing from their archive was definitive evidence of Seldes's supposed ongoing working relationship with the Communist Party. Heeding Levine's request, Kirkpatrick attempted to gather more revelatory information—namely, evidence that *In Fact* was financially subsidized by the party. While researching, Kirkpatrick learned that frequent Seldes target Eugene Lyons was himself already at work on an exposé of *In Fact*. Ultimately, neither Kirkpatrick nor Lyons was able to find evidence directly tying Seldes to the party, a fact the Kirkpatrick memo suggests disappointed Levine.

Nevertheless, Lyons completed his exposé of Seldes, drawing heavily on the information provided by Kirkpatrick. *Plain Talk* published that article, "Red Mouthpiece," in its March 1947 edition, the same issue in which Levine announced Lyons as a new contributing editor. Conservative radio commentator and fellow Seldes target Fulton Lewis Jr. amplified the article to his millions of listeners—a major boon to the fledgling *Plain Talk*'s otherwise meager circulation.[58] Lyons accused *In Fact* of propagandizing for the Communist Party, tracing shifts in Seldes's own publicly stated political positions to shifts in the official party line. He also attacked Seldes's personal integrity, detailing allegations of plagiarism uncovered by Kohlberg's researchers and noting that Seldes's tendency to smear political opponents extended to both the Left and Right, from *New Leader* to *Reader's Digest*.[59] To conclude, Lyons wrote, "in concealing these facts from his subscribers [Seldes] has perpetrated a fraud and imposture upon them, palming off the changing Communist propaganda as his own independent views."[60] Seldes's sin, according to Lyons, was not merely disseminating Communist Party propaganda, but claiming to arrive at the Communist line through his own independent thought—an impossibility according to the emergent right-anticommunist theory of propaganda, which was based on a belief that free and rational thought necessarily resulted in opposition to communism.

Focusing on Seldes's financial and institutional backing, Lyons adopted Seldes's own materialist rationale for press criticism—assuming that a publication's framing and political positions necessarily corresponded to the conditions of its production and the personal and pecuniary ends of its ownership. Like Seldes, Lyons and the ex-FBI agents who would become American Business Consultants sought to reveal the underlying financial, political, and interpersonal connections that explained why their opponents understood the world and the news of the day differently than they did. Rather than acknowledging the inevitability of differences of opinion under conditions of liberal pluralism, they all framed political disagreement as epistemological threat. For instance, the American Business Consultants' newsletter, *Counterattack*, launched on a subscription-only basis in 1947 and did not present arguments in favor of free market principles or against the geopolitical machinations of the Communist Party. Instead, under the slogan "Facts to Combat Communism," its authors focused on revealing the putative hidden motivations behind nominally liberal groups, media outlets, and public figures. Guilt by association, conflation of liberal political beliefs with Soviet atrocities, allegations of dual loyalty with nefarious foreign powers—all tactics popularized, albeit against fascism, by George Seldes in *In Fact*—became the central strategy of right anticommunists in the late 1940s and early 1950s.

Seldes, of course, was an antifascist gadfly with few connections to the US federal security apparatus. Right-anticommunist outfits like American Business Consultants, conversely, maintained close ties to the FBI and to countersubversive congressional proceedings, such as the House Committee on Un-American Activities (which gained standing status in 1946) and the Senate Internal Security Subcommittee, created by Sen. Patrick McCarran in 1950 and made infamous by Sen. Joseph McCarthy in the years that followed. Seldes inspired a media reform movement among progressives who sought a socially responsible press that put public interest over personal profits. His opponents used his tactics to ignite a Red Scare.

American Business Consultants played a crucial role in stoking a moral panic that corresponded with the federal government's countersubversion efforts. In 1950 American Business Consultants published *Red Channels: The Report of Communist Influence in Radio and Television*, which listed 151 supposed communist sympathizers and fellow travelers, most of whom worked in radio or film, and many of whom suffered as the report came to serve as a blacklist in Hollywood and throughout the entertainment and advertising industries.[61] The report's authors bristled at allegations that they were engaged in blacklisting. Like Seldes, they saw their work as simply informing the public about the unacknowledged political and financial loyalties of media figures. "This fight will be decided in American homes," the report's authors wrote in *Counterattack* one month after publishing *Red Channels*. "The American radio and TV audience will decide the issue and, if properly informed, will decide it correctly."[62]

THE DECLINE OF *IN FACT*

Predictably, the same month that *Plain Talk* published the Lyons exposé of Seldes, *In Fact* issued an exposé of Lyons—apparently hoping that reiterating the latter's connections to fascism as a "*Digest* fellow traveler" would counter Lyons's revelations about Seldes.[63] However, by 1947, with the emergence of *Counterattack* two months after the Seldes–Lyons spat, progressives were beginning to lose the battle over defining the presumed structural biases of the media in the minds of the public. Seldes's subscription base dropped precipitously. *In Fact* soon became a regular target of *Counterattack*, with the latter routinely alleging that Communist Party USA leader Earl Browder had once considered Seldes for the editorship of the *Daily Worker*, as if such a fact had self-evident implications for the veracity of Seldes's later work.[64]

The feud between Seldes and *Counterattack* broke open in the spring of 1948, when Seldes published an exposé of right-wing counterpropaganda research efforts, calling American Business Consultants "more respectable, better publicized, and probably most successful of the new anti-communist crusaders."[65] Seldes compared the group, unfavorably, to Joseph Kamp's antilabor research outfit, the Constitutional Educational League, publisher of *Headlines, and What's Behind Them*, a newsletter launched in the late 1930s and devoted to right-anticommunist news criticism. Emphasizing their status as former FBI agents, Seldes also criticized the American Business Consultants' capacity for research, writing: "Its 'dossiers,' however, are usually cribbed from the unreliable files of the House un-American Committee and contain the same stupid standards of judging subversive activity."[66]

Responding to *In Fact*'s allegations about American Business Consultants, *Counterattack* accused Seldes of telling seventeen lies but gave only one example, which was itself based less in a disagreement about facts than with Seldes' semantics. Excusing its failure to reproduce Seldes's putative factual errors, *Counterattack* wrote, "Much more important is the poisonous effect of 'In Fact' on public opinion week after week. Seldes' sheet is distributed in unions, colleges, libraries, youth groups, women's clubs, and among teachers and other professional people. Pretending to be liberal, it has spread Stalin's doctrines more effectively than an OPENLY Communist paper could have."[67] Again, more important than the veracity of the information published within *In Fact* was Seldes's failure to affix a "Communist" label to his newsletter. Responding to the publication of *Red Channels* in 1950, Seldes would similarly criticize *Counterattack* for its obsession with "purity labels in others" despite its refusal to disclose its own opaque political and financial motivations.

By the summer of 1950—when Seldes railed against the publication of *Red Channels*, calling it a brazen attempt by American Business Consultants to "cash in on the cold war and the unpopularity of communists and communism"—*In Fact*'s days were numbered.[68] From a peak circulation of 176,000, by January 1950 Seldes's subscriber base had dwindled to 73,000, threatening *In Fact*'s subscription-based financial viability. In October 1950 Seldes decided to fold. In a passionate farewell editorial, Seldes explained his financial constraints and clarified the stakes of his mission. "I have stated from the first that what Reaction in America is after is not the 54,000 members of the Communist Party or even the 540,000 who according to FBI Chief Hoover are their fellow travelers, but the liberal, democratic, pro-labor, anti-fascist Left, which is ten times or more the strength of the communists, but which is not organized," Seldes wrote. "It was these millions of good Americans I wanted as my subscribers."[69]

Seldes had hoped that by exposing the fascist sympathies and antilabor motivations of business propagandists and revealing the biases of major newspapers and magazines, he would awaken the public's latent class consciousness. What Seldes found instead was "apathy." He lamented, "There is no protest, no indignation. Or very little. People are frightened to death." Seldes attributed this fear to the success of red-baiting efforts, which by 1950, he wrote, were "a hundred times worse than that of the 1920s."[70] As if on cue, four days after the final issue of *In Fact*, *Counterattack* celebrated the newsletter's end by reiterating its red-baiting of George Seldes: "It was the apathy of the CP to those who don't follow its line, not the apathy of the American people to fascism, that is responsible for *In Fact*'s demise."[71]

With the publication of *Red Channels* and the folding of *In Fact*, 1950 marked a turning point in the history of structural media criticism in the United States. For much of the 1940s, liberal and left-wing journalists, lawyers, and activists successfully popularized the idea that the press exhibited a right-wing bias against President Roosevelt, the New Deal, and labor. They mobilized to prevent that bias from extending from print to broadcast media, as we saw in the preceding chapter, ultimately pressuring the Federal Communications Commission into adopting its Fairness Doctrine in 1949. As we will see in the next chapter, that policy would influence the first grassroots mobilization of the modern conservative movement—Facts Forum—which ultimately produced radio and television programming designed to conform to the Federal Communications Commission's balance imperative. When Facts Forum was exposed as a right-wing front group in late 1953, it initiated a conflict between the modern conservative movement and the press that would ultimately lend salience to that movement's claims of liberal media bias.

Yet at the very moment that progressive media reformers were mobilizing the public against right-wing bias, their opponents were already cultivating a critical disposition toward the press all their own. Targeted by progressive media reformers, conservatives and right anticommunists mobilized a counterattack. They launched new journals and research outfits that borrowed and built upon the ideas and tactics that had been used against them, including, most notably, the combative form of structural press criticism popularized by *In Fact*. This burgeoning right-anticommunist infrastructure served as a vital bridge for left-anticommunist journalists—like Ralph de Toledano and Eugene Lyons—connecting them to funders and outlets that would facilitate their rightward ideological migration. Both found their way to William F. Buckley's *National Review* by the late 1950s. This newly formed right-anticommunist movement infrastructure also bolstered the Second Red Scare, which served as a crucial wedge for pulling anticommunists away from common cause with progressives and for relegating so-called fellow travelers, like George Seldes, to the margins of public life.

Between 1950 and the 1970s the modern conservative movement built upon the lessons of its right-anticommunist forebears in continuing to cultivate and popularize a critical disposition toward the mainstream press. Indeed, rigid distinctions between the Old and New Right, between the right-anticommunist periodicals and research outfits of the late 1940s and the "first generation" of conservative media activism in the late 1950s and early 1960s, obscures ongoing collaborations between them. For instance, among the subscribers to *Counterattack* was Arthur G. McDowell, a liberal trade unionist who served as director of civic, education, and governmental affairs for the Upholsters International Union of North America, which funded the Council Against Communist Aggression, or CACA (by far the most befitting acronym in the history of anticommunism).[72] Through his work with CACA in the 1950s and 1960s, McDowell collaborated with some of the most influential right anticommunists of the era, including *Counterattack* editor T. C. Kirkpatrick, *Plain Talk* editor Isaac Don Levine, and Eugene Lyons.[73] McDowell hosted monthly luncheons for anticommunists living in Washington, DC, and its surrounding suburbs. Among the regular attendees of these gatherings, renamed the McDowell Luncheon Group after its founder's untimely death in 1966, was economist Reed J. Irvine.[74] In 1969 Irvine used the group as a springboard for launching Accuracy in Media, the conservative press watchdog.

When Morris Ernst joined Accuracy in Media's advisory board in 1971, he was likely unaware of the circuitous path structural press criticism had taken, from left to right. He may have even experienced it as a sense of vindication. While progressive media reformers like George Seldes aligned with communists in opposition to fascism and in support of organized labor and racial equality, Ernst had long been willing to play ball with the FBI to root out subversives, who he believed held views fundamentally in opposition to his belief in liberal pluralism. If in the 1940s the loudest complaints of media bias came from the left, by the 1960s the sense of media marginalization had shifted notably to the right. We now turn to how that shift occurred.

3

CULTIVATING A CONSERVATIVE CRITICAL DISPOSITION TOWARD THE PRESS

"The American people cannot be required to forever accept the penalty of confusion and futility inflicted by distortion of the news."

H. L. Hunt thought he was fulfilling the balance imperative. Beginning in 1951, the Texas oilman had produced "educational" radio and television programming intended to "stimulate interest in public affairs."[1] These debate-style Facts Forum broadcasts were designed to benefit from the affordances of the Fairness Doctrine, the 1949 FCC-issued requirement that broadcast licensees dedicate airtime to "the discussion of public issues of interest in the community" in a way that ensured that "the public has a reasonable opportunity to hear different opposing positions."[2] Between 1951 and 1956, Hunt spent at least $3.4 million, untaxed, producing the shows—yielding $5 million or more in free "public service" airtime each year.[3] By January 1956 Facts Forum programming aired on no fewer than 724 broadcast stations, 99 of them television. It reached millions of listeners located in nearly every US state and territory as well as in the Philippines.[4]

But in early 1954 Facts Forum found itself on the defensive. A series of exposés—initially in the Communist *Worker* newspaper, then in national mainstream outlets like *Time* magazine—had revealed Hunt's bankrolling of Facts Forum. Worse, they unpacked Hunt's right-anticommunist political beliefs and alliances, once again raising the specter of reactionary dominance over the airwaves. Addressing the allegations in his *Facts Forum News* magazine, Hunt defended the organization's commitments to nonpartisanship and anticommunism. He also targeted the press. "The people are sovereign and have the power to require reliability in the news," Hunt wrote. "They can require honest information or propaganda, whatever they elect, and if propaganda, can finally elect which direction it be slanted."[5]

Of course, Hunt's critics saw Facts Forum as propaganda. But, as his reply indicates, it wasn't merely so. Hunt's confidence in the public's capacity to ascertain the reliability of a news source was rooted in his idiosyncratic conception of public opinion, which assumed that most Americans already shared his conservative (he preferred the term *constructive*) political beliefs. For Hunt, Facts Forum was not geared at indoctrinating the masses. It aimed to encourage what he envisioned as a natural democratic consensus around his right-anticommunist conception of reality.

When Hunt founded Facts Forum in 1951, he initially charged the nonprofit with coordinating autonomous local discussion groups around the country. The stated goal was to fight political apathy through the promotion of putatively balanced critical debate over the news of the day. Facts Forum's outward concern with civic engagement did belie Hunt's ultimate desire to affect a rightward shift in public opinion, which he considered to be a "constant immutable force which can be altered or changed only by itself."[6] But Hunt saw Facts Forum as a means of encouraging conservatives to be more outspoken in expressing their preexisting worldview and, increasingly, to insist that worldview be reflected back to them in the news and commentary they consumed. As he put it in an early plan for Facts Forum, "Since the knowledge of an individual does not become a part of the democratic process unless expressed, Facts Forum shall cultivate not only an informed but an articulate opinion."[7] In doing so Hunt also cultivated a critical disposition toward the mainstream press among the nascent conservative grassroots.

To date, the historiography of Facts Forum has focused almost exclusively on its broadcast programming. As historian Heather Hendershot contends, "there is no doubt that Facts Forum's most important and far-reaching activity was not its small group discussions or mail-order library but rather its delivery of messages to wide audiences via TV and radio."[8] She rightly notes that Facts Forum's commitment to "balance" contradicted the propagandistic character of its aesthetic and rhetorical strategies—namely, the "constructive" side was always depicted more emphatically and attractively, while the "liberal" side was often less-than-well-articulated. But Facts Forum's persistent emphasis on nonpartisan balance, on the importance of group discussion of current events, on nurturing a skeptical disposition toward mainstream sources of information, and on the acceptability of disagreement (albeit within right-anticommunist discursive parameters) was more than mere window dressing.

In a letter published in his local newspaper, Facts Forum participant Eugene Elkins of Dallas wrote that the group "gives the voter an opportunity to get all the facts concerning matters vital to his well-being, study them, discuss and debate them with fellow members and have a voice in remedying adverse conditions." Elkins continued, "He will not then be a push-over for appeals to his emotions by demagogues and the high-powered propaganda of entrenched bureaucracy."[9] While the broadcast medium appears unidirectional and propagandistic, Facts Forum's messages explicitly challenged readers and listeners to consume actively and, as this chapter will show, there is ample evidence to suggest they did.

Historians have also allowed Hunt's many personal eccentricities—his bigamy, his peculiar habits, his loner tendencies—to obscure his demonstrable impact on modern conservatism. In her pathbreaking history of the "first generation" of conservative media activists, Nicole Hemmer mentions the "idiosyncratic" Hunt only in passing to suggest that his media operations (Facts Forum, then Life Line) were "institutionally distinct from the rest of conservative media."[10] It is true that Hunt did not run in the Midwestern and Northeastern social circles of early conservative media activists Henry Regnery, Clarence Manion, and William Rusher—Hemmer's main focus. It is also true that William F. Buckley later relegated Hunt to the so-called lunatic fringe for his "yahoo bigotry and his appallingly bad manners."[11] But Buckley was a regular panelist on Facts Forum's *Answers for Americans* program in 1955, and Hunt gave him a platform to promote the launch of his *National Review* magazine later that year.[12] Facts Forum served as a vital early platform for many conservative media figures—among them Manion, Dan Smoot, Fulton Lewis Jr., and Medford Evans—who, as we will see in chapter 4, would soon find their way into various conservative media outlets, from those launched by Buckley to those run by the John Birch Society. Facts Forum, further, was a first attempt at mobilizing postwar conservative political activism at the grassroots. While it had limited success in that regard, its targeting by the mainstream press brought it national prominence—stoking a conflict between modern conservativism and the press at a crucial moment in that movement's formation.

This chapter takes H. L. Hunt and Facts Forum seriously by considering them largely on their own terms. It withholds judgment regarding their merits and coherence with the purpose of understanding how Facts Forum would have been experienced by its participants and listeners. Through polling and letter-writing contests as well as encouraging consumption of multiple media sources and attention to "both sides" of the issues of the day, Facts Forum enabled those participants to see themselves as part of an imagined community that shared not only modern conservative values but a critical assessment of mainstream sources of news and information—outlets that increasingly deprecated those participants' means of political engagement. This audience did not disappear when Facts Forum unceremoniously folded in 1956. They served as a base for future conservative media and organizing initiatives. Hunt's reputation among other conservative media activists notwithstanding, Facts Forum shaped what it meant to be conservative in the years immediately preceding the formation of a sustained movement infrastructure in the late 1950s and early 1960s. The press's antagonism toward Facts Forum in its final years set into motion a conflictual dynamic between modern conservatism and mainstream journalism—a pattern of interaction that would repeat with each new iteration of the modern conservative movement, reinforcing conservative perceptions that the media was not only biased against their worldview but against them.

H. L. HUNT, CONSTRUCTIVE

Perhaps fittingly, Hunt first entered the public eye the same month that the FCC concluded its hearings to reconsider its Mayflower ban on broadcast editorials. In April 1948 *Life* magazine ran a pictorial feature on a "new crop of multi-millionaires" produced throughout the US

Southwest by the Texas oil and cattle booms of the preceding decades.[13] It included a candid sidewalk portrait of Hunt with the caption: "Is this the richest man in the U.S.?"[14] A cross-promotion with the magazine's sister publication *Fortune*, the question was left to be answered in the business magazine's own April issue, which estimated Hunt's wealth at $263 million and his income at more than $1 million per week. Yet *Fortune* noted that Hunt's "quiet habits and abhorrence of cameras make him an unknown even to most of his fellow Texans."[15]

Privacy was an important strategy for the budding billionaire due to his complicated and socially taboo personal life. By 1948 Hunt was six years into a second bigamous relationship.[16] The origins of Hunt's wealth proved another likely source of his long-standing public discretion. Hunt used an inheritance to buy his first parcel of land, a 960-acre tract in Lake Village, Arkansas, in 1911, with the intention of establishing a cotton farm. When flooding ruined his first crop, Hunt subsisted on poker winnings and quickly earned a reputation around town as a professional gambler. Hunt's gambling was both a source of seed money and strategy for what was initially a boom-and-bust career in land speculation. In the early 1920s Hunt's quest for undervalued land led him to El Dorado, Arkansas, an oil boomtown renowned for its dens of sex work and gambling, which Hunt allegedly leveraged in making his first of many oil fortunes.[17]

By the time Hunt arrived in Dallas, Texas, in 1938, where he established the headquarters of his increasingly vast oil and gas production empire, his personal quietude and loner tendencies were exacerbated by the condescending exclusivity of the city's high society. Already enormously wealthy from investments in the booming East Texas oil fields, Hunt was nevertheless refused admission to the city's most prestigious country club, which claimed it had already accepted its quota of nouveau riche oilmen.[18] For similar reasons, Hunt was excluded from the city's political establishment. Despite his wealth and status as founder and president of Hunt Oil Company and, later, HLH Products, Hunt was not a member of the local Citizens Council and wielded little if any influence in local politics.[19] Indeed, local Dallas conservatives defined themselves as moderate against his perceived ideological and personal eccentricities.[20] Hunt's social life in Dallas was largely relegated to the city's underground gambling scene, which gladly welcomed his six-figure wagers and predilection for high-risk bets. He was, apparently, on the way to his daily afternoon poker game when the *Life* magazine photographer spotted him outside the Mercantile National Bank Building that housed the Hunt Oil offices.

Upon seeing the *Life* photograph, *Dallas Morning News* columnist Frank X. Tolbert requested an interview with Hunt, who uncharacteristically agreed. Hunt used the interview to demur on *Life*'s "richest man" claim, and to carefully manicure his newly public image—son of a Confederate veteran who was nevertheless a Republican of humble beginnings, who bought his first parcel of land with money he had saved (not inherited) working as a farmhand and lumberjack (not a professional gambler), a (one-) family man whose company contributed patriotically to the war effort by easing a fuel shortage caused by "the shutdown of the strike-bound coal mines in the winter of 1946." Hunt's desire to be known for his strike-busting was one of several details in the interview that anticipated his imminent turn toward right-wing political activism. Hunt also stressed that "he ha[d] always attempted to maintain a non-alcoholic and non-Communistic organization." Asked directly about his politics, Hunt replied: "On any ticket I would vote for these men for President. . . . In the order named—MacArthur, Taft, and Eisenhower. I feel the country needs a President with extreme courage. Such a man might well save us a war."[21] Hunt later credited the Tolbert interview with having "broke the ice," giving him an entrée into public life largely on his own terms.[22]

Hunt's dream candidates—especially Gen. Douglas MacArthur and Sen. Robert A. Taft—were darlings of the Right at a moment when conservatism was wildly unpopular. As Clark and Rimanoczy wrote in the dedication to their 1948 self-help book *How to Be Popular, Though Conservative*, "millions of unhappy Americans in all walks of life . . . have found themselves branded with the nasty name, 'conservative,' which, in some circles, rivals the mark of Cain and the Cloven Hoof."[23] By the late 1940s, Hunt had also grown increasingly concerned with the unpopularity of identifying as conservative. In a 1950 pamphlet Hunt pointed to a Gallup public opinion poll that found that 23 percent of respondents identified as liberal, 17 percent as conservative, and 60 percent "failed to make a choice between the two designations." Hunt reasoned, "When middle-of-the-roaders and others without particular conviction lean temporarily toward the leftist side, they can and do take great pride in the banner 'Liberal;' but when leaning toward what should be the 'Constructive' side, they may balk at the title of 'Conservative' and fail to announce and support their preference."[24] Hunt presumed that the 60 percent who declined to identify with either political label were more likely inclined toward conservatism but were disinclined to identify as such either due to stigma or apathy. His initial solution was rhetorical: simply replace the politically fraught term *conservative* with *constructive*, which Hunt considered to have an inherently positive meaning.

The bulk of Hunt's pamphlet sought to demonstrate the rhetorical value of using *constructive* to describe a political identification that he framed as nonpartisan yet diametrically opposed to liberalism. Constructive, according to Hunt, meant advocating for "a government which does not exact a pound of freedom for every service offered and an administration of that government which the people can understand and whose actions they can anticipate by consulting the laws enacted by their representatives." It meant "opposing liberals for their liberty with the money of others who work, produce, earn and save." In short, Hunt assumed that modern conservative ideology reflected the baseline beliefs of politically unaffiliated Americans. If given a term of political identification with a more positive connotation, Hunt imagined, "The previously undecided, now being offered a more attractive choice, would thoughtfully weigh the new question. Many of them would cast aside lack of conviction and then proudly announce that they were 'constructive' for in so doing they would proclaim a faith."[25]

Hunt also acknowledged popular support for "collectivist" government policies at home and abroad, a phenomenon he attributed to "strangely warped minds." If political apathy might be partially cured with better branding, then ensuring that public opinion reflected the conservative worldview required identifying and counteracting those responsible for warping the public's minds—namely, the news media. To do so, Hunt envisioned an "educational facts league whose membership may comprise sincere and open-minded members of all political parties or adherents to any philosophy of government so long as they dedicate themselves to securing, listing and using facts." Doing so, according to Hunt, required securing "impartial presentation of all the news through all news channels concerning issues of public interest." Hunt framed this ideal impartiality as beset on both sides by political ideologues, and he tasked his proposed facts league with advocating for the public's entitlement "to the facts on both sides of all issues" and against settling for "the part and kind of news which Left Wing workers or Right Side partisans are willing to let them have."[26] Hunt's pamphlet was published as an op ed in Louisiana's *Shreveport Times* in December 1950, accompanied by an editorial that lauded him as an exemplar of the "American system of free enterprise and unrestricted initiative."[27]

In the summer of 1949, a year before Hunt published his pamphlet, the FCC formally overturned its ban on broadcast editorials, arguing that they were "not contrary to the public interest" so long as they were "within reasonable limits and subject to the general requirements of fairness."[28] Hunt's pamphlet positioned his facts league as a grassroots corollary of the FCC's new Fairness Doctrine—prioritizing debate of issues of public concern justified by a stated commitment to impartiality through balance. While *constructive* would fail to catch on as a political identity, six months after the *Shreveport Times* celebrated his pamphlet, Hunt organized the first Facts Forum in Dallas. Begun as a series of local discussion groups, Facts Forum soon took to the airwaves nationally, with long-lasting effects upon the salience of conservative political identity and its relationship to the mainstream press. While Hunt imagined Facts Forum meetings as spaces where "constructive" truths might emerge self-evidently, from the beginning the public opinion expressed through the discussions reflected a commingling of the social and cultural milieu of participants with the hard right–anticommunist politics of their organizers.

FACTS FORUM AT THE GRASS ROOTS

Hunt was by no means the first conservative activist to see the political necessity of mobilizing a right-anticommunist grass roots around an explicit project of active news media consumption and criticism. In 1948 the US Chamber of Commerce published *A Program for Community Anti-Communist Action*, which outlined a six-point plan for defeating communism at the local level. Its top priority was the formation of local committees to research, educate, and initiate community discussion of the communist threat. The plan suggested recruiting former FBI agents or military intelligence officers as well as anticommunist reporters and commentators as "trained experts" but cautioned organizers to "avoid self-styled experts who lack common sense or who 'play by ear,' or those who may be anti-labor, anti-Semitic, and the like."[29] It recommended right-wing publications like *Counterattack* and *Plain Talk* as among the most trustworthy sources of anticommunist news and information.[30] It further advocated for activists to pressure their local newspapers and radio stations to carry "a full and accurate coverage of Communism." The program warned, "It is important to expose Communist propaganda in the press, radio, and screen. While few newspapers, periodicals, or radio stations consciously carry such propaganda, many have been deceived from time to time. Hence it is necessary to be vigilant in watching for errors."[31]

While it is unclear whether Hunt read the chamber's program, Facts Forum was a more-or-less faithful application of it. Hunt went out of his way to hire former FBI agents and to implement several of the chamber's tactical recommendations—from founding local discussion groups and anticommunist research libraries to promoting letters-to-the-editor writing campaigns and offering awards for "outstanding public service against Communism."[32] Dallas attorney Robert Dedman hosted the first Facts Forum discussion group on June 5, 1951, at the organization's offices, housed in the same Mercantile National Bank Building complex as Hunt Oil. *The Dallas Morning News* counted 55 people in attendance at the inaugural meeting.[33] Within a week six additional discussion groups had been organized in Dallas, boasting some 225 participants between them. Among Facts Forum's first invited speakers was none other than ex-FBI agent Ted "T. C." Kirkpatrick, cofounder of American Business Consultants and managing editor of *Counterattack*.[34] By the end of June Hunt had hired another charismatic former FBI agent, Dan Smoot, to serve as Facts Forum's coordinator.

Smoot was born into a poor farming family in southeastern Missouri in 1913. By the early 1930s Smoot had found his way to Dallas, where he worked for a wholesale produce firm while completing high school and, ultimately, bachelor's and master's degrees from Southern Methodist University. In 1941 Smoot was accepted into Harvard University's doctoral program in American Civilization but withdrew after the Pearl Harbor attack to join the Army. Rejected for flat feet and color blindness, Smoot was nevertheless hired in March of 1942 by the Federal Bureau of

Investigation, who assigned him to a squad investigating communists in Cleveland.³⁵ The quality and extent of Smoot's FBI service is a matter of some dispute. Smoot's version—which he later used for purposes of self-promotion—placed strong emphasis on hunting communists in the "industrial Midwest" and on his supposed work as "an Administrative Assistant to J. Edgar Hoover."³⁶ While Smoot would later narrate his resignation from the bureau as based in his frustration with its inability to root out "international socialism," his FBI file indicates that by the time he resigned in June 1951, he had developed a reputation for being "extremely antagonistic." His final performance review cited "disloyalty" in recommending against future bureau collaboration with Smoot.³⁷

Throughout the latter half of 1951 and well into 1952, Smoot was regularly dispatched to give talks promoting Facts Forum to local service clubs around the state of Texas—from the Lions and Kiwanis to Daughters of the American Revolution and various women's auxiliary groups. Smoot relied upon his status as an ex-FBI agent to lend credibility to his assessment of an outsized communist threat before pitching Facts Forum as a solution.³⁸ Perhaps the largest such event occurred in September 1952, when Smoot was invited by Pro America, "an organization of non-partisan women devoted toward attaining an informed opinion through the study of issues of good government," to give a talk in El Paso.³⁹ Cosponsored by the Non-Partisan Women of El Paso and the El Paso Executives Club, Smoot's talk titled "The Promise of America" received considerable advance coverage in the local newspaper.⁴⁰

Speaking before an audience of as many as twelve hundred, Smoot called Sen. Joseph McCarthy "a modern-day Paul Revere" and warned of an imminent threat of communist subversion. According to the *El Paso Herald-Post*, Smoot "told his audience that the Reds have indoctrinated many Americans with a theory of 'democratic centrism,' in other words, that 'laissez-faire capitalism' must be abandoned for a planned socialist state."⁴¹ Smoot's complaint that "misguided American liberals" were unwittingly advancing the cause of communism through implementing New Deal economic policies that Smoot equated with socialism illuminates the political stakes of Facts Forum's "non-partisan" assessment of national politics. The group's ability to depict itself as above the political fray was rooted not only in its unauthorized appropriation of the FBI imprimatur but in the fact that the cohering modern conservative ideology of its organizers had not yet captured either political party. Facts Forum provided a political outlet for people who were temperamentally or situationally disposed toward modern conservative ideology but who felt ambivalence toward major party politics.

While Hunt strove to spread Facts Forum far and wide, and by all accounts provided ample funding to do so, the discussion group concept required substantial local buy-in to catch on. For example, despite considerable interest in right-anticommunist politics, illustrated by Smoot's large audience in September 1952, Facts Forum struggled to gain traction in El Paso. The local YMCA offered occasional Facts Forum discussions as part of its adult programming, but its activities were noted in passing in the local press and went unreported even by *Facts Forum News*, a newsletter Hunt began publishing in February 1952 to chronicle and coordinate Facts Forum activities as the organization spread.[42] By January 1953 Facts Forum had resorted to placing classified ads in the *El Paso Herald-Post*, seeking a "local person, full time or part time, to organize discussion groups."[43] There is little evidence Facts Forum ever found a devoted local organizer in El Paso, however, as its documented activities there were largely relegated to collaborative initiatives with the local Pro America group—namely, the organizing of right-anticommunist lending libraries.[44] Elsewhere, Facts Forum attempted to leverage the social connections of its local emissaries, with varying degrees of success. For example, in mid-July 1951, Smoot traveled one hundred miles northeast of Dallas to Paris, Texas, where he pitched Facts Forum to the town's Junior Chamber of Commerce as a "non-political" organization that "doesn't give a hoot what the citizens think so long as they think."[45] Despite being vouched for by a local rancher and endorsed by the local newspaper, the Paris chapter of Facts Forum only managed twenty members and one meeting.[46]

Facts Forum was more successful in Kaufman, Texas, where a "unit" formed in early 1952. Located thirty miles southeast of Dallas, organizers benefited from their proximity to Facts Forum headquarters, inviting guest speakers to boost turnout at local meetings. Facts Forum president Robert Dedman presided over an initial organizational meeting in Kaufman and brought fellow Hunt employee, yet another ex-FBI agent, Bill Billings to lead the town's first discussion meeting.[47] More than fifty people attended that first Kaufman discussion meeting in March 1952, at which Billings "outlined arguments on both sides of the question 'Does

Senator Joseph McCarthy do more good than harm?'" They agreed to meet again on the third Thursday of each month, and local insurance agent Henry W. Nash announced plans to run a lending library out of his office.[48] By April Facts Forum had stocked its Kaufman library with nearly sixty volumes of assorted anticommunist and anti–New Deal literature including the young William F. Buckley's *God and Men at Yale*, which it described as "a widely discussed new book that emphasizes the fact that individualism and private capitalism are being derided and condemned in the vast majority of colleges in the United States."[49]

Notably, the Kaufman unit's most highly attended discussion was on then-raging ideological rivalries within the Democratic and Republican Parties. By the summer of 1952, a presidential election year, both major parties in Texas were engulfed in factional warfare. On the Republican side, after two consecutive failed presidential runs by moderate Thomas Dewey, conservative supporters of the Old Right stalwart Ohio senator Robert A. Taft saw an opportunity to refashion the party in his staunchly anti–New Deal, antilabor, and isolationist image. The party's moderate wing, in turn, saw in retired Allied commander Dwight D. Eisenhower a war hero whose popularity might allow the Republicans to reclaim the White House for the first time in twenty years. Meanwhile, Texas Democrats were divided between "loyalists"—liberals like Ralph Yarborough who supported the Truman-led national party's advocacy of organized labor, Keynesian federal economic programs, and, increasingly, civil rights for Black Americans—and supporters of the conservative, segregationist, and staunchly anticommunist Democratic governor Allan Shivers (who, by summer's end, would endorse Eisenhower, delivering Texas for the Republicans).[50] The national press reported the tensions, in Texas and throughout the South, as evidence of possible party realignment or at least the potential for a meaningful two-party political system in a region that had been dominated by Democratic Party hegemony since the end of Reconstruction.[51]

In late June, just before the national party conventions, the Kaufman Facts Forum unit convened a town hall with area representatives of the state's "Big Four" political factions.[52] Each of the four were given twelve minutes to speak, after which guest moderator Dan Smoot solicited questions from the 250 audience members, yielding a "lively" discussion lasting "for more than an hour." According to a local newspaper account of the meeting, "a greater percentage of the questions" were directed at Enoch Fletcher, an attorney from Grand Saline and general counsel for the Republican State Executive Committee, there representing the Taft Republicans. Accused by Eisenhower Republican representative Jack Nossaman of stacking the party's Texas delegation with Taft supporters despite bipartisan support for Ike, Fletcher replied, "The Eisenhower forces are accusing us of stealing something they never had." He blamed "exaggerated" reports in *The Dallas Morning News* and *Dallas Times Herald* for the growing perception that Taft delegates were not representative of the will of Texas Republicans. He further suggested that the *Morning News* had refused to print a syndicated Drew Pearson column containing allegations against prominent Texas Eisenhower promoter Jack Porter, and that the paper had "published an unflattering photograph of a Rusk County Taft delegate, implying malicious intent."[53]

With only one extant account of the Kaufman town hall, it is impossible to know precisely how Fletcher's allegations of pro-Eisenhower and anti-Taft press bias were received by the Facts Forum audience, just as it is impossible to know for certain the tenor of the questions Fletcher was disproportionately asked. That said, there is evidence to suggest that Facts Forum participants in the Dallas area were at least ideologically disposed toward Taft's archconservative policy positions and hoped Eisenhower would adopt them. In a September 1952 poll, also published in the *Kaufman Herald*, only 23 percent of Dallas-area Facts Forum respondents said they would advise Eisenhower against, "vigorously opposing Fair Deal measures."[54] Furthermore, only 17 percent supported a Democratic Party loyalty pledge designed to prevent conservative and segregationist Southern Democrats, like Shivers, from reigniting the Dixiecrat revolt of 1948.[55] While the Kaufman unit recessed for the month of October, respecting a Facts Forum–wide ban on discussing campaign issues within thirty days of a general election, it seems likely many of its members were inclined toward the conservative factions, of either party, who ultimately settled for Eisenhower that November.[56] And as Kaufmanites reassessed their partisan loyalties in light of these strong conservative factions, the specter of press bias against the farthest right bloc loomed.

By the summer of 1952 Facts Forum membership had reportedly reached 35,000 nationally, most organized into groups no larger than 49 members.[57] The bulk of these groups met in Texas and surrounding states, but by 1953 Facts Forum boasted units in no fewer than forty-one municipalities located in fifteen states from California to Massachusetts.[58] Facts Forum attempted to encourage business managers nationwide to host discussion groups for their employees, but there is little evidence of adoption outside of a handful of Dallas-area firms.[59] Rather, the concept appears to have attracted its strongest support from members of the local professional class and small business owners, although Facts Forum's own self-narrative carefully emphasized its cross-class appeal.[60] Facts Forum also targeted high school students and women's civic groups, and evidence suggest at least gender parity if not higher participation rates among women than men.[61]

While Facts Forum did not explicitly discriminate based upon race, all indicators suggest its participants were overwhelmingly (if not entirely) white. This resulted, in part, from Facts Forum's reliance upon preexisting social networks to spread discussion groups. Hunt's initial plan to spread Facts Forum relied upon the establishment of four "branch offices," located in Beeville and Houston in Texas as well as in Vandalia, Illinois (near the farm where Hunt was born and raised), and Omaha, Nebraska.[62] While local news reports indicate these branch offices were indeed responsible for Facts Forum's spread in Illinois, Nebraska, and Texas's coastal bend, the uneven national spread of discussion groups in part mirrored the extended white social connections of Hunt, his employees, family members, and participants in the initial Dallas units, who shared the concept with likeminded friends in other cities and states.[63]

Half of the states with reported Facts Forum units by 1953 (including Texas, where groups were most active) had statutes mandating racial segregation in public accommodations, education, transportation, or all three.[64] Furthermore, Facts Forum polling results are consistent with not only a white participant base but a segregationist one—in August 1952, only 11 percent of Facts Forum participants supported the enactment of a "compulsory federal [Fair Employment Practice Committee] law," and 69 percent opposed the US Supreme Court's 1954 *Brown* desegregation ruling, on account that it violated "States' Rights."[65] Local groups had relative autonomy in deciding what to discuss, with the stipulation that meetings were to be structured as debates between "both sides" of a given issue. However, in relying on preexisting civic groups and extended social connections to spread, Facts Forum populated its discussions with primarily white middle-class participants, united by a sense of alienation from mainstream party politics, a patriotic embrace of capitalism in the face of communist threats at home and abroad, and a growing anxiety regarding federal efforts to promote racial equality.

FACTS FORUM'S ACTIVE AUDIENCES

Discussion groups may have been Hunt's ideal method for cultivating a "constructive" shift in public opinion, but Facts Forum's national audience and influence owe more to Hunt's substantial investment in mass media. Facts Forum's longest-running eponymous program launched in the fall of 1951 and featured coordinator Dan Smoot delivering extended monologues offering both liberal and conservative interpretations of current events or public policy questions. Early episodes, which sometimes featured invited guests, discussed such topics as "the desirability of federal aid to public schools" and whether publications should "print news hostile to the national safety if released by the government."[66] Smoot's weekly one-man debates were sometimes supplemented with moderated discussions, which by the fall of 1952 were occasionally simulcast over radio and television by WBAP in Ft. Worth, Texas.[67] Beginning in 1953 Facts Forum expanded its programming line-up to include *State of the Nation*, a show broadcast over the Mutual and Don Lee radio networks that focused on interviewing politicians, and a panel discussion program that was ultimately picked up for radio and television distribution by the ABC network under the name *Answers for Americans*.[68]

As Facts Forum programming expanded, so too did its audience base. The number of radio and television stations airing Facts Forum programs doubled between early 1954 and January 1955, when *US News & World Report* estimated their combined audience in the millions.[69] By 1955 Smoot's one-man debate program was aired in thirty-minute installments on 80 TV stations and fifteen-minute installments on 265 radio stations, *State of the Nation* was reportedly carried by more than 400 radio stations, and *Answers for Americans* could be seen on 50 TV stations and heard on 138 radio stations. Another Facts Forum program aired by Mutual, *Reporters' Roundup*, was broadcast by some 350 radio stations.[70] As Facts Forum's radio and television audience base grew, so did its print circulation. Begun in early 1952 as a newsletter primarily reporting on Facts Forum discussion groups, by February 1954 *Facts Forum News* transformed into a glossy magazine with reprints of radio scripts and, increasingly, original articles and extended interviews with politicians and right-anticommunist leaders. One year later the magazine began distributing on newsstands, increasing its circulation fivefold to 375,000.[71] It's easy, when considering audience statistics, to imagine an anonymous mass of passive receivers—each uncritically absorbing information as though they were being injected by a hypodermic needle. But Hunt's purpose was not indoctrination; it was cultivating active political participation from audiences that he presumed already shared his right-anticommunist conception of reality. As such, Facts Forum took pains to cultivate *active* audiences—promoting letters-to-the-editor writing contests and amateur public opinion polling.

In Milwaukee, Wisconsin, for example, listeners of local radio station WISN heeded Facts Forum's call to active participation by proposing local discussion groups and flooding area newspapers and congressional representatives with letters supporting various right-anticommunist causes.[72] One such letter, written by Milwaukee resident Gerda Koch, lauded an Internal Revenue Service crackdown on Communists, lamenting that her taxes too often supported "Red plans and propaganda." She added, "If most of us knew the history of communism and its workings, we could and would more readily recognize the evil right under our very noses."[73] While Koch's sentiments mirror those regularly aired by Dan Smoot, that she took the time to write them out in her own words and to mail them to her local newspaper lends insight into her political subjectivity. Koch was not merely a believer in antitax and anticommunist ideas. Through Facts Forum she came to associate those ideas with critical activities like discerning the validity of information and sharing her findings through letters written to be circulated publicly. Koch's letter, published in the *Milwaukee Journal*, earned her a ten-dollar cash award and a reprint in *Facts Forum News*. Facts Forum participants like Koch were attracted not merely by the group's ideas but also by its methods.

By the 1950s mass letter-writing was already a well-worn tactic of interest group politics in the United States. Left, labor, and even religious groups routinely launched campaigns asking supporters to write in favor of or opposition to specific policy proposals or pieces of legislation.[74] Facts Forum differed by encouraging individuals to write letters on whatever topic they saw fit. The rules of the Facts Forum letter-writing contest changed throughout its five years of existence, with the only constant being that in order to win, a letter first needed to have been published by a newspaper or magazine other than *Facts Forum News*—a rule consistent with Hunt's goal of shifting public opinion through promoting the public expression of "constructive" private opinions. While winning letters tended to reflect the right-anticommunist themes that dominated Facts Forum polling questions and broadcast programming, the contest encouraged the expression of individual viewpoints. When first announced in August 1951, the contest simply offered monetary awards for the top four letters to newspapers "debating either side of any question in Facts Forum polls."[75] In April 1952 the rules were changed to reward the top four letters "espousing the liberal side of Facts Forum questions" and the top four "advocating the conservation or constructive side."[76] Despite this change, no "liberal" letters were submitted for the May 1952 contest. The next month the experiment with ideological labeling was abandoned since "there have been few entries for the liberal side."[77]

The dearth of liberal letter writers, while indicative of the self-selecting right-anticommunist insularity of Facts Forum participants, did not mean total uniformity of opinions expressed. For example, while most Facts Forum poll respondents opposed the *Brown v. Board* decision desegregating public schools, not all letter-writing contestants supported maintaining the racial status quo. Koch's winning letter, published in the November 1956 issue of *Facts Forum News*, ran alongside two letters with personalized approaches to managing race in public accommodations. A contest-winning letter by George E. Miller, originally published in the *Nashville Banner*, expressed repulsion at the Ku Klux Klan practice of burning crosses: "Christ died on the cross for all men, not for any particular race of people," Miller wrote. "The cross is supposed to help us settle our differences, not aggravate them."[78] Meanwhile, Roy F. Carpenter's winning letter sought an alternative solution to the segregation problem. "To force all races to go to a common school smacks of dictatorial power," Carpenter wrote in a letter originally published in *The Dallas Morning News*. "In the three-way system certain schools could be designated for each race, and other schools for those who wish to attend a common school. This would mean we had the right to choose."⁷⁹ While no letter offered a full-throated defense of civil rights for Black Americans, and it would be difficult to imagine Facts Forum awarding a letter outlining the merits of socialism, the organization's openness to certain degrees of disagreement or difference of opinion encouraged letter writers to not merely repeat some right-anticommunist party line but to treat their letters as an expression of self.

If Facts Forum's contests encouraged participants and spectators alike to think of political activity through the lens of creative self-expression, the organization's polling operation was designed to foster their ability to imagine themselves as part of a larger critical community, a burgeoning modern conservative public. While Facts Forum rarely reported sample sizes for its monthly polls, it seems likely that responding to poll questions was the most common mode of participation in Facts Forum, other than tuning in to one of the group's radio or television broadcasts.⁸⁰ For example, by the summer of 1952 some twenty-three Facts Forum discussion groups were operating in Omaha, Nebraska, some of them small enough to be hosted in the living rooms of participants' homes. Meanwhile, approximately four thousand Omaha-area residents reportedly responded to Facts Forum polls.⁸¹ Typically containing twelve to fifteen questions, the polls were distributed monthly via *Facts Forum News* and direct mail postcards as well as in local newspaper advertisements. Some were even placed in local buses and streetcars.⁸² At first sourced from public officials and apparent Hunt associates, Facts Forum also solicited questions from participants and by February 1954 was offering cash prizes for the yes-or-no questions (eighty-two characters or fewer) judged "best" by the organization's polling committee according to their "current interest, fairness and conciseness."⁸³ All told, between 1951 and 1956, Facts Forum polled 934 questions. While question topics ranged widely, a plurality concerned matters of US foreign policy. Other common themes included domestic countersubversion, US military policy, and partisan politics.⁸⁴

The very act of polling public opinion subtly invites participants and spectators to consider their personal opinions in relation to the aggregated opinions of others, but Facts Forum took additional steps to encourage this process of identification. Early poll results reported in local newspaper advertisements, for example, often explicitly asked readers: "How did your opinion compare with the Facts Forum results? Save these ballots for future references."[85] In August 1952 Facts Forum took this invitation a step further, initiating a contest whereby participants were asked to predict the cumulative total of "yes" vote percentages in a given monthly poll. That is, in addition to considering whether they would have personally voted "yes" or "no" to each question, participants were asked to anticipate how their fellow respondents would answer each of the fourteen questions polled that month and then to quantify that prediction. They were asked to anticipate, for example, that a high percentage of Facts Forum respondents would answer the question, "Can constitutional government meet the needs of our times?" in the affirmative (92 percent) but that a low percentage would affirmatively answer the question, "Should the Taft–Hartley law be repealed?" (14 percent). A successful participant would also have to recognize which questions might be met with ambivalence by the Facts Forum public, like "Are all men created equal?" a question that yielded a 47 percent "yes" vote.[86]

While the prediction contest lasted only a year, it was by no means the only method by which Facts Forum encouraged participants not only to express their personal opinions publicly but to consider the ideological implications of public opinion polling itself.[87] By early 1954 Facts Forum found itself on the defensive after a *Time* magazine exposé alleged "ultraconservative" bias in its programming and poll questions.[88] In response, Facts Forum called upon participants to critically interrogate the poll questions themselves, instructing in the February 1954 issue of *Facts Forum News*: "If you find some of the above questions 'loaded,' please ask a friend to check the card for 'loaded' questions and compare your findings. Then determine which philosophy, party or person it is 'loaded' to favor. Please communicate your findings to Facts Forum as an aid in guarding against 'loaded' questions in the future."[89]

In asking participants to compare their biases with those of a friend, Facts Forum was relying upon the same social insularity that enabled its polls to express opinions consistent with the unpopular "truths" of modern conservatism. Facts Forum participants responded as expected. In the February 1954 Facts Forum poll, 75 percent of respondents indicated their belief that the "non-friends" of anticommunists were "endangering free enterprise." Below the poll results, Facts Forum reported feedback received in the intervening month: "Many Facts Forum enthusiasts have suggested that the question should have been phrased 'foes' or 'critics' of anti-Communists and that the use of the milder term 'non-friends' loads the question. This comment again raises the question, 'When is a question loaded?' Facts Forum presumes that a question is 'loaded' when it is phrased so as to influence the answer or to imply as fact something which is erroneous."[90] While Facts Forum's critics found its poll questions to be slanted, its respondents found them to be not slanted enough to adequately convey the "facts" as they saw them.

Critics were correct to challenge Facts Forum's claim of political impartiality, but in doing so they failed to question why the organization's polling and programming might have *felt* impartial to its participants. One answer can be found in an additional request made of participants by Facts Forum in light of *Time* magazine's allegations of poll question bias: "When you find a 'loaded' question, determine in your own mind how Dr. Gallup or Elmo Roper would have phrased the question."[91] In explicitly comparing its questions to those of the most highly regarded polling operations of the day, Facts Forum not only implied a bias in those polls, it invited participants to consider the gap between the opinions they expressed publicly and those expressed as mainstream public opinion by scientific polls. Importantly, Facts Forum participants saw that gap as not merely rooted in a difference of opinion but in a difference of facts—a belief evidenced in increasing skepticism among Facts Form participants concerning the veracity of mainstream news reports.

In November 1952 only 29 percent of Facts Forum participants agreed that "subversive activities [are] properly publicized in our newspapers." The same poll reported that only 34 percent of Facts Forum participants found, "the American press truly objective in its reporting of the news."[92] This distrust was exacerbated by the rise of McCarthyism, and especially the Army–McCarthy hearings, which were televised in the spring and summer months of 1954. Asked in June 1954, "In the McCarthy-Army case do news reports contradict TV?" some 79 percent of Facts Forum participants responded 'yes.'"[93] Such a result suggests the presence of an intelligible gap between conservative interpretations of the Army–McCarthy hearings and how journalists reported those proceedings. This gap reflected a burgeoning conservative news judgment, one rooted in increasing skepticism concerning the veracity of mainstream news reports. As fifth-place Facts Forum letter writer Duke Burgess of Dallas put it in the fall of 1954, "While it should be perfectly obvious, as well as proper, that publishers propound their own philosophies and 'grind their own axes' in their editorial columns, I believe most American publishers do not deliberately attempt to dictate the reporting of current history in their news columns. Nevertheless, there is obvious news slanting in almost every publication you can pick up."[94]

Burgess's appeal to the "obvious" gap between the news as he understood it and how it was routinely reported in the press relied not only on confidence in his personal ability to discern the truth omitted in "slanted" reporting of the news of the day but on a presumption that he was not alone in recognizing that gap. It was not merely obvious to him but "should be" obvious to all. In Facts Forum poll results, participants like Burgess found affirmation that others unknown to them thought the same way they did. In providing a routine, critical activity performed by individuals who were made explicitly aware that the same activity was being simultaneously performed by unknown participants with presumably like minds, Facts Forum conjured modern conservatism as an imagined community.[95] That community was imagined as not only supportive of right-anticommunist policy prescriptions but as critically engaged in distilling the "facts" from news thought to be "slanted" by professional journalists. Through Facts Forum, modern conservatives came to identify with one another and to be assured of each other's existence as individuals with a shared critical appraisal of the news of the day, affirming a common conception of truth as defined explicitly against that expressed in mainstream publications and opinion polls.

While Hunt was busy expanding his audience and encouraging right anticommunists to participate in various acts of civic engagement, Sen. Joseph McCarthy of Wisconsin was stoking the public's fears that Communists were engaged in widespread subversive activities not only within the press but within the federal government itself. In January 1952 some 61 percent of Facts Forum participants considered McCarthy's highly publicized investigations into Communist infiltration of US institutions to be doing "more good than harm," and by May of that year some 81 percent expressed approval of the senator's tactic of "naming individuals in attempting to uncover disloyalty." In September 1953 some 75 percent of Facts Forum respondents indicated their approval of "McCarthy's methods in checking for subversion."[96] By 1954, as McCarthy's methods came under intense scrutiny via the nationally televised Army–McCarthy hearings and increasing consensus among both print and broadcast journalists that the senator had overstepped his authority, McCarthy's popularity began a decline from which he would not recover.[97] Nevertheless, his support among Facts Forum participants persisted, with only 29 percent approving of his censure by the Senate in late 1954.[98] As the press turned against McCarthy, his constituency of diehard supporters found themselves increasingly skeptical of the intentions of the journalists who targeted him. This sentiment would have been especially pronounced among Facts Forum supporters as McCarthy's downfall coincided with increasingly withering press criticism of Hunt's operations and those who participated in them.

FACTS FORUM VERSUS THE PRESS

In late 1953, amid a national expansion of Facts Forum's radio and television programming and as McCarthy's Senate hearings were reaching a fever pitch, the press began digging into H. L. Hunt's financing of right-anticommunist campaigns. By the last week of September a Washington bureau reporter for Rhode Island's *Providence Journal-Bulletin* had publicly identified Hunt as Facts Forum's primary financier. A week later the Communist Party of the USA sensationalized Hunt's connection to McCarthy in its weekend newspaper *The Worker*. It accused Facts Forum of conspiring with the red-baiting senator and of attempting to "put over the McCarthyite slant on every subject from Korea to books."[99] Facts Forum's initial reaction was to deny collusion with McCarthy and to gloat by inserting a reprint of *The Worker* article in the October 1953 issue of *Facts Forum News*. "Facts Forum could not repress a feeling of pride in making this enemy," a subsequent issue of the newsletter explained, attempting to reassure participants who apparently mistook the reprint for evidence that Facts Forum had itself gone Communist. "The attack proves our program for Freedom has been sufficiently effective that instead of continuing to snipe at us through the usual news channels, the Communists' first team has finally come into the open with a direct attack."[100] While Facts Forum initially primed its supporters for direct battle with Communists, it was instead increasingly embattled by the non-Communist professional press.

Ben H. Bagdikian penned the first major journalistic exposé of Facts Forum, published by *The Providence Journal-Bulletin* in late 1953 and early 1954 as an eight-part series titled "The Facts About Facts Forum."[101] Identifying a gap between the organization's professed political impartiality and its growing reputation as a purveyor of "ultraconservative" propaganda, Bagdikian framed his series as answering the question: "Why there should be such unprecedented distrust of a 'non-partisan educational' organization?"[102] In addition to pointing out the organization's promotion of "extreme" conservative viewpoints, Bagdikian noted Facts Forum's increasingly confrontational stance against the Eisenhower administration.[103]

But the bulk of the series focused on detailed critiques of Facts Forum's methods, with separate articles reframing its seemingly impartial "both sides" programming, lending libraries, letter-writing contests, and polling operations as partial toward the burgeoning right-anticommunist cause. The series concluded with an overview of the many faults of the Facts Forum project, resulting in one "major" criticism: "its net effect is to disseminate fear, suspicion and divisive propaganda." Bagdikian reasoned, "The consistent pattern of its 'both sides' broadcasts is to reduce all national issues to: Isolationism, ultra-conservatism and McCarthyism—versus—treason or stupidity. The results of this, if carried into the entire field of mass communications, could be to increase the pressures dividing segments of American society, to increase group hatreds, and to implant suspicions which did not exist before."[104] Bagdikian identified the salience of right-wing propaganda, like Facts Forum, as a *cause* of division and suspicion, rather than a public expression of real political disagreement.

While Bagdikian's reporting on Facts Forum may have come as a surprise to those who were only cursorily familiar with its programming, it is difficult to imagine an active Facts Forum participant being terribly shocked by his findings—although they might bristle at his accusation that their political beliefs were "extreme." Bagdikian's primary sources for his exposé had already been publicly circulated by Facts Forum itself: he drew on the group's own pamphlets, broadcast transcripts, newsletters, and public statements. For example, among the damning evidence

Bagdikian marshaled against Facts Forum was a quote from a Facts Forum pamphlet describing its polling as designed "to focus attention of large numbers of people in all walks of life and in all parts of the nation on a carefully selected group of questions. By thus causing thousands of people to consider the same group of questions at the same time, the poll may be invoking a powerful psychological force for good."[105] To Bagdikian and others opposed to modern conservative ideology, "powerful psychological force" conjured the specter of reactionary propaganda unduly influencing the uncritical masses.

But to active participants, who may or may not have yet identified as "conservative" but who nevertheless saw their opinions reflected in Facts Forum polls and programs, the poll was a means of asserting public support of their not-yet-popular truths. Indeed, one early Facts Forum pamphlet addressed to prospective members offered an alternative reading of the psychological power of its polling operation: "it directs study and causes vast numbers (including nonmembers) to study and think about the same subjects at the same time. It brings into play group psychology—not the same thing as 'mob' psychology at all because it will not be blind, but instead intelligent and most far-seeing." Whereas critics feared the polls' effects on an uncritical mass public, participants were invited to imagine themselves as a part of a "grass roots movement of thinking people."[106] They were encouraged to conceptualize the public as latently critical, with polling itself a means toward the end of motivating the apathetic to become actively engaged in current affairs. Nevertheless, Facts Forum's false impartiality became a hot topic of 1954. Bagdikian's exposé was picked up by the Associated Press wire service, and articles drawing from or building on his reporting appeared in newspapers and magazines nationwide.[107]

Responding to a growing chorus of critics, Facts Forum issued a series of statements, read over the air by Smoot and published in the pages of the January 1954 issue of *Facts Forum News*. These began by distancing the group from its supposed ties to McCarthy, pointing to its bipartisan list of program guests as evidence of its impartiality, and noting its explicit instructions for its audiences to "consider arguments from all sources in making decisions on controversial subjects." While Facts Forum positioned itself as open to constructive criticism, it nevertheless expressed confidence that its efforts would be evaluated positively in "the judgment of the intelligent public." Indeed, while its critics envisioned the public as unaware of and duped by the group's underlying political ideology, Facts Forum's defense relied upon the assumption of a critically engaged public, one less concerned with the group's impartiality than with the unpopular truths expressed in its programming: "Facts Forum is unquestionably being represented as a force for evil. The truth or falsity of this accusation can be readily ascertained by any person who will listen in on the Facts Forum air programs."[108] The group's confidence was no doubt bolstered by its own polling, which found that participants overwhelmingly believed that Facts Forum would "survive the Daily Worker and other enemy attacks."[109]

In subsequent months Facts Forum fixated on its critics, specifically homing in on *Time* magazine, which the group described as "a more worthy foe than *The Worker*, discredited columnists and some other critics."[110] The *Time* article, which simply condensed the *Journal-Bulletin* exposé, agreed with Bagdikian's conclusion that "Facts Forum is less a nonpartisan educational foundation than one of the biggest private political-propaganda machines in the U.S."[111] By February 1954 Facts Forum had offered claim-by-claim rebuttals of *Time*'s many criticisms.[112] But Facts Forum was not content to denounce *Time* for towing what it believed to be the Communist Party line. Rather, it used the magazine's criticisms as a means of modeling the critical disposition toward the mainstream press it hope to nurture in its participants.

In an interview conducted by Mutual-affiliate radio reporters in Dallas and printed in the March 1954 issue of *Facts Forum News*, Facts Forum president Robert Dedman took a conciliatory tone in defending his group's attempts at impartiality. He placed special emphasis on the Facts Forum prescription for the public to critically consult multiple sources before making decisions concerning controversial issues: "A large part of the Facts Forum program is devoted to getting the public to read any and all publications in securing information on current issues from all sources." A reporter followed up, "Do you mean by that, Mr. Dedman, that you'd like for people to read magazines or papers which you yourself might consider unreliable, slanted or even, in fact, false?" Dedman replied, laughing, "Mr. Branch, you may be surprised to know that my answer to that question is yes. If the intelligent people, to whom Facts Forum appeals, do not see or read a certain publication, they do not have first-hand knowledge so that they can appraise it for good or bad or true or false. It's well recognized nowadays that through reading some publications the party line can definitely be detected and the reader or listener can then recognize the subversive party line whenever and wherever he reads or hears it."[113]

Emphasizing the importance of critically consuming media with which one disagrees, Dedman nodded to an intended effect of Facts Forum's "both sides" programming, one overlooked by critics who saw the group's halfhearted attempts at balance as merely a trick to secure free airtime and hoodwink the public. By exposing audiences to two sides of a political issue, rather than one, Facts Forum was fostering critical reading and listening practices designed to enable supporters to recognize patterns in liberal argumentation. Juxtaposed with examples of conservative argumentation, Facts Forum hoped to encourage participants to recognize the sorts of facts and hermeneutics that bolstered liberal viewpoints and, perhaps more importantly, the *absence* of information and interpretive strategies that supported conservative positions on the same topic. It was not only that Smoot made the conservative case more articulately than the liberal case; it was the *gap between* his performances of liberal and conservative sides that yielded the sort of critical conservative public that Facts Forum hoped to achieve—a public trained to read *all* media through a conservative interpretive lens and able to ascertain subversion in between the lines.

During its final two years of operation, Facts Forum increasingly published and aired commentary designed to appeal to an audience that felt underserved—if not personally targeted—by professional journalists. *Facts Forum News* shifted away from chronicling the activities of discussion groups and reprinting radio transcripts toward publishing original articles and interviews—right-anticommunist reporting and commentary designed to counter a presumed leftist slant in the mainstream press. In doing so, Facts Forum relied on a growing stable of reporters and media professionals who were increasingly branding their right anticommunism as "conservative"—talents like Hardy Burt, Fred Schwarz, Fulton Lewis Jr., Clarence Manion, and the young upstart William F. Buckley, who has long been credited with leading modern conservatism from the political wilderness to electoral dominance over the course of the mid-twentieth century. Yet the small cadre of activists Buckley led were situated within a broader movement infrastructure that they influenced but never fully controlled. While their efforts often used the "liberal media" as a foil to organize against, the movement's mutually antagonistic relationship with the press was inherited from right-anticommunist activists in the late 1940s, discussed last chapter, and from Facts Forum in the early 1950s.

When Facts Forum launched in June 1951, H. L. Hunt was searching for a means of uniting "the portion of the Democratic party opposing radicalism, the part of the Republican party opposing both radicalism and lethargy and the part of the States Rights party that rises above sectional prejudice" under the banner "constructive." In practice, Facts Forum attracted predominantly white, middle-class participants, whose right-anticommunist beliefs tended to alienate them from the leading factions of both the Republican and Democratic Parties. While Hunt never gave up his preference for the term *constructive*, by the time Facts Forum ceased operations at the end of 1956, his project had cultivated a base of supporters who were beginning to recognize one another as *conservative*—a term increasingly associated with a critical disposition toward the mainstream press.

4

BEYOND BUCKLEY

"I conclude that very often personal editorial opinion influences the supposedly objective stories of newspaper and radio reporters."

William F. Buckley Jr. was mere months from launching *National Review*—the opinion journal that would prove highly influential in legitimating modern conservatism within elite political circles—when he shared the *Answers for Americans* television screen with longtime conservative radio commentator Fulton Lewis Jr. in April 1955. Together they debated New York University professor Charles Hodges and liberal commentator George Hamilton Combs on the question "How accurate is America's news?" Lewis, whose contentious investigative reporting of the consumer cooperatives movement in the 1940s indirectly inspired the FCC's Fairness Doctrine, began by arguing: "Objective reporting is nonexistent." To which Buckley added, "I believe there is consistently more distortion in the papers of the left than there is in the papers of the right."[1] After heated discussion that involved a consideration of the news media's coverage of Sen. Joseph McCarthy's crusade against communist subversion and the alleged liberal bias of *Time* magazine, Buckley was afforded the last word: "The answer to more accurate news reporting is, I think, the same as the answer to so many problems we face. We've got to wait until such time as the public becomes indignant. The American people have become apathetic, supine, bored—with the result that outrage can be committed by the press or by the radio or by the intellectuals. They just don't care."[2]

Not content to wait for the public at large to spontaneously come around to the emergent conservative belief in left-wing media bias, Buckley's *National Review* became a regular outlet for essays expounding on the "delinquencies of the Liberal press" from November 1955 onward.[3] Buckley's role in the formation of the modern conservative movement, and in framing that movement against a "liberal media" foil, is difficult to overstate. Along with editing *National Review*, the movement's official organ, he helped build much of modern conservatism's foundational infrastructure—from the Intercollegiate Society of Individualists and the Young Americans for Freedom to the American Conservative Union—in the 1950s and 1960s. Young Americans for Freedom and Intercollegiate Society of Individualists, working alongside College Republicans, established student newspapers and radio programs at universities across the country in the 1960s.

These outlets helped spread the conservative critical disposition toward the mainstream press among college students—many of whom would vote to usher in the Reagan Revolution in 1980. They also provided formative media experiences for many conservative news commentators who would find gainful employment in a burgeoning conservative media system from the late 1980s onward.[4] Buckley himself provided an early model for latter-day conservative media in hosting the nationally syndicated television program *Firing Line*.[5] In addition to giving Buckley an outlet to pit his conservative ideas against some of the leading liberal and left figures of the era, *Firing Line* regularly fixated on the issue of media bias. Between 1966 and 1974, *Firing Line* broadcast no fewer than fourteen episodes devoted to discussing the political stakes and putative left-wing biases of the mainstream press.[6]

Historians have largely credited Buckley—along with collaborators like *National Review* publisher William Rusher, book publisher Henry Regnery, and radio commentator Clarence Manion—with the proliferation of a "first generation" of postwar conservative media in the late 1950s and early 1960s, which crafted and promoted a "fusionist" modern conservatism that eventually found its standard-bearer in Ronald Reagan.[7] These news and opinion sources exacerbated the yawning gap—first explicitly nurtured by Facts Forum in the early 1950s—between an increasingly salient conservative worldview and the world as depicted in mainstream news coverage. As we began to see last chapter, the conservative critical disposition toward the press was not a top-down by-product of conservative media like Facts Forum's radio and television shows, or even *National Review* and *Firing Line*. It emerged among conservatives as they navigated both mainstream and burgeoning movement media, engaging in critical reading practices modeled (but not determined) by the latter.

That is to say: Buckley and his tight-knit circle of activists neither invented conservative media nor devised the notion of liberal media bias. Their primary achievement was in developing a conservative form of respectability politics.[8] As we saw in the preceding chapters, from the Great Depression up until the early days of the Cold War, US political culture revolved around a bipartisan New Deal consensus that rendered conservatism unpopular. Conservatism's association with the interests of big business, and with carrying water for fascists abroad in the run-up to World War II, inhibited the movement's growth beyond a minority status in both major political parties. That began to change in the late 1940s and 1950s. The Second Red Scare, or McCarthyism, elevated anticommunism as a salient bipartisan issue.[9] Then, in 1954, the US Supreme Court issued its *Brown v. Board of Education of Topeka* decision, declaring racial segregation in public schools to be unconstitutional and focusing national attention on the civil rights of Black Americans. As anticommunism grew into the Cold War, and as *Brown* stoked the civil rights movement, Buckley and those in his orbit successfully reframed modern conservatism as a principled and well-disciplined movement beset by a liberal "establishment" (including the media) and a right-wing "fringe," exemplified by more overt white supremacists and conspiratorial right-anticommunist groups like the John Birch Society.[10]

In the early 1960s, as the Birchers embarked on a campaign to impeach US Supreme Court Chief Justice Earl Warren (in part for authoring the majority opinion in *Brown*), Buckley publicly distanced himself and the conservative movement from the group's founder, Robert Welch, in the pages of *National Review*.[11] Two years later, at the inaugural business meeting for the American Conservative Union, Buckley personally filed a motion to exclude all John Birch Society leadership from membership. The next day the American Conservative Union board met again and unanimously rescinded its formal ban, "provided that it is the understood policy of the Board that such restrictions shall apply as a matter of unstated policy."[12] Buckley's efforts to sanction John Birch Society leadership—to police the boundaries of modern conservatism—helped establish him as a voice of reason in the eyes of the mainstream press that his movement despised, but whose approval it needed in order for conservatism to be accepted as a legitimate opposition to liberalism. Buckley failed, however, to put a stop to the Birchers, who continue to operate at the conservative grassroots to this day.[13]

This chapter foregrounds the corners of the modern conservative movement outside Buckley's direct reach—corners he publicly disavowed but that nevertheless contributed to his movement's success. If Buckley's band of media activists helped popularize belief in mainstream press bias among respectable conservatives in the 1960s, less-reputable conservative activists like the Birchers faced considerable press scrutiny that made the "liberal media" appear as a more direct and tangible threat. Indeed, the conservative critical disposition toward the press—initially cultivated by Facts Forum—was a tie that bound conservatives both within and beyond Buckley's version of respectability. Targeted by both movement and mainstream press, the Birchers built their own alternative conservative media network of publications, ranging from national magazines like *American Opinion* and *Review of the News* to hyperlocal community newspapers like the *Birmingham Independent*. Focusing on the media activism of the John Birch Society during the height of the civil rights era, this chapter demonstrates how the "liberal media" claim emerged less as a top-down movement strategy than as a bottom-up interpretation of the various headwinds facing modern conservatism as it navigated rapidly shifting conditions regarding the maintenance of white supremacy, particularly in the US South.

FACTS FORUM'S LEGACY

Facts Forum folded abruptly at the end of 1956, without so much as saying a formal good-bye within the pages of its magazine. Those who received *Facts Forum News* monthly got only a brief letter informing them, without explanation, "The December 1956 issue, which is now in the mail, will be the last copy you will receive."¹⁴ Texas oilman H. L. Hunt had bankrolled the magazine's circulation, so there were no ongoing subscriber accounts in need of managing. Since Facts Forum had shifted its focus from discussion groups to broadcast programming, the decision to close shop seems to have been Hunt's alone.¹⁵ The FBI attributed Hunt's loss of interest in Facts Forum to the unexpected death of his wife Lyda, who died of complications following a stroke in May 1955. By the summer of 1955, internal FBI reports described Hunt as "despondent" and noted "considerable dissension" among the staff, including the impending defection of Dan Smoot.¹⁶ Facts Forum critic *Time* magazine attributed the group's demise to "acute public indifference," quoting an unnamed Hunt associate as saying, "He just got tired of useless and lost causes."¹⁷

Far from a lost cause, two years after Hunt shuttered Facts Forum the retired candy manufacturer Robert Welch founded the John Birch Society.¹⁸ If Facts Forum sought to awaken a right-anticommunist critical community, Welch sought to enlist that community as a countersubversive vanguard—establishing explicitly anticommunist lending libraries, promoting avowedly conservative periodicals and radio commentators, and organizing letter-writing campaigns to ensure that the conservative grassroots would be heard by politicians and newspaper editors.¹⁹ All of these efforts were premised on responding to a perceived structural disadvantage faced by conservatives, that of media and educational systems biased against their worldview. As Welch wrote in his *Blue Book* manifesto, "With the metropolitan press and big circulation general periodicals not only largely denied to us, but in many cases either consciously or blindly promoting the Communist line, we need to use every feasible channel to get more of the truth over to more of the American people."²⁰

While not mentioning Facts Forum directly, Welch took pains to disabuse supporters of the idea that their activism was somehow nonpartisan or apolitical, a strategy that had proven a key source of Hunt's excoriation by the press. In a 1957 letter introducing readers to his newly formed conservative magazine *American Opinion*, Welch wrote, "We shall consider honesty and objectivity, in our treatment of every person and every subject, to be of vital importance. But 'impartiality' we shall scorn as a combination of pretense and cowardice." Welch continued, "The very name of this magazine is designed to make clear its stand in the world-wide ideological struggle between Americanist and Communist philosophies, and in the political battles between Americanist and Communist factions."[21] While Hunt launched an organization designed to appeal to right anticommunists who still thought of themselves in apolitical terms, after five years of intense public scrutiny and debate over the boundaries of responsible political discourse, Hunt bequeathed to Welch a base of disaffected and newly self-conscious conservatives, wary of the press and seeking a clear advocate for their political interests.

That base is evident in the growing circulations of conservative opinion journals like *National Review, Human Events,* and Welch's *American Opinion* in the late 1950s and early 1960s.[22] Each of these three influential conservative publications hired or published former Facts Forum employees, who helped interweave a critical disposition toward the press into the fabric of modern conservative ideology. Former *Facts Forum News* editor Medford Evans was among the early contributing editors to *American Opinion*, and he and his son M. Stanton Evans both became regular contributors to *National Review*.[23] The younger Evans, who was a senior at Yale when his father was hired by Facts Forum in 1954, went on to a long and influential career as a conservative journalist at *The Indianapolis Star*, managing editor of *Human Events*, and founder of the National Journalism Center, a nonprofit educational initiative that has been training young conservatives for careers in journalism since 1977 (alumni range in tone and temperament from Ann Coulter to Malcolm Gladwell).

Meanwhile, after resigning from Facts Forum in the summer of 1955, Dan Smoot went on to publish his own newsletter, *The Dan Smoot Report*. As with the circumstances surrounding his resignation from the FBI, Smoot's decision to leave Facts Forum was privately messy but publicly leveraged.[24] In Smoot's telling, while working at Facts Forum he received, "well over a hundred thousand letters, most of them from people who liked the nationalist, pro-American, anti-communist, anti-socialist, anti-big government side of my broadcasts. They urged me to give up the 'foolish' two-sides, saying it was ridiculous and hypocritical for one man to argue a question from two opposite points-of-view and sound as if he believed what he was saying on both sides." Freed from the balance imperative, Smoot rebranded himself as offering commentary "that uses old-fashioned American constitutional principles as a yardstick for measuring all important issues."[25] Smoot's readership overlapped considerably with the John Birch Society's membership, so much so that in

March 1971, when health issues required Smoot to slow down, the Birch publication *Review of the News* subsumed his newsletter as an occasional column.[26]

Welch launched *Review of the News* in 1965. The news magazine offered a weekly digest of national and international happenings deemed most pertinent to its conservative readership. Starting with a meager paid circulation of 5,555 in 1966, by 1974 *Review of the News* reported a paid circulation of nearly 45,000.[27] In addition to modeling what a proper conservative news judgment would look like in tailoring its weekly coverage, the magazine subsumed the short-lived Bircher periodical *Correction Please*, which was launched in June 1964 to highlight examples of "falsehood, exaggeration, distortion, and misrepresentation, clipped from newspapers, magazines, and occasionally other sources, with short corresponding corrections of each item to set the record straight."[28] In column form, "Correction, Please!" demonstrated how to read between the lines of the mainstream press. In the inaugural issue of *Review of the News*, for instance, the column disputed a caption featured in *Newsweek* magazine that read, "A white man squares off against a Negro demonstrator." Without including the photo in question, the unnamed *Review of the News* writer chided, "Since both the white man and the Negro demonstrator have their right hands cocked and left hands in defensive positions, we wonder why the caption shouldn't read: A Negro demonstrator squares off against a white man. Or is it a Newsweekism that all whites are the aggressors and all Negro demonstrators the defenders?"[29]

Typical of the column's general approach, "Correction, Please!" modeled a critical reading strategy that transformed real racial conflict—in fact characterized by white brutality—into a battle over contested meanings. While a typical reader might presume that the photographer witnessed the white man instigating before snapping the photograph, thus justifying the caption, "Correction, Please!" encouraged its readers to instead consider the source. Rather than focusing on whether that particular white man, in fact, instigated the conflict (and the implications of that fact), readers were asked to discern whether the news reflected the reality of the broader racial conflict as they understood it and to attribute any gap between that understanding and the reported news not to their own personal biases but to those of the intermediary (in this case *Newsweek*). As racial conflict at home dovetailed with increasingly militant domestic opposition to US imperialism abroad, movement conservatives and racial reactionaries (typically white Southern Democrats, who may or may not yet have affiliated with the modern conservative movement) would have found the daily news to be ever more dissonant with their expectations, a phenomenon that manifested in growing distrust of the press.[30] For John Birch Society members, this distrust was rendered palpable by the group's notably active engagement with the mainstream press, which quickly turned conflictual.

JOHN BIRCH VERSUS THE PRESS (AND VICE VERSA)

Like Facts Forum before it, the John Birch Society encouraged its members to write regular letters to local editors and public officials—an effort to amplify conservative public opinion at a time when it was mostly understood to be marginal at best. One of the group's first coordinated letter-writing campaigns targeted *Newsweek*. In an October 1959 issue, the magazine had reported on the Algerian Liberation Front's decolonial struggle against the French, failing to mention that sympathizer "Si Mustapha" was the nom de guerre of the German-born communist Winfried Müller. Welch alerted Birch Society members, who inundated *Newsweek* with letters of complaint. While *Newsweek* disputed Welch's characterization that its coverage had "glorified" the Algerian Liberation Front, it admitted having erred in failing to fully identify Mustapha-Müller. "Because *Newsweek* prides itself on the balance and accuracy of its stories, it is with real embarrassment and concern that I must agree that we were off line with this one," Dwight W. Norris wrote to Welch on behalf of the magazine's editors. Welch reprinted Norris's letter in the group's January 1960 bulletin, claiming victory. "As we gather strength we can become far more effective watchdogs over some of the most pronounced misreporting in other publications," Welch wrote.[31]

Throughout the early 1960s Welch would routinely call upon Birchers to write letters protesting the coverage of various national news outlets. He took particular issue with CBS News. In May 1961 Welch reported that a CBS reporter had used underhanded tactics to interview him against his wishes, resulting in footage that made the Birch leader look cagey and defensive. "As I am sure future events will show, the Columbia Broadcasting Company is out to destroy The John Birch Society," Welch warned members.[32] When, that November, CBS aired an investigation of an illegal bookmaking establishment in Boston, Welch assumed it was "a 'frame-up' to discredit the Boston Police Force" and reissued his earlier complaints against CBS as a pamphlet titled "The Story of a Hoax." It started by noting that, while Welch had not watched CBS's *Biography of a Bookie Joint*, he could personally attest to the integrity of the Boston Police. He wrote, "As to whether CBS is capable of perpetrating a hoax in order to discredit anti-Communists, we shall let you be the judge." In the group's March 1962 bulletin, Welch shared the pamphlet, encouraging Birchers to circulate it along with personalized letters of criticism to local CBS affiliates, newspapers, and the Federal Communications Commission, "anybody where you think the correction and protest will do any good."[33]

Bircher media activism also involved boosting fledgling conservative outlets. In late 1959 Welch called on Birchers to write letters to the heads of three major US airlines—American, United, and Eastern—calling on them to offer *Human Events* or *National Review* as reading material for their customers. "Point out that each airline has tens of thousands of American conservatives among its customers who would like to find on its planes at least <u>one</u> publication which they consider fully trustworthy in that publication's selection and interpretation of the news," Welch wrote.[34] While that effort proved unsuccessful, the Birchers had more luck encouraging businesses to sponsor conservative radio commentators.[35] In July 1960, for instance, Birchers were requested to write letters of thanks to Kemper Insurance Companies of Chicago—sponsors of Fulton Lewis Jr.'s radio show—encouraging them to continue and expand their sponsorship. "All members who have read the Blue Book," Welch wrote, referring to the John Birch Society founding manifesto, "know how important we consider it to be to maintain and increase the audiences reached by Fulton Lewis, Dean Manion, Dan Smoot, and other outstanding Americanist voices on radio and television."[36] The Birchers similarly boosted the circulation of conservative syndicated columnist Westbrook Pegler.[37]

Indeed, the Birchers would often use letter-writing campaigns to ingratiate themselves with conservative commentators, especially those who were wary of the group's tone and tactics. This became more and more necessary from early 1961 onward as the Birch Society's launch of its "Movement to Impeach Earl Warren" alienated some would-be supporters, who viewed it as a quixotic distraction. That January conservative syndicated columnist George Sokolsky published a blistering critique of the campaign. Alerting Birchers to the criticism, Welch asked them to send friendly letters to the columnist. "We need George Sokolsky on our side in this particular fight," Welch wrote. "And we think all it will take to win him as an active supporter will be to prove that we are not just a few excited people with an 'angry fancy,' making a futile gesture." Welch further encouraged Birchers to send letters of praise to *Richmond News Leader* editor James J. Kilpatrick, an ardent segregationist who played a key role in promoting the idea that the mainstream press was biased against the South. "Mr. Kilpatrick, who has not criticized us in any way, is nevertheless another very able leader in the Conservative cause who does not yet think we have any chance of making our MOVEMENT sufficiently effective to be of real importance," Welch wrote.[38]

Sokolsky and Kilpatrick would be the least of Welch's troubles. While the John Birch Society had experienced critical press coverage as early as July 1960—when the *Chicago Daily News* revealed that Welch had accused President Dwight D. Eisenhower of being a secret communist agent in his self-published book *The Politician*—by early 1961 the Birchers were under widespread attack.[39] As it had with Facts Forum in early 1954, *Time* magazine turned the national spotlight on the Birchers when it published an exposé on the group in March 1961. In the two weeks that followed, more than one hundred newspapers across the country followed suit, accusing the Birchers of secrecy, conspiracism, antisemitism and proto-fascism.[40] In April William F. Buckley weighed in—defending the Birchers, to a degree, but nevertheless distancing his conservative movement from Welch's more conspiratorial claims. While Buckley said he agreed that communists were conspiring to take over the United States, he disagreed that they had already succeeded (as Welch often insinuated). "If our government is in the effective control of Communists," Buckley wrote in *National Review*, "then the active educational effort conducted by conservatives in this country, to the extent it is based on the premise that we *and* our governors wish to save America, is a sheer waste of time."[41]

The *National Review* had long been wary of the Birchers' more grandiose claims of communist conspiracy. In April 1959 the magazine published an article by Eugene Lyons warning against the "overestimation of the Kremlin's power to deceive and confuse the West." A former fellow traveler himself, Lyons found Welch's conspiracism to be little more than "foolish myth-making and dangerous self-delusion."[42] By February 1962, after a year of relentlessly negative press attention for conservatives who were being increasingly associated with the Birchers, Buckley saw fit to cut Welch loose. "If not a single criticism had been made of Mr. Welch by the Liberal press, the dilemma would exist just the same, and conservatives sooner or later would have to face it," Buckley wrote, sensitive to the appearance of caving to mainstream press criticisms. "Robert Welch is damaging the cause of anti-Communism." While Buckley noted that John Birch Society members were "some of the most morally energetic, self-sacrificing, and dedicated anti-Communists in America," he ultimately encouraged them to distance themselves from their leader.[43]

Unfazed, Welch interpreted Buckley's criticisms within the broader context of the conservative movement's ongoing contentious relationship with the mainstream press. In his March 1962 bulletin Welch responded to growing conservative criticisms of his John Birch Society leadership with a thinly veiled "fable" of a conservative organizer gradually selling out his allies in pursuit of being "the recognized leader of the 'loyal opposition.'" Unlike Buckley, Welch saw pandering to the "Liberal Establishment" as a fool's errand.[44] The prior August Welch expounded on the uphill battle conservatives faced due to the "nearly infinite web of distortions, falsehoods, and misinformation that has been woven over the minds of the American people by the Court Historians and Court Journalists of the Liberal Establishment during half a century." He noted, "There is a tiny percentage of our membership which thinks that we should adjust everything we say and do primarily to the consideration of how it will be regarded by the press." Welch disagreed. "Neither now nor at any other point shall we be willing to settle down into a tight and prosperous little bureaucracy, advocating study without action, prayer without works, or the taming of rattle-snakes by patting them lovingly on the head," Welch wrote. "We are fighting against the most cruel, amoral, cunning, ambitious, extensive, powerful, and successfully organized gang of completely merciless criminals the world has ever seen, and we know it."[45]

While Welch was clearly frustrated by critiques from the Right, he saw a silver lining in being targeted by mainstream outlets that he and his fellow Birchers had long suspected of communist fellow-traveling. Bragging about one such criticism in his July 1961 bulletin, Welch wrote, "If the vicious—though typically uninformed and half-baked—enmity of Ralph McGill and the *Atlanta Constitution* is not worth one new chapter a week to us in the state of Georgia, then the good citizens of that state have gone more soft, or have really been more brainwashed, than we believe to be the case."[46] Indeed, throughout the 1960s, as civil rights movement campaigns against Jim Crow segregation drew national press scrutiny to the South, the John Birch Society experienced considerable growth there.[47] In Birmingham, Alabama, the Birchers boasted more than one hundred chapters by 1965. The city's high concentration of right-wing activism created a stifling political environment but one primed for entrepreneurial conservative media activism. "A liberal bold enough to speak publicly is likely to find his picture on the front page of *The Birmingham Independent*, a right-wing weekly newspaper that is, among other things, the unofficial organ for the Birch Society," *The New York Times* reported.[48] As we will see, the *Independent* not only coordinated right-anticommunist public opinion in Birmingham; it also intervened in a broader struggle over the news then occurring throughout the South.

US SOUTHERN NEWS CULTURES AND THE "PAPER CURTAIN"

As historians Kathy Roberts Forde and Sid Bedingfield have shown, from Reconstruction through the modern civil rights era, the US South was characterized by two conflicting news cultures. Most large circulation newspapers in the region were owned and staffed by white publishers and journalists whose civic activism and reporting helped build and maintain white supremacist political economies and social orders across the region.

This racist political, economic, and social order was challenged by a robust Black press that, albeit to varying degrees, was dedicated to cultivating multiracial democracy.[49] While historians of modern conservatism have often looked to movement-produced and -aligned media to explain the growing salience of right-wing politics from the mid-twentieth century onward, local and regional news cultures shaped the broader circulation of those conservative ideas.[50] For instance, in New Hampshire, a small state that would hold outsized influence in the US presidential primary process from the early 1970s onward, Nackey Scripps Loeb and her husband William used their *Union Leader* newspaper to assist the modern conservative takeover of the Republican Party.[51] In the South, where the Democratic Party was hegemonic, white-owned daily newspapers played an important role in cultivating a distrust of the national press that helped create fertile ground for modern conservatism from the mid-1950s onward.[52]

Among the leading proponents of the idea that the national press was biased against the South was Thomas R. Waring, editor of the Charleston, South Carolina, *News and Courier*—a publication *Time* magazine once called "the South's most segregationist newspaper."[53] Waring was a devoted white supremacist who believed that the social marginalization of Black Americans was justified by their racial inferiority. He took issue with Northern, and Northern-based national, media outlets that tended to depict Jim Crow as rooted in the bigotry of white Southerners—often eliding the insidious white supremacist social arrangements that perpetuated de facto segregation in the North as well. "A paper curtain shuts out the Southern side of the race relations story from the rest of the country," Waring wrote in 1955, accusing Northern journalists of abandoning objectivity in their coverage of racial politics in the South.[54] Between 1955 and 1958, Waring conspired with *New York Times* music critic John G. Briggs Jr., who wrote a series of press criticism columns for the *News and Courier* under the pseudonym Nicholas Stanford. In addition to lending credence to Southern complaints of Northern media bias, Briggs leaned into overtly racist and antisemitic framings at a moment where Northern-based conservative movement publications, like Buckley's *National Review*, were recalibrating toward more colorblind racist rhetoric.[55]

In 1959 Waring coordinated with Mississippi Citizens' Council leader Robert Patterson to convene segregationist Southern journalists with the aim of counteracting the prevailing press bias against the South. The meeting, held at the Henry Grady Hotel in Atlanta, included nine segregationist editors from across the region. They tapped James J. Kilpatrick, editor of the *Richmond News Leader*, to find an advertising agency willing to help correct purported misinformation about the South circulated by national outlets. While Kilpatrick never followed through with the idea, he used his role as head of public relations for the Virginia Commission on Constitutional Government to reframe the segregationist message as resistance to unconstitutional federal overreach—forging a deracinated racist rhetoric that would soon be adopted by leading conservative movement figures, including Barry Goldwater.[56] Kilpatrick himself would go on to write about racial politics for *National Review* and *Human Events* and by the 1970s was a regular television pundit and syndicated columnist.[57] The modern conservative movement served as a vehicle for the sublimated racial grievances of white Southerners like Kilpatrick, ultimately reshaping national media discourse around race to the benefit of Southern conservatives.[58]

While Waring was tapped by *Harper's* magazine in 1956 to pen a defense of segregation from a white Southern perspective, he felt that Northern editors generally tended to elevate more liberal white Southern voices, like the editors of the *Atlanta Constitution*, *Charlotte Observer*, and Mississippi's *Delta Democrat Times*.[59] Indeed, in the years following the *Brown* decision, newspapers in several major Southern cities avoided full-throated defenses of Jim Crow in favor of varying degrees of accommodation with federal imperatives to integrate—ranging from support to begrudging appeals for gradualism. Waring and his fellow segregationist editors not only faced a hostile Northern press but increasingly found their perspectives contested within the white Southern press as well. This sense of dual embattlement shaped the critical disposition toward the press among white Southern segregationists, which figures like Kilpatrick and groups like the John Birch Society helped to bridge with that of the modern conservative movement. As we'll see in Birmingham, even daily Southern newspapers that vehemently opposed the civil rights movement, and national press coverage thereof, were themselves tarred as liberal by activists even further to their right.

BIRMINGHAM, 1963

In May 1963 the heads of Birmingham's two daily newspapers, the morning *Post Herald* and the evening *News*, took to the pages of *Editor & Publisher* to decry national and international reporting of racial conflict in their city. "The electronic media representatives always come south with evidently preconceived ideas of our problems," *Birmingham News* publisher C. B. Hanson told the journalism trade magazine. "Most of the newspapers, but in particular the broadcasters, were not truthful in their reports. They presented a warped and distorted picture of what was going on."[60] The preceding weeks had seen an influx of nonviolent direct action from protestors led by Dr. Martin Luther King Jr. and his Southern Christian Leadership Conference (SCLC). The so-called Birmingham campaign, which involved mass civil disobedience in the city's downtown shopping district, has since become a well-worn case study for social movement theorists who, by and large, credit it with shifting US public opinion against Jim Crow.[61] It has also been—incorrectly, as we have seen—described as a point of origin for the idea of liberal media bias.[62]

That's due in part to Birmingham Commissioner of Public Safety Eugene "Bull" Connor, who controlled both the city's police and fire departments, and who ordered the use of fire hoses and police dogs to dispatch the civil rights protestors. Images of peaceful Black demonstrators being blasted with highly pressurized water and attacked by German shepherds, sicced by white policemen, beamed from television sets across the country and around the globe. A caption accompanying a ten-page pictorial essay documenting the brutality in *Life* magazine noted, "If the Negroes themselves had written the script, they could hardly have asked for greater help for their cause."[63]

Defending their respective decisions to downplay coverage of the civil rights movement more broadly and their city's use of pressurized water and dogs against nonviolent protestors, both Birmingham newspaper executives exhibited a paternalism common among white Southern elites of the era. "We recognized that some of those leading the Negroes thrive on publicity and we did not want our columns to be their sounding board," *Post Herald* editor James E. Mills told *Editor & Publisher*. "But we are trying to do an honest news job." Earlier that spring, both of the city's daily papers had supported changes to Birmingham's governing structure—from a three-man commission to a mayor-council system—and both had endorsed Albert Boutwell to lead it. Boutwell, a relative moderate, defeated the ardent segregationist Bull Connor a day before the SCLC launched its Birmingham campaign that April. *The Birmingham News* publisher, Hanson, suggested that these moves were part of a gradualist approach toward integration, embraced by the city's white leadership. He told *Editor & Publisher*, "Virtually the day after the election, when at last the road was open for a solution to the segregation problem, the Rev. Martin Luther King and other outsiders—some of them frankly publicity seekers—came to Birmingham and started raising Hell."[64]

We would be remiss to take the editors at their word that they supported a "solution" or that they even agreed that segregation was a "problem." A contemporaneous source considered the *Post Herald* "as hard-line segregationist as respectable journalism allows," and noted that neither it nor the *News* had been critical of their city's handling of racial matters until they were forced by the civil rights movement and the courts to take the problem seriously.[65] Both newspapers also owned radio and television stations in the area and in the years leading up to 1963 had variously enforced "blackouts" of local press coverage of civil rights activities across mediums, which were circumvented by a couple of Black-oriented radio stations taking advantage of rare instances of absentee white ownership.[66] In 1988 *The Birmingham News* even issued a formal apology for its coverage of the civil rights movement, which involved colluding with white authorities, downplaying coverage, and denouncing protestors.[67] And yet both papers' handling of Birmingham city affairs raised the ire of residents in the tony white Birmingham suburbs of Cahaba Heights, Mountain Brook, Homewood, and Vestavia. In 1963 all were served by a small weekly newspaper called the *Cahaba Valley News*.

Operated by Hal Totten and with a meager circulation of around 1,800, the *Cahaba Valley News* catered to the hard right conservatism of Birmingham's white elite. Alongside coverage of local children's sports leagues and the goings on of various social clubs, the paper denounced President John F. Kennedy and his attorney general brother Robert as "nepotists" who they accused of actively conspiring with civil rights leaders domestically and with communists abroad. The paper described King and the SCLC as outside agitators and blamed them for an ongoing Ku Klux Klan campaign of violence against the city's Black residents and their supporters. In a front-page editorial opposing calls for federal troops to keep the peace in Birmingham, the paper wrote of King: "Just what hold this Communist-accommodating rabble-rouser has over the Kennedy nepotists is difficult to conjure. But the control is there."[68] The paper regularly featured conservative syndicated columnists like Paul Harvey, Tom Anderson, and Clarence Manion. It ran editorials defending the John Birch Society against allegations of fascism and antisemitism, and it celebrated Gov. George Wallace's infamous stand in the schoolhouse door opposing integration at the University of Alabama and the growing national profile that his demand of "segregation forever" afforded both him and the state.[69]

Although a small weekly and not in direct competition with the *Post Herald* and the *News*, the *Cahaba Valley News* regularly positioned itself as a conservative alternative to the city's dailies. It accused both of "prodding" the city into a new governance structure, which it depicted as conspiring to absorb the unincorporated wealthy white suburbs that the *Cahaba Valley News* served.[70] When both daily papers criticized proposed state legislation to create an Alabama sovereignty commission designed to defend against federal integration efforts, the *Cahaba Valley News* published an open letter, written by nine white attorneys, denouncing the papers. "A portion of the press of the South has quit the fight against forced integration and is busily engaged in conditioning the people to accept the inevitable," the letter read, naming *Atlanta Constitution* editor Ralph McGill as an exemplar of the trend. The *Cahaba Valley News* endorsed the letter, adding, "Any Southerner or Southern newspaper, even Northern owned or controlled, who opposes the bill creating the Alabama Sovereignty Commission is bent on undermining NOT ONLY the treasured right of the South, but government as set forth in the Constitution of the United States."[71]

The paper's reference to "Northern owned or controlled" news was intended as a dig at the local dailies. The *Birmingham Post Herald* was owned by the Cincinnati-based Scripps Howard chain, and *The Birmingham News* had been purchased by the New York–based Newhouse chain in 1955.[72] While the *Cahaba Valley News* regularly published criticism of national news outlets, dubbed the "controlled Liberal Press," and the Kennedy administration's efforts to "manage" their coverage, it was the perceived liberal bias of the local dailies that informed its aspirations for growth.⁷³ In mid-November 1963 the paper announced plans to expand its coverage and to change its name to the *Birmingham Independent*. It boasted new ownership by "a large number of stockholders, none of them with large blocks of stock, and located throughout the state," and it positioned itself within the broader Birmingham news market as a "solid, fighting, home-owned, home-edited, Conservative newspaper."⁷⁴ In the years that followed, the *Independent* would occasionally smear the *Post Herald* as one of "Birmingham's two northern owned daily newspapers," but it more routinely denounced *The Birmingham News* for its coverage of race relations and civil rights.⁷⁵

For example, in July 1963, while still the *Cahaba Valley News*, the paper published an exposé alleging that both Martin Luther King Jr. and Birmingham civil rights leader Fred Shuttlesworth were openly collaborating with known communists.⁷⁶ When, in April 1964, a local daily published a syndicated column corroborating King's communist ties, the *Independent* ran a front page "told you so" editorial. "The columnist was Joseph Alsop, admittedly one of the most left-wing of all left-wing 'news' dispensers," the *Independent* chirped, although Alsop, a devoted anticommunist, was by no means a leftist. "The newspaper was the *Birmingham News*, which—because it is printed in Birmingham—attempts to oppose the civil 'rights' bill while taking every opportunity subtly to espouse integration."⁷⁷ The bragging continued in weeks ahead, as the *Independent* solicited new subscribers with in-house ads celebrating that its scoop had been validated by a "Liberal" local daily.⁷⁸ Pledging to "TEAR THE PAPER CURTAIN," the *Independent* would closely align itself with local John Birch Society activists, adopting an even more hostile stance toward its journalistic competitors around the country.⁷⁹

INDEPENDENT PRESS CRITICISM

The *Birmingham Independent* launched on January 1, 1964, with a front-page editorial introducing the paper's expanded vision and more aggressive tone. "We are the Conservatives," the editorial declared. "We are the Americans who fight to the death the socialistic pressures that have been growing yearly; that have been steadily stealing from all Americans their freedoms and rights. We expose at every opportunity the sinister influences that have been consorting with communists, delivering us into the hands of a Godless slavery." Describing itself as "the only major Conservative NEWSPAPER in this area," it stressed that the *Independent* was "not a propaganda medium." Rather, its new owners pledged to tell "the story of the doctrine of the complete American patriot" with extended coverage of happenings throughout the region and, ultimately, throughout the state.[80] The newspaper, which ran for a decade, grew steadily under its new, more active ownership. By late 1967, when the paper started calling itself the *Alabama Independent*, it reported a circulation of around 6,300, more than a threefold increase over the reach of the *Cahaba Valley News*.[81]

The *Independent* did not list its local owners, but it seems likely that many if not all shared some affiliation with the John Birch Society.[82] While the *Cahaba Valley News* occasionally defended the Birchers and shared many of their political positions, when it rebranded as the *Independent* the paper started publishing ads soliciting membership and direct involvement in John Birch Society campaigns.[83] At least one known local Birch chapter leader, pharmacist Jimmy C. Jones, began contributing original reporting to the *Independent* starting in 1964.[84] He focused primarily on documenting the putative subversive activities of area liberals, especially those affiliated with the University of Alabama.[85] Notorious Bircher crusades—impeach Earl Warren, support local police, oppose water fluoridation—all became regular topics of reporting in the *Independent*, slowly displacing more typical hyperlocal coverage of Boy Scout troops and school dances. The paper also started running reprints of Birch Society pamphlets and articles that first appeared in official Birch publications like *American Opinion* and *Review of the News*.[86] For instance, the *Independent* routinely reprinted the unsigned Bircher "Correction, Please!" column, critiquing national news reporting of various subjects and offering conservative interpretive frameworks for reading between the lines of implicitly liberal or left reporting.

Indeed, as the paper's affiliation with movement conservatism strengthened, so too did its claims of local and national press bias. The *Independent* was replete with press criticism—and not just concerning coverage of the civil rights movement. Its media critical emphases varied, shaped by a mix of local concerns, Bircher pet issues, and electoral politics. The *Independent*'s first year of operation, 1964, was a key turning point in the history of modern conservatism. After years of dominance by its liberal wing, the Republican Party nominated Arizona Sen. Barry Goldwater as its nominee to challenge incumbent President Lyndon Johnson. Unsurprisingly, the *Independent* backed Goldwater and vehemently opposed Johnson, whose advocacy for the Civil Rights Act of 1964 was seen as a betrayal by conservative white Southern Democrats.[87] Throughout 1964 the *Independent* accused Johnson of "managing" the press to do his bidding. In March it published a syndicated column by Fulton Lewis Jr., who claimed that Johnson was rewarding liberal reporters and punishing conservative ones by rarely calling on them at press briefings.[88] The paper also accused television networks of giving the president preferential treatment.[89]

The bulk of the *Independent*'s press criticism in 1964 focused on what it perceived as unfair treatment afforded to Republican presidential nominee Barry Goldwater.[90] In June it published an editorial promoting conservative activist Phyllis Schlafly's book *A Choice Not an Echo*, which argued that Goldwater's candidacy was opposed by a shadowy "Establishment," composed of a "New York financial clique" that included the publishers of *Time* magazine and *The New York Times* as well as Ralph McGill, the segregationist-and-Bircher-reviled editor of the *Atlanta Constitution*.[91] As the national press homed in on Goldwater's hard right policy positions and affiliations, which fell well beyond the bounds of the prevailing liberal political consensus, the *Independent* cried foul. It accused wire reporters working for the Associated Press and United Press International of omitting important context concerning Goldwater's disavowal of "extremists" on the left and right. "Although, of course, the Left-wing press can be expected to deliberately misinterpret Goldwater's statements to include Right-wing conservatives, a simple reading of Goldwater's actual statement proves the lie!"[92]

When Goldwater was soundly defeated that November, the *Independent* laid the blame at the feet of national broadcasters. "Both ABC and CBS bluntly refused to give Goldwater a chance to speak out," the *Independent* argued. "NBC gave him 15 minutes but has run its own campaign against the senator in other ways."[93] Goldwater felt similarly. The day after his election loss, he too blamed the press for its negative depictions of his candidacy: "I think, frankly, that these people should hang their heads in shame because I think that they've made the Fourth Estate a rather sad, sorry mess."[94] In an editorial reflecting on the 1964 election, the *Independent* agreed: "If the Americanist cause is ever to win a national election there are several requisites to be met." The first, they argued, was "control of at least a portion of the National Communications media." The editors continued, "The hue and cry is now about 'images.' The liberals who control the machinery which creates the images are now publicly decrying but privately rejoicing in the false image they have given the Conservative Republicans."[95]

In the years that followed, the *Independent* routinely took individual national media outlets to task for their coverage of issues ranging from civil rights to Vietnam to policing, accusing the press broadly of "failing" the American public.[96] The paper's emphasis on widespread liberal/left media bias conveyed to its readers the need for constant vigilance and critical approaches to interpreting, or "filtering," news coming from untrusted (nonconservative) sources.[97] "Tired of reading between the lines?" the paper asked readers in an August 1967 front-page solicitation. "Subscribe to the *Birmingham Independent*."[98] Like national Birch publications, the *Independent* routinely provided readers with interpretive strategies for consuming content produced by mainstream outlets. For example, in July 1964 it ran a syndicated column by Tom Anderson listing a series of "news items" drawn from mainstream reporting along with "comments" applying appropriate conservative context.[99] Later that month, promoting a local talk show by *None Dare Call It Treason* author John Stormer, the *Independent*'s editors provided a series of "misnomers" common in mainstream press reporting, with strategies for interpreting the facts surrounding them. "We almost need a new dictionary to interpret the political 'news' today," the editors wrote. "Indeed it is only by careful sifting that we can separate the real news from the propaganda."[100]

The *Independent* further promoted this practice of conservative close reading of the news by regularly printing letters to the editor in which readers from around the country demonstrated their critical disposition toward other outlets. For example, in May 1966 reader Pryde Hinton of Dora, Alabama, recounted a letter they had written to an unnamed Midwestern radio station that had aired critical reporting of then Alabama governor Lurleen Wallace, wife of George: "Your newscaster was as unfair and untruthful as most of the news media are about Southern affairs and persons."[101] In sharing the letter with the *Independent*'s readers, Hinton modeled an active approach to consuming and counteracting biased reporting. Other readers shared their own critical reading practices. "Every person with an ounce of intelligence has taken note that all the national wire services, all the radio and TV networks and practically all the large magazines do not mention the name of George Wallace except to deliberately distort, defame and vilify him" reader T. J. Campbell of Atlanta wrote to the *Independent* in the spring of 1968. "This is what is known as 'quarantine from the news.'"[102]

The *Independent*'s penchant for publishing letters criticizing *other* media outlets underscores its commitment to fostering such critical practices among its readers. Another reader, whose letter was published alongside Campbell's in April 1968, described watching a televised hearing of the Senate Foreign Relations Committee in which Republican senator Karl Mundt took Secretary of State Dean Rusk to task for the administration's "no win" policy in Vietnam. "I scanned both the morning and evening dailies and both ignored Senator Mundt and his confrontation with the Secretary," wrote Harry Stanley of Phoenix, Arizona, who went on to accuse the press of conspiring with communists to prolong the war. "That portion of the News Media which laments the loudest when they feel that Freedom of the Press is being abused are the ones who abuse that freedom the most by practicing irresponsible journalism," Stanley concluded. "All of which brings to light the all-important part such publications as the *Alabama Independent* are playing with their unmuzzled reporting of the news."[103]

CULTIVATING A SENSE OF MEDIA EMBATTLEMENT

The idea of liberal media bias was not some abstract claim for the *Birmingham Independent* and its conservative readers. Between persistent press scrutiny of the John Birch Society and Goldwater's ascendance to Republican Party standard-bearer, the 1960s saw renewed focus by national news media on the perils and absurdities of the increasingly vocal right-wing "fringe."[104] From the point of view of that fringe, including readers of the *Independent*, the national press was not merely failing to report the news in accordance with the modern conservative worldview. It was leading a direct attack against them and the movement they supported. The *Independent*, like the John Birch Society that it unofficially promoted, leveraged this sense of embattlement to recruit and retain conservative activists. In the same inaugural issue in which the *Independent* declared its allegiance to Birch-style Americanism, it depicted the national press as its foe. "The nation's press—much of it—has devoted a great deal of space to describing the 'closed minds' and 'dinosaur beliefs' of the dedicated anti-communists who are referred to sneeringly as 'super-patriots,'" the editors wrote, before listing several instances where the national press purportedly misjudged communist intentions.[105] From its first issue onward, the *Independent* made a point of defending its conservative readers from attacks—from the left and right.

In December 1964, for instance, the *Independent* published a lengthy editorial denouncing the *St. Petersburg Times* for reporting that Birchers had been told to arm themselves and their children. Listing the many liberal and left political associations of *Times* publisher Nelson Poynter and his managing editor David Loth, the *Independent* framed itself as a bulwark—protecting its readers from communist attacks. "Mr. Poynter and his ilk are smug in thinking that they can get away with their lies and their victims are helpless and have no voice," the editorial read. "But that is where small weekly newspapers like *The Birmingham Independent* come in." The *Independent* also situated the attack in the context of a memorandum written by Walter Reuther and delivered to then–Attorney General Robert F. Kennedy in 1962, which suggested using Internal Revenue Service and Federal Communications Commission regulations (including Fairness Doctrine complaints) to weaken right-anticommunist radio commentators and organizations like the John Birch Society. "When one remembers that Gus Hall said that the Communist Party could not take over until the John Birch Society is destroyed then we can see why the left-wing presses are cooperating in such a unified attack on all anti-Communist groups," the *Independent* warned.[106]

The *Independent* rarely missed an opportunity to remind its readers of the ongoing efforts—putatively by government, communists, and the press—to undermine conservative groups, publications, and commentators. The paper regularly alluded to the so-called Reuther Memo and to the Johnson administration's purported targeting of conservatives.[107] It covered right-anticommunist radio commentator Rev. Carl McIntire's dispute with the Federal Communications Commission over Fairness Doctrine violations in 1966 (discussed in this book's first chapter).[108] It covered Gen. Edwin Walker's libel lawsuit against the Associated Press, which had incorrectly reported him as leading a violent white mob protesting against efforts to integrate the University of Mississippi (he claimed to merely be a riot attendee).[109] It regularly featured essays written by anticommunist evangelical broadcaster Dr. Billy James Hargis, excitedly covered his local rallies, and reported on IRS investigations into the anticommunist evangelical broadcaster who was "under heavy attack by the Communists and liberal news media."[110]

While the *Independent* strongly aligned its readers with the embattled, less-reputable corners of modern conservatism—the Birchers, McIntire, Walker, Hargis—it occasionally cast shade on William F. Buckley. In October 1965 it ran a political cartoon depicting the John Birch Society as a gigantic tiger behind a wall labeled "GOP," with a miniature Buckley imploring a handful of moderate Republicans, pulling helplessly on the tiger's tail, to "Throw the Scoundrels Out!"[111] The *Independent*'s beef with Buckley grew in 1967 as Alabama governor George Wallace began making moves toward a third-party run for the US presidency in 1968. In April 1967 the *Independent* reported on a Buckley speech in Houston, Texas, where he denounced Robert Welch as having "done more than anyone else to damage the conservative cause" and predicted that George Wallace would be "a real nuisance" and damage the Republican Party's chances to carry the South in 1968.[112] That December the paper ran an editorial rebutting Buckley's ongoing denunciations of Welch, accusing him of lying and manipulating conservatives. "The attempt of the self-proclaimed expert on the John Birch Society at reverse psychology seems to make about as much sense as the inarticulate gobblelygook we hear on his Television 'Firing Line.'"[113]

Buckley's *National Review* famously endorsed Republican Richard Nixon for president in 1968, declaring the right-wing populist George Wallace "unqualified."[114] The *Independent* proudly backed Wallace's American Independent Party run. As it had with Goldwater in 1964, the paper dutifully chronicled what it considered to be widespread press bias against their preferred candidate. "Most of the newsmen I had contact with viewed the Wallace supporters as so many strange little animals in a cage," Michigan radio host David Norris wrote in the *Independent* after covering Wallace's campaign through his state. "The majority of the media I observed overlooked the cheering, shouting, applauding, enthusiastic thousands to photograph a few dirty, degenerate, filthy-mouthed, highly misinformed, obnoxious scum." Norris lamented, "If our forefathers intended a free and truthful press to keep tabs on our government, I'm sure they'd be disappointed at the disgusting hands into which has fallen this grave responsibility."[115] When Nixon ultimately won, the *National Review* lamented that Wallace had stolen what would have been a landslide, although it offered some conciliatory words for the Alabama governor's conservative supporters. The magazine further implored Nixon to study Wallace's appeal. "Either he will respond actively to the challenges of those problems which gave rise to the Wallace movement," the magazine wrote of Nixon, "or the nation will find that movement still present four years from now, much larger, much uglier and far more dangerous."[116]

As we will see in the coming chapters, by 1972 Nixon would answer Wallace with a "Southern Strategy" of his own, appealing to the racial prejudice of white Southerners to pull them into the Republican Party. Along with Vice President Spiro Agnew, he would also elevate long-standing conservative complaints of left-wing media bias. While *National Review* backed him in 1968, Nixon's political tactics as president would ultimately borrow more from the Birchers than Buckley. Assisted by Accuracy in Media—with its own roots in right-anticommunist movement infrastructure and Bircher collaborations—Nixon and Agnew would help make the "liberal media" a common sense well beyond the modern conservative movement.

This chapter has demonstrated that, in doing so, Nixon and Agnew benefited from a groundswell of conservative animosity toward the press in the preceding decade. The less-reputable corners of the modern conservative movement—Birchers and segregationists—played as much, if not more, of a role in cultivating that critical disposition toward the press among the grassroots as did the more respectable activists in Buckley's orbit. Far from a rhetorical ploy or an attempt to "play the refs," the "liberal media" claim was an engine for entrepreneurial conservative media activism well beyond the movement's formal organs and organizations. Its productivity can be measured in the proliferation of conservative commentators and outlets throughout the 1960s and 1970s. While Birmingham was particularly prone to such activism as an epicenter of the Black Freedom struggle of the 1960s, the *Independent*'s market positioning—critical of both local and national news—was not uncommon throughout the South in those years. Furthermore, the *Independent*'s practice of reprinting conservative and media critical editorials from other small newspapers across the country—not only in the South but in the North and West as well—suggests it was but one example of a broader, decentralized conservative antipathy toward the mainstream press emergent throughout the mid-twentieth century.

5

LIBERAL MEDIA GOES MAINSTREAM

"The American who relies upon television for his news might conclude that the majority of American students are embittered radicals; that the majority of Black Americans feel no regard for their country; that violence and lawlessness are the rule rather than the exception on the American campus. We know that none of these conclusions is true."

Vice President Spiro Agnew was doing an unusual form of damage control when he addressed the Midwestern Regional Republican Conference in Des Moines, Iowa, on November 13, 1969.[1] The previous week President Richard Nixon had delivered a televised address to the nation outlining his plan to scale back US military involvement in Vietnam by gradually turning ground operations over to the South Vietnamese. In terms of public opinion, Nixon's speech was a resounding success. Polls marked a shift in popular support for the president's handling of the conflict, with one showing a rise from 58 percent approving before the speech to 77 percent approving after.[2] The speech was, however, panned by pundits. In Iowa Agnew levied a trenchant critique of television news. "We can deduce that these men read the same newspapers. They draw their political and social views from the same sources," Agnew said. "Worse, they talk constantly to one another, thereby providing artificial reinforcement of their shared viewpoints."[3]

Emphasizing why "such a great gulf existed between how the nation received the President's address and how the networks reviewed it," Agnew not only accused the media of left-wing bias. He also framed the liberal media as the enemy of a conservative constituency that Nixon had recently christened the "great Silent Majority." One week later, speaking in Montgomery, Alabama, Agnew extended his critique to the printed press: "I don't seek to intimidate the press or the networks or anyone else from speaking out," he told the local Chamber of Commerce. "But the time for blind acceptance of their opinions is past. And the time for a naïve belief in their neutrality is gone."[4] Lent credence by a sitting US vice president, an idea that had spent the better part of two decades circulating among the growing conservative grass roots—that news conveyed by mainstream television networks and newspapers was biased against the worldview of a presumed conservative majority of Americans—was, for the first time, a focal point of national political discourse.

While many in the press rejected the tone and tenor of Agnew's speeches, unlike the previous two decades of conservative news criticism, he managed to strike a nerve. "Rhetoric aside, Agnew did touch on a major phenomenon," *Time* magazine wrote. "It is the strange, pervasive love-hate relationship that Americans seem to have with TV—the force that entertains them, unifies them by making them simultaneous witnesses to great events, and yet also brings them words and images they resent."[5] The preceding year, 1968, had presented US television audiences with disturbing images of social unrest. The assassination of Martin Luther King Jr. that April sparked rebellions in Black communities across the country, a rejoinder to the long, hot summer of riots in 1967. The assassination of Sen. Robert F. Kennedy that June and growing antiwar agitation by a burgeoning New Left culminated in a chaotic Democratic National Convention in Chicago, where police beat bystanders and protestors alike, as the latter chanted "the whole world is watching!" at rolling cameras.[6]

One week before Agnew's speech, journalists and scholars at Columbia University published a report reviewing the preceding year of broadcast news and diagnosing a looming "crisis." The report criticized broadcasters for failing to adequately inform the electorate by devoting less than 10 percent of airtime to news and commentary and by scaling back funding for investigative and documentary programming.[7] Although *Time* admitted that the report's critique of commercialism bore little relation to Agnew's allegation of conspiracy among a "small, unelected elite" group of journalists, it nevertheless situated the vice president's complaints of liberal bias within a broader antipathy toward television news. *Time* also noted parallels between Agnew's complaints and those of Theodore H. White, perhaps the most famous and influential political journalist of the era. Months earlier, in an appearance on William F. Buckley's *Firing Line* program, White attacked what he saw as an increasing concentration of political and cultural taste making. "You can take a compass with a one-mile radius and put it down at the corner of Fifth Avenue and 51st Street in Manhattan and you have control of 95% of the entire opinion and influence-making in the US," White told Buckley and his television audience.[8]

The growing sense of public dissatisfaction with broadcast news was reinforced by a groundswell of audience responses to the vice president's attacks. Agnew's office reported receiving 73,938 letters in support of his Iowa speech, and only 3,784 against. Broadcasters, from local affiliates up to the Big Three networks, reported a similar influx of critical correspondence from viewers, including a noticeable uptick in "hate mail." A study of one network's Agnew-inspired hate mail by researchers at the Columbia Graduate School of Journalism found that some 25 percent of letters accused the networks of communist sympathy, while 11 percent included antisemitic language, and 10 percent contained anti-Black sentiments.[9] Agnew's speech, and the anti-press backlash it induced, also sparked efforts to hold journalists accountable to the publics they serve. In 1973 a group of professional journalists and philanthropists launched the National News Council, which served as an independent ombudsperson for the press—fielding complaints and leveraging public pressure to hold news outlets accountable—through the 1970s and early 1980s.[10]

Agnew's speeches and the growing consensus among journalists and news media scholars that something was amiss in their profession came at a particularly opportune time for Reed Irvine and a small group of anticommunist activists known as Accuracy in Media (AIM). In September 1969 Irvine and his collaborators launched AIM to "function as a watchdog or ombudsman for the public with respect to accuracy of news reporting."[11] Throughout the 1970s, as the Nixon administration's battles with the press escalated over the Pentagon Papers and Watergate scandal, AIM used press releases, letters to editors, FCC complaints, and shareholder activism to raise awareness of what it perceived as rampant bias and inaccuracy among mainstream news outlets. AIM capitalized on the increased willingness of journalists to listen to public criticisms of their profession and their work, making the problem of liberal media bias a topic of deliberation and debate well beyond the modern conservative movement. Despite its deep roots in the right-anticommunist corners of that movement, initially AIM took pains to present itself as nonpartisan and impartial. This chapter foregrounds those efforts, which involve AIM leveraging the legacy of progressive media reform efforts in the 1940s—a context that also explains an increased willingness by journalism industry leaders to take the group's claims seriously.

REED IRVINE AND THE ORIGINS OF AIM

While Accuracy in Media would ultimately collaborate with the New Right, as we will see next chapter, AIM emerged less from the modern conservative movement than from the vestigial right-anticommunist infrastructure that preceded it. AIM was a spinoff from the Council Against Communist Aggression (CACA), a group founded in the early 1950s by Arthur G. McDowell, director of civic, educational, and governmental affairs for the Upholsters' International Union of North America. A liberal trade unionist and former socialist, McDowell framed CACA as "careful and scrupulous," as opposed to what he considered to be the "bad and uninformed" anticommunism of old guard conservative groups like the National Association of Manufacturers.[12] But as executive secretary of CACA in the 1950s, McDowell not only subscribed to *Counterattack*, he developed a working rapport with the antilabor American Business Consultants, accessing the group's research files and even leaking information on supposed communists "for possible use" in their newsletter.[13] In the 1960s McDowell hosted a luncheon group to promote discussion and collaboration among anticommunists residing in Washington, DC, and its suburbs.[14] Renamed the McDowell Luncheon Group after his untimely death in 1966, the regular meeting was designed "to get Democrats and Republicans, liberals and conservatives, Catholics, Protestants and Jews, to work together to support the principles that made our pluralistic society possible. That meant opposing those who wanted to seize control of the power of the state to destroy pluralism"—namely, communists.[15]

Among the group's regular attendees was economist Reed J. Irvine. Born in Salt Lake City in 1922, Irvine earned a bachelor's degree from the University in Utah in 1942, just in time to serve as a Marine Corps intelligence officer in the Pacific theater during World War II. After the war Irvine studied economics at Oxford on a Fulbright fellowship before starting his career with the Federal Reserve Bank in 1951, settling in Silver Spring, Maryland.[16] Well educated, and socially connected to the intelligence community via his military service and postwar affiliation with CACA, Irvine was an especially critical consumer of the news, particularly when it came to matters of foreign policy and what he perceived to be domestic subversion. By the late 1960s, as Irvine approached retirement from the Federal Reserve System's Division of International Finance, he grew increasingly concerned with the rise of the New Left and Black Power movements, the plight of Soviet dissidents, and the ongoing war in Vietnam.[17]

A prolific writer of letters to newspaper editors, Irvine routinely expressed bewilderment and fear at what he understood to be growing social and cultural disorder in the United States. He wrote letters against liberalizing drug laws and sex education curriculum.[18] He was an especially keen proponent of the use of policing powers to return the country to a state of "domestic tranquility."[19] In 1969 Irvine began regularly contributing book reviews to the Washington *Evening Star* newspaper, lauding books critical of communism in the Soviet Union and China and panning books that extolled the politics of the New Left. From lamenting the "tragic victims of drugs" to criticizing "these ill-informed youngsters" who opposed US military interventions in Southeast Asia—Irvine's letters and reviews tended to understand the threats facing the United States as resultant from a spoiled and ill-informed younger generation.[20]

As Irvine wrote in a letter on civil disobedience published in a December 1969 issue of the *Evening Star*, "tyranny is thrusting its ugly form upon this country wrapped in the disguise of liberty." Irvine continued, "We have no greater obligation to our children than to teach them to see through that disguise. Our biggest mistake has been that we as parents have been lax in this ourselves, and we have compounded the error by allowing, in the name of freedom, the perpetrators of the fraud to secure a strong influence in our schools and other channels of education and information."[21] If Irvine's reasoning echoed the rationale of the 1950 anticommunist blacklist *Red Channels*, that's because he was a fan—he directly collaborated with its *Counterattack* authors in affiliating with CACA.[22] In 1950 *Counterattack* sought to "awaken" the general public to what its authors understood to be underreported communist threats. By the late 1960s, when Irvine steered the McDowell Luncheon Group to focus on the problem of news bias, he benefited from nearly two decades of right-anticommunist organizing efforts, including those of American Business Consultants, Facts Forum, and the John Birch Society, which by the 1960s had helped cultivate a critical disposition toward the press among the burgeoning conservative grass roots.[23]

In September 1969 Irvine and a handful of his fellow McDowell Luncheon Group members founded Accuracy in Media as an advocacy group serving the interests of this imagined conservative critical community. According to Irvine, AIM "was a product of the frustration sensed by millions of people because the chasms they perceived between what was actually going on in the world and what was being presented by the dominant media."[24] While the group's stated emphasis on accuracy suggested a focus on errors of fact, Irvine also envisioned AIM as serving the more subjective function of contesting the predominating news judgment of professional broadcast and print media outlets: "AIM would not be precluded from comment on distorted reporting where no factual misstatement was involved but where a misleading impression had been created by omitting important information or over-emphasizing certain stories or parts of a story." Irvine continued, "It is recognized that this is a delicate area which may involve honest differences of news judgment, but it is also recognized that a valuable service can be performed by calling to the attention of responsible editors cases of under-reporting or over-reporting that appear serious in the minds of AIM's expert panel."[25]

Perhaps unbeknown to Irvine, in founding AIM he was enacting a vision first laid out by H. L. Hunt in 1954.[26] As discussed in chapter 3, when Facts Forum became a target of widespread criticism in the mainstream press, Hunt advocated for right-wing news consumer empowerment. "The people pay for the news which reaches them. They pay in taxes, in patronizing advertisers, and in subscriptions," Hunt wrote in *Facts Forum News*. "Paying for the news they have a measure of control, and perhaps laboriously and over a period of time, they can get through the news channels whatever news they desire, be it a fair, honest presentation of both sides on vital issues, or only one side."[27] Hunt assumed a general public composed by a latent conservative consensus—a precursor to Nixon's "Silent Majority"—one he hoped to coax out of its supposed apathy by rebranding "conservative" ideas as "constructive," and by funding Facts Forum groups and programming.[28] Over the course of the 1960s Hunt's *Life Line* radio program joined a chorus of conservative broadcast and print media products aimed at serving and bolstering a conservative public that was consistently depicted as massive, silent, and "forgotten" by both established interest groups and the press.[29] This burgeoning conservative public and the yet-to-be-expressed majority it was thought to indicate, shaped the imagined consumer on whose behalf AIM was formed to advocate.

So, when in November 1969 Vice President Agnew announced that the time had come for television news to be "more responsive to the views of the nation and more responsible to the people they serve," Accuracy in Media quickly positioned itself as vehicle for that accountability.[30] AIM founding executive secretary Benjamin Ginzburg applauded Agnew's speech as a "great public service," noting that "the public has long recognized that TV news frequently does not tell it like it is, but like a few highly opinionated men in New York and Washington want it to be." Like Agnew, Ginzburg presumed a correlation between majority opinion and objective reality while leaving unspoken the conservative political stakes of that belief. Rather than associating with the conservative movement that cultivated belief in liberal media bias, or with the Republican Party that popularized the idea beyond the conservative grassroots, Ginzburg identified AIM's founding members as merely "public-spirited citizens" and the group itself as "a private civilian review board for the news media." As evidence that the media played "loose with the facts," Ginzburg cited coverage of the riots that accompanied the 1968 Democratic Convention in Chicago and a sensationalized CBS report on hunger in America.[31] While Irvine would later contend that both examples had provoked critical commentary by liberals and conservatives alike, there is little doubt that AIM's concerns aligned it with critics on the right.[32]

This tension between AIM's public claims to impartiality and the undeniably conservative ties and judgment that informed its media criticism is further reflected in marginalia found on working copies of the group's early promotional materials. One such solicitation introduced AIM as "a non-profit, non-partisan organization" designed to "encourage the news media to maintain the highest possible standards of accuracy in their reporting and news commentary." The letter remained opaque as to the standards AIM planned to employ to determine both accuracy itself and what news errors were deserving of the group's sustained public agitation, but an unnamed editor suggested the additional wording, "writing from the standpoint of the preservation of our constitutional system, our free enterprise economy, and opposition to all forms of collectivism to which cause we are dedicated."[33] Such wording never found its way into AIM's public-facing materials, but it effectively summarizes the group's unarticulated standards of judgment—standards that aligned with those of Nixon and Agnew's conception of the Silent Majority as well as with the burgeoning New Right.[34] Nevertheless, early on AIM's anticommunism also attracted the support of Cold War liberals, while its persistent concern with the principles of fairness and ideological balance endeared the group to civil libertarians.

MORRIS ERNST AND THE FRAUGHT LEGACY OF LIBERAL MEDIA REFORM

Despite having its cause almost immediately boosted by the vice president of the United States, AIM spent its first year and a half largely outside the national public eye. Under the leadership of Benjamin Ginzburg, the group's efforts were characterized by mostly private and ad hoc appeals made by Irvine to the presidents of CBS, NBC, WETA, *The Washington Post*, and *The New York Times*.[35] These letters, often typed on personal letterhead and lacking any mention of AIM, focused on programming and coverage with which Irvine disagreed. His critiques, to a letter, exhibited their author's personal right-anticommunist perspective, primarily accusing the networks and publications of being soft on communism abroad and New Left radicalism at home. In the case of the

Washington, DC, public television station WETA, Irvine evinced his own political sensibilities in alleging partisan bias. "It appears that WETA fears political bias only when it comes from the Republican side," Irvine wrote. "Democratic bias is evidently acceptable."[36] Yet, as AIM began developing a more formidable fundraising and publicity strategy in 1971, it took pains to nurture a more politically neutral image. "We are not a 'right-wing' organization," Ginzburg's successor Abraham Kalish would insist in 1973, citing as evidence the group's occasional criticisms of reporting published by the *National Review* and *Chicago Tribune*. But AIM's primary cudgel for fending off charges of partisan bias was the early presence of liberals and Democrats on its National Advisory Board.[37]

AIM's national stature can be traced back to May 1971, when Kalish replaced Ginzburg as the group's executive secretary. Freshly retired from a career as a professor of communications at the Defense Intelligence School and writer for the US Intelligence Agency, Kalish immediately set about building AIM's organizational capacities. The group officially incorporated that June, and Kalish began raising money to fund AIM's publicity campaigns and shareholder activism, with quick success.[38] By fiscal year 1972–1973, AIM boasted an annual budget of $80,000—an astronomical increase from its $6,000 budget the year Kalish took over operations.[39] The organization's rapid growth resulted in part from Kalish's other major initiative of 1971, building an esteemed National Advisory Board to bolster AIM's credibility and fundraising prowess. Announced in August 1971 at a luncheon featuring a keynote address by Democratic representative Harley Staggers, the board included an illustrious array of foreign policy and communication experts—among them former secretary of state and Cold War architect Dean Acheson, Ambassador Eldridge Durbrow, and prominent right-anticommunist journalist Eugene Lyons.[40] Like the McDowell Luncheon Group out of which AIM was formed, the inaugural advisory board was bipartisan and ideologically diverse apart from a shared commitment to anticommunism. Among its marquee names was that of former general counsel of the American Civil Liberties Union and longtime media reform proponent Morris L. Ernst. AIM clearly relished Ernst's affiliation, with Kalish routinely using his name as evidence of the group's political impartiality. Ernst's motivation for lending his name to AIM illuminates the fraught political legacy of the liberal media reform efforts that Ernst had helped spearhead with his 1946 book *The First Freedom*, efforts that, as we saw in chapter 2, unwittingly set the discursive and regulatory conditions that allowed Accuracy in Media to thrive.

Interestingly, it was Ernst who took the initiative in seeking out AIM, writing in a cold letter addressed to the organization in early June 1971, "Would you kindly send me your literature."[41] Kalish replied with extreme informality, which provoked a second letter of interest from Ernst in which he requested more organizational details and reiterated, "I am very much interested in what I imagine to be your effort."[42] As though first realizing the stature of his correspondent, Kalish's second response began, "I am indeed pleased that Morris Ernst is very much interested in our efforts." Detailing AIM's organizational structure and recent incorporation, Kalish added, "We have no connection with any branch of government or any special interest. On that basis we welcome support from all who realize the vital role played by the mass communications media in the democratic process." Kalish also extended an invitation for Ernst to join Durbrow, Acheson, and journalist Edgar Ansel Mowrer on the group's nascent advisory board.[43]

Despite describing himself as "not much of a committee person," Ernst agreed to join after Kalish assured him the obligations would be minimal and flexible.[44] "We should like to have you give us any ideas or suggestions. When we start our Bulletin you might want to contribute thereto. We would also want to be able to call on you for specialized advice," Kalish wrote of Ernst's anticipated responsibilities, after noting that the board would not hold regular meetings.[45] Ernst would go on to become one of AIM's most publicly cherished advisers—the first to be profiled in the pages of *AIM Report*, a newsletter the group launched in August 1972 that would also routinely reprint Ernst's column "I Have A Concern," which he contributed to the Greenwich Village weekly neighborhood newspaper *The Villager*.[46]

The brief 1973 profile of Ernst in *AIM Report* quoted him directly from the forward of *The First Freedom*: "Having spent much of my life fighting for freedom of thought—freedom from government control—I have concluded that we have done a magnificent job in removing government from its historic role of nursemaid to the mind of man. However, I have recently concluded that far more is kept from our minds by lack of diversity of ownership of the means of communication than by government interference."[47] When Ernst initially wrote those words in the mid-1940s, the common sense among postwar media reformers was that concentration of media ownership would disproportionately stifle *liberal* voices—effectively extending a long-standing conservative monopoly on the printed press to the new broadcast medium. But by the early 1970s, when Ernst agreed to join the AIM board, Agnew had popularized the exact opposite—the news media now was increasingly considered to be controlled by a cabal of liberals, stifling conservative news and commentary from their East Coast ivory towers. The concepts of "fairness" and "balance," once used as a safeguard to ensure that liberal voices were included in a presumably conservative public sphere, were now being leveraged to advocate for the inclusion of conservative perspectives into a presumably liberal one.

For instance, in the fall of 1972 AIM issued a series of reports documenting what it deemed to be favoritism on the part of CBS News toward Democratic presidential candidate George McGovern, to the detriment of incumbent Republican Richard Nixon. AIM noted it was not the first to allege partisan bias in CBS coverage, citing Edith Efron's 1971 book *The News Twisters*, which argued the network had been biased against Nixon in its coverage of his 1968 presidential campaign. A libertarian inspired by Ayn Rand's objectivist philosophy, Efron covered the broadcast industry as a journalist for *TV Guide* magazine. In 1968 she received a grant from the Historical Research Foundation, an outfit funded by *Plain Talk* financier and influential right-anticommunist Alfred Kohlberg, to develop "an analytical method for testing bias in news coverage and for the purpose of evaluating the tri-network coverage of the then upcoming 1968 presidential campaign." The book received wide praise from conservatives, especially AIM, and even some liberals but was aggressively opposed by executives at CBS, among others. Efron leveraged the many criticisms of her book by broadcast executives, the Democratic Party, and liberals to reinforce her claims of a left–liberal conspiracy within broadcasting designed to stifle Republican politicians and conservative viewpoints.[48]

After conducting a two-week content analysis of CBS, NBC, and ABC, AIM corroborated Efron's findings: "While all networks devoted more time to stories favorable to McGovern and unfavorable to President Nixon and the Administration, ABC and NBC were relatively well balanced. But CBS showed an imbalance of roughly three to one."[49] Unsatisfied with CBS News President Richard Salant's dismissive response to its study, the next month AIM extended its analysis (and critique) to the network's radio news operations: "Mr. Salant has responded to our letters, but the favoritism that seems too evident to us in the content and tone of the broadcasts is not apparent to Mr. Salant even when he has been provided with the detailed evidence summarized in this report." AIM implored its supporters to write letters to Salant's boss, CBS President Arthur Taylor, and to "urge that CBS News be required to strive for balance and fairness in its reporting of the campaign."[50]

True to form, Ernst promoted the AIM studies in his *Villager* column by pointing out the dire implications of unchecked broadcast network bias on freedom of thought. "In our non-singleton newspaper town there is some value in the *News* being avowedly for one candidate and the *Times* for another," Ernst allowed, referring to the local media environment in New York City. But if bias might be acceptable under the proper competitive conditions, Ernst interpreted unwillingness on the part of CBS News's broadcast competitors to amplify AIM's criticisms as a sign of subtle collusion. "Freedom of thought no longer exists in our city as it did with ease when we had a dozen dailies and when the television licensees were not so sweetly protective of each other," Ernst wrote.[51] Not only did he agree with AIM's assessment of CBS News's liberal bias, he also understood the watchdog to be "injecting competition into the marketplace of thought," implicitly concurring with AIM as to that marketplace's overall leftward tilt.[52]

Ernst saw AIM within a long tradition of liberal media criticism, dating back at least to the media reform movement of the 1940s, and he promoted it as such—spreading the belief that *all* news consumers, not merely conservatives, were harmed by the absence of national outlets relying on conservative news judgment. He did so by regularly advising executive secretary Abraham Kalish to frame AIM's work within the context of media monopoly and to "keep in mind that our ideas of a free press are based on the matching of wits in the marketplace of thought."[53] He also sent solicitations containing AIM materials to no fewer than six dozen personal acquaintances, among them Murray J. Rossant of the Twentieth

Century Fund (financier of the National News Council) and Vice President Spiro Agnew.[54]

In his letter to Agnew, Ernst introduced AIM as a solution to the vice president's own concerns regarding press bias, which he again attributed to media consolidation.[55] To drive home this connection, he enclosed a revised edition of *The First Freedom*, which journalism professor Bryce W. Rucker had updated in 1968 with Ernst's blessing to reflect shifts in the political economy of news media that had occurred by the late 1960s—most notably, the increasing predominance of television. While the updated book reiterated and extended Ernst's initial concern that increasingly monopolistic media ownership trends were damaging the viability of the "marketplace of ideas," it remained vague as to what political ideology yielded the most benefit from such conditions.[56] Ernst's enthusiastic promotion of AIM, however, left little doubt as to where he personally stood on that question.

Ernst only appears to have wavered in his otherwise unadulterated support of AIM on two occasions, which bookended his four years of service on the group's National Advisory Board. The first occurred the same month AIM publicly announced the board's formation, August 1971. Ernst received a letter from Reuven Frank requesting his intercession in a dispute that the NBC News president was having with Abraham Kalish. In early August the Progressive Labor movement radical-turned right-anticommunist Phillip Abbott Luce had published an issue of his newsletter *The Pink Sheet on the Left* accusing an NBC News correspondent of ties to Black and Palestinian militant groups.[57] Kalish, on behalf of AIM, wrote a series of increasingly pushy letters to Frank and his boss demanding a public response to the allegations.[58] In a subsequent letter to Ernst, Frank complained that it seemed as though Kalish was more interested in claiming NBC's unwillingness to cooperate than in receiving the requested response. "May I presume to ask you to use your influence so that future inquiries from Accuracy in Media be more reasonably expressed?" Frank asked of Ernst, who readily obliged.[59] Writing to Kalish, Ernst expressed his "shock" in the tone of his correspondence with Frank and implored him to avoid "cynicism and despair" in favor of a more hopeful approach. "As you may know, I have been a critic of the networks but happily remain friendly with the officials against whom I have directed what I always thought to be *helpful* criticism," Ernst wrote.[60] Kalish did not reply to Ernst's initial plea and responded evasively to a follow-up letter a month later—apologizing for his delay but not his treatment of Frank.[61]

While Ernst considered Kalish's delayed reply "unwarranted," he declined to question the sincerity of the AIM executive secretary's intentions, writing in a final letter to Frank, "All too many well-intentioned good folk become nuisances in our lives."[62] Ernst's continued enthusiastic support of AIM, despite the group's aggressive behavior and indication that its efforts might be more interested in scoring political points than improving distorted reporting, indicates his concern with ends rather than means. As was clear in his earlier collaboration with the FBI, Ernst could stomach strong-arm tactics so long as they resulted in increased ideological competition within his liberal conception of a pluralist public sphere (which excluded all totalitarians, but particularly communists). AIM both promoted competition through airing conservative perspectives concerning the news of the day and policed the conceptual boundaries of Ernst's idealized marketplace of ideas—taking to task media outlets who employed journalists with left-radical beliefs or affiliations.

A PRESS OPEN TO CRITICISM

AIM's thin veneer of impartiality—achieved in part through the group's affiliation with Morris Ernst—provided enough plausible deniability that some corners of the journalism profession felt compelled to take it seriously.[63] In August 1971 the journalism trade magazine *Editor & Publisher* ran a favorable profile of AIM that obscured the political stakes of its project and seems to have relied upon AIM executive secretary Abraham Kalish as its only source. "AIM is not interested in the ideology of any communication medium," *E&P* staff writer Luther Huston wrote. "All it wants is that the media report news that the public is entitled to know, and not suppress, ignore, or distort news because the newspaper or the network disagrees with the content or the angle of the story."[64] *Columbia Journalism Review* (*CJR*), on the other hand, lampooned AIM by quoting liberally from the group's promotional materials and immersing them in snark that hinted heavily at the group's right-wing bias.[65] Nevertheless, *CJR* saw fit to run a lengthy response by Kalish, who took the trade journal to task for damaging AIM's reputation among newspaper editors by suggesting that the group "is really a political organization that only pretends to be interested in accuracy in news reporting."[66]

If AIM's tone, tactics, and emphases consistently undermined its claims to impartiality, the group's success in popularizing the notion of liberal media bias benefited from a broader trend toward introspection among professional journalists. This favorable foundation was laid, in part, by Vice President Agnew, whose vociferous critiques of the news media in the fall of 1969 drew explicitly on rhetoric associated with the progressive media reform tradition that still carried considerable weight among journalists.[67] Speaking in Montgomery, one week after his initial attack on the networks in Des Moines, Agnew riffed on Ernst in citing consolidation as a key factor in declining competition within the newspaper industry. "Many, many strong, independent voices have been stilled in this country in recent years," Agnew told the Alabama Chamber of Commerce. "And lacking the vigor of competition, some of those who have survived have—let's face it—grown fat and irresponsible." Agnew also accused the Washington Post Company of establishing a monopoly—a key concern of progressive media reformers—through its cross-ownership of newspaper, radio, and television properties in the nation's capital. "The American people should be made aware of the trend toward the monopolization of the great public information vehicles and the concentration of more and more power in fewer and fewer hands," Agnew said.[68]

Perhaps unsurprisingly, journalism professional organizations bristled at such remarks when uttered by a sitting vice president. Norman Isaacs, then president of the American Society of Newspaper Editors, called Agnew's Iowa speech "a drive for a real one-party press—not through free expression but through open intimidation by the top officials of our government."[69] Sigma Delta Chi, a fraternity for journalists, passed a resolution denouncing Agnew's Iowa address for having, "gone far beyond anything that might be considered constructive and, in fact, can be construed as a threat to American freedom to collect and comment on the news."[70] But *Editor & Publisher* took a more conciliatory stance. The trade journal drew parallels between Agnew's complaints and those of the Roosevelt and Truman administrations, both of which had accused the newspaper industry of conservative bias against their liberal policies. "The theme is the same," the editors wrote. "The only thing that has changed is the medium."[71] They also hinted at the potential trust-busting implications of Agnew's speech: "Since the Vice President made so much of diversity of voices in news commentary, was it merely coincidental that he chose to speak out in two cities—Des Moines and Montgomery—where there is a high degree of concentration of the news media?"[72]

Columbia Journalism Review similarly teased constructive criticisms out of Agnew's attacks. In its winter 1969–1970 issue, the trade journal published a series of commentaries assessing Agnew's speech and the state of journalism more broadly. *CJR* editor Alfred Balk acknowledged a "germ of truth" in Agnew's critiques and devoted his essay to "the sorting out of truth from partisan polemics." Balk conceded that network television reporting often elevated "bad news" over "good news," that it prioritized profit over public enlightenment, and that trends toward media consolidation and monopolistic conditions had reduced the number of perspectives available to American news consumers. "But is it true, as Spiro Agnew seemed to be saying, that American news media have been politicized—that they have fallen under the effective control of liberal zealots, to the detriment of fair reporting and analysis of other than liberal viewpoints?" Balk asked. After consulting studies of presidential newspaper endorsements and public opinion polling, he concluded that the press maintained a conservative bias, while broadcast news tended to reflect the consensus of two-thirds of Americans, who identified as liberal "with respect to the operational level of Government programs." Balk ultimately suggested that claims of "liberal bias" were more a reflection of political frustration from the margins, although he acknowledged that the rising volume of criticism was harming press credibility more broadly.[73]

While Balk ultimately rejected the premise of liberal media bias, that he deigned it worthy of consideration illustrates the subtle yet impactful work of Agnew's speech. Journalists did not accept his critique wholesale, of course—but they began to validate key components of the "liberal media," reframing a "fringe" claim as a topic of legitimate debate within and beyond professional journalism. For instance, in the same *CJR* issue, Theodore White affirmed Agnew's central premise that a gap had emerged between the New York and Washington, DC–based establishment media and the (latently conservative) rest of America. "I think what we're going through in this country is not only a political crisis but a cultural crisis of enormous dimensions," White wrote, presciently. "It's a difference in cultures that divides the country and it will probably take fifty years before we can look back and see what's happening."[74]

Edwin Diamond, a former senior editor of *Newsweek*, conceded that although "ham-handed," Agnew had a point in calling for media diversity. He situated Agnew's critiques within the context of a proliferation of alternative press outlets, particularly on the New Left, as well as increasing efforts at producing Spanish-language and Black-owned broadcast media—implying that conservative consumers were similarly underserved by the mainstream media. Diamond concluded with five suggestions for increasing diversity in news coverage, most of which foregrounded increasing opportunities for dialogue between media and their audiences. These included calling for more "mutual criticism and self-examination" among journalism professionals, as well as "civilian review of the media."[75] While not entirely embracing Agnew's claims of liberal media bias, Diamond nevertheless proposed solutions to mitigating the growing credibility gap between conservatives and the mainstream press they derided.

AIM AND THE NATIONAL NEWS COUNCIL

Diamond wasn't the only voice advocating for a civilian media review board in the wake of Agnew's speech. In early 1970 a handful of journalists began conversations with the Twentieth Century Fund—a foundation established by liberal businessman Edward Filene and directed by former journalist Murray J. Rossant—to build an American equivalent of the British Press Council, an ombudsperson for disputes between the media and their audiences.[76] By 1971 Rossant established a task force to explore the feasibility of the idea, with *CJR* editor Alfred Balk serving as rapporteur. It unanimously recommended the establishment of an independent press council to "receive, to examine, and to report on complaints concerning the accuracy and fairness of news coverage in the United States as well as to study and to report on issues involving freedom of the press."[77]

The formation of the National News Council (NNC) was announced in late November 1972. Days later AIM executive secretary Abraham

Kalish wrote a letter ensuring that his group was on the organization's radar. "I know that several members of your proposed task force . . . are well acquainted with AIM," Kalish wrote, listing the names of prominent media figures affiliated with the council. "They have all been on the receiving end of complaints that we have filed about inaccuracies or lack of balance." Kalish noted the conspicuous absence of "anyone representing the public who has been active in the field of press criticism" and offered that AIM would "be happy to nominate a representative to serve on your committee, a person who can give you the benefit of our rich experience as a press ombudsman."[78] Despite his dismissive and competitive tone, AIM would initially attempt to leverage the council to further bolster the impartiality of its complaints of liberal media bias.

Indeed, as the NNC was still in the process of forming in late 1972 and 1973, AIM forwarded a flurry of complaints to the council alleging biased or inaccurate reporting by *The New York Times*, *Washington Post*, and CBS News.[79] Kalish even filed a complaint against the Twentieth Century Fund itself for failing to mention AIM in the task force report inaugurating the council. That report was written by Alfred Balk, the *Columbia Journalism Review* editor who had published the withering denunciation of AIM a year prior. "It is astonishing that Mr. Balk should not mention AIM in his summary of organizations that have been active in the field of press criticism," Kalish complained to Rossant.[80] While Rossant apologized and promised to include mention of AIM in future editions of the task force report, Kalish's aggressive early engagement caused the council to proceed with caution.

In an internal memo sent in August 1973, the same month the council began formally receiving public complaints, executive director Bill Arthur warned his staff, "In general, we are going to have to reject AIM's complaints since they will be on a well-orchestrated schedule to harass the liberal press in the country." But, he continued, "because of their querulous nature, and so that they do not read any dark plots into our motives, however, we shall have to give good and sufficient reason in each case."[81] In part to avoid allegations of liberal bias itself, the NNC would spend its first two years lending its nonpartisan reputation to AIM for its clearly partisan purposes.

AIM became a regular topic of discussion among the council's board of directors, not to mention the grievance committee that adjudicated the complaints the council saw fit for formal evaluation. In early November 1973, without consulting the grievance committee, council staff pointedly declined to investigate an AIM complaint against CBS News commentator Eric Sevareid, who months earlier had rebuffed Soviet dissident Alexander Solzhenitsyn's claim that US news media had neglected to report on a massacre in Huế perpetrated by the Viet Cong. Committed to the belief that the press was biased against US military involvement in Vietnam, AIM considered the putative dearth of reporting about communist atrocities in Huế to be a "serious blot on American journalism." Kalish wrote in his complaint, "Mr. Sevareid attacked the credibility of Solzhenitsyn without justification or factual basis. He has a moral obligation to set the record straight."[82] In declining to weigh in as to whether US press coverage of Huế was sufficient, council staff also questioned "how AIM can set itself up as judge and jury of what is heavy coverage and what is not," which prompted a lengthy and histrionic reply by Kalish.[83]

During a debrief of the episode at the council's November board meeting, *National Review* publisher William Rusher, the group's token conservative member, noted that if the grievance committee had been consulted, "the answer might have been worded differently." Board chair Roger Traynor agreed. A retired chief justice of California and respected liberal jurist, Traynor nevertheless vouched for AIM as "a formidable group composed of able, articulate people" whose "major grievance concerns inadequate coverage given by the media to the conservative point of view." Traynor advised, and the board agreed, to handle AIM with "great care" going forward, including directing all correspondence from the group to the grievance committee for evaluation prior to any council reply.[84] Such white glove treatment was no doubt rooted in concerns that AIM would undermine the credibility of the fledgling council much in the same way the group was raising suspicions of liberal bias in mainstream news—placing regular letters to editors in major publications while purchasing ads denouncing those very same outlets. AIM's conflict-driven publicity strategy was designed to turn up the volume of "liberal media" claims within national political discourse at the precise moment when mainstream journalists and their advocates were increasingly attuned to criticism and seeking to rebuild their credibility with disaffected audiences.

Between December 1973 and June 1975 AIM filed six formal complaints with the NNC—against *Newsweek*, the New York Times News Service, syndicated columnist Jack Anderson, *Time* magazine, *The New York Times*, and CBS News. The council ruled in AIM's favor in the first three cases, lending the group's allegations of liberal media bias the imprimatur of an ombudsperson with closer ties to professional journalism than to the modern conservative movement.[85] The council declined to consider AIM's allegations against *Time* in October 1974 and ruled complaints against *The New York Times* and CBS to be "unwarranted" in 1975. While it is unclear why AIM stopped engaging with the NNC after 1975, an internal NNC memo suggested "they didn't like us getting all the press."[86] This seems unlikely. By filtering complaints through the NNC, AIM was able to amplify their allegations against major media outlets and legitimate the idea that liberal bias was not merely a conservative claim but a widely accepted and real phenomenon.

As we'll see in the next chapter, AIM's turn away from the NNC coincided with the emergence of the "New Right"—a tightly networked group of conservative activists responsible for building a second generation of movement infrastructure in the late 1970s that helped elect Ronald Reagan to the presidency in 1980. AIM's eventual public embrace of conservatism, while complicated, is indicative not only of the declining salience of the group's claims of impartiality but of a broader sense that impartiality itself was an untenable expectation. Five years of highly publicized agitation against the press, of holding mainstream outlets accountable to the Silent Majority of media consumers conjured by Nixon and Agnew, had shifted the broader political and journalistic discourse. The "liberal media" was no longer merely a right-wing complaint; it was ongoing topic of mainstream debate.

By 1975—the year that Morris Ernst excused himself from Accuracy in Media and that AIM stopped engaging with the NNC—the group's consistently right-wing attacks on various media figures and outlets had earned it a reputation not for advancing pluralism but for assigning public consequences for reporting and commentary that dared to challenge the Nixon and Ford administrations or the fraught anticommunist activities of US military and intelligence agencies. In a highly publicized example, in the fall of 1974 AIM launched a campaign against Pulitzer Prize–winning investigative journalist and syndicated columnist Jack Anderson, who had been a primary journalistic antagonist of the Nixon administration. In August 1974 Anderson wrote a column exposing the State Department–run International Police Academy for its role in training foreign police forces in the use of torture tactics.[87] In addition to responding with an anti-Anderson publicity campaign, AIM filed a formal complaint with the NNC, which by February 1975 had publicly issued a report concurring with AIM that Anderson had, "made biased and inaccurate use of quotations from source letters."[88] Retaliating against pressure from AIM, Anderson assigned his research staff to investigate the group, and Reed Irvine in particular. By early March 1975 Anderson reported his findings in his nationally syndicated column—accusing AIM of being a "front" for oil companies, and Irvine of violating federal law by leveraging his position with the Federal Reserve to facilitate and subsidize his attacks on the press.[89]

AIM's vocal hostility toward Anderson in late 1974 and early 1975 fueled ongoing speculation as to its right-wing intentions and benefactors—increasing Ernst's value as a surrogate. In early March 1975 Ernst represented the group at a luncheon of the International Committee of the Public Relations Society of America in New York. As one attendee wrote him after, "Your presence was particularly valuable in discounting the 'right-wing' label that seems to have attached itself to AIM in some minds."[90] Ernst replied cordially to the fan letter but noted his impending resignation from the AIM board in hopes he would be replaced by "some younger person."[91]

Ernst's decision to resign his affiliation with AIM came at an especially inopportune time, one week before Anderson would publish his exposé of the group. Irvine had been aware of an impending hit piece for months and had regularly engaged in heated correspondence with Anderson denying allegations of wrongdoing and accusing the columnist of harassment.[92] Tipped off that Anderson was preparing to publish the findings of his investigation of AIM, the group engaged in preemptive damage control—sending a letter containing a detailed refutation of Anderson's charges to all newspapers that carried his column. The letter urged editors to refrain from running Anderson's column, or at very least to "be fair and print this communication in the same edition, giving it equal prominence."[93] The next day, Irvine wrote a letter to Ernst alerting him to Anderson's imminent attack and imploring him to reconsider his resignation. "Please stick with us until this storm is over," Irvine wrote.[94]

Ernst did not reply until two days after the Anderson column ran and never responded directly (at least in writing) to Irvine's request that he reconsider his resignation. Although he would linger on AIM's National Advisory Board through May of 1975, he kept a notably lower profile and repeatedly refused to participate in AIM's public retribution against Anderson, despite concurring with Irvine that the columnist was a "disagreeable character." Ernst feared his participation in a campaign against Anderson would "prove embarrassing" due to Ernst's prior legal representation of journalists Drew Pearson and Bob Allen, two of Anderson's mentors who had pioneered the scandal-driven journalism for which he was known and had even founded the "Washington Merry-Go-Round" syndicated column that gave Anderson his national audience.[95] Whether out of fear of reprisal from Anderson or an unwillingness to associate with a watchdog whose reputation was growing more and more partisan, Ernst's resignation from AIM coincided with the group's increasing collaboration with the emergent New Right.

6

CONSERVATIVE PRESS CRITICISM AND THE NEW RIGHT

"The people are angry and they are catching on to the arrogance and leftism of the media elite."

Richard Viguerie devoted the October 1984 issue of his magazine *Conservative Digest* to interrogating the question "Were the TV Networks Objective?" in their coverage of that summer's presidential nominating conventions. The magazine, launched in 1975 to provide readers with a monthly sampling of content published across conservative movement and movement-friendly mainstream media, unsurprisingly found all three major networks to have slanted their reporting against incumbent Republican Ronald Reagan and in favor of Democrat Walter Mondale (deeming CBS worst and ABC best, albeit still biased).[1] Reagan would, we now know, defeat Mondale in an epic landslide reelection mere weeks later. While the 1980s saw conservatives wielding power at the federal level for the first time since the New Deal, they remained steadfast in their belief that the news media was a bulwark against their ultimate goal—making their worldview an uncontested reality. "Our Founding Fathers were eager to protect the freedom of the press because they did not want government to impose its views on the media, so that media could be a check on government excess," Viguerie wrote. "But a strange thing happened. Instead of a governmental elite imposing its opinions on the media, a media elite has worked to impose its views on the government and on society as a whole."[2]

Thirty years earlier, as we saw in chapter 4, Facts Forum asked a similar question—"How accurate is America's news?"—on its *Answers for Americans* television program—prompting William F. Buckley Jr., to declare the public too "apathetic, supine, bored" to pressure journalists into adopting a conservative news judgment. It took nearly three decades, but by the late 1970s, conservatives were enthusiastically rallying against the press and toward the Republican Party in significant numbers. While belief in liberal media bias did not *cause* the growing popularity of conservatism as a political identity—conservatism's mass salience is not reducible to any one cause, actually—that the two emerged together is significant.

As we have seen, from the movement's earliest formations in the late 1940s and early 1950s, being conservative in part meant adopting a critical disposition toward the mainstream press. This disposition was and remains a driving force behind conservative media activism. Belief in bias begat efforts to counteract it, ranging from discussion groups like Facts Forum and the John Birch Society to new publications and radio programs. As we saw last chapter, this proliferation of conservative movement media dovetailed with a growing self-consciousness among mainstream journalists that they were losing the trust of their audiences. Boosted by an especially media-hostile Nixon administration and the watchdog efforts of Accuracy in Media (AIM), conservative press criticism flourished in the 1970s.

This was the foundation upon which the conservative marketing expert Richard Viguerie would help build a "New Right." Born in 1933 near Houston, Texas, Viguerie felt drawn to politics from an early age. While his parents did not encourage political conversation, as a teenager Viguerie found inspiration in Christian libertarian Henry Grady Weaver's *The Mainstream of Human Progress*—a 1947 book his father brought home after his employer, a petrochemical refinery, distributed copies to all personnel. Viguerie began actively identifying as a conservative in the late 1940s, influenced by "the Rush Limbaugh of that time, Fulton Lewis, Jr.," as well as by broadcaster John T. Flynn and, later, Facts Forum's Dan Smoot. As a college student in the early 1950s, Viguerie found few campus resources for an aspiring conservative activist, so he joined the Young Republican Club of Houston in search of political like-minds. A Taft Republican in Texas, Viguerie became a conservative when doing so meant joining an ill-fated sect within a woefully unpopular minority party.[3] But by the late 1950s the beginnings of a reputable conservative movement infrastructure were emerging out of the social connections of Taft Republicans and conservative Democrats scattered across the country, increasingly networked by William F. Buckley Jr. and the expanding orbit of his *National Review* magazine.[4]

In September 1960 Buckley convened ninety young conservatives at his family estate in Sharon, Connecticut, to launch Young Americans for Freedom, an organization widely credited with helping conservatism spread on college campuses throughout the United States in the 1960s and 1970s. Among those signing on to the group's foundational "Sharon Statement" (drafted by journalist M. Stanton Evans, son of *Facts Forum News* editor Medford Evans) was the young conservative journalist David Franke.[5] Viguerie, "desperate to get out of Houston and get involved in politics," had met Franke at a Republican conference in Washington, DC, in 1959 and the two stayed in touch. In early 1961, working as an editorial assistant for *National Review*, Franke visited Viguerie in Houston as part of a reporting trip covering conservative John Tower's election as the first Republican US senator from Texas since Reconstruction.

While reading Franke's article in *National Review* that July, Viguerie saw a classified ad seeking a "young man ... interested in [a] career with Conservative organizations and movements—public relations, organizing and fund raising."[6] Viguerie called Franke, who helped him secure the job as executive secretary for Young Americans for Freedom. During a brief stint in New York, where he and Franke shared a Greenwich Village apartment, Viguerie relished his proximity to such "intellectual giants" as fusionist conservative philosopher Frank Meyer, and *National Review* founders William Rusher and Buckley. Resolute that the Right had the best analysis of politics and public life, Viguerie diagnosed conservatism's persistent unpopularity as resulting from a marketing problem. "We had *nobody* who could *market* the *National Review*, *Human Events*, the books, our organizations, our causes—promote our ideas," he told me during a 2014 interview. Sensing a niche, Viguerie began what would become a lifelong study of marketing, purchasing, among other things, a subscription to the trade magazine the *Reporter of Direct Mail Advertising*.[7]

Viguerie's innovations in direct mail marketing for conservative causes would galvanize the movement in the 1970s, helping to usher in the

Reagan Revolution in 1980. Reimagining conservatives as an underserved market segment, Viguerie introduced them to concerns they would not have seen covered by the professional press. That those conservatives would be critically disposed toward that mainstream media was, by then, a given. By 1975—the year Viguerie launched *Conservative Digest* and rebranded modern conservatism as the "New Right"—Accuracy in Media had leveraged the Nixon administration's contentious relationship with the mainstream media to the point that liberal media bias was less a claim than an object of study—a question to be researched and debated well beyond conservative movement media and grass roots.[8]

Accuracy in Media's collaboration with what would become the New Right predates its branding in the mid-1970s. Conservative journalist Lee Edwards, a Viguerie-collaborator, was among the fourteen individuals to whom Reed Irvine sent his initial proposal for AIM in 1969.[9] As founding editor of the Young Americans for Freedom magazine *The New Guard*, Edwards was no stranger to early conservative efforts to define and confront the "liberal media." In that magazine's first issue, published in 1961, he ran an article diagnosing the news media with liberal bias and urging young conservatives to pursue careers in journalism: "Thirty years ago student thinking was for the most part well to the left, and the student of 1931 has become the press, radio and TV pundit of 1961."[10] The implication: the young conservatives of 1961 could be sitting pretty as media hegemons by 1991. As it happens, the modern conservative movement *did* manage to fundamentally alter the news media environment in the United States by the 1990s, albeit not under conditions of its own choosing. This chapter and the next show how AIM and the New Right worked—not always together, but symbiotically—toward that end.

BUILDING A "NEW RIGHT" WITH DIRECT MAIL

As historian Lizabeth Cohen has shown, beginning in the late 1950s fears of declining consumer demand converged with advancing social scientific research into consumer behavior, the growing popularity of television, and innovations in small-batch production processes—leading the advertising industry to reorient around the principle of market segmentation. Rather than pitch products to a homogeneous mass market, the 1960s and 1970s saw the emergence of a new commercial culture that transformed social difference into a series of discrete markets defined by different tastes and needs, yielding new opportunities to profit through "reincorporating disaffected groups into the commercial marketplace."[11]

Direct marketing, which had long specialized in microtargeted advertising campaigns bulk mailed to individual households in particular zip codes, was well positioned to be at the cutting edge of the market segmentation trend. For example, a cover story in the February 1963 issue of the *Reporter of Direct Mail Advertising* titled "Twenty Million Negroes: A Neglected Market" urged its implicitly white readers to "investigate" the underserved demographic. Noting that, as "barriers of prejudice are lowered," the Black community represented a potential "sleeping giant of a market," the magazine's managing editor encouraged "field trips" to identify Black neighborhoods for the purpose of crafting mail campaigns designed to test inhabitants' response rates.[12] A regular reader, Viguerie would have been attuned to the potentials of direct marketing in locating untapped profitability in marginalized communities.

In March 1964 the *Reporter of Direct Mail Advertising* identified another "sleeping giant": politics. Noting that political direct mail had a reputation for being "unimaginative, amateurish, ineffectual," Milton Pierce, a Democrat, heralded Republican advertising executive Walter Weintz's belief that, "used properly, direct mail can be the most powerful way to promote a candidate—as well as the idea." While the article focused on the use of direct mail in election campaigns, offering advice for developing and tailoring mailings, it also noted the method's more subtle benefits. Pierce argued that direct mail can "gauge the pulse of the public" and "establish an almost personal relationship between the voter and the politicians."[13]

Among the successful direct mail campaigns Pierce explored was one conducted by the Goldwater for President Committee, launched in November 1963. "In its first week, the campaign reaped 30,000 supporters in 30 states—with contributions ranging from $2 to $100," Pierce reported. "At its inception, the Goldwater for President Committee was mailing at a rate of 3,000 letters a day—before Mr. Goldwater had even announced that he would run!"[14] Goldwater, of course, answered the call, which had been carefully orchestrated by a group of businessmen and activists to channel the newly vital energies of the conservative movement into what they hoped would be a winning electoral strategy.[15] While Goldwater's landslide loss to Lyndon Johnson in 1964 represented a setback for the movement, it provided Viguerie with an opportunity to apply direct mail methods in pursuit of what he saw as a developing and undertargeted conservative market segment.

The historiography of the modern conservative movement has long coalesced around a narrative that depicts the 1964 Goldwater campaign as a generative loss, one that heralded and helped set the stage for the ultimate conservative takeover of the Republican Party, epitomized by the election of Ronald Reagan in 1980.[16] For Viguerie, the Goldwater campaign generated one valuable and tangible asset—a mailing list.[17] In 1964 federal campaigns were required to report on a quarterly basis the names and addresses of all individuals making contributions of fifty dollars or more to a candidate. Donor information was kept on file with the clerk of the US House of Representatives, where it was accessible for public review. With the help of a half dozen paid assistants, in 1964 Viguerie collected a handwritten list of 12,500 early and enthusiastic Goldwater supporters. He had the data punched into a magnetic tape reel and, in January 1965, used it to launch the Viguerie Company, a political direct marketing firm he based in the Northern Virginia suburbs of Washington, DC. "I now was the sole possessor of the best list in the nation for raising money for conservative causes," Viguerie later reminisced. "I also knew what to *do* with that list."[18]

Unlike Hunt and the Birchers, whose reputations were tarnished by a hostile press, and unlike Buckley, who attempted to ingratiate himself and his movement to that press, Viguerie leveraged an inhospitable media environment to conservatism's advantage. The mid-1960s were a period of "high modernism" in American journalism, according to news media and political communication scholar Daniel C. Hallin. Bolstered by relative elite consensus concerning the New Deal and Cold War, successful journalists of the era subscribed to a positivist and technocratic professional ideology, one that equated objective reporting with responsibility to the interests of a generalized public.[19] As Hallin notes, "Journalism took on a role in this period that felt to most of those involved and appeared to most of the society to be genuinely 'above politics.'"[20] This ideology extended to the mediums of radio and television by way of the Federal

Communications Commission's Fairness Doctrine, which asserted a "public interest" in mandating ideologically balanced programming.

Conservative efforts to resist this professional hegemony were fledgling in the early 1960s. It took the *National Review* nearly five years to reach a paid circulation of thirty thousand, and despite its movement-building successes it struggled financially early on.[21] While right-wing broadcasters routinely flouted the Fairness Doctrine in the 1960s, doing so raised the risk of IRS investigation, FCC sanction, and political marginalization, as we saw in chapter 1.[22] More elite-oriented activists like Buckley depicted conservative ideas—long associated with emotional and prejudicial appeals aimed at benefiting *private* interests—as rational, serious, and scholarly, applying rhetorical and aesthetic strategies designed to enable liberals and those without ideological affiliation to recognize conservative ideas as representing a competing vision of the *public* interest.

While Buckley and his affiliates pressed on the tensile discursive boundaries of the liberal consensus to make modern conservative ideas more legible and respectable within elite media and policymaking circles, Viguerie took a more populist approach. Appealing to grassroots conservatives as an underserved market segment—one that, paradoxically, saw itself as both marginalized and capable of standing in for the public as a whole—Viguerie built the New Right with a direct marketer's eye toward growing and merging lists. As a friendly reporter described his approach in 1975, Viguerie saw himself as cobbling together a "'new majority' out of one-issue people. For example, if you could find the people opposed to busing and merge them with anti-gun control, anti-abortion, anti-Equal Rights Amendment, anti-obscenity groups, the hard hats and others, you would have a powerful base."[23]

Far from mere coalition building, Viguerie sought to solidify conservatism as a coherent marketable (and consumable) political identity. While Viguerie saw his work as merging discrete preexisting conservative interests into a unified base capable of confronting the Left, the New Right itself helped constitute the new conservative identity that it claimed to represent. There is nothing inherent, per se, about a political coalition between gun enthusiasts and opponents of abortion, for instance. That both constituencies felt underserved by "high modern" media coverage of their pet issues, however, provided fertile ground for Viguerie's direct mail campaigns, which were often framed as providing information and perspectives overlooked or omitted by mainstream news outlets.

AIM AND THE NEW RIGHT

By 1975, with its claims of impartiality losing salience, Accuracy in Media found itself among the single-issue groups Viguerie hoped to aggregate into a new conservative majority. While AIM declined to use Viguerie's firm for its direct mailings, "mainly because we want to control our costs and keep them low," the group nevertheless benefited from the rising tide of conservative media criticism.[24] It had already laid the groundwork for Viguerie's efforts by documenting and publicizing incidents of liberal media bias—the foil against which many New Right newsletters framed their single-issue appeals. Through a diversity of tactics ranging from publicity campaigns to FCC complaints, Reed Irvine led AIM in pressuring the three major broadcast outlets (CBS, NBC, ABC) and national newspapers of record (most notably *The Washington Post* and *New York Times*). These campaigns—which knowingly borrowed tactics from contemporaneous progressive consumer activism spearheaded by Ralph Nader—played a vital role in shaping modern conservatism not only as a consumer identity but one overlooked by the prevailing ideology of professional journalism.

A prime example of the consumer activist mentality AIM cultivated among its supporters can be seen in its various media shareholder campaigns, which ran from the 1970s through the 1990s. In July 1973 AIM announced it had purchased shares in the parent companies of *The New York Times*, *Washington Post*, and all three major television broadcasters.[25] AIM was by no means the first conservative group to turn to activist investing to disrupt putative liberal bias. In 1965 the Lubbock, Texas–based businessman David W. Dye founded Medias Unlimited Inc. with the express purpose of "influencing major media . . . to assume higher degrees of moral and responsible presentations and program content." Dye bought two hundred shares of CBS stock and sought one thousand conservatives to join him, with a preliminary goal of controlling 20 percent of the network.²⁶ While Dye's effort proved unsuccessful, it attracted the attention of the John Birch Society set, including syndicated columnist and broadcaster Paul Harvey, who framed the initiative as "Little David and the CBS Goliath."²⁷ Unlike Dye, AIM harbored no illusions that it might take over major media outlets outright. Instead, the watchdog used shareholder resolutions to resist liberal bias in major media outlets by demanding the enforcement of professional codes of conduct and a halt to "advocacy journalism."

As with its appeals to the National News Council, AIM's shareholder activism was couched in rhetoric designed to appeal to the prevailing journalistic professional ideology of the era. It framed its efforts as advocating not for conservatives but for news consumers more broadly. In the spring of 1974, for instance, AIM proposed resolutions to the shareholders controlling *The New York Times* and *Washington Post*, urging them to impose an AIM-drafted code of ethics on their news managers, editors and reporters. The codes called for "accurate, fair and balanced" presentations of the news and a commitment to viewpoint diversity, "including those with which the management disagrees." They also called for greater accountability to consumer complaints, requiring that criticism of news coverage to be "reported and heeded," with timely and public corrections of substantiated errors.²⁸ Early AIM shareholder resolutions targeting the Big Three broadcasters (CBS, NBC, and ABC) called for the establishment of ombudspersons and, in the case of CBS, the creation of a committee "on corporate responsibility" to investigate allegations that the network was biased in its coverage of national defense issues.²⁹

While AIM's resolutions did not pass and were met with resistance from management of the media conglomerates involved, the strategy was more oriented at shaping public perceptions of the broadcasters as being resistant to the needs and perspectives of their consumers. "In taking this action, we have tested the networks in two ways," AIM reported in its January 1975 issue of its newsletter. "First, we are requiring them to go on record on some fundamental issues involving ethics, the handling of complaints from the public, and the investigation of charges of bias against them," they continued. "Second, we are testing their willingness to observe democratic principles and permit their shareholders to cast an informed vote on the important resolutions we have proposed."[30]

That the networks generally contested or outright refused to include AIM resolutions in their shareholder proxy materials made them seem defensive and against the very journalistic principles they claimed to espouse. Although AIM's shareholder campaigns remained rooted in its claims to be a nonpartisan and neutral arbiter of media accuracy, as discussed in the preceding chapter, AIM's earliest associations and supporters undercut its claims to political impartiality from the start. From Irvine's inclusion of Lee Edwards among those who first received a proposal for AIM, to early favorable coverage by Viguerie's newsletter *The Right Report*, AIM recognized its undertaking as serving a conservative constituency, and conservative leaders saw AIM's work as attuned with their cause.

Indeed, the day after AIM publicly announced its bipartisan National Advisory Board in early August 1971, it issued a statement aligning itself with the well-known conservative movement organ *National Review* in a spat against *The Washington Post*. Upset that the *Post* had declined to cover AIM's press conference, "news that would be of interest to its readers," executive secretary Abraham Kalish accused *Post* national news editor Ben Bagdikian of letting personal animosity cloud the paper's judgment. Bagdikian had long been scorned by conservatives—not only had he raised Nixon's ire through his central role in the *Post*'s publication of the Pentagon Papers in 1971, he had also written the multipart exposé for *The Providence Journal* undermining Facts Forum's claims of impartiality in 1954. Kalish claimed that Bagdikian had spiked the AIM National Advisory Board story in retaliation for the group's criticisms of the *Post*'s refusal to cover an open letter circulated one week earlier by *National Review* founders Buckley and Rusher in which twelve "prominent conservatives" suspended their support of President Nixon. "Mr. Bagdikian indicated that the *Washington Post* would not carry stories that emanated from the *National Review* or persons connected with it," Kalish wrote.[31] AIM's connections to the modern conservative movement would grow markedly from the mid-1970s onward, not due to any shift in ideology on the part of AIM but due to the New Right infrastructure that grew up around it.

MEDIACRACY AND THE NEW REPUBLICAN MAJORITY

President Nixon's resignation in August 1974, which resulted in moderate Gerald Ford's ascendance to the presidency and an increase in liberal Democratic primacy in both houses of Congress, made 1975 a year of soul searching for the Republican Party and of unprecedented opportunity for the conservative movement.[32] With only 18 percent of the national electorate willing to identify as Republican, conservative activists quickly laid the conceptual and infrastructural groundwork that, by 1980, would enable their capture of the party.[33] Rather than focus explicitly on party capture, the unpopularity of the Republican brand caused these activists to center their analysis and activities on promoting not only conservative ideology but conservative political identity.

For example, in 1975 *National Review* publisher Bill Rusher released *The Making of the New Majority*, a book that advocated for a new political party based on a shared commitment to conservative ideological orthodoxy. To make his case, Rusher drew heavily on Kevin Phillips's 1969 book *The Emerging Republican Majority*, which projected an upward trend in likely conservative political identification—led by voters in Sunbelt states in the South and West. In a move reminiscent of H. L. Hunt's rationale for preferring the term *constructive* to *conservative* in 1950, Rusher noted that a May 1974 Gallup Poll had found that only 23 percent of respondents identified as Republican, while 38 percent identified as conservative (Rusher then added in a proportional number of undecided voters to predict 59 percent support for a conservative party). In a quarter century, the connotation of *conservative* had shifted from negative to positive—activists no longer saw promoting a conservative political identity as a problem but instead as a solution.[34] As strategists like Rusher and Pat Buchanan emphasized ideological affiliation in lieu of partisan loyalty following Nixon's resignation, conservatism was simultaneously being reimagined as an *insurgent* political identification, a populist antipode to a new "liberal elite" epitomized by the mainstream news media.[35]

This idea's primary theorist was none other than former Nixon electoral strategist and "Southern Strategy" innovator Kevin Phillips. In 1975 Phillips published a follow-up to *The Emerging Republican Majority* titled *Mediacracy*, which outlined a new post-partisan framework for understanding the US political system. In *Mediacracy*, Phillips conceded that the social conditions produced by an industrial economy had yielded a politics that pitted conservative elites against a mass population whose desire for more egalitarian conditions demanded social change. Phillips contended that this long-standing US political fault line had undergone a tectonic shift as a result of the emergence of a postindustrial economy—marked by a decline in dominance of the manufacturing industry and increasing investment in the information technology and communication sectors. "Change does not threaten the affluent intelligentsia of the Post-Industrial Society the way it threatened the landowners and industrialists of the New Deal," Phillips argued. "On the contrary, change is as essential to the knowledge sector as inventory turnover is to a merchant or a manufacturer."[36] Phillips depicted this knowledge elite as having both cultural and pecuniary interests in promoting liberal social policies that challenged the traditional racial and religious values of middle-class white Americans, especially those living in the Sunbelt or otherwise removed from the power centers of New York and Washington, DC.

Phillips's conception of mediacracy—rule by media—not only tapped into long-standing conservative fears of press and broadcast bias; it employed social scientific reasoning to contend that the primary political conflict of the era was evident in the competing worldviews of putatively liberal media producers and, presumably, conservative white middle-class media consumers. While mainstream journalists were unconvinced by Phillips's conclusions, his book was widely celebrated in conservative circles.[37] It was both previewed and reviewed favorably in the *National Review*—Dartmouth professor Jeffrey Hart lauded Phillips for identifying a "new elite" against which he called for a new conservative "countercoalition" to organize. Hart wrote, "What the moment requires, therefore, is a political leader who grasps the new situation, who is spoiling for a real fight, and who can fashion the rhetoric necessary to illuminate for the American people the identity of their new oppressors."[38] Phillips's ideas also found their way more subtly into the media criticism of the John Birch Society set, including that of former *Facts Forum News* editor Medford Evans.[39]

In May 1975, the same month that Phillips published *Mediacracy*, Richard Viguerie launched *Conservative Digest*, "a magazine for the new majority" expressly positioned against "the major influences on public opinion (the education establishment, big business, big labor and the media)," which Viguerie described as "increasingly under the influence of liberals and leftists." Published monthly and oriented toward a mass audience, *Conservative Digest* embraced the new post-partisan political paradigm described by Phillips while breaking with the traditional common sense of conservative movement organizers.⁴⁰ "The conservative movement, they said, is like a pie. And it's got these slices here," Viguerie recalled of a conversation he had with an "Old Right emissary" the year he founded the magazine. "And what you're doing here, Richard, is you're slicing it thinner." Viguerie continued, "I said to myself, and maybe him too, I said if there are only 125,000 people in America that will support the conservative cause, then the cause of liberty and freedom doesn't have much longer to last, and maybe I should be with my family or on the golf course."⁴¹

While *Conservative Digest* only briefly achieved the mass audience to which it aspired—it hit its peak average paid circulation of 109,749 in 1977 and steadily declined thereafter—the magazine played a vital role in cohering a majoritarian conservative identity out of a set of previously somewhat discrete policy preferences.⁴² As Viguerie wrote in the magazine's inaugural issue, "The public opinion polls show a remarkably large and growing majority of Americans consider themselves conservative. Spontaneous, independent conservative groups are springing up all across the country, concerned with everything from busing to school textbooks to taxes."⁴³ Far from spontaneous and independent, the proliferation of conservative groups in the mid-1970s was coordinated by a small group of organizers convened by Viguerie in the Northern Virginia suburbs of Washington, DC. Anticipating the economic policy they would help make famous, these New Right organizers employed a "supply side" approach to the so-called marketplace of ideas.⁴⁴

Conservative Digest quickly became a clearinghouse for reporting and commentary concerning a wide array of single-issue campaigns, from opposition to abortion rights, to support for maintaining US sovereignty over the Panama Canal, to opposition to liberal media bias. AIM and its collaborators were early and routine contributors. Abraham Kalish, who retired from AIM in May 1974 to devote more time to education advocacy, contributed an article on television's insidious influence on children to the magazine's second issue in June 1975.[45] Beginning that July *Conservative Digest* condensed articles from *AIM Report* irregularly but often, and by the late 1970s and early 1980s Reed Irvine's byline was commonplace in the magazine's pages.[46] The magazine even devoted its September 1977 issue to fighting "bias in the news." The issue featured a column by Irvine and brief tips for battling liberal media bias from California Senator S. I. Hayakawa, *TV Guide* reporter and *News Twisters* author Edith Efron, Nixon telecommunications policy staffer and future CSPAN-founder Brian Lamb, Nixon staffer and media critic Bruce Herschensohn, and Irvine.[47]

The special issue's cover story advised readers to "use the media to your advantage" by pitching press releases and creating media events to promote conservative causes locally. It encouraged readers to "police the media," offering AIM as an exemplar of "how to conduct a professional study of news bias."[48] The special issue also promoted "special projects" like urging newspapers to hire ombudspersons, calling for more business and financial reporting, demanding editorial codes, supporting "worthy" journalism students, contesting local FCC license renewals, and supporting cable television. "Probably the most realistic alternative to the power of TV network news is a national system of cable TV," it reasoned, presciently. "If America were 'wired' for cable TV (as we are now wired for telephone), we might see as many as 100 national cable TV stations. A few of these would offer political viewpoints different from ABC, CBS and NBC, just as magazines like *Conservative Digest* and *National Review* offer alternatives to *Time* and *Newsweek*."[49]

As was the case for the myriad other single-issue groups that together composed the New Right, *Conservative Digest* amplified AIM's media criticism among a self-consciously conservative readership, promoting suspicion of mainstream newspaper and television outlets as among the defining characteristics of conservative political identity. Indeed, liberal media bias became a core issue for the New Right—a problem that affected the salience of all other single-issue campaigns and for which *Conservative Digest* was itself conceived as a solution. As Irvine wrote in a blurb for the magazine in September 1988: "I read and sometimes write for *Conservative Digest* and I enthusiastically recommend it to others. Why? Because it provides concise, easy-to-read articles about important topics that are generally ignored or downplayed by our liberal-dominated media.

It's written and edited for busy people who want to keep abreast of current developments free from the censorship exercised by the liberal gatekeepers. I learn from it, and I think you will too."[50] Even when *Conservative Digest* wasn't drawing on AIM's expertise in informing its readers "how to fight bias in the news," its promotion of conservative movement pet issues itself served as a form of positive critique of a mainstream news media thought to insufficiently cover them.[51]

NEW RIGHT MEDIA ACTIVISM BEYOND AIM

The New Right focus on media bias was by no means confined to the watchdog efforts of AIM. Eagle Forum—a group founded in 1972 by Phyllis Schlafly to oppose the Equal Rights Amendment—engaged in considerable media activism, especially at the local level, and often highlighted print, radio, and television coverage it believed to be slanted.[52] By 1981 it had even published a how-to guide designed to help conservative activists seeking "access to the biased television and radio media." Based on the successful media strategies of the anti-ERA campaign and advertised in *Conservative Digest*, the primer offered a practical rundown of federal broadcast regulations and methods for developing and implementing a news strategy to effectively promote candidates and issues in local media.[53] Schlafly's concern with liberal media bias preceded the founding of both Eagle Forum and AIM and informed her launching of *The Phyllis Schlafly Report* in August 1967.[54] While not explicitly focused on media bias, Schlafly saw her newsletter as filling in gaps in the liberal media's coverage of issues that concerned her. By 1974 she was soliciting new conservative readers and Eagle Forum donors by promoting her newsletter's "enviable record of accuracy, reliability, news scoops, and patriotic awards." Among those scoops: her reporting on "the secret contracts made between women's libbers and television stations."[55]

In October 1973 *The Phyllis Schlafly Report* published an exposé of a then-increasingly prevalent community organizing tactic by which citizens groups would pressure radio and television stations into signing agreements designed to increase racial and gender diversity in local programming. These "citizen's agreements," a form of preemptive settlement between broadcasters and community groups, gained in popularity following two DC Circuit Court decisions in 1966 and 1969 that affirmed the role of "public intervenors" in the Federal Communications Commission's broadcast license renewal process. These agreements often included provisions whereby broadcasters agreed to hire both on-air talent and behind-the-scenes employees from underrepresented racial, ethnic, or gender backgrounds as well as to produce programming tailored toward the views and interests of locally underrepresented communities.[56]

In December 1975 the FCC issued a policy statement encouraging broadcast licensees to consider pursuing such agreements, and Schlafly issued a call to arms for her newsletter readers to begin organizing local conservative community pressure groups. "If non-lib groups do not immediately assert their rights under the new FCC policy, the women's lib special-interest groups will control the editorial programming and employment policies of all television and radio stations," she wrote.[57] When Schlafly again turned her readers' attention to the issue of citizens' agreements in 1982 in an effort to convince the new Reagan-appointed FCC chair Mark S. Fowler to ban them, Accuracy in Media was inundated with letters from supporters requesting more information.[58] "I have never received anything from Eagle Forum before, so I wanted to check with AIM to see what, if anything, you know of these contracts," an AIM supporter from Colorado Springs wrote to Reed Irvine in March 1983. In response to the influx of letters, Irvine affirmed that he considered citizens' agreements to be a "serious problem" and alerted supporters of ongoing efforts by the conservative American Legal Foundation to pressure the FCC into halting the practice.[59]

As the citizens' agreements issue illustrates, with the emergence of the New Right in the mid-1970s, AIM found itself entangled within a movement infrastructure that scaled up conservative media activism beyond any one group's control.[60] This growth of single-issue conservative groups—many of whom, like Eagle Forum and the American Legal Foundation, engaged in their own forms of media activism—greatly expanded AIM's own reach. Designed to function as a media watchdog, AIM launched national publicity campaigns, filed FCC complaints, and engaged in shareholder activism within national and international media corporations. None of these efforts required a strong membership base, let alone local chapters capable of systematically expanding AIM's influence over local and regional media outlets. Indeed, by 1977 the group's membership base was limited to the nine thousand subscribers to the *AIM Report*. AIM relied on the national media it antagonized, and on conservative movement publications like *Conservative Digest*, to amplify its media criticism and influence beyond its own subscriber base.[61] The constellation of organizations that composed the New Right, especially groups like Eagle Forum that organized local and regional chapters, were similarly vital in helping AIM achieve its mission of counteracting liberal media bias beyond New York and the Beltway.

COMBATING THE LIBERAL MEDIA IN THE REAGAN ERA

As a result of growing conservative infrastructure, by the early 1980s AIM was no longer able to set the media activism agenda for the movement. The New Right's media strategy was complicated by the election of conservative movement darling Ronald Reagan to the presidency in 1980. No longer able to depict themselves as simply marginalized by the mainstream media, proximity to power required conservatives to perform a delicate two-step: counteract mainstream media criticism of Reagan while leveraging the same media to hold his administration accountable to the ideological orthodoxies of movement conservatism. This dilemma is evidenced in much of *Conservative Digest*'s coverage of the Reagan transition team and early appointments in late 1980 and early 1981. Indeed, writing after Reagan's victory in December 1980, Viguerie warned conservatives not to let victory lull them into complacency. "Many of the key people in the Reagan administration are strongly opposed to the conservative movement," he wrote. "The liberals own and control most of the country's influential newspapers, TV and radio networks and magazines.... My point here is that liberals will not roll over and play dead."[62]

While generally supportive of the Reagan administration, AIM remained more focused on issues of national security and foreign policy—especially defending the CIA from critical media coverage of its many dubious forays into Latin America—than on mounting a wholesale defense of the president in light of press criticisms of his conservative domestic agenda. In 1981, Reagan's first year in office, AIM was more concerned with defending the CIA from critical media coverage of its activities in El Salvador and Nicaragua than in defending the president. While AIM did occasionally address the press's critical treatment of Reagan, it was mostly noted in passing.[63] Effectively counteracting liberal media bias in the Reagan era required a broader range of focus and diversity of tactics, beyond AIM's financial and organizational capacities, not to mention Irvine's right-anticommunist proclivities.[64]

As such, in April 1983 National Conservative Foundation chair Terry Dolan—a close collaborator of Viguerie in organizing the New Right—proposed a "Strategy to Combat the Liberal Media."[65] Citing a newly released and influential study by S. Robert Lichter and Stanley Rothman that surveyed professional journalists and found them to overwhelmingly possess cosmopolitan cultural tastes and liberal political beliefs, Dolan came to a conclusion that Irvine and AIM had reached fifteen years earlier—"It's time to make the press accountable for the inaccuracies, innuendos and slander regularly passed along to the helpless public as NEWS."[66] Dolan proposed a $2.5 million per year "counter-offensive against the liberal media" that called for funding a research operation devoted to documenting liberal media bias; producing films, television series, and newsletters to counteract that bias; and funding student publications to promote conservative journalism on college campuses. "Conservatives today are at the mercy of the media. We know the power of the media to shape the views of millions. We can see the damage the media has done to President Reagan and the conservative movement. But, so far nothing has been done," Dolan wrote, ignoring decades of prior conservative movement efforts to counteract liberal media bias.[67]

While Dolan's full vision was not implemented in the concerted manner he proposed, several conservative groups, including AIM, combined to fulfill many of the needs he identified. Even as Dolan was writing, in the early 1980s AIM was already leveraging an influx of donations from the conservative philanthropists Harold W. Siebens and Richard Mellon Scaife to bolster its research documenting biases in television news, especially CBS.[68] AIM was also actively investing in successful counterprograming. By 1985 it had produced, and convinced PBS to air, *Television's Vietnam*—a documentary narrated by Charlton Heston and designed as a counterpoint to the critically acclaimed thirteen-part PBS documentary *Vietnam: A Television History*.[69] Similarly, the Institute for Educational Affairs had been funneling money to conservative and libertarian college student newspapers since 1980, building what it called the Collegiate Network of right-wing student publications to thirty-three by 1983. By 1986 the organization had expanded its programming to offer a toll-free hotline for conservative student journalists facing challenges as well as an annual conference to foster national networking.[70] In 1987 L. Brent Bozell III founded the Media Research Center, growing the conservative movement's capacity for documenting instances of liberal media bias.[71] Indeed, as Reagan passed the baton to George H. W. Bush in 1988—the same year conservative talk radio host Rush Limbaugh entered national syndication—AIM was one among many media press watchdogs in movement conservatism, including the Media Research Center and Joseph Farah's Western Journalism Center.[72]

While the rise of the New Right greatly expanded the scale and scope of conservative media activism, it often did so in ways that did not serve AIM's organizational interests. This seems to have resulted in part from Irvine's ambivalence about fully and publicly committing AIM to the conservative cause, despite his clear personal support. In private correspondence, Irvine was wont to sing the praises of various conservative movement organizations, especially Eagle Forum and the Heritage Foundation.[73] Irvine was also an inaugural member of the Council for National Policy, a secretive group founded by Christian evangelical leader Tim LaHaye (of *Left Behind* book series fame) to enable conservative movement leaders to network and coordinate on strategy. Beginning in 1981 the council hosted regular retreats, at which conservative leaders like Irvine, Viguerie, Dolan, Howard Phillips, Paul Weyrich, and others rubbed elbows with major donors like Nelson Bunker Hunt (son of H. L.), Cullen Davis, Joseph Coors, and Bob Perry, to name a few.[74]

Irvine resigned from the Council for National Policy in 1983, citing the time and expense of participation.[75] "I don't feel justified using the funds we get from our contributors to take expensive trips that don't directly advance our progress toward our objectives in some way," Irvine wrote in a letter detailing his many criticisms of the council. He found the group both insufficiently "action-oriented" and overly partisan. "Since I am not engaged in partisan political activity, much of the discussion was not relevant to my work, even though it was interesting," Irvine wrote. He also bristled at the council's strict confidentiality rules: "This speaks to the question of whether the organization is action-oriented or not," Irvine wrote. "Disseminating important information is action. Bottling it up simply means that the meetings are more for the entertainment of those present, rather than for trying to get things done."[76] Irvine's appeal for action, despite his putative disinterest in the partisan politics such action would advance, illustrates the tension at the heart of his media activism. As he wrote in a response to a critic in 1986, Irvine saw AIM as primarily concerned with "facts" and bristled at being identified with "New Right radicals"—even as AIM relied upon and actively collaborated with New Right publications, leaders, donors, and groups to advance the unacknowledged conservative conception of reality upon which its advocacy for media accuracy was based.[77]

Irvine's discomfort with explicit partisan political activity seems to have lessened by the late 1980s. As early as 1985 Irvine was fishing for a speaking invitation to the Conservative Political Action Conference, whose American Conservative Union organizers, he lamented, seemed "allergic to me."[78] By 1989 Irvine was again working alongside New Right leaders Morton Blackwell and Paul Weyrich, co-organizing the annual Conservative Leadership Conference.[79] If Irvine finally learned to stop worrying and love the conservative movement by the late 1980s, his longstanding ambivalence impeded AIM's capacity for steering broader conservative media activist efforts against the "liberal media." Perhaps nowhere is this weakness clearer than in Irvine's unsuccessful campaign to convince the Reagan administration to keep the Fairness Doctrine, to which we now turn.

7

THE END OF FAIRNESS

"There is a major difference between me and the dominant media culture. I freely, openly, and proudly admit my bias, my conservative predisposition. All of my listeners know that I editorialize and analyze from a decidedly conservative worldview. But the major media—at least the overwhelming majority of them—will not admit their bias. They simply cannot bring themselves to confess their liberalism."

Rush Limbaugh was somewhere around the peak of his influence in 1993, when he published his second book *See, I Told You So*.[1] Democrat Bill Clinton had recently defeated Republican George H. W. Bush in the 1992 US presidential election. During his one-term presidency, Bush had managed the decline of the Reagan era but had failed to fill the Great Communicator's shoes as beloved figurehead of the modern conservative movement. After twelve years in proximity to power, that movement was adrift.

Limbaugh, meanwhile, had spent the Bush years building a conservative talk radio juggernaut. After a middling early career as an oft-fired disc jockey and a brief stint working in sales for the Kansas City Royals baseball team, Limbaugh first found success in 1984. That year the foul-mouthed shock jock Morton Downey Jr. was fired from KFBK radio in Sacramento, California, after using an anti-Asian racial slur in an off-color joke and refusing to apologize.[2] Limbaugh was hired to replace him. By 1988—when Limbaugh was given the nationally syndicated early afternoon slot at ABC Radio Network and moved to WABC-AM in New York City—he had developed a new format, fusing right-wing ideology with irreverent humor, punditry with active audience participation. By 1993 the *Rush Limbaugh Show* boasted seventeen million listeners per week.[3] That September the *National Review* declared Limbaugh "leader of the opposition" in a cover story that included a note from an especially prominent fan. "Now that I've retired from active politics," former present Ronald Reagan wrote to Limbaugh, "I don't mind that you have become the Number One voice for conservatism in our Country."[4]

In *See, I Told You So*, Limbaugh devoted an entire chapter to a federal regulatory shift that had in part enabled his rapid rise to prominence: the Fairness Doctrine. "When the FCC concocted the Fairness Doctrine in 1949, it believed that radio stations did too much 'entertainment'—music—and not enough 'informational programming,'" Limbaugh wrote. "And then, ladies and gentlemen, I arrived. My show—three hours a day of event-driven discussion, covering every front-burner political, social, and cultural issue imaginable, with callers of all ideological persuasions phoning in to agree or disagree—is precisely what the regulators *said* they were trying to promote."[5] As we saw in this book's first chapter, Limbaugh was definitively *not* the paragon of broadcasting envisioned by the Fairness Doctrine and its proponents. The regulation, which mandated balanced treatment of matters of public controversy over the airwaves, was a bureaucratic compromise. The FCC acceded to demands from the broadcasting industry that they be allowed to editorialize over the air while also addressing the concerns of progressive media reformers who worried that allowing broadcasters to promote political causes would necessarily skew the airwaves rightward. Limbaugh's meteoric rise starting in 1988, one year after the Fairness Doctrine was abandoned, has long been interpreted by progressives as a vindication of the policy's efficacy.[6]

Indeed, as Limbaugh was writing his book in 1993, there was a brief and unsuccessful push to reinstate the Fairness Doctrine. Democrats in the House and Senate had introduced "Fairness in Broadcasting" bills that year, and pro-fairness language had been added as a rider to a campaign finance reform bill that passed the Senate that summer. Limbaugh framed this legislation as targeting him personally. "Every member of Congress will deny that the desire to re-impose the Fairness Doctrine has anything whatsoever to do with my show, or with the rise of conservative talk radio,"

Limbaugh wrote. "But don't be fooled."[7] In fact, members of Congress from both parties had been trying unsuccessfully to codify the doctrine since Reagan vetoed the "Fairness in Broadcasting Act of 1987," including another failed bipartisan effort in 1989. Limbaugh's focus on the doctrine as a looming threat to conservatism built on anxieties that the FCC might be used to silence right-wing broadcasters like him. As we saw in this book's first chapter, revelations of a Kennedy-era "Reuther Memo" conspiring against right anticommunists, followed by the Johnson-era targeting of right-wing radio commentators like Carl McIntire, stirred conservative opposition to the Fairness Doctrine in the 1960s. Limbaugh sought to channel these long-standing concerns in a self-serving effort to thwart legislation that would have undermined his still-newfound fame and fortune.

Limbaugh's egocentric treatment of the Fairness Doctrine was correct in one important regard—the emergence of conservative talk radio in the late 1980s and early 1990s *did* foundationally alter US political and media culture. As he noted, news/talk and public affairs radio programming had increased dramatically during the Reagan and Bush years. In 1980 some 355 radio stations reported offering news or talk formats. By 1993 that number had increased to 1,699 stations. By 1996, the year Fox News launched, that number had reached 2,334 stations.[8] The astronomical growth of talk radio enabled conservative news and commentary at a truly national scale, dwarfing the combined media activist initiatives of conservative movement figures like William F. Buckley or Richard Viguerie.

Limbaugh was keenly aware that he was building something capable of transcending movement infrastructure, of making an impact beyond merely contesting elections. In *See, I Told You So*, Limbaugh introduced his readers to the political theorist Antonio Gramsci, noting that the Italian Marxist had "succeeded in defining a strategy for waging cultural warfare." Limbaugh continued, "What we need to do is fight to reclaim and redeem our cultural institutions with all the intensity and enthusiasm that we use to fight to redeem our political institutions."[9] While conservatives had long lamented the mainstream "liberal media," Limbaugh was the first to credibly suggest it could be reclaimed by the Right.

Not all conservatives shared Limbaugh's vision. With the notable exception of New Right leader Paul Weyrich, many conservative movement figures opposed rescinding the Fairness Doctrine—afraid of losing the one regulatory mechanism that could force the Big Three US television networks to "balance" their programming with right-wing commentary. While hindsight makes Reagan's repeal of the doctrine seem like a no-brainer, his administration faced concerted opposition from conservative groups like Accuracy in Media and Eagle Forum, which complicated the political calculus at the time. In short, the rise of a distinct and commercially viable right-wing media sector in the United States—documented in this book's conclusion—was by no means an inevitable result of either the conservative critical disposition toward the press or the end of the Fairness Doctrine. While ultimately successful at reconfiguring US political culture to their benefit, right-wing media outlets like Limbaugh were not necessarily good for the modern conservative movement itself. When that movement's leaders failed to convince Reagan to uphold the Fairness Doctrine, they were soon forced by circumstances to relinquish control over conservatism's messaging and constituents.

CODIFYING FAIRNESS AT THE EXPENSE OF THE RIGHT

As we saw in the case of Carl McIntire in this book's first chapter, the 1960s were a period of intense conflict between right-wing radio broadcasters and the Kennedy and Johnson administrations.[10] Concerned with the growing organizational capacities of the modern conservative movement, which would succeed in placing its darling Sen. Barry Goldwater on top of the Republican Party presidential ticket in 1964, the Democratic National Committee (DNC) invested heavily in opposition research and counter-propaganda campaigns. These included right-wing media monitoring initiatives like Wesley McCune's Group Research Inc. and the National Council for Civic Responsibility, which engaged in advertising campaigns designed to raise public concern regarding the political activities of right-wing groups like the John Birch Society.

As part of this effort, liberal journalist Fred J. Cook wrote the campaign-year attack book *Goldwater: Extremist on the Right*. Grove Press agreed to publish the work late in the summer of 1964 after receiving assurances that the DNC would purchase fifty thousand copies.[11] As Cook was beginning research for his Goldwater book, in May of 1964 he published an article in the liberal ideas magazine *The Nation* titled "Radio Right: Hate Clubs of the Air."[12] In it, Cook introduced his readers to what was by then a sprawling network of right-wing radio and television broadcasters and their bankrollers—from Facts Forum alumni H. L. Hunt and Dan Smoot, to former Notre Dame Law School dean and John Birch Society leadership council member Clarence Manion, to right-wing evangelicals like Carl McIntire and Billy James Hargis.

Just as United Auto Workers president Walter Reuther had written in a secret 1961 memo drafted for the Kennedy brothers, Cook speculated about how the federal government might put a stop to right-wing broadcasting. He accused Southern Democrats of pressuring the Internal Revenue Service to keep the agency from investigating what Cook believed to be right-wing exploitation of religious loopholes to avoid paying taxes on their broadcasting initiatives. He also felt that the Federal Communications Commission had not been doing enough to nip the problem in the bud.[13] While the Fairness Doctrine had been on the books since 1949, the FCC was still fine-tuning what proper enforcement might look like. It took the commission until 1964 to issue a "Fairness Primer," advising broadcasters as to the practical applicability of the regulation.[14]

Cook advised his readers that they could help the FCC achieve a stricter enforcement of the doctrine. "One recourse for liberal forces would appear to be to demand free time to counter some of the radical Right's wild-swinging charges," Cook wrote. "The Federal Communications Commission's 'primer on fairness' provides that, where such controversial programs are aired, the opposing point of view must be presented if offended parties demand equal time."[15] Between Cook's article and the DNC's other efforts to counteract right-wing radio, 1964 saw a groundswell of public complaints against local radio stations across the country. By one account the campaign had yielded 1,678 hours of free time for liberal replies to right-wing broadcasters like Manion, Smoot, and McIntire.[16]

Near the end of November 1964, after President Lyndon Johnson's landslide election victory, the right-wing evangelical broadcaster Billy James Hargis denounced Cook over the air for his critical coverage of that year's Republican presidential nominee. Hargis cited a 1959 *Newsweek* magazine story documenting Cook's firing from the New York *World-Telegram* for shoddy reporting, concluding "this is the man who wrote the book to smear and destroy Barry Goldwater." In a retrospective interview with journalist Fred Friendly, Hargis claimed that he hadn't given the attack much thought at the time. "You know how I do these broadcasts, I don't even script them," Hargis told Friendly, emphasizing his critical engagement with various news sources. "I go into the little booth with a pile of clippings from *Time, U.S. News & World Report* or the Tulsa newspapers. On this particular day I had Cook's book about Goldwater and a five-year-old *Newsweek* clipping about Cook's phony attempt to smear New York officials."[17] Hargis's *Christian Crusade* radio show aired on hundreds of local stations around the country, including WGCB in Red Lion, Pennsylvania. Following his own advice from earlier that year, Cook sent more than two hundred letters to the owners of stations that carried *Christian Crusade*, asking whether they'd aired the November 25 episode and, if so, requesting equal time to answer Hargis's criticisms.[18]

When Rev. John M. Norris, who owned WGCB in Red Lion, opened Cook's letter, he read it in the context of the ongoing onslaught of complaints spurred earlier that year by the DNC. Norris had already denied requests for equal time by the DNC and American Civil Liberties Union, which had written in protest of attacks on President Johnson made by the former Facts Forum host Dan Smoot. "Our rate card is enclosed," Norris wrote to Cook. "Your prompt reply will enable us to arrange for the time you may wish to purchase." Cook reminded Norris that federal regulations obligated him to offer free time for a brief reply, but Norris refused. Cook ultimately escalated the matter to the FCC, which in October 1965 ordered Norris to grant Cook's equal time request. Norris again refused. Fearing an unfavorable court precedent, the National Association of Broadcasters urged Norris to settle. When it became clear that he was committed to taking the matter to court, the association dedicated $10,000 toward his legal fees.[19] In 1966 Red Lion Broadcasting filed a lawsuit against the FCC, challenging the constitutionality of the Fairness Doctrine.

After three years meandering through the courts, by 1969 *Red Lion* had reached the US Supreme Court, where it was considered alongside a related antifairness case brought by the Radio-Television News Directors Association. That June the Supreme Court ruled unanimously in favor of the Federal Communications Commission, upholding the constitutionality of the Fairness Doctrine. Writing for the Court, Justice Byron White argued, "It is the right of the public to receive suitable access to social, political, esthetic, moral, and other ideas and experiences which is crucial here. That right may not constitutionally be abridged either by Congress or by the FCC." Importantly, White dismissed a claim by the directors' association that the FCC had misinterpreted Congress's intent when it amended the Communications Act in 1959. That year Congress had updated Section 315 of the law by carving out an exception to the "equal time" mandate for certain appearances on news programs. But, White noted, Congress had stipulated that the exception did not excuse broadcasters from the obligation to "operate in the public interest and to afford reasonable opportunity for the discussion of conflicting views on issues of public importance." This seemingly arcane point mattered considerably. White not only affirmed the constitutionality of the Fairness Doctrine as an administrative rule of the Federal Communications Commission; he also codified the doctrine in statutory law as well.[20] In short: *Red Lion* removed any lingering doubt as to the Fairness Doctrine's enforceability.

THE NEW RIGHT'S EMBRACE OF FAIRNESS

Partly as a result of *Red Lion*, the Fairness Doctrine became an increasingly popular site of legal and political contestation throughout the 1970s and early 1980s. Throughout the 1970s, Accuracy in Media (AIM) had relied upon the doctrine as a primary means of pressuring the three major broadcast networks into adding conservative context to their news and commentary, albeit with mixed results.[21] In addition to filing myriad Fairness Doctrine complaints against programming aired by CBS, NBC, ABC, and PBS, AIM spent significant time and money advocating for stronger FCC enforcement of the doctrine. In March 1972, for example, AIM general counsel David Lichtenstein testified before the FCC in support of the rights of implicitly conservative media consumers to federal protections from the putatively liberal whims of the broadcast industry. "In this era of heightened concern for the interests of the consumers, it is desirable that the FCC strengthen its investigative arm, improve its enforcement machinery and act vigorously to combat the inroads that 'advocacy journalism' has already made in broadcasting."[22] Phyllis

Schlafly's Eagle Forum also seized on the *Red Lion* ruling's emphasis on the general public's right to be informed as a rationale for protecting the Fairness Doctrine, an issue that drew more of the organization's attention following its successful defeat of the Equal Rights Amendment in 1982.[23] But in the 1970s it was AIM that first developed a reputation as the conservative movement's primary advocate for a Fairness Doctrine with teeth.

AIM's focus on Fairness Doctrine enforcement grew out of the organization's own oft-frustrated complaint efforts. Between October 1971 and August 1972, for example, AIM filed six fairness complaints with the FCC. When these complaints went unrequited by December 1972, AIM sued the FCC to compel the commission to answer them.[24] The FCC finally began responding to AIM's many complaints in early 1973, including acting upon one filed (by AIM on behalf of business groups and actuaries) against an NBC documentary program called *Pensions: The Broken Promise*.[25] The investigative report, aired in November 1972, depicted private pensions as a "consumer fraud, a shell game and a hoax"—a statement that AIM highlighted in characterizing NBC's reporting as "an all-out assault on the private pension system in the United States."[26] By May the FCC issued a ruling concurring with AIM that NBC had violated the Fairness Doctrine by producing a program that "explicitly advocated and supported proposals to regulate the operation of all pension plans" without conveying the views of opponents of pension system reforms. The win marked AIM's first favorable ruling from the FCC out of eleven formal complaints filed in the watchdog's first two and a half years.[27]

When NBC vigorously appealed the ruling, at first unsuccessfully with the FCC and later successfully in the federal courts, AIM invested considerable resources in pursuit of case law that would compel the commission to extend its application of the Fairness Doctrine to the Big Three television networks. As AIM was well aware, the FCC exhibited little difficulty in enforcing the doctrine among independent radio broadcasters, especially those with a religious or conservative bent. "Some who were happy to see the fairness doctrine used to silence small conservative radio stations have now developed serious reservations about the doctrine when they see it can also be applied to curb the one-sidedness of the major networks," Irvine wrote to supporters in December 1973 following the FCC's rejection of NBC's initial appeal.[28] AIM had long warned its readers that the television networks were angling to "eliminate the Fairness Doctrine," that its executives were "not concerned about the right of the public to have access to the airwaves, about the right of the listener to be fully and accurately informed, not propagandized or brainwashed by the broadcasters."[29]

But as NBC's appeal entered the federal courts, AIM found its efforts undermined by the FCC itself. In the spring of 1975, following a disadvantageous Court of Appeals ruling, AIM successfully petitioned for a rehearing that was unexpectedly cut short when FCC counsel filed a motion to declare the case moot. While presumably an effort to cut the commission's losses, AIM took the poorly communicated decision by FCC lawyers as a betrayal. "We feel that the performance of the FCC in this case demonstrates that the usefulness of the Fairness Doctrine is probably at an end," Irvine wrote in *AIM Report* under the subheading "Is the Fairness Doctrine Dead?" While AIM managed to keep fighting NBC's appeal until February 1976 (when the US Supreme Court declined to hear the case), the FCC's abortive legal strategy caused Irvine to conclude that the commission lacked the "stomach for the battles that even-handed enforcement will require." He wrote, "They broke ranks and fled on the eve of battle. Will they ever regroup and fight again?"[30]

Even as it became apparent that the FCC was unable and unwilling to fully enforce the Fairness Doctrine, AIM kept applying pressure to the commission using a diversity of tactics. For example, the group publicly opposed President Nixon's appointments of Glen O. Robinson and Abbott Washburn to the FCC in the summer of 1974 on account of their failure to indicate support for stronger enforcement of the doctrine and Robinson's outright opposition to it. While both nominees were easily confirmed, AIM used their appointments to highlight its vision of what FCC accountability would look like. "We would like to see on the FCC men and women who wholeheartedly agree with the Commission's 1949 statement that broadcast licenses abuse their trust when they withhold relevant news or facts concerning a controversy, or when they slant or distort presentation of such news," the group wrote in *AIM Report*. "We would like to see men and women on the FCC who will reject the head-in-the-sand approach taken by the Commission in recent years."[31]

Beginning in August 1975, Irvine also routinely used his syndicated column to call his readers' attention to the Fairness Doctrine and its ineffective implementation by the FCC.[32] For instance, Irvine highlighted a federally funded study that found the FCC to be the poorest performing of fifteen government agencies in terms of response to public complaints. While the other agencies were found to have an average clear reply rate of 87 percent, the study found only 46 percent of FCC responses to be sufficiently clear and timely. "AIM's experience confirms the findings of the study," Irvine wrote.[33] As examples of the FCC's unwillingness to fully administer the Fairness Doctrine piled up, Irvine's columns showed increasing exasperation. "You get better odds at the gaming tables in Las Vegas than you do from the FCC," he sighed in 1977.[34]

Those odds would grow even longer with the election of the notoriously regulation-averse Reagan administration in 1980. There were 2,400 Fairness Doctrine complaints filed in 1974, with 94 of them forwarded to the licensee for action. By 1984 there were 6,760 complaints filed, with only 6 forwarded to the licensee for action. In 1985 there were 7,296 complaints filed, with none forwarded. None were forwarded for action in 1986 either.[35] While AIM was increasingly frustrated by the FCC's chronic hesitation to enforce Fairness Doctrine complaints, it remained a staunch advocate for keeping it on the books.

THE MOVE TOWARD REPEAL

Declining Fairness Doctrine enforcement in the 1980s corresponded with Reagan's appointment of Mark S. Fowler as chair of the Federal Communications Commission. Although a staunch advocate of free market ideology, Fowler wasn't much of a movement guy. A naturalized US citizen, born in Toronto, Canada, he worked in broadcasting throughout the 1960s—first as a radio announcer, then in sales, and ultimately in management as a program director—before getting a law degree from the University of Florida in 1969. In 1975 he started the Washington-based communication law firm Fowler & Meyers, which specialized in representing broadcasters.[36] He found his way into Republican Party politics in 1976, when he served as communications counsel for then-Gov. Ronald Reagan's losing bid to replace Gerald Ford as the party's presidential nominee.[37] Fowler served in the same role for Reagan's successful 1980 presidential campaign and played an active role building the incoming administration, codirecting the Legal and Administrative Agencies Group and serving as a "key member" of the FCC transition team.[38]

Reagan's appointment of Fowler was seen as a boon to the broadcasting industry.[39] His predecessor, the Carter-appointee Charles D. Ferris, was broadly deregulatory in his approach. Determined to put an end to scarcity—a key rationale justifying New Deal–era broadcast regulations, as we saw in this book's first chapter—Ferris scaled back telecommunication rules, paving the way for innovations in satellite and cable television. By 1980 Ferris's approach had yielded a slew of new cable television channels, including the Cable News Network (CNN), which engaged in direct competition with the Big Three broadcast networks for news audiences and advertising revenue. Unlike broadcast television and radio, cable channels weren't subjected to content-based regulations like the Fairness Doctrine because satellite and cable technologies weren't limited by the scarcity of electromagnetic frequencies. While supportive of efforts to deregulate their industry, broadcasters ultimately saw Ferris as biased against them. As ABC chair Leonard Goldenson put it in a September 1980 speech at the National Press Club, "Washington has tilted the balance—against free television and in favor of pay television."[40] While Fowler would continue Ferris's deregulation of telecommunications, his primary concern was with rolling back New Deal–era broadcast regulations. "We are for full competition," Fowler told *The New York Times* when he was sworn in as FCC chair in May 1981, "but I believe there is a public interest in making sure that the present systems are not harmed through precipitous actions."[41]

Upon taking office, Fowler almost immediately set his sights on repealing the Fairness Doctrine. "Regulating over-the-air broadcasters on the premise that an audience can get programming only from the one source when the audience has literally dozens of video options is like stringing buoys in a fish pond to keep the trout from swimming from one end to the other," he told the Oregon Association of Broadcasters in June 1981.[42] However, due in part to the Supreme Court's 1969 *Red Lion* decision, Fowler lacked the authority to remove the doctrine on his own. As Fowler told the libertarian magazine *Reason* in a 1981 interview, the Fairness

Doctrine involved two prongs with different legal authorities: the first mandating coverage of issues of public importance, the second requiring balancing of viewpoints. "The first one is mandated by this agency, so we could eliminate it ourselves," Fowler told *Reason*. "The second would require Congress's cooperation."[43]

That September Fowler proposed a series of changes to the Communications Act, including amendments to sections 315 and 326, those ensuring equal time and fairness over the air. "The so-called Fairness Doctrine permits this Commission to act as editor and censor of material broadcast to the people," Fowler said in a statement accompanying his legislative proposal. "Someone must edit. Not all material can be broadcast. I would rather have the editor make these choices than the government."[44] Assuming an active, even discerning, public capable of deciding for itself whether broadcasters were providing adequate coverage of political matters, Fowler argued: "The people, in any event, expect the press to present all sides of controversial issues, and they judge the press accordingly. We must be confident in the people's ability and resourcefulness to make the widest choice possible."[45]

Fowler took his crusade against the Fairness Doctrine to the people by way of the mainstream media. In September of 1981 he published an op-ed in *The Washington Post* framing his antipathy toward fairness as an extension of First Amendment protections to the electronic press.[46] This appealed to journalists' growing sense of embattlement, in part caused by conservative press watchdogs like Accuracy in Media. In the days following Fowler's op-ed, the editorial boards of *The Washington Post* and *New York Times* both editorialized against the doctrine. "The fairness doctrine all too often has simply become a means of assaulting the news judgment of broadcasters and their right to reach these judgments, by claiming that they present unfair coverage of a major controversy," the *Post* editorial board wrote. They concluded, in a nod to the declining salience of the scarcity rationale that initially justified the regulation, that "the day is coming when virtually all people will have access to [cable television] and—along with those providing the news and views—can determine for themselves what's fair."[47] The *Times* editorial board followed a week later, supporting Fowler's call to repeal the doctrine. "Whatever the risks, abandoning these codes follows logically from the rapid deregulation of radio and television," the *Times* editors wrote. "The emphasis so far has been on expanding consumer choice by removing barriers to technological progress. Editorial freedom is the obvious next step."[48]

Despite being seen by broadcasters as "one of their own," Reagan initially seemed less than enthusiastic to repeal the Fairness Doctrine.[49] In a January 1982 interview with *TV Guide*, Reagan dodged what should have been a softball question about his thoughts concerning the regulation. "You know, I haven't given it that much thought," Reagan responded when asked about Fowler's ongoing crusade against the doctrine. "I have no quarrel with both sides being presented."[50] Indeed, it was Fowler, not Reagan, who ensured that repealing the doctrine remained an administration priority.[51]

Following Reagan's lukewarm comments to *TV Guide*, which were taken by broadcasters as a shot across their bow, Fowler made a concerted effort to keep Reagan on message in opposition to the doctrine.[52] In March 1982 Fowler took a crack at drafting a speech for Reagan to deliver at the National Association of Broadcasters conference to be held the following month in Dallas, Texas.[53] While Reagan did not deliver the speech—purportedly at the behest of the Secret Service, who saw a visit to the city where President Kennedy was killed as risky for Reagan, who had himself experienced an assassination attempt the prior year—he sent a signed letter that included some of Fowler's suggested phrasing. "It is essential to extend to electronic journalism the same rights that newspapers and magazines enjoy," the letter read. "Were the founding fathers here today, they would recognize the critical importance of a free flow of information both at home and from abroad to the preservations of our democratic way of life."[54] Speaking at the same conference, Fowler urged broadcasters to lobby Congress in support of his efforts to secure a Fairness Doctrine repeal.[55]

While Fowler's efforts to pressure Congress failed to gain much traction, he also put the administrative gears into motion for the FCC to rescind the regulation itself. In May 1984 Fowler issued a "notice of inquiry" indicating the commission's interest in formally reconsidering the Fairness Doctrine's merits.[56] Two months later, his effort received a boost from the US Supreme Court. The Court had been asked to consider the constitutionality of Section 399 of the Public Broadcasting Act of 1967, which prohibited federal funding of noncommercial television and radio stations that editorialized. In a 5–4 decision, the Court found that the ban on editorializing violated the First Amendment. Writing for the majority, Justice William Brennan cited in a footnote a legal article coauthored by Fowler, writing, "The prevailing rationale for broadcast regulation based upon spectrum scarcity has come under increasing criticism in recent years." While Brennan seemed to suggest that Fowler's argument had merit, he concluded, "We are not prepared, however, to reconsider our long-standing approach without some signal from Congress or the FCC that technological developments have advanced so far that some revision of the system of broadcast regulation may be required."[57]

The following year, the FCC did just that.

After a series of hearings initiated by Fowler's "notice of inquiry," in August 1985 the commission published a report finding that the Fairness Doctrine no longer served the public interest. "In making this determination, we do not question the interest of the listening and viewing public in obtaining access to diverse and antagonistic sources of information," the commission wrote. "Rather, we conclude that the fairness doctrine is no longer a necessary or appropriate means by which to effectuate this interest. We believe that the interest of the public in viewpoint diversity is fully served by the multiplicity of voices in the marketplace today and that the intrusion by government into the content of programming occasioned by the enforcement of the doctrine unnecessarily restricts the journalistic freedom of broadcasters."[58] Noting its disputed authority to repeal the doctrine outright due to the Supreme Court's 1969 *Red Lion* decision, the FCC concluded by calling on Congress to formally repeal it.

THE NEW RIGHT'S FAILED DEFENSE OF FAIRNESS

As the federal bureaucratic gears began turning toward the policy's ultimate repeal, Accuracy in Media regularly and in a variety of venues submitted oral and written testimony opposing any weakening of the doctrine as detrimental to the interests of a general public.[59] For example, in written testimony submitted to the FCC in September 1983, AIM attorney John D. Hemenway characterized the Fairness Doctrine as "the only really effective remedy available to the average citizen" and implored the FCC not to "unleash the unbridled power of the big media upon a relatively defenseless public, especially in view of the expressed desire of the representatives of the sovereign people, the United States Congress, which explicitly wants the Fairness Doctrine to remain."[60] AIM also framed its support of the Fairness Doctrine more explicitly in terms of the interests of an underserved constituency of conservative media consumers, actively coordinating with other New Right groups to pressure both Congress and the FCC into retaining it. In August 1983, for example, AIM issued a joint statement with the conservative American Legal Foundation, American Media Business Council, Committee for a Free Press, Conservative Caucus, and Leadership Council, urging the public to write letters to their congressional representatives, the FCC, and President Reagan in opposition to rule changes that in effect would have all but repealed the doctrine.[61]

AIM also defended the interests of conservative media consumers in its public testimony. For example, while speaking at an FCC hearing in February 1985, Irvine openly worried that any increased competition resulting from the elimination of broadcast fairness requirements would continue to marginalize news and commentary of interest to conservatives. "True, ABC News now has a conservative commentator while CBS and NBC stick with their liberals. But in general the network response to criticism of their predominantly liberally biased documentaries has been to reduce the number of documentaries they air, not to alter the bias," Irvine testified. He continued, "Network news staffs are overwhelmingly liberal in their political and social orientation. This is what determines the slant of the news, the narrowing of the range of information and opinion provided to viewers and listeners. The enforcement of the fairness doctrine could enlarge the flow. Eliminating the doctrine entirely will tend to encourage further constriction of the flow."[62] Irvine also took pains to frame AIM's opposition to Fairness Doctrine repeal in terms he expected to resonate with the religious and constitutional originalist interest of his fellow New Right conservatives. Suggesting that movement conservatives should pressure the Reagan administration into removing FCC chair Fowler from office, Irvine warned that deregulating the broadcast industry would unleash "a torrent of pornography and media abuse." Irvine wrote, "The slightly enforced restraints imposed upon the broadcasting industry have been a finger in the dike. Mr. Fowler is proposing to remove the finger."[63]

While many New Right groups agreed with Irvine that the media's liberal biases would only strengthen if unfettered by federal regulation, a small but influential cadre of conservative movement leaders had a different take. Most notably, in 1984 influential New Right organizer and close Viguerie associate Paul Weyrich endorsed FCC chair Fowler's efforts to deregulate broadcast media in the pages of *Conservative Digest*. "The de-regulation of the broadcast industry, combined with great advances in technology, will break the strangle-hold which major media outlets have on the viewing and listening public," Weyrich predicted. Unlike Irvine, Weyrich saw an opportunity for conservative media entrepreneurs on the horizon: "As new broadcast services come on line and the viewing and listening public shifts away from the networks and other major media operations, not only will the public have more choice, but the majors will have to shape up or they will lose out in the long run."[64] Somewhat ironically, in opposing the Fairness Doctrine, Weyrich was actively siding with the mainstream media he otherwise opposed—including CBS news anchor Walter Cronkite, *The New York Times*, *The Washington Post*, all three major television networks, the National Association of Broadcasters, and the Radio-Television News Directors Association.[65]

Two years after the FCC released its 1985 report urging repeal the Fairness Doctrine, Congress had instead passed the Fairness in Broadcasting Act—a bill designed to more explicitly codify the policy in federal law. The move, along with two federal appellate court cases that reaffirmed the FCC's legal authority to repeal the policy on its own, renewed debate within the Reagan administration over the Fairness Doctrine's fate. While a wide array of groups supported congressional codification of the doctrine—including progressive organizations like the AFL-CIO, American Civil Liberties Union, and Americans for Democratic Action—it was the support of such New Right–aligned groups as AIM, Eagle Forum, the National Conservative Political Action Committee, and the National Rifle Association that forced the administration to weigh the political consequences of vetoing the Fairness in Broadcasting Act of 1987.[66] The motley alliance of Fairness Doctrine supporters was forged by a common critical disposition toward the mainstream press. "Ideological bias has been clearly shown by a number of studies of network programming," wrote Gary Bauer, Reagan's assistant for policy development, in a memo advising the president against vetoing the bill. "This bias is likely to worsen without the fairness doctrine to ensure open debate." Bauer concluded, "I recommend we keep the veto weapon for issues on which there is more clear consensus among our natural allies."[67]

Despite the watchdog's long-standing campaign in support of a robustly enforced Fairness Doctrine, AIM was mentioned only in passing in West Wing memoranda debating whether Reagan should veto the Fairness in Broadcasting Act.[68] Eagle Forum's Phyllis Schlafly was most often cited as the Fairness Doctrine's chief New Right proponent. "Many of the President's traditional supporters support the fairness doctrine as the only way they have to get access," Bauer wrote in his memo opposing Reagan's veto in the summer of 1987. "For example, Phyllis Schlafly credits it with providing her the chance to battle ERA proponents on the air. She and others will work for an override of any veto."[69]

Schlafly had indeed steered Eagle Forum toward more explicit Fairness Doctrine advocacy. After finding herself the lone supporter of the Fairness Doctrine at a meeting of conservative movement leaders in early 1982, Schlafly commissioned Eagle Forum's national media chair, Elaine Donnelly, to draft a paper "In Defense of the Fairness Doctrine," which Donnelly completed that September. The paper's arguments were later repackaged in Eagle Forum materials opposing the doctrine's repeal.[70] But AIM had been persistently advocating on behalf of strengthening the doctrine since 1972, making its sidelining within White House discussions of the policy surprising, if also a logical extension of AIM's relative marginalization within the broader New Right as it expanded in the late 1970s and 1980s.

By the end of the summer of 1987, after six and a half years of nonenforcement of fairness requirements, President Reagan vetoed the Fairness in Broadcasting Act, and the FCC finally repealed the Fairness Doctrine once and for all. "History has shown that the dangers of an overly timid or biased press cannot be averted through bureaucratic regulation but only through the freedom and competition the First Amendment sought to guarantee," Reagan wrote to the Senate, explaining his decision to veto.[71] AIM responded not with a bang but a whimper—once again urging in vain for supporters to write their elected officials to intervene and bitterly anticipating the world to come. "In the absence of any fairness requirement, broadcast licensees will be free to use their stations to ride their personal hobby horses with no restraint," Irvine warned. "This added power may well increase the value of stations to their owners. It is unlikely to add to public enlightenment or to the enrichment of the debate on public affairs in most cases."[72] Irvine's words proved prescient, although not in exactly the way he was imagining. The Fairness Doctrine's repeal would indeed unleash a new era of political hobbyhorse riding and profitability for radio station owners—but the beneficiaries would be the very conservative media consumers on whose behalf AIM had advocated, as well as the conservative agenda it advanced in allying with the New Right.

While AIM continues to serve as a vocal right-wing media watchdog to this day, its influence within the modern conservative movement declined with the death of the Fairness Doctrine. In the late 1980s, not unlike Facts Forum in the 1950s and despite Reed Irvine's insistence to the contrary, AIM was publicly exposed as a far-right front for corporate interests.[73] In their classic 1988 study of the political economy of mass media, *Manufacturing Consent*, Edward Herman and Noam Chomsky noted AIM's strong ties to the oil industry and its clear advocacy for right-wing foreign policy positions, accusing it of producing "flak" designed to push the mainstream media rightward.[74] As the 1990s dawned—with the collapse of the Soviet Union depriving anticommunists of their favorite foil and conservative talk radio dominating both the airwaves and the agenda of the modern conservative movement—AIM's influence waned even further.

By the late 1990s and early 2000s, as conservative media flourished on cable and online, competition over resources and audiences grew. AIM found itself as one among many groups devoted to chastising the "liberal media" while digging up and amplifying scandals and conspiracy theories designed to undermine the Democratic presidency of Bill Clinton.[75] To compete, AIM diversified its media production efforts. It experimented with radio and contributed to Paul Weyrich's short-lived National Empowerment Television cable channel, a failed precursor to Fox News.[76] In perhaps the clearest sign of AIM's shift in emphasis, by the fall of 1993 Irvine and collaborator Cliff Kincaid devoted episodes of the group's *Media Monitor* radio program to *opposing* the reinstatement of the Fairness Doctrine.[77]

Only five years after mounting an exhaustive defense of the doctrine, AIM depicted a newly proposed Fairness in Broadcasting Act as a conspiracy led by the "liberal-left" in general, and gay rights groups in particular. AIM feared that a return of the "insidious" doctrine would "give the liberal-left the opportunity to tie conservative broadcasters up in court by filing complaints against them with the Federal Communications Commission." As a sample of the havoc these liberal-left groups might wreak, AIM noted that talk radio giant Rush Limbaugh had already bowed to pressure levied against his program by the Gay and Lesbian Alliance Against Defamation (GLAAD). "Listeners to the program have detected a noticeable change in his treatment of homosexuals," the AIM broadcast warned.[78] AIM's claim that Limbaugh had softened his homophobic rhetoric was old news—Limbaugh had already admitted as much in a *New York Times* profile, expressing regret for his ruthless mockery of AIDS patients. "It was a totally irresponsible thing to do," Limbaugh told a *Times* reporter in December 1990.[79]

But AIM's insinuation that the broadcaster had bent under the pressure of GLAAD contradicted Limbaugh's carefully manicured reputation for irreverence and editorial independence. When, two days after the *Media Monitor* broadcast, a caller brought AIM's critique to Limbaugh's attention live on the air, he bristled. Limbaugh denied softening his tone and took aim at Kincaid, accusing him of having "abandoned any pretense to accuracy some time ago" and of being "incapable of truth." Limbaugh then turned introspective about his success in relation to the work of AIM: "One of the primary reasons that I have succeeded is because I tell myself what to do. I never have meetings with anybody about what to say, what not to say, how to say something, what to do." Limbaugh continued, "I think Kincaid thinks he ought to be me—wishes he ought to be me—thinks that I am a pretender to the conservative throne. He's a movement guy, full force. I am *not* a movement conservative and that's what bothers him."[80]

Irvine and Kincaid spent months attempting to extract an apology from Limbaugh, to no avail. And in a move that illustrates just how influential Limbaugh had become, by December 1993 Kincaid was mailing evidence of his long-standing support of Limbaugh to conservative movement leaders, pleading, "I need your help in clearing my name."[81] While the spat itself was indicative of the sort of turf battles that became more common as the field of conservative media grew more crowded in the 1990s, Limbaugh's framing of the difference between himself and "movement conservatives" illuminates the paradoxical successes of the New Right. In the 1970s, when Richard Viguerie rebranded the conservative movement as an umbrella for myriad single-issue campaigns, he and his fellow organizers possessed considerable agenda-setting ability. At weekly breakfast meetings hosted by Viguerie in his Northern Virginia offices, New Right organizers discussed the news of the day and decided which issues would be foregrounded in conservative movement mailers and publications in the coming weeks and months. Often the issues selected by New Right organizers corresponded with active legislation or other policy matters of interest to political insiders within the Beltway.

But somewhere along the way the audiences built and targeted by a constellation of New Right single-issue groups and, coordinated by Viguerie, developed a distinctly conservative *taste*—preferences in enemy construction, in humor, in manners of speech that were no longer reducible to support for any one particular issue or array of issues.[82] At the heart of this conservative taste was a critical disposition toward the mainstream press—a trait fostered above all else by AIM and amplified by the broader media activist projects of the New Right. Indeed, widespread belief in liberal media bias primed the market for conservative talk radio hosts like Limbaugh to achieve commercial viability. Less movement-aligned and driven by entertainment imperatives, Limbaugh increasingly framed politics in explicitly Gramscian terms of hegemonic struggle—imploring his audience to consider that "the Culture War is a bilateral conflict" and urging them to participate.[83] When, in the 1970s, Viguerie and his New Right associates decided to "reverse engineer the left," establishing think tanks, advocacy groups, and political action committees, they unwittingly engaged in a sort of war of position—laying the building blocks of conservative counterhegemony.[84]

With the success of Limbaugh and other talk radio hosts in the 1990s and the subsequent emergence of Fox News Channel in 1996, the programming of mass audience conservative media outlets by the early 2000s was beginning to resemble a war of maneuver—directly antagonizing professional journalistic values to the point of producing an alternative "conservative media establishment" capable of neatly narrating current events to fit within a worldview palatable to the conservative taste.[85] But in the early 1990s a full-grown conservative media establishment was not yet visible on the horizon. The issues-based conservatism that had driven movement leaders like Viguerie and Irvine was in the midst of being eclipsed by new conservative media personalities, like Limbaugh, who identified with the conservative political culture fostered by the New Right but saw it less of a movement affiliation than a personal identity. As Limbaugh described his show's methodology in 1993, "It's not controlled or dominated by topics. I don't sit in my office in the morning and say, 'Alright, what am I mad about today and who do I want to skewer today and about whom am I going to tell the truth today?' I read the newspaper to find out what's hot in the news and that's what I talk about. It's an event driven show."[86]

As conservative media activists had been promoting as early as Facts Forum in 1951, Limbaugh understood his conservatism as a personal disposition that became evident to him in part through his daily consumption of the news. Where Accuracy in Media failed in its project of bolstering FCC regulation and achieved mixed success in holding major media outlets accountable for coverage dissonant with the right-anticommunist worldview, its hesitant collaboration with the New Right helped usher in a new generation of self-aware conservative media consumers and producers—an unwieldy constituency that the conservative movement and Republican Party each struggle to wrangle to this day.

CONCLUSION

The morning of Wednesday, November 4, 1992, might as well have been Christmas. Results from that year's US presidential race were tallied the night before—although well past my bedtime. Eight years old and eager to learn who won, I woke early and rushed outside to collect my family's copy of *The Dallas Morning News* from the front lawn. As I made my way back inside, I impatiently removed the plastic wrapper revealing the headline: "Clinton triumphs." I wept, rushing to my mother's bedside to deliver the news.

Yes, I was a dramatic little Republican back in 1992.[1] My parents had divorced the prior December, and my paternal grandfather had died that February. I struggled with the overwhelming emotions that accompany losses of all sorts, including, it turns out, by incumbent presidents. My mom struggled too. A tired, working, single mother of two whose own parents were both in declining health, she felt sentimental when she listened to music, so she turned the radio dial in our boxy blue Astro van to the news/talk station WBAP-AM. There she found Rush Limbaugh, whose political commentary and jokes at the expense of liberals kept her from crying on long drives around the North Texas suburbs while running errands with us kids.[2] Raised in a Democrat household, my mom joined the Republican Party in 1980—drawn in, as with so many of her generation, by Ronald Reagan's presidential campaign against Jimmy Carter. In

Limbaugh she found a lighthearted, conservative kindred spirit, and I found a lifelong interest in right-wing political culture—back then it was the air I breathed.

All research is therapy if you really think about it. This book started as a dissertation that sought to tell the prehistory of Fox News. When Fox launched in 1996 under the slogan "Fair and Balanced," to whom did it appeal and why? A lot happened in the decade it took me to answer that question. When I started, Donald Trump was a failed real estate mogul with a reality TV show and a side hustle slandering the country's first Black president. Now he's in his second term as president, having rebuilt the Republican Party, and much of the modern conservative movement, in his own garish image. When I started, my mom was alive and still conservative, still half-jokingly asking me questions like, "You were raised on Rush Limbaugh, what happened to you?" Now she's dead from cancer and Limbaugh is too.

The critical disposition toward the press that I uncovered while researching conservative media activism, I've come to realize, taught me how to search for it. Republicans (unsurprisingly, if you've made it this far into the book) largely blamed the press for George H. W. Bush's loss in 1992—for focusing on his many gaffes and for taking interest in a relatively young and charismatic governor from Arkansas. Bush campaign staffer, and later George W. Bush FCC appointee, Robert M. McDowell captured this sentiment in the form of a bumper sticker: "Annoy the Media: Re-Elect Bush."[3] As a die-hard Bush supporter and Limbaugh Ditto Head, I too cultivated a critical disposition toward the mainstream press. I too believed in liberal media bias. I honed my youthful conservatism not only by listening to Limbaugh but also by reading *The Dallas Morning News* against the grain each morning alongside my mom at our kitchen table. Not that the *Morning News* was particularly liberal. But my understanding and awareness of my conservative political identity came through active engagement with the news of the day—through paying close attention to how the paper's reporters wrote and framed their stories and whether that matched the worldview I was being raised within.

My young fixation with news and politics had, by high school, turned into a viable career path. I signed up for my first journalism class in the fall of 2001 and started writing for my local newspaper, the *Lewisville Leader*, a year later. As I learned how to *do* journalism, the terrorist attacks of September 11, 2001, inspired a stunning rightward shift within the mainstream media (not that conservatives at the time would admit it). Republican President George W. Bush was largely hailed for his heroic response, despite having failed to prevent the attacks. Bipartisan support for the wars in Afghanistan and Iraq revealed the limitations of the balance imperative—journalists, as "secondary definers," had few experts they deemed credible enough to counter the steady drumbeat toward war.[4] Trained by my youthful conservatism to take mainstream news with a grain of salt, I was particularly attuned to inconsistencies in reporting on the machinations of Saddam Hussein and his putative ties to Al-Qaeda. I was unconvinced by Colin Powell's now infamous presentation before the United Nations Security Council, where he delivered transparently shoddy evidence of "weapons of mass destruction" to justify a US invasion of Iraq. By the late spring of 2003, when Bush prematurely declared "Mission Accomplished" and I graduated from high school, I had come to identify more as a journalist than as a conservative, with my long-cultivated critical disposition ultimately turning against the latter.

Of course, for many (perhaps most) conservatives, a critical disposition toward the press acts as a sort of centrifugal force—keeping them invested in conservative politics, inoculating them against ideology-contradicting facts and arguments.[5] For much of the mid-twentieth century, when the Fairness Doctrine regulated broadcast media and "high modern" imperatives shaped professional journalism, that meant participating in the modern conservative *movement*. That may have meant subscribing to movement publications like *National Review* and *Human Events* or joining movement aligned groups like Young Americans for Freedom, the American Conservative Union, or the John Birch Society. It likely meant voting for Goldwater, then maybe Wallace, and almost certainly Reagan. If you were a Democrat, it meant eventually joining the Republican Party. It may also have meant tuning in to "public affairs" broadcasts like H. L Hunt's *Life Line* radio program or William F. Buckley's *Firing Line* television show—blips within a broader commercial broadcast system geared more toward entertainment than news. In short: All of the media activist initiatives chronicled in this book were designed to win adherents to the conservative cause and to defeat liberals and the Left, *not* to make money (although Richard Viguerie managed to do both).

By the early 1990s, when I was beginning the journey that resulted in this book, a new conservative political and media culture was starting to form. As we saw in chapter 6, in the 1970s and 1980s the New Right cultivated a new generation of self-aware conservative media consumers. As we saw in the last chapter, the repeal of the Fairness Doctrine in 1987 paved the way for a series of conservative media initiatives, most notably talk radio, that sought to serve those consumers while prioritizing commercial viability. As Rush Limbaugh told the CBS television news magazine *60 Minutes* in 1991, "I'm trying to attract the largest audience I can and hold it for as long as I can so that I can charge advertisers confiscatory advertising rates—this is a business."[6] The introduction of market logics into conservative media disrupted earlier movement efforts to use media as a means toward the end of conservative electoral and policy success. The result, exacerbated by technological developments around the turn of the twenty-first century, is an unstable media/movement hybrid, where once internecine battles over conservative ideology and style now shape our media culture as a whole. Where once we could mostly avoid the aesthetics and ideas swirling within right-wing political culture by simply consuming mainstream media, now it is hardly possible to look away.

THE EMERGENCE OF A DISTINCT RIGHT-WING MEDIA SECTOR

It is important to emphasize that none of this was inevitable. While Limbaugh's success spawned an entire industry's worth of imitators, resulting in conservative hegemony within AM talk radio, early efforts by conservative movement leaders to launch a cable television channel failed miserably.[7] In late 1993 New Right leader Paul Weyrich and his Free Congress Foundation launched National Empowerment Television (NET). While its founders claimed NET would be "C-Span with attitude," it definitively lacked the latter.[8] As Reece Peck has argued, early conservative movement forays into television were heavy on ideology and light on entertainment. NET was the most successful of these early conservative cable channels, running from 1993 to 2000, with other upstarts like the Republican Exchange Satellite Network (RESN) and GOP-TV lasting only a few short years each. A fourth attempt, the Conservative Television Network, failed to raise enough capital to even launch.[9] When Rupert Murdoch and Roger Ailes debuted Fox News Channel in 1996, they were well aware that a long-standing critical disposition toward mainstream media had created significant consumer demand for conservative alternatives. "I think there is an underserved audience that is hungry for fair and balanced news," Ailes told *The New York Times* in 2000. "If the conservative point of view is not presented anywhere else in journalism, then those people will come to us."[10]

But for conservative media consumers to *find* Fox, Murdoch first needed to persuade cable providers to carry it—an expensive and politically fraught prerequisite.[11] Fox also had to compete not only with CNN but with sports and entertainment content readily available on other cable channels like ESPN and HBO. Ailes, who had won Emmys in the 1960s as executive producer of the *Mike Douglas Show* before working as a Republican media consultant for the Nixon and Reagan campaigns, had a knack for compelling television.[12] Fox News succeeded at reaching disaffected conservative media consumers because of two key ingredients that movement activists and media entrepreneurs lacked: decades of tabloid and entertainment television production experience and economies of scale attendant with a global media conglomerate. Fox News ran at a loss for four years before finally breaking even in 2000.[13] It surpassed CNN in ratings in January 2002, capitalizing on a groundswell of patriotic sentiment as George W. Bush embarked on his "War on Terror." Fox has largely dominated the cable news sector ever since—with CNN and MSNBC both adopting programming and stylistic elements developed by Fox in order to keep pace.[14] By 2004 the conservative-turned-liberal political consultant David Brock was decrying a democracy-corrupting "Republican Noise Machine," with Limbaugh and Fox News at its center.[15] Political communication scholars Kathleen Hall Jamieson and Joseph Cappella soon found evidence of a "conservative media establishment," composed of Limbaugh, Fox, and *The Wall Street Journal* editorial page.

Writing in the waning years of the Bush administration, Jamieson and Cappella documented how commercially driven right-wing media tended to reinforce a "fusionist" conception of conservatism, epitomized by Ronald Reagan. They contended that if the conservative media establishment "were confronted by a serious Republican presidential contender whose proposals and past deviated from the Reagan doctrine, they would marshal against the candidacy."[16] In the months preceding the publication of their pathbreaking book *Echo Chamber*, they seemed to be spot on. While running for the 2008 Republican presidential nomination, Arkansas Gov. Mike Huckabee deviated from fusionist dogma by proposing some modest tax increases to support social services. As predicted, the conservative media establishment turned on Huckabee, allowing Arizona Sen. John McCain to ultimately win the nomination. But two months after *Echo Chamber* was published, Fox News *hired* Huckabee to anchor his own folksy political commentary show. Here we begin to see an entertainment-driven deviation from modern conservative orthodoxy that has contributed to an ideologically and stylistically diverse right-wing media sector structured by an (then fledgling, now rampant) online attention economy.

By 2009 the Tea Party movement—which epitomized the burgeoning conservative media/movement hybrid—had begun to mobilize against the presidency of the newly elected Democrat Barack Obama. Initially a grassroots response to a viral rant by CNBC host Rick Santelli against an Obama administration plan to help homeowners facing foreclosure due to the Great Recession, the Tea Party was largely structured by the aggregate efforts of a slew of preexisting conservative movement and adjacent groups ranging from Americans for Prosperity, to Freedom Works, to the Libertarian and Republican Parties, to the John Birch Society.[17] The Tea Party was also boosted and influenced by Fox News primetime hosts Sean Hannity and Glenn Beck as well as by countless conservative talk radio figures including Limbaugh. This expanded, profit-driven "conservative media establishment" was further bolstered by an uptick in smaller-scale conservative print and radio entrepreneurship during the preceding two decades.[18]

As this book has shown, antipathy toward the mainstream media has long driven conservative media ownership, innovation, and activism. Technological developments in the late 1990s and early aughts had lowered the barriers to entry for individuals and groups to launch their own news and commentary websites, often referred to as blogs. Unsurprisingly, conservatives were early and enthusiastic "netizens" of the "blogosphere," a much slower precursor to the sorts of networked internet content production and distribution that would soon develop into what we now call social media. The Heritage Foundation, a think tank founded by New Right activists in 1973, launched *Townhall*, an online news community for conservatives, in 1995. That same year Matt Drudge founded the *Drudge Report*, a conservative news aggregation website that became a popular resource for professional political reporters after it broke the news of the Clinton–Lewinsky sex scandal in 1998. That year, inspired by Drudge's role in driving the Clinton scandal narrative, conservative journalist Christopher Reddy founded *Newsmax*, a clickbait-driven online magazine. Specializing in right-wing conspiracy theories and a burgeoning conservative celebrity culture, *Newsmax* was second only to FoxNews.com in conservative web traffic by 2011.[19]

As the Tea Party began staging rallies and garnering media attention in 2009, former Drudge assistant Andrew Breitbart launched *Big Government*, the first in a network of right-inspired topical blogs (*Big Hollywood*, *Big Journalism*, etc.) that helped establish him as a Tea Party leader. Although conservative, Breitbart wasn't much of a movement guy. He considered himself to be a "default liberal" who shifted right in 1991 after watching the US Senate confirmation hearings for Supreme Court Justice Clarence Thomas, which he later called an "electronic lynching." Like his idol Rush Limbaugh, who wasn't *all* business after all, Breitbart saw his media activism through the lens of Antonio Gramsci's conception of cultural warfare. "Make no mistake: America is in a media war," he wrote in his 2011 memoir. "The left wins because it controls the narrative. The narrative is controlled by the media. The left *is* the media. Narrative is everything. I call it the Democrat-Media Complex—and I am at war to gain back control of the American narrative."[20] *Big Government* quickly landed its first blow. In 2009 it published undercover videos shot by conservative activist James O'Keefe alleging misconduct by the progressive Association of Community Organizations for Reform Now (ACORN). The videos went viral, contributing to the closure of ACORN the following year.

The late aughts and early 2010s were a watershed moment in digital news. Sites like *Gawker*, *HuffPost*, and *Buzzfeed* were leveraging rapidly growing social media platforms like YouTube, Facebook, Instagram, and Twitter to produce a new, and at times controversial, mode of journalism. Liberally mixing celebrity gossip with political news, aggregation with original content, these digital news outlets rode the online attention economy to profitability, inspiring innovation (or, depending on your perspective, deterioration) within traditional newsrooms as well.[21] This trend impacted conservative media, too, resulting in a proliferation of digital conservative news sites during the Obama era. Breitbart had created his own eponymous news aggregation site in 2005, the same year he leveraged his experience working for Drudge to help launch the liberal news aggregation site *Huffington Post*. Breitbart.com started publishing original content in 2007, rebranding as *Breitbart News*. When Andrew Breitbart died unexpectedly in 2012, a year after a major capital infusion by billionaire Robert Mercer, *Breitbart News* absorbed the Tea Party–era blogs as verticals and tapped Steve Bannon to run the streamlined operation.[22]

Breitbart News was one among several attempts by conservative activists and media figures to capitalize on the viral potential of digital news. And like their conservative media activist forebearers chronicled in this book, many looked leftward for inspiration. In 2010 conservative television commentator (then of CNN and MSNBC fame, and later a Fox News star) Tucker Carlson launched *The Daily Caller* with his college roommate and former Dick Cheney aide Neil Patel. Initially framed as a "conservative answer to the Huffington Post," the *Daily Caller* invested in original reporting and established a foundation to train aspiring conservative journalists.[23] In 2012 conservative writers and activists Michael Goldfarb and Matthew Continetti launched the *Washington Free Beacon*, a news arm of their newly launched Center for American Freedom—a think tank modeled after and designed to counteract the successes of the liberal Center for American Progress.[24] The more established conservative think tank Heritage Foundation would launch its own digital news site, the *Daily Signal*, in 2014. Like the *Caller*, the *Free Beacon* and *Daily Signal* hired reporters and created beat structures that mirrored traditional professional news operations, albeit with a conservative ideological twist. Although conservative, their editors and reporters saw themselves as journalists and claimed to share professional news values such as commitments to accuracy, to fairly representing differing perspectives, and to setting a measured tone in debate—although they often faced criticism for partisan, inaccurate, and at times racially and culturally insensitive reporting.[25]

By the 2010s social media platforms like YouTube, Facebook, Instagram, and Twitter matured to the point of cultivating influencers—sometimes algorithmically, sometimes through creator partnerships.[26] Individual content producers were able to accumulate massive audiences, which attracted companies and other wealthy benefactors who had something to sell. Right-wing influencers quickly emerged, some organically and some with the help of conservative organizations and media outlets. Founded in 2012 by Charlie Kirk and Bill Montgomery to build support for conservatism among young people, Turning Point USA was particularly social media-forward, cultivating and promoting right-wing influencers like Candace Owens. While working as an editor-at-large at *Breitbart News*, Ben Shapiro leveraged YouTube and Facebook to build a sizable following of his own. Like other influencers on the right, he took to podcasting and in 2015 launched his own conservative media company, The *Daily Wire*, which also became a regular platform for other right-wing influencers to promote their pet projects and ideas. *The Blaze*, a video-forward digital media company originally founded by Glenn Beck in 2012 to capitalize on the Fox News stardom he built during the Tea Party era, would also platform various right-wing influencers, as would a new generation of conservative cable and online streaming channels like One America News Network (founded in 2013), Newsmax TV (2014) and Right Side Broadcasting Network (2015). Not all right-wing influencers engaged these platforms, but they combined to form an "alternative influence network" that played an outsized role in mobilizing right-wing audiences during the Trump campaigns and administrations.[27]

More established conservative print media also slowly joined the digital fray. In 1995 conservative writers Bill Kristol and Fred Barnes launched the *Weekly Standard*, published by Rupert Murdoch's News Corporation. The magazine soon rivaled the *National Review*, serving as an unofficial organ of neoconservatism during its height in the George W. Bush administration. Despite its influence, the magazine never turned a profit. As neoconservatism faded in popularity—due in no small part to its support for what became military quagmires in Afghanistan and

Iraq—and as Murdoch's print interests shifted to *The Wall Street Journal*, which he purchased in 2007, the *Standard* was sold to the conservative billionaire Philip Anschutz in 2009.[28]

Anschutz already owned the *Washington Examiner*, a daily tabloid he launched in 2005 to compete with *The Washington Post* and with DC's stalwart conservative broadsheet *The Washington Times* (founded by Unification Church leader Sun Myung Moon in 1982). He pledged to improve the *Standard*'s web presence, but it was the *Examiner* that first pivoted that direction. In 2013 Anschutz downsized the *Examiner*, scaling back local reporting to focus on national reporting with the goal of making it a web-only "center-right version of political publications like *The Hill*."[29] In 2018, as the *Standard* resisted the Trump-led shift away from neoconservative orthodoxies like free trade, Anschutz cut it loose—shuttering the publication to focus resources on the more Trump-friendly *Examiner*.[30] Ex-*Standard* writers soon formed *The Bulwark*, an online news and commentary site that has since carved out a rare anti-Trump niche within the right-wing media sector, holding space for a remnant of fusionist and neoconservative commentators.

Of all the media described above, *The Bulwark* comes the closest to operating according to a stable ideology. Nearly all of the most prominent outlets comprising the contemporary right-wing media sector either shift with the vicissitudes of right-wing political culture or function in an omnibus fashion—few have strict ideological litmus tests beyond general agreement with a broadly conservative worldview or open hostility toward liberals and the Left. They vary widely in style and tone. While many of these conservative outlets garner revenue from subscriptions or online advertising, most also benefit from the philanthropic largesse of wealthy conservatives. The result is a complex array of competing interests and motivations structured around an attention economy driven primarily by platforms beyond their control.[31] Recent efforts by right-wing activists and tech investors to build or buy their own social media sites can be read as a tacit acknowledgment of this fundamental instability. While the right-wing media sector often appears lockstep or coordinated, it remains to be seen whether it will remain so once Trump's cult of personality fades. When that happens and infighting ensues to fill the power vacuum, at least one commonality will remain: a critical disposition toward mainstream media and an activist urge to counter prevailing media narratives by producing content consistent with an ever-evolving right-wing worldview.

ASYMMETRICAL POLARIZATION AND THE FUTURE OF NEWS

When historians tell the story of right-wing media in the twenty-first century—beyond my provisional sketch above, that is—2016 will no doubt loom large. It's not just that Donald Trump succeeded that year in a hostile takeover of the Republican Party and an upset victory over Democrat Hillary Clinton for the US presidency. The emergence of the right-wing media sector, with its various styles, personalities, and ideologies, created a complex media culture that destabilized the conservative media/movement hybrid. Long seen as a Republican Party kingmaker, Fox News was slow to board the Trump train. As Yochai Benkler, Robert Faris, and Hal Roberts showed in their groundbreaking network analysis of election year social media, it was *Breitbart News* that pulled the right-wing media sector and its conservative audiences into formation behind Trump.[32] With Steve Bannon at its helm, *Breitbart* conveyed a distinctly paleoconservative worldview, adopted from a small group of highly online white nationalists who called themselves Alt Right. The site leveraged favorable algorithmic conditions on Facebook and Twitter to advance a moral panic over "illegal immigration" among conservative media consumers. *Breitbart*'s social media successes that year dovetailed with Trump's campaign messaging, which sought to prime voters with anti-immigrant sentiments using the catchphrase "Build the Wall." As conservative audiences came to expect anti-immigrant and pro-Trump content, other outlets like Fox fell into line.

As Trump gained momentum, his political gravity shifted the right-wing media around him. Several leaders of conservative media organizations initially refused to go along. Glenn Beck of *The Blaze*, Ben Shapiro of the *Daily Wire*, prominent talk radio host Mark Levin, *RedState* blog founder Erick Erickson, the *National Review*—all publicly opposed Trump before ultimately acceding to the growing pro-Trump demands of their audiences. The notion that Fox News was insufficiently loyal to the conservative cause, a perception Trump himself stoked during his first presidency, created growth opportunities for further right cable channels like One America News and Newsmax TV. The overarching shift by right-wing media away from fusionist respectability politics and toward more full-throated paleoconservative and white identitarian ideology during the Trump years had a radicalizing effect among conservative media consumers as well. Analyzing millions of social media posts and hyperlinks, Benkler, Faris, and Roberts found a networked public sphere online characterized by asymmetric polarization. While liberal and left social media users remained engaged with more traditional, professional news outlets like *The New York Times* and CNN, conservative users primarily engaged with right-wing media outlets and were highly insulated from mainstream sources of news. As a result "roughly a third of the American media system" faced increased vulnerability to "disinformation, lies, and half-truths."[33]

As this book has shown, the modern conservative movement has long prioritized worldview preservation over a diligent commitment to empirical reality. The critical disposition toward the press, rooted as it was in real active conflict between conservatives and the professional journalists who covered their movement unfavorably, often served as plausible deniability when fact-based claims by conservatives failed to hold up to scrutiny. It is no historical accident that the Right adopted structural media criticism from the Left amid the highly dubious anticommunist witch-hunts of the Second Red Scare. But whereas in the mid-twentieth century the critical disposition toward the press came to structure the modern conservative movement—a driving force behind media activist initiatives to depict the world in accordance with modern conservative ideology—now that critical disposition structures our entire media system. While this is partly a result of the media activist initiatives chronicled in this book—there are more and a wider variety of right-wing media outlets now than ever before—it is also the result of changes in our media system as a whole and in journalism as both an industry and a profession.

As journalism studies scholars Matt Carlson, Sue Robinson, and Seth Lewis have noted, it is less useful to consider Trump as a *cause* of our contemporary media dysfunction than as a diagnostic of just how far journalism has fallen from its "high modern" heyday in the mid-twentieth century. During the period covered in this book, the late 1940s through the early 1990s, journalists were bestowed by large swaths of the public with what Thomas Gieryn calls "epistemic authority," or the "legitimate power to define, describe, and explain bounded domains of reality."[34] But trust in US news media has declined for decades. The cause of this decline is somewhat overdetermined. The newspaper industry has lurched from crisis to crisis for the better part of eighty years, resulting in ever fewer outlets and reporters. Deregulation of the broadcast industry has consolidated media ownership, reducing diversity of perspectives over the airwaves. New technologies—from radio to television to cable to the internet to social media—have repeatedly revolutionized access to news and information, eroding traditional journalistic forms of gatekeeping and empowering audiences to do their "own research." Carlson, Robinson, and Lewis frame this problem in terms of journalism's declining relevance, helpfully pointing out that, like it or not, professional news reporting is no longer the driving force behind our collective knowledge. It is more accurate to think of mainstream journalism as a decentered component within a much broader media culture—competing with other top-down cultural industries and institutions, not to mention bottom-up, amateur media practices enabled by the internet and social media, for making meaning of our shared quotidian reality.

Although common, a generalized framing of the problem at hand—that our current era of media and political dysfunction results from a tech-fueled epistemological crisis—glosses over a key datapoint. A 2023 Gallup/Knight study found that 28 percent of Democrats hold an unfavorable view of US news media. Among Republicans, that number is 79 percent. Put another way: 45 percent of Democrats have a favorable opinion of journalists, while only 8 percent of Republicans do.[35] If the structural headwinds facing the news industry are politically neutral, impacting audiences across the ideological spectrum relatively evenly, what explains this stark partisan discrepancy? This book has provided an answer, albeit perhaps an unsatisfying one for those in search of quick or apolitical solutions. A critical disposition toward mainstream sources of news and information is deeply ingrained in right-wing political culture and has been since the earliest formations of the modern conservative movement in the late 1940s. If mainstream journalism is a perennially besieged component of our broader media culture, right-wing media is too. Both compete for who can craft the most compelling and salient narrative of our collective experiences. Ironically, if we wish to put an end to the idea of liberal media bias, we will need to recognize and embrace journalism as an unavoidably political project.

ACKNOWLEDGMENTS

This book exists because the late Marilyn Young encouraged me (given my background) to study the history of US conservatism, because Lisa Duggan told me I should pursue a PhD, and because Andrew Ross so generously guided me along the scholar-activist path. I owe these three debts I can never repay—which is especially ironic in the case of Andrew, given his vital work toward debt abolition. If you liked this book, please read theirs too.

Other dear mentors whose works you should also read: Cristina Beltrán, Nikhil Pal Singh, Anna McCarthy, Brett Gary, George Shulman, Josie Saldaña, Arlene Dávila, Jennifer Morgan, and Rodney Benson. This book builds on pathbreaking works by Victor Pickard, Nicole Hemmer, Kathryn Cramer Brownell, Heather Hendershot, Bethany Moreton, Rick Perlstein, John S. Huntington, and Joe Lowndes. Read them too.

I started writing this book's first draft back in 2011 and have been thinking about its core questions in earnest since 2009. In myriad untraceable yet vital ways this book has been shaped by my conversations with Eman Abdelhadi, Heather María Ács, Leticia Alvarado, Robert Asen, Nadia Awad, Jen Ayers, Scott Alves Barton, James Beacham, Kathleen Belew, Nolan Bennett, Max Besbis, TJ Billard, Jonah Birch, Sophie Bjork-James, Rich Blint, Annika Brockschmidt, Nikki Buskey, Ariana Ochoa Camacho, Robyn Caplan, André Carrington, Daniel Aldana Cohen, Andy Cornell, Mike Cowburn, Emma Shaw Crane, Ned Crowley, Thulani Davis, Dan DiMaggio, Sam

Dinger, Gordon Douglas, Sara Duvisac, Chelsea Ebin, Roy Edroso, Francesca Fallaci, Jess Feldman, Ben Gly Fogel, Josh Frens-String, Katie Gaddini, Emmaia Gelman, Michael Gould-Wartofsky, Miles Grier, Ayasha Guerin, Eva Hagerman, Christina Hanhardt, Brandon Harris, Ben Heath, Kari Hensley, JJ Hermes, Rebecca Hill, Emily Hue, Robert Inks, Caroline Jack, Sarah Jackson, Rana Jaleel, Gaurav Jashnani, Ronak Kapadia, Jenny Kelly, David Klassen, Curd Knüpfer, Liz Koslov, Emma Kreyche, Zenia Kish, Rebekah Larsen, Marisol LeBrón, Justin Leroy, Becca Lewis, Sean Larson, Lauren Lassabe Shepherd, Justin Abraham Linds, Johana Londoño, Claudia Sophía Garriga López, Cindy Ma, Alex Manevitz, Stefania Marghitu, Elizabeth Mesok, Manijeh Moradian, Joan Morgan, Rosy Mota, Debashree Mukherjee, Tim Neff, Sam Ng, Chris Nickell, Michelle O'Brien, Ayesha Omer, Robert Oxford, Jan Maghinay Padios, Mani Parcham, Anne Pasek, Roy Pérez, Elliott Powell, Jose Miguel Palacios, Landon Palmer, Cynthia Peacock, Nathan Pensler, Colette Perold, Laura Portwood-Stacer, Nate Preus, Seth Prins, Meredith Pruden, Natasha Raheja, Justin Rawlins, Brian Ray, Erica Robles-Anderson, Emily Rogers, Shelly Ronen, Srirupa Roy, Yashoda Sampath, Carolyn Schmitt, Stuart Schrader, Zach Schwartz-Weinstein, Kyle Shybunko, Anna Skarpelis, Rory Solomon, Shanté Smalls, Jackson Smith, Jennifer Flores Sternad, Sara Jane Stoner, Joe Sudbay, Bligesu Sümer, Sunaura Taylor, Christy Thornton, Leanne Tory-Murphy, Kaja Tretjak, Louie Dean Valencia, Nantina Vgontzas, Alyx Vesey, Laura Waldman, David Austin Walsh, Natalie Walshe, Damien Weaver, Abby Weitzman, Khadijah Costley White, Howell Williams, Ella Wind, Maya Wind, Tim Wood, and Yunkang Yang.

The ideas in this book have also been deeply shaped by a series of scholarly and journalistic collaborations. I am especially appreciative of my longtime collaborator and coauthor Anthony Nadler and of Reece Peck for being such generous and rigorous interlocutors. Other collaborators who have helped shape my thinking include Magda Konieczna, Clara Juarez Miro, and Isis Giraldo. Special thanks to Noelene Clark, Jhodie-Ann Williams, James Brandt, and the *Radical History Review* Digital Collective for the opportunities to write for wider audiences.

This book contributes to the burgeoning scholarly field of right-wing studies. My efforts to help organize this field partly explain why it took me so long to write. I am grateful to Lawrence Rosenthal for his work in establishing the Berkeley Center for Right-Wing Studies, and to Eliah

Bures and Kelly Jones for launching the *Journal of Right-Wing Studies*—important venues that provide the field with some institutional foundation. I am also appreciative of Eric Klinenberg and Michael Koncewicz at New York University's Institute for Public Knowledge, for their generous support of the global New Right working group I co-organize with Maya Vinokour and Leif Weatherby. Thanks, too, to Daniel Kreiss, Francesca Tripodi, Tressie McMillan Cottom, Shannon McGregor, and Meredith Clark for creating and sustaining the Center for Information, Technology, and Public Life at the University of North Carolina–Chapel Hill, and especially to Alice Marwick and Paul Elliott Johnson for organizing the CITAP working group for studying right-wing media. These spaces, and their many contributors whose names I can't even exhaustively list, have sustained my work beyond measure by placing it into community.

This work is also sustained by the field of journalism studies, and especially journalism history. Thanks to Matt Carlson, Sue Robinson, Seth Lewis, and Folker Hanusch for welcoming me into the former, and to Brian Creech, Josh Shepherd, Michael Socolow, Jeff Pooley, Dave Park, Matt Pressman, Dave Mindich, Elliot King, Rob Wells, Elisabeth Fondren, and Will Mari for helping me feel at home in the latter. Special thanks, too, to Paula Chakravartty, Rachel Kuo, and the editorial collective of *Communication, Culture & Critique* for helping keep me grounded in my home field of critical-cultural studies.

My research for this book was enabled by generous funding from the Graduate School of Arts and Science, the Global Research Initiative, and the Department of Social and Cultural Analysis at New York University as well as from the American Council of Learned Societies and Andrew W. Mellon Foundation. It was sustained by my employment in the Departments of Media and Communication Studies at Ursinus College; Media, Culture and Communication at New York University; and Journalism and Creative Media at the University of Alabama. I had too many wonderful colleagues to list at each institution, but I am especially thankful for my colleagues in Tuscaloosa for their support and comradery as the final iteration of this project took shape. Special thanks to The Polygon: Jess Maddox, Shaheen Kanthawala, and Kaitlin Miller.

As with any historical work, this book benefited immeasurably from the diligence and guidance of countless librarians and archivists, especially Tab Lewis at NARA, Crystal Brooks at Dallas Public Library, Linnea

Anderson at the University of Minnesota, Andrew Lee and Rosa Monteleone at NYU, Nicole Dittrich at Syracuse University, and Donna Davey, Rachel Yood, Erika Gottfried, and Kate Donovan at Tamiment Library. Thanks to Diana Bachman and Karen Wight at the University of Michigan, and Addison Merryman at Duke University for enabling my remote access to archives at their respective institutions. And thanks to Amy Ritchart for research assistance in processing the National News Council papers. Special thanks to James Gilbreath, and to his mother Andrea, for providing me with access to the private papers and personal library of Birmingham John Birch Society activist Jimmy C. Jones.

I am thankful to all the acquisition and series editors who saw the potential in this project early and sought to publish it, especially Nik Usher, Matt Becker, Kathy Roberts Forde, and Sid Bedingfield, who reviewed early chapter drafts and provided crucial feedback as I developed the manuscript. Thanks to Gwyneth Mellinger and Jacob Nelson for feedback on early chapter drafts, and to dear friends Tessa Moll, Sam Markwell, and Tej Nagaraja for reviewing chapters and serving as accountability buddies as I wrote and revised the manuscript. Thanks, too, to Steven Thrasher and Dan Berger for providing me with regular doses of levity along the way. Special thanks to the Columbia University Press production team (including two anonymous reviewers) and, especially, to my editor, Philip Leventhal, for his constructive feedback and persistence.

This book is an homage to my mother, Mary Anny Baker, who died before I could finish it but who at least knew it was for her. I am thankful for the ongoing care and support of my remaining family, especially my dad, Terry Bauer, and his wife, Caroline; my sister, Emily Sanders; Carole and Dick Bauer; Jane Bauer; Karen and Mike McCoy; and Bruce Baker. I am fortunate to have been welcomed and embraced by the Arettines and Katramados families—special thanks to Jasmine and George for enabling a well-timed writing retreat that allowed me to finally complete the manuscript.

This book is dedicated to my partner, Maria. Thank you for your patience, planning, support, and encouragement, without which this project and my work would be impossible. Thank you for your commitment to building community, for your strong ethical compass, and for your vision. Thank you for teaching me how to live free.

NOTES

INTRODUCTION

1. Benjamin Mullin, "Bezos Orders Washington Post Opinion Section to Embrace 'Personal Liberties and Free Markets,'" *New York Times*, February 26, 2025.
2. New York Times Pitchbot (@nytpitchbot.bsky.social). "The Washington Post and LA Times editorial pages have gone full MAGA, MSNBC has purged all of its anti-Trump anchors, and Twitter is owned by a literal Nazi. Here's why liberal media bias is still a problem." BlueSky, February 26, 2025, 9:07 a.m. CT. https://bsky.app/profile/nytpitchbot.bsky.social/post/3lj3nrp4bu222.
3. Eric Alterman, *What Liberal Media? The Truth About Bias and the News* (Basic Books, 2003); and Edward S. Herman and Noam Chomsky, *Manufacturing Consent: The Political Economy of the Mass Media* (Pantheon, 1988).
4. For more on this competition see A. J. Bauer and Anthony Nadler, "Competing for Cultural Authority: Journalism Studies Must Account for the Right," *Journalism Studies* 26, no. 5 (2025): 624–637.
5. See Rick Perlstein, *Before the Storm: Barry Goldwater and the Unmaking of the American Consensus* (Hill & Wang, 2001); Rick Perlstein, *Nixonland: The Rise of a President and the Fracturing of America* (Scribner, 2008); Rick Perlstein, *The Invisible Bridge: The Fall of Nixon and the Rise of Reagan* (Simon and Schuster, 2014); and Rick Perlstein, *Reaganland: America's Right Turn 1976–1980* (Simon and Schuster, 2021).
6. For a helpful overview of this historiography, see Kim Phillips-Fein, "Conservatism: A State of the Field," *Journal of American History* 98, no. 3 (2011): 723–743. See also A. J. Bauer, "The Alternative Historiography of the Alt-Right: Conservative Historical Subjectivity from the Tea Party to Trump," in *Far-Right Revisionism and the End of History: Alt-Histories*, ed. Louie Dean Valencia-García, 121–137. (Routledge, 2020).

7. Rick Perlstein, "I Thought I Understood the American Right. Trump Proved Me Wrong," *New York Times Magazine*, April 11, 2017.
8. Eleanor Clift, "Pat Buchanan: Donald Trump Stole My Playbook," *Daily Beast*, June 1, 2016; Nicole Hemmer, *Partisans: The Conservative Revolutionaries Who Remade American Politics in the 1990s* (Basic Books, 2022); and John Ganz, *When the Clock Broke: Con Men, Conspiracists, and How America Cracked Up in the Early 1990s* (Farrar, Straus and Giroux, 2024).
9. Matthew Dallek, *Birchers: How the John Birch Society Radicalized the American Right* (Basic Books, 2023); and Edward H. Miller, *A Conspiratorial Life: Robert Welch, the John Birch Society, and the Revolution of American Conservatism* (University of Chicago Press, 2021).
10. John S. Huntington, *Far-Right Vanguard: The Radical Roots of Modern Conservatism* (University of Pennsylvania Press, 2021), 7–8.
11. For more on modern conservatism's ideological incoherence and the role of enemy construction in bolstering it, see Paul Elliott Johnson, *I, The People: The Rhetoric of Conservative Populism in the United States* (University of Alabama Press, 2022).
12. George H. Nash, *The Conservative Intellectual Movement in America Since 1945* (Intercollegiate Studies Institute, 1998); Kevin Mattson, *Rebels All! A Short History of the Conservative Mind in Postwar America* (Rutgers University Press, 2008); and Corey Robin, *The Reactionary Mind: Conservatism from Edmund Burke to Sarah Palin* (Oxford University Press, 2011).
13. Conservatives will occasionally admit as much. See Mollie Ziegler Hemingway, *Trump vs. The Media* (Encounter Books, 2017).
14. Nicole Hemmer, *Messengers of the Right: Conservative Media and the Transformation of American Politics* (University of Pennsylvania Press, 2016), xii.
15. Hemmer references Arthur Schlesinger, *The Vital Center: The Politics of Freedom* (Houghton Mifflin, 1949); and Daniel Bell, *The End of Ideology: On the Exhaustion of Political Ideas in the Fifties* (Free Press, 1960).
16. Victor W. Pickard, *America's Battle for Media Democracy: The Triumph of Corporate Libertarianism and the Future of Media Reform* (Cambridge University Press, 2014).
17. See also Daniel Oppenheimer, *Exit Right: The People Who Left the Left and Reshaped the American Century* (Simon & Schuster, 2016); and Mattson, *Rebels All*.
18. For an apt visual metaphor of this historical formation, see Walter Benjamin, "Theses on the Philosophy of History," in Hannah Arendt, ed., *Illuminations*, trans. Harry Zohn (Shocken, 2007), 253–264; thesis IX.
19. For an overview of the liberal media literature, see Anthony Nadler and A. J. Bauer, "Conservative News Studies: Mapping an Unrealized Field," in Anthony Nadler and A. J. Bauer, eds., *News on the Right: Studying Conservative News Culture* (Oxford University Press, 2019), 233–236.
20. Perceptions of news media bias vary according to the eye of the beholder. See Tien-Tsung Lee, "The Liberal Media Myth Revisited: An Examination of Factors Influencing Perceptions of Media Bias," *Journal of Broadcasting & Electronic Media* 49, no. 1 (2005): 43–64; David Niven, *Tilt? The Search for Media Bias* (Praeger, 2002); and David

Edwards and David Cromwell, *Guardians of Power: The Myth of the Liberal Media* (Pluto, 2005). Not surprisingly, there have been works claiming to both prove and disprove the existence of liberal media bias. See, for example, Alterman, *What Liberal Media?* and Tim Groseclose, *Left Turn: How Liberal Media Bias Distorts the American Mind* (St. Martin's, 2011). The "liberal media" claim remains a perennial topic of books published by conservative presses and imprints. Examples: Reed Irvine, *Media Mischief and Misdeeds* (Regnery Gateway, 1984); Bernard Goldberg, *Bias: A CBS Insider Exposes How the Media Distort the News* (Regnery, 2001); Brian C. Anderson, *South Park Conservatives: The Revolt Against Liberal Media Bias* (Regnery, 2005); John Gibson, *How the Left Swiftboated America: The Liberal Media Conspiracy to Make You Think George Bush Was the Worst President in History* (Harper Collins, 2009); and Howard Kurtz, *Media Madness: Donald Trump, the Press, and the War on Truth* (Regnery, 2018).

21. See Eve Kosofsky Sedgwick, "Paranoid Reading and Reparative Reading, or, You're So Paranoid, You Probably Think this Essay Is About You," in *Touching Feeling: Affect, Pedagogy, Performativity* (Duke University Press, 2003), 123–151.

22. David Brock, *The Republican Noise Machine: Right-Wing Media and How It Corrupts Democracy* (Crown, 2004); and Jen Senko, *The Brainwashing of My Dad* (Sourcebooks, 2021). See also Jeff Sharlet, *The Family: The Secret Fundamentalism at the Heart of American Power* (HarperCollins, 2009); Jane Mayer, *Dark Money: The Hidden History of the Billionaires Beyond the Rise of the Radical Right* (Doubleday, 2016); Nancy MacLean, *Democracy in Chains: The Deep History of the Radical Right's Stealth Plan for America* (Viking, 2017); and Anne Nelson, *Shadow Network: Media, Money, and the Secret Hub of the Radical Right* (Bloomsbury, 2019).

23. For earlier works that reduce conservatism to one or a few psychological dispositions or intellectual tendencies, see especially Daniel Bell, ed. *The Radical Right: The New American Right, Expanded and Updated* (Doubleday, 1963); Richard Hofstadter, *The Paranoid Style in American Politics and Other Essays* (Knopf, 1966); Theodor W. Adorno, Else Frenkel-Brunswik, Daniel Levinson, and Nevitt Sanford, *The Authoritarian Personality* (Harper & Brothers, 1950); Nash, *Conservative Intellectual Movement*; and Robin, *Reactionary Mind*.

24. See especially Joseph E. Lowndes, *From the New Deal to the New Right: Race and the Southern Origins of Modern Conservatism* (Yale University Press, 2008); Joseph Crespino, *In Search of Another Country: Mississippi and the Conservative Counterrevolution* (Princeton University Press, 2007); Kevin Kruse, *White Flight: Atlanta and the Making of Modern Conservatism* (Princeton University Press, 2007); and Matthew D. Lassiter, *The Silent Majority: Suburban Politics in the Sunbelt South* (Princeton University Press, 2006).

25. Michael Omi and Howard Winant, *Racial Formation in the United States*, 3rd ed. (Routledge, 2014).

26. Edward H. Miller, *Nut Country: Right-Wing Dallas and the Birth of the Southern Strategy* (University of Chicago Press, 2015).

27. Daniel Martinez Hosang and Joseph E. Lowndes, *Producers, Parasites, Patriots: Race and the New Right-Wing Politics of Precarity* (University of Minnesota Press, 2019);

Geraldo L. Cadava, *The Hispanic Republican: The Shaping of an American Political Identity, from Nixon to Trump* (Ecco, 2020); and Cristina Beltrán, *The Trouble with Unity: Latino Politics and the Creation of Identity* (Oxford University Press, 2010). There is also a long history of conservatism among Black Americans. See Leah Wright Rigueur, *The Loneliness of the Black Republican: Pragmatic Politics and the Pursuit of Power* (Princeton University Press, 2014); and Angela D. Dillard, *Guess Who's Coming to Dinner Now? Multicultural Conservatism in America* (New York University Press, 2002).

28. Lauren Berlant, *The Queen of America Goes to Washington City: Essays on Sex and Citizenship* (Duke University Press, 1997).

29. Michelle M. Nickerson, *Mothers of Conservatism: Women and the Postwar Right* (Princeton University Press, 2014); Ronnee Schreiber, *Righting Feminism: Conservative Women and American Politics* (Oxford University Press, 2008); Catherine E. Rymph, *Republican Women: Feminism and Conservatism from Suffrage Through the Rise of the New Right* (University of North Carolina Press, 2006); and Donald T. Critchlow, *Phyllis Schlafly and Grassroots Conservatism: A Woman's Crusade* (Princeton University Press, 2005).

30. See Richard M. Mwakasege-Minaya, "Cold War Bedfellows: Cuban Exiles, US Conservatives, and Media Activism in the 1960s and 1970s," *Historical Journal of Film, Radio, and Television* 41, no. 1 (2021): 114–135; and Richard M. Mwakasege-Minaya, "Exiled Counterpoint: Cuban Exile Reception, Media Activism, Conservatism, and the National Educational Television Network," *Chiricú Journal: Latina/o Literatures, Arts, and Cultures* 4, no. 2 (2020): 37–61.

31. Brett Gary, *The Nervous Liberals: Propaganda Anxieties from World War I to the Cold War* (Columbia University Press, 1999); and J. Michael Sproule, *Propaganda and Democracy: The American Experience of Media and Mass Persuasion* (Cambridge University Press, 1997).

32. Morris L. Ernst, *The First Freedom* (Macmillan, 1946), 279, Exhibit A.

33. Ernst, *The First Freedom*, 288, Exhibit F.

34. Ernst, *The First Freedom*, 289, Exhibit G.

35. See Pickard, *America's Battle for Media Democracy*. The mid-1940s saw the publication of several books advancing structural criticisms of the press, contributing to the increased public focus. See, for example, Oswald Villard, *The Disappearing Daily: Chapters in American Newspaper Evolution* (Knopf, 1944); George Marion, *The 'Free Press': Portrait of a Monopoly* (New Century, 1946); Robert Cushman, *Keep Our Press Free* (Public Affairs Committee, 1946); and Leon Svirsky, ed., *Your Newspaper: Blueprint for a Better Press* (Macmillan, 1947).

36. Betty Houchin Winfield, *FDR and the News Media* (University of Illinois Press, 1990), 109; Pickard, *America's Battle for Media Democracy*, 125–128; and Richard W. Steele, *Propaganda in an Open Society: The Roosevelt Administration and the Media, 1933–1941* (Greenwood, 1985).

37. Pickard, *America's Battle for Media Democracy*, 124–151.

38. The Commission on Freedom of the Press, *A Free and Responsible Press: A General Report on Mass Communication* (University of Chicago Press, 1947).
39. "In the Matter of Editorializing by Broadcast Licensees," Docket No. 8516, *Federal Communications Commission Reports* 13 (July 1, 1948–June 30, 1949): 1246–1270; 1249.
40. Gordon Carroll, "Dr. Roosevelt's Propaganda Trust," *American Mercury*, September 1937, 1–31; Gordon Carroll, "How the WPA Buys Votes," *American Mercury*, October 1937, 194–213; and Gordon Carroll, "Propaganda from the White House," *American Mercury*, November 1937, 319–336.
41. Michael Denning, *The Cultural Front: The Laboring of American Culture in the Twentieth Century* (Verso, 1996).
42. Ernest Boyd, "The United Affront," *American Mercury*, November 1937, 275–283; 277.
43. Albert Jay Nock, "The Difficulty of Thinking," *American Mercury*, November 1937, 358–361.
44. Albert Jay Nock, "Isaiah's Job," *Atlantic Monthly*, June 1936, 641–649.
45. Fred G. Clark and Richard Stanton Rimanoczy, *How to Be Popular, Though Conservative* (D. Van Nostrand, 1948), 19. While the book's circulation size is unclear, it was excerpted in *Reader's Digest*, exposing it to millions of readers. See "How We Live: Excerpts from the book 'How to Be Popular Though Conservative,'" *Reader's Digest*, October 1948, 136–137.
46. Kim Phillips-Fein, *Invisible Hands: The Businessmen's Crusade Against the New Deal* (Norton, 2009); Elizabeth A. Fones-Wolf, *Selling Free Enterprise: The Business Assault on Labor and Liberalism, 1945–60* (University of Illinois Press, 1994); Bethany Moreton, *To Serve God and Wal-Mart* (Harvard University Press, 2009); and Caroline Jack, *Business As Usual: How Sponsored Media Sold American Capitalism in the Twentieth Century* (University of Chicago Press, 2024).
47. "Why Headlines?" *Headlines, and What's Behind Them*, July 30, 1938, 4, emphasis in original.
48. American Business Consultants, *Red Channels: The Report of Communist Influence in Radio and Television* (Counterattack, 1950), 1.
49. Heather Hendershot, *What's Fair on the Air? Cold War Right-Wing Broadcasting and the Public Interest* (University of Chicago, 2011).
50. "Famous Wildcatter Finds Word to Help Bewildered World: It Is 'Constructive,'" *Shreveport Times*, December 3, 1950.
51. William F. Buckley Jr., "Our Mission Statement," *National Review*, November 19, 1955.
52. Hemmer, *Messengers of the Right*.
53. Robert Welch, *The Blue Book of the John Birch Society* (Western Islands, 1959), 64–73.
54. See *Thunder on the Right*, a 1962 CBS News documentary hosted by Eric Sevareid.
55. Paul Matzko, *The Radio Right: How a Band of Broadcasters Took on the Federal Government and Built the Modern Conservative Movement* (Oxford University Press, 2020).
56. See, for example, Irving G. McCann, *Case History of the Smear by CBS of Conservatives* (McCann Press, 1966).

57. William F. Buckley, "The Question of Robert Welch," *National Review*, February 13, 1962, 83–88.
58. "Minutes of the Meeting of the Board of Directors of the American Conservative Union, December 18–19, 1964," Box 20, Folder 12, American Conservative Union papers, MSS 176, Brigham Young University (hereafter, BYU).
59. David Greenberg, "The Idea of 'the Liberal Media' and Its Roots in the Civil Rights Movement," *The Sixties: A Journal of History, Politics and Culture* 1, no. 2 (2008): 167–186.
60. William Gillis, "The Anti-Semitic Roots of the 'Liberal News Media' Critique," *American Journalism* 34, no. 3 (2017), 262–288.
61. Timothy J. Lombardo, *Blue-Collar Conservatism: Frank Rizzo's Philadelphia and Populist Politics* (University of Pennsylvania Press, 2018); Ronald P. Formisano, *Boston Against Busing: Race, Class, and Ethnicity in the 1960s and 1970s* (University of North Carolina Press, 1991); and Jonathan Rieder, *Canarsie: The Jews and Italians of Brooklyn Against Liberalism* (Harvard University Press, 1985).
62. Christopher Cimaglio, "'A Tiny and Closed Fraternity of Privileged Men:' The Nixon-Agnew Anti-Media Campaign and the Liberal Roots of the US Conservative 'Liberal Media' Critique," *International Journal of Communication* 10 (2016), 1–19.
63. Cecilie Gaziano, "How Credible Is the Credibility Crisis?" *Journalism Quarterly* 65, no. 2 (1988): 267–279; and Nik Usher, "Re-Thinking Trust in the News," *Journalism Studies* 19, no. 4 (2018): 564–578.
64. Edith Efron, *The News Twisters* (Nash Publishing, 1971); and Kevin P. Phillips, *Mediacracy: American Parties and Politics in the Communications Age* (Doubleday, 1975).
65. S. Robert Lichter and Stanley Rothman, "Media and Business Elites," *Public Opinion* 4, no. 5 (1981): 42–46, 59–60; and S. Robert Lichter, Stanley Rothman, and Linda S. Lichter, *The Media Elite: America's News Powerbrokers* (Adler & Adler, 1986). As of February 2025, *The Media Elite* has been cited in nearly seven hundred scholarly works.
66. Brian Rosenwald, *Talk Radio's America: How an Industry Took Over a Political Party That Took Over the United States* (Harvard University Press, 2019).
67. Reece Peck, *Fox Populism: Branding Conservatism as Working Class* (Cambridge University Press, 2019).
68. Yochai Benkler, Robert Faris and Hal Roberts, *Network Propaganda: Manipulation, Disinformation, and Radicalization in American Politics* (Oxford University Press, 2018).
69. Kathleen Hall Jamieson and Joseph Cappella, *Echo Chamber: Rush Limbaugh and the Conservative Media Establishment* (Oxford University Press, 2008).
70. Daniel Kreiss and Shannon C. McGregor, "A Review and Provocation: On Polarization and Platforms," *New Media & Society* 26, no. 1 (2023), 556–579; Deen Freelon, Alice Marwick and Daniel Kreiss, "False Equivalencies: Online Activism from Left to Right," *Science* 369, no. 6508 (2020): 1197–1201; and Benkler, Faris, and Roberts, *Network Propaganda*.
71. Nadler and Bauer, *News on the Right*.

1. THE FAIRNESS DOCTRINE AND ITS SUBTEXTS

1. Quotes transcribed by the author from a forty-minute recording of McIntire's broadcast on September 19, 1973, that has been preserved by the Shortwave Radio Audio Archive, a project of the Internet Archive. It is accessible at https://archive.org/details/sraa-radio-free-america-circa-1973. For details about the ship, see Albin Krebs, "McIntire Unable to Get 'Pirate' Radio Ship Going," *New York Times*, August 31, 1973, 56; and "M'Intire Vows Fight to the End," *New York Times*, September 4, 1973, 79.
2. See Mark Goodman and Mark Gring, "The Ideological Fight over Creation of the Federal Radio Commission in 1927," *Journalism History* 26, no. 3 (2000), 117–124; and Hugh G. J. Aitken, "Allocating the Spectrum: The Origins of Radio Regulation," *Technology and Culture* 35, no. 4 (1994), 686–716.
3. "M'Intire Vows Fight to the End"; and Donald Janson, "McIntire Loses 6 Blocks in Cape May in a Tax Sale," *New York Times*, September 7, 1973, 74.
4. Donald Janson, "McIntire Silences Pirate Radio at Sea," *New York Times*, September 21, 1973, 45; "McIntire's Station Barred by a Judge from Broadcasting," *New York Times*, September 22, 1973, 63; and "Court Keeps McIntire Off the Air," *New York Times*, February 22, 1974, 71.
5. Heather Hendershot, *What's Fair on the Air Cold War Right-Wing Broadcasting and the Public Interest* (University of Chicago Press, 2011).
6. Donald Janson, "Fundamentalist Has Plan for Pirate Radio Station," *New York Times*, June 25, 1973, 37.
7. "In the Matter of Editorializing by Broadcast Licensees," Docket No. 8516, *Federal Communications Commission Reports* 13 (July 1, 1948–June 30, 1949): 1246–1270; 1249.
8. "Station Accused of Rightist Stand," *New York Times*, October 15, 1967, 53.
9. "Whitehead Again Assails FCC Rules," *New York Times*, June 9, 1973, 67; and Donald Janson, "McIntire Gains Support in Radio Station Dispute," *New York Times*, December 3, 1973.
10. Victor W. Pickard, *America's Battle for Media Democracy: The Triumph of Corporate Libertarianism and the Future of Media Reform* (Cambridge University Press, 2014), 3–4, emphasis in original.
11. Portions of this chapter first appeared in A. J. Bauer, "Propaganda in the Guise of News: Fulton Lewis Jr. and the Origins of the Fairness Doctrine," *Radical History Review* 141 (2021): 7–29.
12. New Deal–era media reformers were constrained by earlier decisions of the Federal Radio Commission, which had distinguished between programming that promoted the "private or selfish interests" of station owners and the similarly self-interested promotion of commercial advertising. While allowing the former would risk stifling speech (since there are more individual perspectives than broadcast frequencies), failing to allow the latter would deprive stations of a lucrative source of operating revenue. In opposing editorialization, New Dealers were responding to a regulatory environment that already problematized non-commercial editorial speech. See Robert McChesney,

Telecommunications, Mass Media, and Democracy: The Battle for the Control of US Broadcasting, 1928–1935 (Oxford University Press, 1988), 27.

13. "In the Matter of the Mayflower Broadcasting Corporation, for Construction Permit, and the Yankee Network, Inc. (WAAB), for Renewal of Licenses (Main and Auxiliary)," *Federal Communications Commission Reports* 8 (March 1, 1940–August 1, 1941), 333–341; 340.

14. Pickard, *America's Battle for Media Democracy*, 45–51. As to the partisanship of the hearings, a Fly colleague at the FCC, Marcus Cohn, later recalled: "One of the reasons it was a big issue is that during the preceding elections a vast majority of the newspapers in America were anti-Roosevelt. Fly, of course, adored Roosevelt and adored the New Deal and what the New Deal stood for. The history was that it was the newspapers which were beginning to be more and more prominent in radio, and of course the popularity of radio continued to increase daily ... It was terribly important from Fly's point of view that radio be kept independent of the newspapers." See Sally Fly Connell, interview with Marcus Cohn, July 31, 1967, 6–7, James Lawrence Fly Project, Oral History Research Office Collection of the Columbia University Libraries.

15. Testimony of Carl McIntire, "Official Report of Proceedings Before the Federal Communications Commission in the Matter of Editorializing by Broadcast Licensees, Docket No. 8516," Vol. 4 (March 4, 1948), 693, RG173, Docketed Case Files, Docket No. 8516, Box 3385, Records of the Federal Communications Commission (hereafter, FCC), National Archives and Records Administration, College Park, Maryland (hereafter, NARA).

16. Testimony of James Lawrence Fly, "Official Report of Proceedings Before the Federal Communications Commission in the Matter of Editorializing by Broadcast Licensees, Docket No. 8516," Vol. 2 (March 2, 1948), 309, RG173, Docketed Case Files, Docket No. 8516, Box 3385, FCC, NARA.

17. An abundance of protest letters came from Catholics expressing agreement with an article titled "Against One-Sided Arguments on the Air," which was published in *Our Sunday Visitor* on February 8, 1948. See RG173, Docketed Case Files, Docket No. 8516, Box 3384, FCC, NARA.

18. Testimony of Frank Stanton, "Official Report of Proceedings Before the Federal Communications Commission in the Matter of Editorializing by Broadcast Licensees, Docket No. 8516," Vol. 1 (March 1, 1948), 43, RG173, Docketed Case Files, Docket No. 8516, Box 3385, FCC, NARA.

19. Stanton cited Charles Siepmann, "Shall Radio Take Sides?" *Nation*, February 21, 1948, 210–211; and Saul Carson, "Radio: Theater On the Air," *New Republic*, November 24, 1947, 38. Pickard notes the degree to which progressive fears that deregulating broadcasters would necessarily result in conservative bias influenced the hearings but does not consider how those reform efforts themselves bolstered the conservative movement they were hoping to forestall. Pickard, *America's Battle for Media Democracy*, 98–123.

20. Testimony of Frank Stanton, 45.

1. THE FAIRNESS DOCTRINE AND ITS SUBTEXTS   209

21. For example, see Letter from James H. Elliott to the FCC, undated, Box 3381, Docketed Case Files, Docket No. 8516, RG173, FCC, NARA. See also Pickard, *America's Battle for Media Democracy*, 110.
22. Letter from Erma Dutton to Chet Huntley, cc/FCC, February 17, 1948, Box 3387, Docketed Case Files, Docket No. 8516, RG173, FCC, NARA.
23. "A Confidential Statement by Sam Balter, Nation-wide News Commentator," Box 59, Folder "Mutual Broadcasting System, September 9, 1938 to May 31, 1948," File Class 44–3: "Complaints: Individual Name Files (Broadcast)," FCC Office of the Executive Director, General Correspondence, 1947–1956, RG 173, FCC, NARA.
24. Letter from H. A. Wallace to James L. Fly, February 18, 1944, File Class 44–3: "Complaints: Individual Name Files (Broadcast)," FCC Office of the Executive Director, General Correspondence, 1947–1956, RG 173, FCC, NARA.
25. Pickard, *America's Battle for Media Democracy*, 126.
26. Letter from Robert B. Lacy to James L. Fly, March 7, 1944, emphasis in original; Box 59, Folder "Mutual Broadcasting System, September 9, 1938 to May 31, 1948," File Class 44–3: "Complaints: Individual Name Files (Broadcast)," FCC Office of the Executive Director, General Correspondence, 1947–1956, RG 173, FCC, NARA.
27. Lewis married Alice Huston, daughter of Republican Party Chairman Claudius H. Huston, in 1930. President Herbert Hoover was invited to the wedding but, unable to make it due to illness, sent his regrets and a silver salad bowl. See "2,000 See Alice Huston Wed to Fulton Lewis, Jr.; Mrs. Gann and Cabinet Members Among Guests," *New York Times*, June 29, 1930.
28. For a hagiographic biography of Lewis, see Booton Herndon, *The Story of Fulton Lewis, Jr.: Praised and Damned* (Human Events, 1958). For a more critical contemporaneous biography, see Edwin A. Lahey, "Bedside Manner in Radio," in David Bulman, ed., *Molders of Opinion* (Bruce Publishing, 1945), 71–81.
29. The first mention of Fulton Lewis Jr. in *In Fact* was a passing suggestion that Lewis was in cahoots with the pro-business National Industrial Information Committee, which Seldes considered to be a fascist front, in the May 11, 1942, issue. The first major coverage of Lewis by Seldes came in the July 12, 1943, issue of *In Fact*, which devoted two pages to exposing his connections with the National Association of Manufacturers (NAM) and the DuPont campaign for "Free Enterprise." For more on the role that the DuPont campaign and NAM, played in fostering the modern conservative movement, see Kim Phillips-Fein, *Invisible Hands: The Businessmen's Crusade Against the New Deal* (Norton, 2009), 3–25.
30. George Seldes, *Facts and Fascism* (In Fact, 1943), 184–202.
31. Letter from Edward J. Gammons to the FCC, July 18, 1939, Box 57, Folder "Fulton Lewis, Jr., July 18, 1939 to March 7, 1947," File Class 44–3: "Complaints: Individual Name Files (Broadcast)," FCC Office of the Executive Director, General Correspondence, 1947–1956, RG 173, FCC, NARA. Lewis complaints fill three folders within the FCC archives, spread across Boxes 57 and 58. Some Lewis complaints were also filed within folders devoted to complaints against the Mutual Broadcasting System.

32. For a helpful history of the consumer cooperative movement of the era, see John Curl, *For All the People: Uncovering the Hidden History of Cooperation, Cooperative Movements, and Communalism in America* (PM Press, 2012), 164–191.
33. Lewis's initial broadcast series against consumer cooperatives occurred on February 20, 21, 24, 25, 26, 28, and March 4, 1947. For transcripts of broadcasts 1–4 and 6–7 see Box 119, Folder 4. For a transcript of broadcast 5, aired on February 26, 1947, see Box 120, Folder 5. All located in Part I, Fulton Lewis Jr. Papers (FLJ), Special Collections Research Center, Syracuse University (hereafter SU).
34. "Fulton Lewis Jr. America's Foremost Radio Commentator Denounces 'Outright Dishonest' of Co-Op 'We Pay Taxes' Screams," Broadcast No. 3, February 24, 1947, Part I, Box 119, Folder 4, FLJ, SU.
35. "Minutes of the Meeting of the Incorporators for the Purpose of Electing Directors," National Tax Equality Association, November 18, 1943, Part I, Box 119, Folder 5, FLJ, SU.
36. Letter from C. A. Keller to Fulton Lewis, Jr., April 24, 1944. Part I, Box 119, Folder 5, FLJ, SU.
37. Correspondence from Murphy (which ranges from short notes affixed to memoranda to full letters) can be found throughout Lewis's research files on cooperatives, housed in Boxes 119–122, Part 1, FLJ, SU. While Murphy's exact title is unclear, his letters often arrived on NTEA letterhead.
38. Several letters between Lewis and NTEA leadership refer to conversations held by telephone, the contents of which have gone unrecorded. While correspondence does not indicate a financial relationship between Lewis and NTEA, such a relationship cannot be ruled out. For evidence of NTEA's advance notice, see "Highly Confidential" Letter from Ben C. McCabe to NTEA membership, February 18, 1947, Part I, Box 121, Folder 1, FLJ, SU.
39. See, for examples, "News via Fulton Lewis," *Cooperative Consumer*, March 6, 1947; and "An Open Letter to Fulton Lewis, Jr.," *Appleton Cooperator*, March 1947, both in Part 1, Box 121, Folder 1, FLJ, SU. The NTEA brought their disagreement with NAM to Lewis's attention, providing him with a detailed summary of the NAM position on cooperatives (namely, that they ought not be taxed the same as for-profit business entities). See "Summary of the NAM Position," by NTEA, Part I, Box 121, Folder 2, FLJ, SU.
40. The Gaeth broadcasts aired from March 3–5, 1947. For transcripts of all three, reproduced in pamphlet form by the National Council of Farmer Cooperatives, see Part I, Box 119, Folder 4, FLJ, SU.
41. "Arthur Gaeth . . . Learns the Facts About Farmers Purchasing Cooperatives from W. G. Wysor," Broadcast No. 3, March 5, 1947 (National Council of Farmer Cooperatives), Part 1, Box 119, Folder 4, FLJ, SU.
42. For transcripts of the Southern States Cooperative meeting at which Lewis was ousted, see Part I, Box 122, Folder 4. See also "Fulton Lewis, Jr., Ousted from So. States Co-Op, Will Ask Supreme Court to Determine Farmers' Right to Criticize Their Cooperatives," National Tax Equality Association, Bulletin No. 76, October 15, 1947. Part I, Box 122, Folder 3, FLJ, SU.

1. THE FAIRNESS DOCTRINE AND ITS SUBTEXTS   211

43. Telegram from Ben C. McCabe to Edgar Kobak, president of Mutual Broadcasting System, March 11, 1947, Part I, Box 122, Folder 1, FLJ, SU.
44. Ross Murphy of the NTEA passed along an eight-page opposition research report on Voorhis to Lewis, emphasizing his friendliness with Upton Sinclair and his earlier socialist activities. See Memorandum from Steve O'Donnell to Ross Murphy Regarding Jerry Voorhis, February 25, 1948. Part I, Box 120, Folder 2, FLJ, SU.
45. For Lewis's extended reflections on the cooperative controversy, see his untitled, unpublished book manuscript on the subject. In it, Lewis depicts himself as an earnest investigative reporter besieged by pro-cooperative "propaganda." Part I, Box 71, Folder "MCC Book About Cooperatives," FLJ, SU.
46. News of the founding of the Voice of Freedom Committee came on the same day (March 3, 1947) that liberal commentator Arthur Gaeth began his rebuttal of the Lewis broadcasts. Indeed, both events were covered in the same "Heard and Overheard" column in *PM*. See Seymour Peck, "New Group to Battle for Liberals in Radio," *New York PM*, March 3, 1947.
47. While coordinated, the VOF wished to appear uncoordinated. One newsletter advised prospective monitors, "Never write in the name of the Voice of Freedom—our strength is in the sum of your individual letters." See "It's Your Write," *Voice of Freedom*, November 1947, 3. My analysis of the *Voice of Freedom* newsletters used those in the collection of Tamiment Library and Robert F. Wagner Archive, New York University.
48. "The High Cost of Living with Fulton Lewis, Jr." *Voice of Freedom*, November 1947, 4.
49. For another example of progressive media critics who tended to blame political disagreement on propaganda, see especially the Institute for Propaganda Analysis. A. J. Bauer, "Glittering Generalities: Reconsidering the Institute for Propaganda Analysis," *International Journal of Communication* 18 (2024), 1976–1994.
50. "Listen with Your Eyes Open!" *Voice of Freedom*, November 1947, 1.
51. "Who's Telling You What to Think?" *Voice of Freedom*, December 1947, 2.
52. "Who's Telling You What to Think?," 3.
53. Letter from Stella Holt to Mr. Slowie of the FCC, October 4, 1947; Letter from Stella Holt to Commissioner Walker, November 12, 1947; and Letter from T. J. Slowie to Stella Holt, November 21, 1947; all in RG173, Docketed Case Files, Docket No. 8516, Box 3383, FCC, NARA.
54. Testimony of Stanley Faulkner, "Official Report of Proceedings Before the Federal Communications Commission in the Matter of Editorializing by Broadcast Licensees, Docket No. 8516," Vol. 2 (March 2, 1948), 245, 242, 258–259.
55. "Fulton Lewis Jr. America's Foremost Radio Commentator Reveals How Co-Ops Dodge Income Taxes and Grow into Monopolies," Broadcast No. 2, February 21, 1947, Part I, Box 119, Folder 4, FLJ, SU.
56. "Fulton Lewis Jr. (A co-op member) Exposes Co-op Tyranny over Members," August 14, 1947. Part I, Box 120, Folder 3, FLJ, SU.
57. Letter from W. G. Wysor to Benedict T. Cottone, general counsel of the FCC, October 31, 1947, with enclosed correspondence between Wysor and Mutual Broadcasting System from August and September, RG173, Docketed Case Files, Docket No. 8516,

Box 3383, FCC, NARA. Wysor's initial letter to Mutual was dated August 21, 1947. Mutual's rejection of his request came in a letter dated September 10, 1947. He waited until October 31, after Southern States had formally expelled Lewis from its cooperative, before reiterating his equal time request and alerting the FCC.

58. Announcement of order for hearings concerning broadcast editorials, issued by FCC secretary T. J. Slowie, September 5, 1947, RG173, Docketed Case Files, Docket No. 8516, Box 3383, FCC, NARA.

59. Pickard, *America's Battle for Media Democracy*, 113. See also "List of Organizations to Whom Editorialization Letter Was Sent," and "List of Individuals to Whom Editorialization Letter Was Sent," both in RG173, Docketed Case Files, Docket No. 8516, Box 3383, FCC, NARA.

60. Letter from T. J. Slowie to W. G. Wysor, November 7, 1947, RG173, Docketed Case Files, Docket No. 8516, Box 3383, FCC, NARA.

61. Testimony of Angus MacDonald, "Official Report of Proceedings Before the Federal Communications Commission in the Matter of Editorializing by Broadcast Licensees, Docket No. 8516," Vol. 4 (March 4, 1948), 658–690; 660, 665.

62. Testimony of Norman Matthews, "Official Report of Proceedings Before the Federal Communications Commission in the Matter of Editorializing by Broadcast Licensees, Docket No. 8516," Vol. 8 (April 21, 1948), 1365–1385; 1380, RG173, Docketed Case Files, Docket No. 8516, Box 3386, FCC, NARA.

63. Testimony of John Carson, "Official Report of Proceedings Before the Federal Communications Commission in the Matter of Editorializing by Broadcast Licensees, Docket No. 8516," Vol. 8 (April 21, 1948), 1314–1325; 1319.

64. Testimony of John Carson, 1316, 1324.

65. "US Radio Analyst in Red Influx, Dies Charges," *Washington Post*, November 19, 1941; and "FCC Analyst No Communist, Fly Declares," *Washington Post*, November 20, 1941. See also "Conferees Agree to Oust 3 Officials," *Washington Post*, June 24, 1943.

66. Sally Fly Connell, interview with Thomas Corcoran, July 31, 1967, 19, James Lawrence Fly Project, Oral History Research Office Collection of the Columbia University Libraries.

67. Jack Gould, "Right-Wing Radio Is Under Inquiry," *New York Times*, January 17, 1963, 5; and Jack Gould, "Radio: Export of Anger," *New York Times*, April 9, 1963, 72.

68. Donald Janson and Bernard Eismann, *The Far Right* (McGraw-Hill, 1963), 140–141, 227.

69. "The Radical Right in America Today," memorandum from Victor G. Reuther (on behalf of Walter) to Robert F. Kennedy, December 10, 1961, Box 63, Folder "Reuther Memorandum, 12/10/1961: 'The Radical Right,'" p. 21, Robert F. Kennedy Papers, John F. Kennedy Presidential Library, Boston, Massachusetts.

70. Conservatives were not entirely wrong to take the Reuther Memo seriously. See Paul Matzko, *Radio Right: How a Band of Broadcasters Took on the Federal Government and Built the Modern Conservative Movement* (Oxford University Press, 2020).

71. For references to circulation of the memo by Hargis and McIntire's ally Edgar Bundy, president of the Church League of America, see the folders pertaining to the Reuther

Memorandum in Box 63, Robert F. Kennedy Papers, John F. Kennedy Presidential Library. See also Donald McKnight, "IRS Discrimination Against Fundamentalists Charged," *Christian Beacon*, April 20, 1967, 5.

72. "This Week in Washington," *Human Events*, June 15, 1963, 164.

2. THE PROGRESSIVE ORIGINS OF CONSERVATIVE PRESS CRITICISM

1. Testimony of Morris L. Ernst, "Official Report of Proceedings Before the Federal Communications Commission in the Matter of Editorializing by Broadcast Licensees, Docket No. 8516," Vol. 3 (March 3, 1948), 401–402, RG173, Docketed Case Files, Docket No. 8516, Box 3385, FCC, NARA.
2. Mark Feldstein, *Poisoning the Press: Richard Nixon, Jack Anderson, and the Rise of Washington's Scandal Culture* (Farrar, Straus and Giroux, 2010).
3. David Greenberg, "The Idea of 'the Liberal Media and Its Roots in the Civil Rights Movement," *The Sixties: A Journal of History, Politics and Culture* 1, no. 2 (2008): 167–186; and Christopher Cimaglio, "'A Tiny and Closed Fraternity of Privileged Men': The Nixon–Agnew Anti-Media Campaign and the Liberal Roots of the US Conservative 'Liberal Media' Critique." *International Journal of Communication* 10 (2016): 1–19.
4. David Brock, *Republican Noise Machine: Right-Wing Media and How It Corrupts Democracy* (Crown, 2004); and Jen Senko, *The Brainwashing of My Dad* (Sourcebooks, 2021).
5. See Cimaglio, "A Tiny and Closed Fraternity."
6. Brett Gary, *Dirty Works: Obscenity on Trial in America's First Sexual Revolution* (Stanford University Press, 2021).
7. For an extremely helpful critical biography of Ernst, see Brett Gary, "Morris Ernst's Troubled Legacy," *Reconstruction: Studies in Contemporary Culture* 8, no. 1 (2008), 22–37. Gary suggests that Ernst's hatred of communists may have resulted from his personal associations with them.
8. Gary, "Morris Ernst's Troubled Legacy," 24.
9. Corliss Lamont, ed., *The Trial of Elizabeth Gurley Flynn by the American Civil Liberties Union* (Horizon Press, 1968).
10. Harrison E. Salisbury, "The Strange Correspondence of Morris Ernst and John Edgar Hoover, 1939–1964," *Nation*, December 1, 1984, 575–577.
11. Gary, "Morris Ernst's Troubled Legacy," 31. See also Morris L. Ernst, "Why I No Longer Fear the FBI," *Reader's Digest*, December 1950. Ernst was by no means the only liberal supporter of Hoover. For a history that situates Ernst within a broader tradition of liberal collusion with domestic intelligence, see William W. Keller, *The Liberals and J. Edgar Hoover: Rise and Fall of a Domestic Intelligence State* (Princeton University Press, 1989).
12. Ernst, *First Freedom*, xi.

13. Victor W. Pickard, *America's Battle for Media Democracy: The Triumph of Corporate Libertarianism and the Future of Media Reform* (Cambridge University Press, 2014), 128.
14. Daniel Oppenheimer, *Exit Right: The People Who Left the Left and Reshaped the American Century* (Simon & Schuster, 2016).
15. George Seldes, *Witness to a Century: Encounters with the Noted, the Notorious, and the Three SOBs* (Ballantine, 1987).
16. A spring 1940 communiqué from the KGB New York Station to Moscow indicates that Seldes was also secretly affiliated with the Communist Party, although both Seldes and Minton vociferously denied it. Whether he was or wasn't is somewhat less important for our purposes than the controversy itself. See John Earl Haynes, Harvey Klehr, and Alexander Vassiliev, *Spies: The Rise and Fall of the KGB in America* (Yale University Press, 2009), 168–173.
17. George Seldes, *Never Tire of Protesting* (Lyle Stuart, 1968).
18. Seldes, *Never Tire of Protesting*, 202.
19. For a helpful, if somewhat hagiographic, overview of Seldes's influence among liberal and progressive activists, see Rick Goldsmith's 1996 documentary film *Tell the Truth and Run: George Seldes and the American Press* (New Day Films).
20. "The Color Line of the AP," *In Fact*, May 20, 1940, 4. My analysis of *In Fact* is based on my accessing complete bound volumes of the newsletter housed at Tamiment Library and Robert F. Wagner Archive, New York University (hereafter, TAM).
21. George Seldes, *The Facts Are . . . A Guide to Falsehood and Propaganda in the Press and Radio* (In Fact, 1942), 1–2.
22. Seldes, *The Facts Are*, 65.
23. Seldes, *The Facts Are*, 127.
24. "Tobacco Shortens Life," *In Fact*, January 13, 1941, 1–2, 4.
25. "Tobacco Shortens Life (Part 2)," *In Fact*, January 27, 1941, 3–4.
26. For example, see "America's Ruling Families—Ford, Mellon, DuPont, Rockefeller—Do Business with Enemy," *In Fact*, June 16, 1941.
27. "Press Bows to Ford," *In Fact*, July 21, 1941, 2.
28. George Seldes, *Facts and Fascism* (In Fact, 1943), 80.
29. Kim Phillips-Fein, *Invisible Hands: The Businessmen's Crusade Against the New Deal* (Norton, 2009), 13–15. See also George H. Nash, *Conservative Intellectual Movement in America Since 1945* (Intercollegiate Studies Institute, 1998).
30. Seldes, *Facts and Fascism*, 92–93.
31. Seldes, *Facts and Fascism*, 86.
32. Ronald Lora and William Henry Longton, eds., *The Conservative Press in Twentieth-Century America* (Greenwood, 1999), 243–252.
33. For more on the *Mercury*'s propaganda analysis, see A. J. Bauer, "Glittering Generalities: Reconsidering the Institute for Propaganda Analysis," *International Journal of Communication* 18 (2024): 1976–1994. For examples from *Scribner's Commentator*, see James L. Harvey, "Red Between the Lines," June 1940, 14–18; Sen. D. Worth Clark, "The

Men Behind Our War Scare," August 1940, 107–109; Frazier Hunt, "A Lesson in Propaganda," September 1940, 85–88; Charles J. Rolo, "Has American Duped Britain?" October 1940, 3–8; Kenneth Monroe, "British Propaganda: 1940 Version," November 1940, 51–55; Freeman Tilden, "The New York Influence—America's Journalistic Poison," December 1940, 7–12; "Priming the Propaganda Pump," February 1941, 3; and John T. Flynn, "Radio—Intervention's Trump," April 1942, 45–49.

34. See Joanne P. Sharp, *Condensing the Cold War: Reader's Digest and American Identity* (University of Minnesota Press, 2000).
35. Friedrich A. Hayek, "The Road to Serfdom," *Reader's Digest*, April 1945, 1–20.
36. "America's First Fascist Editor Joins Up," *In Fact*, November 16, 1942, 1, 3.
37. "New Reader's Digest Editor Makes Total of Seven Native Fascists, Anti-Semites, Nazi Favorites," *In Fact*, May 13, 1946.
38. *In Fact*, June 10, 1946.
39. *In Fact*, September 9, 1946; and *In Fact*, September 16, 1946.
40. "Dept of Justice Buckles to Reader's Digest; Refused to Try Eggleston, Drops Anti-Trust Suit," *In Fact*, November 4, 1946. In May 1947 a federal grand jury also cleared Douglas Stewart of any wrongdoing associated with the von Strempel testimony. See "Scribner's Commentator," in Lora and Longton, *Conservative Press*, 279.
41. Ralph de Toledano, "'In Fact'—Dope Sheet for the Masses—New Masses Style," *New Leader*, May 3, 1941, 4.
42. James A. Wechsler, "The Facts about *In Fact*," *New Leader*, April 22, 1944, 9.
43. While Lundberg lauded *PM*'s Washington bureau, he accused its editor, Ralph Ingersoll, of hiding his paper's favoritism toward the Communist Party behind support of New Deal liberal projects. See Ferdinand Lundberg, "PM: Crypticism—Versus—Crypticism," *New Leader*, June 13, 1942, 4; "The Record of PM," *New Leader*, June 20, 1942, 5; and "The Record of PM," *New Leader*, June 27, 1942, 4. For a thorough history of *PM*, and its many journalistic innovations, see Paul Milkman, *PM: A New Deal in Journalism, 1940–1948* (Rutgers University Press, 1997).
44. "Slants in the News" ran from the July 4, 1942, issue (vol. 25, no. 27) through the August 22, 1942, issue (vol. 25, no. 34) issue. The column's rationale is unstated, other than the headline, and opaque; the items commented upon suggest no discernible pattern or coherent critical approach. It was replaced in the August 29, 1942, issue by a regular column by Daniel Bell titled "Clippings and Comment," which contained no clippings per se but perhaps better described the odds-and-ends approach of his column and its predecessor. My analysis of *New Leader* in the 1940s is based on my accessing complete microfilm reels housed at TAM.
45. See "What a 'Life!'—Henry Luce Goes Intourist with Starry-Eyed Review of Stalin Regime," *New Leader*, April 17, 1943; Christopher Emmett, "Communist Agents and the Freedom of the Press," *New Leader*, June 16, 1945; William Henry Chamberlin and Raymond Leslie Buell, "Is Atlantic Monthly on the Side of Totalitarianism or Democracy?" *New Leader*, February 2, 1946; and William E. Hobn, "ADA in the 'Liberal Press,'" *New Leader*, January 18, 1947.

46. Oswald Garrison Villard, *The Disappearing Daily: Chapters in American Newspaper Evolution* (Knopf, 1944).
47. Oswald Garrison Villard, "Our Daily Press: Trend Is Toward Standardization, Illiberality, Loss of Independence," *New Leader*, December 14, 1946, 7, 19.
48. See, for example, "Have You Done Your Red-Baiting for Today?" *New Leader*, March 6, 1948, 32. The ad reads in part, "Ten years ago *The New Leader* called for Fascist-baiting to halt aggression. The job of halting aggression requires Red-baiting today. Intelligent Red-baiting, Fascist-baiting, bigotry-baiting should be done by real liberals who know the score."
49. Eugene Lyons, "I Expose Another 'Fascist:' One 'Red-Baiter' Debunks Another," *New Leader*, June 23, 1945, 9.
50. Eugene Lyons, "In Defense of Red-Baiting: A Red-Baiter Is One Who Does Not Delude Himself or Others," *New Leader*, December 7, 1946, 8.
51. Lyons, "In Defense of Red-Baiting." To be fair, Lyons lost his editorship of the *Mercury* in 1944 when the magazine was sold to Lawrence Spivak, who rehired former editor Charles Angoff and steered the magazine in a more liberal, centrist direction until 1950, when the magazine's editorial positions resumed their conservative, anti–New Deal stance. See "American Mercury," in Lora and Longton, *Conservative Press*, 243–252.
52. This march was both ideological and institutional. De Toledano was founding managing editor of *Plain Talk*, a position he filled from October 1946 through May of 1947, and by 1956 was a regular contributor, along with Lyons, to William F. Buckley's *National Review*. Lyons's first contribution to *National Review* appeared in its second issue (November 26, 1955), while de Toledano's first byline appeared the following April (18, 1956), in issue 22.
53. Nicole Hemmer, *Messengers of the Right: Conservative Media and the Transformation of American Politics* (University of Pennsylvania Press, 2016), 31–32. See also Mark Major, "Objective but Not Impartial: Human Events, Barry Goldwater, and the Development of the 'Liberal Media' in the Conservative Counter-Sphere," *New Political Science: A Journal of Politics and Culture* 34, no. 4 (2012): 455–458.
54. Joseph Charles Keeley, *The China Lobby Man: The Story of Alfred Kohlberg* (Arlington House, 1969), 190–209.
55. Keeley, *China Lobby Man*, 196–197.
56. Memorandum from T. C. Kirkpatrick to Alfred Kohlberg, John G. Keenan, William F. Higgins, Rev. John F. Cronin, and Isaac Don Levine, December 13, 1946, 1, Box 19, Folder 37, Research Files of Counterattack, TAM.
57. "Subject: George Seldes," July 25, 1946, Box 5, Folder 30, Research Files of Counterattack, TAM. Further research materials attempting to expose Seldes's personal foibles and political affiliations can be found in Box 5, Folder 31.
58. The Lewis broadcast was on March 14, 1947. The next day, he received a telegram with effusive praise from *Plain Talk* publisher Isaac Don Levine. As a result of demand from the broadcast, *Plain Talk* distributed fifty-five thousand reprints—a five-fold increase in its typical circulation of ten thousand. See Telegram from Isaac Don Levine to

Fulton Lewis Jr., March 18, 1947; and Letter from Isaac Don Levine to Fulton Lewis Jr., May 3, 1947, Part I, Box 81, Folder "'In Fact,' 1947," Fulton Lewis Jr. Papers, SU.

59. *Counterattack*'s editors were actually sympathetic to *The New Leader*, which they would later describe as representing "the anti-Communist and anti-totalitarian viewpoint of the 'labor-liberal' group." Announcing the formation of *The Freedman*, which would grow to become an influential right libertarian journal, *Counterattack* suggested that it would be of interest to *New Leader* readers. See *Counterattack*, October 20, 1950, 3.

60. Eugene Lyons, "Red Mouthpiece: The Facts Behind *In Fact*," *Plain Talk*, March 1947, 3–13; 13.

61. American Business Consultants, *Red Channels: The Report of Communist Influence in Radio and Television* (Counterattack, 1950). As a blacklist, *Red Channels* was by no means the first of its genre, nor the longest. Elizabeth Dilling's *The Red Network: A 'Who's Who' and Handbook of Radicalism for Patriots*, which she self-published in April 1934, listed more than 460 left radicals. Unlike *Red Channels*, *The Red Network* was not primarily focused on the influencing capacities of media (either print or broadcast).

62. *Counterattack*, July 28, 1950, 2.

63. "Nazi Favorite Writer Joins Reader's Digest," *In Fact*, March 3, 1947, 1–3; 3. Seldes had been publicly accusing Lyons of fascist sympathies since March 1942. See "Reader's Digest Smear," *In Fact*, March 9, 1942, 2–3.

64. *Counterattack*'s first mention of *In Fact* occurred in its third issue, dated June 6, 1947. Its first mention of George Seldes by name, and the first mention of the repeated allegation of Seldes's supposed connection to Earl Browder, occurred in the August 29, 1947, issue. My analysis of *Counterattack* is based on my accessing complete bound volumes of the newsletter housed at TAM.

65. "Wartime Espionage Agents Being Organized by Private Outfit to Spy on 'Subversives,'" *In Fact*, April 19, 1948, 2–4.

66. "Wartime Espionage Agents," 3. Beginning in 1938, the New Haven–based Constitutional Educational League published perhaps the first newsletter devoted to right anticommunist news media criticism called *Headlines and What's Behind Them*.

67. *Counterattack*, April 23, 1948, 3, emphasis in original.

68. "'Counterattack' Prints Sequel to Liz Dilling's 'Red Network,' Sets Self Up a Radio Censor," *In Fact*, July 15, 1950, 1.

69. "Editorial: To All Our Faithful Subscribers," *In Fact*, October 2, 1950, 2.

70. "Editorial: To All Our Faithful Subscribers," 2.

71. *Counterattack*, October 6, 1950, 2–3; 3.

72. Letter from Arthur G. McDowell to F. J. McNamara, May 5, 1953, Box 137, Folder 5, Philbrick Papers, Library of Congress (hereafter, LOC); and Letter from Arthur G. McDowell to John G. Keenan, October 6, 1958, Box 24, Folder 43, Research Files of Counterattack, TAM. For additional evidence of McDowell's friendly rapport with American Business Consultants, see Box 22, Folders 28 and 35, TAM.

73. Kirkpatrick was on CACA letterhead until his resignation from American Business Consultants in 1953, after which he was replaced by his *Counterattack* editor successor, F. J. McNamara. See letterhead of letters contained in Box 137, Folders 4–5, Philbrick Papers, LOC.
74. "Arthur McDowell Dies in Auto Crash While on Union Mission," *UIU Journal*, October 1966, pp. 1–2, Box 137, Folder 4, Philbrick Papers, LOC.

3. CULTIVATING A CONSERVATIVE CRITICAL DISPOSITION TOWARD THE PRESS

1. H. L. Hunt, "The Background of Facts Forum," *Facts Forum News*, December 1954, 26–28; 28. I accessed *Facts Forum News* in complete bound volumes housed at New York Public Library.
2. "In the Matter of Editorializing by Broadcast Licensees," Docket No. 8516, *Federal Communications Commission Reports* 13 (July 1, 1948–June 30, 1949), 1257–1258.
3. The $5 million estimate was based on Hunt's memory in 1966. See "Playboy Interview: H. L. Hunt," *Playboy*, August 1966, 51. A contemporaneous report claimed that Facts Forum radio and television programming cost around $4 million per year, with more than $3 million in airtime covered "by the stations that broadcast them and by about 30 commercial sponsors." See "Where One Texan's Money Goes: Oilman Hunt's Millions Keep Debate Forums on the Air," *US News & World Report*, January 28, 1955, 36. In addition to Hunt, Facts Forum reportedly was the beneficiary of some two thousand smaller donors.
4. "Facts Forum Radio-TV," *Facts Forum News*, January 1956, 57–61, 64.
5. Hunt, "The Background of Facts Forum," 28.
6. "A Prospect Inspects . . . Facts Forum Plan," n.d., 19, back cover, Box 204, Folder 16, J. B. Matthews Papers, David M. Rubenstein Rare Book and Manuscript Library, Duke University (hereafter, DU).
7. "Facts Forum Plan," June 1, 1951, 2, H. L. Hunt subject file, 62-HQ-108867, Part 3 of 3, Federal Bureau of Investigation, Ernie Lazar FOIA Collection (hereafter, LAZ), https://archive.org/details/lazarfoia, accessed August 17, 2016.
8. Heather Hendershot, *What's Fair on the Air Cold War Right-Wing Broadcasting and the Public Interest* (University of Chicago Press, 2011), 34.
9. Eugene Elkins, "Facts Needed," *Dallas Morning News*, August 8, 1951, 2.
10. Nicole Hemmer, *Messengers of the Right: Conservative Media and the Transformation of American Politics* (University of Pennsylvania Press, 2016), 111.
11. Quoted in Hendershot, *What's Fair on the Air*, 28.
12. William F. Buckley Jr., "The Liberal Mind," *Facts Forum News*, June 1955, 6, 52–57, 60.
13. For Hunt's firsthand account of his first interactions with the press, see H. L. Hunt, *H. L. Hunt Early Days* (Parade Press, 1973), 65–71. For a helpful secondary account, with

additional context, see Harry Hurt III, *Texas Rich: The Hunt Dynasty from the Early Oil Days through the Silver Crash* (Norton, 1981), 148–174.
14. "Southwest Has a New Crop of Super Rich," *Life*, April 5, 1948, 23.
15. "The Land of the Big Rich: Free-Wheeling Free Enterprise in That Capitalistic Oasis, the Southwest, USA," *Fortune*, April 1948, 98.
16. See Ardis Burst, *The Three Families of H. L. Hunt* (Weidenfeld & Nicolson, 1988).
17. Hurt, *Texas Rich*, 40–57.
18. Burst, *The Three Families of H. L. Hunt*, 33.
19. Warren Leslie, *Dallas Public and Private: Aspects of an American City* (Grossman, 1964), 88–89.
20. See Edward H. Miller, *Nut Country: Right-Wing Dallas and the Birth of the Southern Strategy* (University of Chicago Press, 2015).
21. Frank X. Tolbert, "'Richest man'—? Dallasite Doubts It," *Dallas Morning News*, April 4, 1948, as reprinted in Hunt, *H. L. Hunt Early Days*, 66–70.
22. Hunt, *H. L. Hunt Early Days*, 71.
23. Fred G. Clark and Richard Stanton Rimanoczy, *How to Be Popular, Though Conservative* (D. Van Nostrand, 1948), iii.
24. Hunt, *H. L. Hunt Early Days*, 78.
25. "Famous Wildcatter Finds Word to Help Bewildered World: It Is 'Constructive,'" *Shreveport Times*, December 3, 1950.
26. "Famous Wildcatter Finds Word."
27. "Constructive," *Shreveport Times*, December 3, 1950; emphasis in original.
28. "In the Matter of Editorializing by Broadcast Licensees," 1257–1258.
29. *A Program for Community Anti-Communist Action* (Chamber of Commerce, USA, 1948), 14.
30. The feelings between the Chamber of Commerce and American Business Consultants appear to have been mutual, as the latter cross-promoted *A Program for Community Anti-Communist Activity* in the pages of *Counterattack*. See *Counterattack*, November 5, 1948.
31. *A Program for Community Anti-Communist Action*, 19, 22.
32. *A Program for Community Anti-Communist Action*, 20.
33. "Facts Forum Group Holds First Meeting," *Dallas Morning News*, June 6, 1951, 3.
34. "Facts Forum Organizes Seven Units in Dallas," *Dallas Morning News*, June 10, 1951, 12.
35. This is Smoot's own autobiographical narrative of his early years. For a truncated version, see "Who Is the Man?" *Dan Smoot Report*, August 5, 1957, 5–6. For a more detailed one, see Dan Smoot, *People Along the Way* (Tyler Press, 1993).
36. Smoot's brief promotional bio, which always included his FBI service prominently, can be found in each issue of his newsletter *Dan Smoot Reports* (originally called *Dan Smoot Speaks*) as well as on the dust jackets of his books, including *The Hope of the World* (Miller Publishing, 1958) and *The Invisible Government* (Western Islands, 1962), among others. While Smoot's FBI file indicates service in two of the bureau's central

Washington, DC–based divisions, there is little evidence of a direct working relationship with Hoover. See the bureau's "Permanent Brief" for Howard D. Smoot, Memo to Mr. Callahan from C. R. Davidson on the Subject of "Howard D. Smoot, Former Special Agent," April 17, 1961, 6–7, Dan Smoot, FBI Employees Sub-collection, LAZ.

37. Smoot resigned from the FBI on June 15 and was hired by Facts Forum on June 25, 1951.
38. See, for examples, "Jaycees Learn of Facts Forum," *Paris News*, July 19, 1951, 16; "Kiwanians Told of Facts Forum Work by Ex-FBI Agent," *Greenville Evening Banner*, August 15, 1951, 3; "Oak Cliff Lions Club," *Dallas Morning News*, August 29, 1951, 13; "Club to Hear Smoot," *Dallas Morning News*, October 10, 1951, 3; and "Town North Club to Hear Ex-FBI Man," *Dallas Morning News*, October 21, 1951, 9.
39. "Pro America Group Sponsors Free Liberty Hall Address," *El Paso Herald-Post*, September 9, 1952, 4.
40. "Former FBI Agent Speaks in El Paso," *El Paso Herald-Post*, September 23, 1952, 1.
41. "Texas Has 500 Reds, Former FBI Agent Says," *El Paso Herald-Post*, September 24, 1952, 5. For Facts Forum's account of the gathering, including the claim of twelve hundred attendees, see *Facts Forum News*, October 6, 1952, 3. The *Herald-Post* article did not include an audience count but referred to it as "large."
42. "YMCA Adult Program Activities Include Dance, Golf Instruction," *El Paso Herald-Post*, October 20, 1952, 19; and "YMCA Officials Plan Expansion of Programs," *El Paso Herald-Post*, January 5, 1953, 15. The Pro America group also sponsored local broadcasts of Dan Smoot's radio program, see "El Paso Group Sponsors Facts Forum Air Show," *Facts Forum News*, July 1954, 5.
43. Facts Forum ran ads with this wording in the classified section of the *El Paso Herald-Post* on January 5–7, 1953.
44. A report of a Facts Forum library being established in the home of Mrs. Harold L. Richey can be found in *Facts Forum News*, October 27, 1952, 3. By the summer of 1953 a second such library had opened in El Paso in the home of Mrs. H. P. Talley. See "Pro-America Recommends Amendment," *El Paso Herald-Post*, July 1, 1953, 14.
45. "Jaycees Learn of Facts Forum."
46. "Facts Forum Plans Future Meets Here," *Paris News*, August 1, 1951, 11; "Facts Forum Worthy of Large Membership," *Paris News*, August 3, 1951, 6; "Three Subjects Are Discussed by Facts Forum," *Paris News*, August 31, 1951, 2; and "Facts Forum Was Started in '51," *Paris News*, January 1, 1952, 7D.
47. "Facts Forum in Offing for Kaufman," *Kaufman Herald*, February 28, 1952, 10; and "Dallas Attorney, Ex-FBI Agent, to Speak at First Discussion Meeting of New Facts Forum Organized in Kaufman," *Kaufman Herald*, March 13, 1952, 1, 6.
48. "Interest Is Good in Local Facts Form," *Kaufman Herald*, March 20, 1952, 1.
49. "Circulating Library Is Established by Kaufman Unit of Facts Forum," *Kaufman Herald*, April 10, 1952, 3; and "Escapee from Tyranny of Communist Yugoslavia to Address Facts Forum Here," *Kaufman Herald*, April 17, 1952, 1.
50. For a helpful account of the complex political fault lines within the Republican Party in 1952, which resulted in Old Right stalwart Robert A. Taft losing the presidential nomination to Dwight D. Eisenhower, see David W. Reinhard, *The Republican Right Since*

1945 (University of Kentucky Press, 1983), 75–96. For an account of Texas Democratic Party factionalism, from a "loyalist" perspective, see Patrick L. Cox, *Ralph W. Yarborough, the People's Senator* (University of Texas Press, 2001). See also Ricky F. Dobbs, *Yellow Dogs and Republicans: Allan Shivers and Texas Two-Party Politics* (Texas A&M University Press, 2005).

51. "The Republicans and The South," *Life*, May 19, 1952, 34.
52. "Texas 'Big Four' Political Factions to Tell Views at Public Meeting in Kaufman," *Kaufman Herald*, June 26, 1952, 1.
53. "Speakers Representing All Four Factions in Texas Political Split Air Views in Kaufman," *Kaufman Herald*, July 3, 1952, 1.
54. "Facts Forum Poll Advises Ike to Hit Hard at Fair Deal," *Kaufman Herald*, September 11, 1952, 10.
55. For more on the loyalty pledge, see Robert Howard, "Two Southern States Evade Loyalty Issue," *Chicago Tribune*, July 19, 1952, 3; and W. H. Lawrence, "3 States Spurn Loyalty Pledge, Lose Their 64 Convention Votes; Platform Voted Without a Fight," *New York Times*, July 24, 1952.
56. "Facts Forum Slates Nov. 20th Meeting," *Kaufman Herald*, November 13, 1952, 6.
57. For Hunt's account of the history of Facts Forum's growth, see H. L. Hunt, "Background of Facts Forum," n.d., Box 93, Folder 14, Philbrick Papers, LOC. The national membership figures in 1952 were reported in Worth Gatewood, "'Richest Man in US' Publicity-Shy Texas Oil Jillionaire Boosts Facts Forum and MacArthur," *Omaha World-Herald Magazine*, July 13, 1952, 4, 6. The group's National Advisory Board increased the maximum group size from forty-two to forty-nine in early 1952. See "Six New Members Named to Board," *Facts Forum News*, February 18, 1952, 1–2.
58. Figures are based upon a thorough review of issues of *Facts Forum News*, which Facts Forum published from February 1952 to December 1956. All issues are accessible in bound volume format at New York Public Library.
59. Facts Forum reported units at the Dearborn Stove Company, Mosher Steel Company, the Texas & Pacific Railway, and the John E. Mitchell Company. See *Facts Forum News*, April 21, 1952, 1; September 16, 1952, 3. The Dearborn unit was featured in *Manage*, "the magazine of management men in America." See Ruth Davis, "Facts Forum," *Manage*, August 1952, 6–7. According to an article published in *Facts Forum News*, the readership of *Manage* included "the top management of some 1,200 American businesses and industries." See "National Magazines Publish Stories About Facts Forum," *Facts Forum News*, August 5, 1952, 1.
60. "Cross-Section of America Is Grand Island Forum," *Facts Forum News*, October 6, 1952, 2. Even the company-organized forums were narrated as worker-led initiatives. See "Don't Have to Be a 'Veep' to Debate in Dearborn Unit," *Facts Forum News*, April 21, 1952, 1; and "How a Forum Gets Started; Industrial Group Typical," *Facts Forum News*, September 16, 1952, 3.
61. Rose Rossi of Beeville helped spread the word about Facts Forum to the local Republican Women's Club in Corpus Christi, for example. And local architect Verne Lane led the group's Houston efforts, with some assistance from Barbara Strange, a

seventeen-year-old Dallas high school student and Facts Forum coordinator. Phylys Greene, "Facts Forum Units Spread Over Houston," *Houston Post*, July 22, 1951, 1; "The Verne Lanes—Forum Pioneers," *Facts Forum News*, March 31, 1952, 1; and "Mrs. Rose Rossi Speaks Thursday to Republicans," *Corpus Christi Caller-Times*, September 19, 1951. One indicator that women may have been overrepresented, at least in Dallas-area groups—a 1952 poll found that 76 percent of Facts Forum participants in the region supported equal pay for equal work regardless of sex. See "Facts Forum Poll Advises."

62. "Big Membership," *Facts Forum News*, February 18, 1952, 3.
63. For an example outside of Texas, an especially active Facts Forum unit in Staunton, Virginia, resulted from conversations between the business manager of Mary Baldwin College and a Texas-based trustee who reported that "young professional and businesspeople" had adopted the program in Dallas to fight civic apathy. See "Have You Forgotten How to Think about Things That Concern You?" *Pathfinder*, April 23, 1952, 18–19. While she goes unnamed in the *Pathfinder* article, Hunt's wife, Lyda Bunker Hunt, happened to be a trustee at Mary Baldwin College. See "Mrs. H. L. Hunt Dead," *New York Times*, May 7, 1955, 89; and "In Memoriam, Lyda Bunker Hunt," *Facts Forum News*, June 1955, 1.
64. Texas, Louisiana, Georgia, Virginia, and Arkansas featured Jim Crow laws in all three categories, while West Virginia and New Mexico mandated segregated educational facilities. A review of photographs in each issue of *Facts Forum News* from 1952 to 1953, the years when the newsletter reported on discussion groups, yielded no identifiable people of color.
65. "Facts Forum (Results), August 20, 1952," *Facts Forum News*, August 26, 1952, 3; and "Facts Forum Poll Results, July 10, 1954," *Facts Forum News*, August 1954, 1.
66. "Broadcasts: Only the Facts," *Dallas Morning News*, October 5, 1951, 4; and "Broadcasts: A Question of News," *Dallas Morning News*, October 12, 1951, 29.
67. "Facts Forum TV Show Now Carried on Video and Radio," *Facts Forum News*, October 6, 1952, 1; and "Simulcast Gets Big Response," *Facts Forum News*, October 27, 1952, 1.
68. "New Radio Program Series to Feature States Governors," *Facts Forum News*, August 1953, 1; and "Panel Program Now on Radio, TV," *Facts Forum News*, December 1953, 1.
69. In January 1954, Facts Forum programs were reportedly aired on 298 stations located in 268 municipalities; by 1955 station coverage had jumped to 602 stations located in 519 municipalities. See "Facts Forum Radio Schedule" and "Facts Forum Television Schedule," *Facts Forum News*, January 1954, 7–8; and "Facts Forum Radio Schedule" and "Facts Forum Television Schedule," *Facts Forum News*, January 1955, 58–61.
70. "Where One Texan's Money Goes," 35–36. *Reporters' Roundup* was launched in 1954.
71. "Facts Forum Featured in National Magazine," *Facts Forum News*, March 1955, 27. The circulation boost was assisted by Ben H. Wooten, president of the First National Bank in Dallas, who in early 1955 sponsored guest subscriptions for all fourteen thousand bank presidents in the United States at the time. See "Facts Forum News Has 100,000 New Readers," *Facts Forum News*, February 1955, 52–53. By the time Facts Forum folded

in November 1956, however, that circulation had reportedly dropped to one hundred thousand. See "Lost Cause," *Time*, November 26, 1956, 82.
72. Tula A. Connell, *Conservative Counterrevolution: Challenging Liberalism in 1950s Milwaukee* (University of Illinois Press, 2016), 52–55.
73. Gerda Koch, "Revenue Service Clamps Down," *Facts Forum News*, November 1956, 61.
74. For example, when reconsidering its ban on broadcast editorials in 1947–1948, the Federal Communications Commission received hundreds of postcards in support of maintaining the Mayflower Doctrine with nearly identical wording, including some sent by individuals with demonstrably little awareness of the issue at hand. See RG173, Docketed Case Files, Docket No. 8516, Boxes 3381, 3384, FCC, NARA.
75. "Facts Forum Organization Offers 230 Cash Awards," *Dallas Morning News*, August 18, 1951, 3.
76. Letter writers were instructed to self-designate their letter as either liberal or conservative/constructive. If they failed to do so, "the Facts Forum Judging Committee shall exercise its opinion to consider the letter in one category or the other." "Contest Awards," *Facts Forum News*, May 12, 1952, 4.
77. "Letters to the Editor," *Facts Forum News*, June 3, 1952, 4.
78. George E. Miller, "Don't Misuse the Cross," *Facts Forum News*, November 1956, 61.
79. Roy F. Carpenter, "Three-Way Schools," *Facts Forum News*, November 1956, 61.
80. In the late summer and fall of 1953, Facts Forum briefly experimented with reporting its polling sample sizes. Its August 26, 1953, poll, for example, was reportedly based on some 3,386 signed ballots (although nearly 500 additional ballots were reportedly received within two days of the poll's closing date). The September 30, 1953, poll was reportedly based on 4,351 signed ballots. A monthly response in the thousands would conceivably make polling a more common participant activity than letter writing, although exact numbers are elusive.
81. See "Omaha Living Rooms Become Forum for World's Problems," *Omaha World-Herald*, July 20, 1952, 8B.
82. See "Take One," *Facts Forum News*, April 1953, 1; "FF Placards Pay!" *Facts Forum News*, August 1953, 8; and "FF Advertisers Listed," *Facts Forum News*, October 1953, 14.
83. For more on Facts Forum's announcement of its poll question contest, see "February Poll," *Facts Forum News*, January 1954, 8.
84. All poll questions and results from February 1952 until December 1956 were accessed in *Facts Forum News*. Facts Forum polls from 1951 and early 1952, preceding the founding of the newsletter, were accessed via back issues of *The Dallas Morning News* and *Corpus Christi Caller-Times*, two Texas newspapers in which early Facts Forum poll questions and results were regularly printed.
85. While not all sponsors used the same wording, and some did not make this invitation explicit, many of the ads sponsored by Sears, Roebuck and Co. featured some variation of this invitation. Example taken from one such ad, printed alongside a sale price for Kenmore vacuums, in the December 12, 1951, issue of the *Corpus Christi Caller-Times*.
86. These questions were each included in the August 20, 1952, Facts Forum poll, the first featuring the predict-the-polls contest. See *Facts Forum News*, August 26, 1952, 3. The

rules for the contest were first outlined earlier that month; see "Predict-the-Polls Results," *Facts Forum News*, August 5, 1952, 4.
87. The last poll to list combined totals of "yes" votes closed on July 28, 1953. See *Facts Forum News*, August 1953, 1. No explanation was given for why the August 26 poll did not contain a combined total.
88. "Facts Forum Facts," *Time*, January 11, 1954, 52–53.
89. "Facts Forum Poll (February 25, 1954)," *Facts Forum News*, February 1954, 15. See also "Time Magazine vs. Facts Forum," *Facts Forum News*, February 1954, 11.
90. "Facts Forum Poll Closed February 25," *Facts Forum News*, March 1954, inside front cover.
91. "Facts Forum Poll (February 25, 1954)."
92. *Facts Forum News*, November 17, 1952, 2.
93. "Facts Forum Poll Results," *Facts Forum News*, July 1954, 1.
94. Duke Burgess, "News Slanting," *Facts Forum News*, October 1954, 25. The letter was originally published by the *Dallas Times Herald*.
95. Benedict Anderson, *Imagined Communities: Reflections on the Origins and Spread of Nationalism* (Verso, 2006), 35.
96. "Results of Facts Forum Poll," *Corpus Christi Caller-Times*, January 31, 1952, 5; "Facts Forum (Results), May 7, 1952," *Facts Forum News*, May 12, 1952, 3; and "Facts Forum, Closed September 30," *Facts Forum News*, October 1953, 1.
97. See Edwin R. Bayley, *Joe McCarthy and the Press* (University of Wisconsin Press, 1981), 192–195.
98. "Facts Forum Poll Results, Closed November 10th," *Facts Forum News*, inside front cover.
99. "Oil Tycoon Backs McCarthy TV Series," *Worker*, October 4, 1953, 6.
100. See "Did We Blunder," *Facts Forum News*, November 1953, 1. For a copy of the original insert, which included the reprint alongside brief statements by Robert Dedman and H. L. Hunt, see Box I:24, Folder "Facts Forum, 1953–1954, undated," Maurice Rosenblatt Papers, LOC.
101. The *Providence Journal-Bulletin* ran Ben H. Bagdikian's "The Facts About Facts Forum," in eight-parts from December 27, 1953, to January 4, 1954. Fresh off a 1953 Pulitzer Prize win when he began investigating Facts Forum, Bagdikian went on to an illustrious career as a journalist and scholar, eventually playing a role in publishing the Pentagon Papers while working for *The Washington Post* in 1971 and serving as dean of the Graduate School of Journalism at the University of California, Berkeley. His 1983 book *The Media Monopoly* remains a highly influential work in the field of news media criticism.
102. Ben H. Bagdikian, "A Rich Man, A Growing Power," *Providence Sunday Journal*, December 27, 1953, 1, 20; 20.
103. Ben H. Bagdikian, "How to Identify a 'Conservative,'" *Providence Journal-Bulletin*, December 29, 1953, 1, 7.
104. Ben H. Bagdikian, "8 Small Points and the BIG One," *Providence Journal-Bulletin*, January 4, 1954, 1, 8; 8.

105. Ben H. Bagdikian, "The Letters, Polls and Cartoons," *Providence Journal-Bulletin*, January 1, 1954, 1, 19; 19.
106. "A Prospect Asks Why Participate?" (n.d.), 11–12, H. L. Hunt subject file, 62-HQ-108867, Part 3 of 3, Federal Bureau of Investigation, LAZ. This pamphlet was written by Dallas-area Facts Forum participant and SMU law student Bill Brice, who received a $1,000 award for the manuscript upon which it was based. See "Wins $1,000.00!" *Facts Forum News*, February 18, 1952, 1.
107. James Devlin, "Texas Tycoon's Radio-TV Forum Subject of Heated Controversy," Associated Press, printed in *Joplin* (Missouri) *News Herald*, March 2, 1954, 2. See also, for examples, "Facts Forum Facts," *Time*, January 11, 1954, 52–53; "McCarthy, Hunt, and Facts Forum," *Reporter*, February 16, 1954, 19–27; and "More and More," *New Republic*, March 29, 1954, 4. The *Journal-Bulletin* exposé was syndicated in part or full in several newspapers nationwide, including *The Denver Post* and *Milwaukee Journal*. See Ben H. Bagdikian, "Texan's Millions Back Powerful Radio, TV Forum," *Denver Post*, January 3, 1954. *The Washington Post* followed *The Providence Journal* a month later, with its own three-part exposé by reporter Edward T. Folliard. That series ran in the *Post* from February 14–16, 1954.
108. "Facts Forum News Releases," *Facts Forum News*, January 1954, 1, 5–6, 23–24.
109. A February 25, 1954, Facts Forum poll found that 96 percent of participants believed in Facts Forum's resilience in the face of criticism; that number stayed steady at 97 percent when the group asked the question a second time in its April 26, 1954, poll.
110. "Facts Forum News Releases," *Facts Forum News*, January 1954, 6.
111. "Facts-Forum Facts," *Time*, January 11, 1954, 52.
112. See "Facts Forum's Answer to Time Magazine," *Facts Forum News*, February 1954, 9–10; and "Time Magazine Vs. Facts Forum," *Facts Forum News*, February 1954, 11–12.
113. "An Interview with Robert H. Dedman," *Facts Forum News*, March 1954, 11.

4. BEYOND BUCKLEY

1. Transcripts of the episode were published in *Facts Forum News*, April 1955, 28–29, 41; 28.
2. *Facts Forum News*, April 1955, 41.
3. "Regular Features," *National Review*, November 19, 1955, 6. See also Julie B. Lane, "Cultivating Distrust of the Mainstream Media," in *News on the Right: Studying Conservative News Cultures*, ed. Anthony Nadler and A. J. Bauer, 157–173 (Oxford University Press, 2019).
4. Lauren Lassabe Shepherd, *Resistance from the Right: Conservatives and the Campus Wars in Modern America* (University of North Carolina Press, 2023), 42–51.
5. See Heather Hendershot, *Open to Debate: How William F. Buckley Put Liberal America on the Firing Line* (Broadside, 2016).
6. The first episode devoted to the issue of media bias was episode 7, an interview with liberal commentator David Susskind titled "The Prevailing Bias." For a transcript, see

Program Number 7, "The Prevailing Bias," Transcript Box 159, Folder 10, Firing Line Broadcast Records, Collection No. 80040, Hoover Institution, Stanford University.

7. See Nicole Hemmer, *Messengers of the Right: Conservative Media and the Transformation of American Politics* (University of Pennsylvania Press, 2016). See also Rick Perlstein's four-book series on the rise of modern conservatism in the United States: *Before the Storm: Barry Goldwater and the Unmaking of the American Consensus* (Hill & Wang, 2001); *Nixonland: The Rise of a President and the Fracturing of America* (Scribner, 2008); *The Invisible Bridge: The Fall of Nixon and the Rise of Reagan* (Simon and Schuster, 2014); and *Reaganland: America's Right Turn 1976–1980* (Simon and Schuster, 2021).

8. See David Austin Walsh, *Taking America Back: The Conservative Movement and the Far Right* (Yale University Press, 2024). "Respectability politics" is a concept commonly associated with a strand of political activism among Black Americans that is keenly attuned to public perceptions by outgroups and seeks to win those groups' favor through abandoning behaviors that correspond with negative stereotypes. Buckley and his fellow conservatives were not explicitly building on this Black political tradition but rather developing a parallel strategy due to the persistent unpopularity of conservatism throughout the 1930s and 1940s. For a helpful overview of respectability politics among Black Americans, see Hakeem Jefferson, "The Politics of Respectability and Black Americans' Punitive Attitudes," *American Political Science Review* 117, no. 4 (2023), 1448–1464.

9. For more on the importance of anticommunism in cohering a distinctly *modern* conservative ideology, see George H. Nash, *Conservative Intellectual Movement in America Since 1945* (Intercollegiate Studies Institute, 1998).

10. For a helpful overview of *National Review*'s shifting coverage of the civil rights movement, see Robert Greene II, "*National Review* and the Changing Narrative of Civil Rights Memory 1968–2016," in *News on the Right: Studying Conservative News Cultures*, ed. Anthony Nadler and A. J. Bauer, 174–189 (Oxford University Press, 2019).

11. William F. Buckley Jr., "The Uproar," *National Review*, April 22, 1961, 241–243; and William F. Buckley Jr., "The Question of Robert Welch," *National Review*, February 13, 1962, 83–88. For Birchers' rationale for impeaching Warren—namely, over his work in support of racial integration—see Bulletin of the John Birch Society, January 1, 1961, 7, 15–16. The John Birch Society published bound volumes of its monthly bulletins to membership as annual *White Books*. My personal collection includes five volumes spanning the years 1960–1964.

12. "Minutes of the Meeting of the Board of Directors of the American Conservative Union, December 18–19, 1964," Box 20, Folder 12, American Conservative Union papers, MSS 176, BYU.

13. For an excellent account of the John Birch Society's influence on modern conservatism not only in the 1960s but beyond, see Edward H. Miller, *A Conspiratorial Life: Robert Welch, the John Birch Society, and the Revolution of American Conservatism* (University of Chicago Press, 2021).

14. Letter from S. R. Entwistle, November 19, 1956, Box 38, Folder "Facts Forum correspondence," Emanuel Celler Papers, LOC.

15. "Facts Forum to Quit," *New York Times*, November 10, 1956, 39.

16. Letter from L. B. Nichols to Mr. Tolson, July 11, 1955, H. L. Hunt subject file, 62-HQ-108867, Part 3 of 3, Federal Bureau of Investigation, LAZ; and "Mrs. H. L. Hunt Dead," *New York Times*, May 8, 1955, 89.
17. "Lost Cause," *Time*, November 26, 1956, 82.
18. For a thorough history of the founding and politics of Welch and his John Birch Society, see D. J. Mulloy, *The World of the John Birch Society: Conspiracy, Conservatism, and the Cold War* (Vanderbilt University Press, 2014).
19. Robert Welch, *The Blue Book of the John Birch Society* (Western Islands, 1959), 64–73.
20. Welch, *Blue Book*, 68.
21. Letter from Robert Welch to *American Opinion* readers, December 2, 1957, Robert H. W. Welch Jr. subject file, 62-HQ-104401, Federal Bureau of Investigation, LAZ. Welch personally owned and controlled *American Opinion* until May 1960, when he formally donated it to the John Birch Society.
22. The circulation of *National Review* increased from 7,500 in 1955 to 30,000 in 1960. See Ronald Lora and William Henry Longton, eds., *Conservative Press in Twentieth-Century America* (Greenwood, 1999), 525. For sake of comparison, by 1959 *National Review* claimed a circulation of 29,000, making it more widely circulated than such progressive and liberal competitors as *The Nation* (24,000) and *New Republic* (27,000). See William F. Buckley, "Can a Little Magazine Break Even?" *National Review*, October 10, 1959, 393–394, 407.
23. Occasional *Facts Forum News* contributors Clarence Manion and Alfred Kohlberg, both experienced right-anticommunist media figures in their own right, were also early members of *American Opinion*'s editorial advisory board. All names were present on the masthead of the magazine's October 1959 issue, for instance. For more on Manion, see Hemmer, *Messengers of the Right*.
24. By the time Smoot made his decision to leave Facts Forum, the organization had already been thrown into chaos by the untimely death of Hunt's wife. According to internal FBI reports, Hunt had placed many investments in Lyda's name, expecting her to outlive him, that now required considerable legal and financial disentanglement and impacting his ability to fund pet projects. Furthermore, Hunt was reportedly increasingly dissatisfied with his Facts Forum staff, including Smoot. While Smoot depicts his exit from Facts Forum as following a calling, it seems likelier he was motivated by self-interest. See Letter from L. B. Nichols to Mr. Tolson, July 11, 1955, H. L. Hunt subject file, 62-HQ-108867, Part 3 of 3, Federal Bureau of Investigation, LAZ; and Memorandum from C. D. DeLoach to Mr. Nichols, July 28, 1955, H. L. Hunt subject file, 62-HQ-108867, Part 3 of 3, Federal Bureau of Investigation, LAZ.
25. "Who Is the Man?" *Dan Smoot Report*, August 5, 1957, 5–6.
26. Letter to readers from Scott Stanley Jr., *Review of the News*, March 10, 1971, 1–3. In welcoming Smoot into the fold, Stanley wrote, "There is no periodical and no patriotic writer that we would more gladly welcome into our editorial family." My analysis of *Review of the News* (reviewing all issues from September 1965 through December 1975) utilized microfilm reels housed at New York Public Library.

27. Paid circulation figures drawn from statements of ownership, management, and circulation published in *Review of the News*; see vol. 2, no. 41 (October 19, 1966), 24; and vol. 10, no. 41 (October 9, 1974).
28. "Correction Please," *Bulletin of the John Birch Society*, June 1, 1964, 18. Before its brief stint as a periodical, "Correction, Please" started as a regular feature in *American Opinion*, launching in the magazine's October 1962 issue.
29. "Correction, Please!" *Review of the News*, September 3, 1965, 32.
30. David Greenberg, "The Idea of 'the Liberal Media' and Its Roots in the Civil Rights Movement," *The Sixties: A Journal of History, Politics and Culture* 1, no. 2 (2008): 167–186.
31. *Bulletin of the John Birch Society*, December 31, 1959, 7.
32. *Bulletin of the John Birch Society*, May 1, 1961, 11.
33. *Bulletin of the John Birch Society*, March 1, 1962, 21. For a copy of the four-page "Story of a Hoax" pamphlet, see 15–18.
34. *Bulletin of the John Birch Society*, December 31, 1959, 14; emphasis in original. See also May 1, 1960, 14–15.
35. For Welch's acknowledgment of the failure of the airline campaign, see *Bulletin of the John Birch Society*, December 1, 1961, 7.
36. *Bulletin of the John Birch Society*, July 1, 1960, 9–10.
37. *Bulletin of the John Birch Society*, July 1, 1961, 14; and August 1, 1962, 8–9.
38. *Bulletin of the John Birch Society*, February 1, 1961, 9–10, emphasis in original. The Kilpatrick campaign seems to have borne fruit as the *Richmond News Leader* would go on to occasionally endorse Birch initiatives. See *Bulletin of the John Birch Society*, December 1, 1961, 20; and August 1, 1962, 16.
39. "Newspaper Attacks," *Bulletin of the John Birch Society*, August 1, 1960, 5–8.
40. For Welch's account of this onslaught, see especially *Bulletin of the John Birch Society*, April 1, 1961.
41. Buckley, "The Uproar," *National Review*, emphasis in original.
42. Eugene Lyons, "Folklore of the Right," *National Review*, April 11, 1959, 645–647.
43. Buckley, "The Question of Robert Welch."
44. *Bulletin of the John Birch Society*, March 1, 1962, 3–4.
45. *Bulletin of the John Birch Society*, August 1, 1961, 2–5.
46. *Bulletin of the John Birch Society*, July 1, 1961, 12.
47. For a definitive account of this coverage, see Gene Roberts and Hank Klibanoff, *The Race Beat: The Press, The Civil Rights Struggle, and the Awakening of a Nation* (Knopf, 2006).
48. Roy Reed, "Birch Society is Growing in the South," *New York Times*, November 8, 1965, 1, 19.
49. Kathy Roberts Forde and Sid Bedingfield, eds., *Journalism and Jim Crow: White Supremacy and the Black Struggle for a New America* (University of Illinois Press, 2021).
50. Matthew Pressman, "The New York *Daily News* and the History of Conservative Media," *Modern American History* 4, no. 3 (2021), 219–238.

51. Meg Heckman, *Political Godmother: Nackey Scripps Loeb and the Newspaper That Shook the Republican Party* (Potomac Books / University of Nebraska Press, 2020).
52. David Wallace, "Piercing the Paper Curtain: The Southern Editorial Response to National Civil Rights Coverage," *American Journalism* 33, no. 4 (2016): 401–423.
53. "Education: Sewanee's Pride," *Time*, June 2, 1961.
54. Waring, quoted in Sid Bedingfield, *Newspaper Wars: Civil Rights and White Resistance in South Carolina, 1935–1965* (University of Illinois Press, 2017), 170–199.
55. Sid Bedingfield, "Who Is Nicholas Stanford? The *New York Times* Music Critic and His Secret Role in the Rise of the 'Liberal Media' Claim," *American Journalism* 35, no. 4 (2018), 398–419.
56. William P. Hustwit, *James J. Kilpatrick: Salesman for Segregation* (University of North Carolina Press, 2013), 79–106.
57. Elizabeth Atwood, "Reaching the Pinnacle of the 'Punditocracy': James J. Kilpatrick's Journey from Segregationist Editor to National Opinion Shaper," *American Journalism* 31, no. 3 (2014): 358–377.
58. For a helpful account of the emergence of colorblind racism and its role in legitimating conservative politics in both major parties from the 1970s onward, see Michael Omi and Howard Winant, *Racial Formation in the United States*, 3rd ed. (Routledge, 2014), 191–238.
59. Bedingfield, *Newspaper Wars*, 176.
60. "Stories Distorted, Ala. Editors Say," *Editor & Publisher*, May 18, 1963, 12, 61.
61. Aldon D. Morris, "Birmingham Confrontation Reconsidered: An Analysis of the Dynamics and Tactics of Mobilization," *American Sociological Review* 58, no. 5 (1993): 621–636. As Morris argues, the focus on the campaign as a media event has caused some to overlook the role of direct confrontation in achieving the campaign's local demands.
62. Greenberg, "The Idea of 'the Liberal Media.'"
63. "They Fight a Fire That Won't Go Out: The Spectacle of Racial Turbulence in Birmingham," *Life*, May 17, 1963, 30.
64. "Stories Distorted, Ala. Editors Say."
65. Quoted in Enrique DuBois Rigsby, "A Rhetorical Clash with the Established Order: An Analysis of Protest Strategies and Perceptions of Media Responses, Birmingham, 1963" (PhD diss., University of Oregon, 1990), 82.
66. Julian Williams, "Black Radio and Civil Rights: Birmingham, 1956–1963," *Journal of Radio Studies* 12, no. 1 (2005), 47–60.
67. Lorraine Ahearn and Barbara Friedman, "A Commemorative Bind: How the *Birmingham News* Redressed Past Journalistic Failure Through Contemporary Civil Rights Memory," *Journalism History* 48, no. 4 (2022), 283–302.
68. "Troops Call Peril to Constitution," *Cahaba Valley News*, May 15, 1963, 1.
69. For a representative sample of the newspaper's tone of coverage, including all described above, see its July 24, 1963, issue. I accessed issues of the *Cahaba Valley News, Birmingham Independent*, and *Alabama Independent* spanning the years 1963–1968 on microfilm housed at Gorgas Library, University of Alabama, Tuscaloosa.

70. "We May Be Conscripted," *Cahaba Valley News*, July 10, 1963, 2.
71. "Respected Lawyers Back Sovereignty Commission: Question Motives of Critics," *Cahaba Valley News*, August 14, 1963, 1, 5, emphasis in original.
72. The *Birmingham Independent* closely covered the New York–based Newhouse chain's media acquisitions throughout the state in the years that followed, heavily implying a nefarious plot. See for examples, "Freedom of the Press," March 31, 1965, 4; "Newhouse Chain Buys Anniston Cablevision Co.," August 4, 1965, 4; and "Peer of the Press," October 3, 1966, 1. Given that S. I. Newhouse was the son of Jewish immigrants from Russia, it seems likely that the editors were knowingly alluding to well-worn if salient antisemitic tropes. For a helpful account of the role of antisemitism in the development of the "liberal media" claim, see William Gillis, "The Anti-Semitic Roots of the 'Liberal News Media' Critique," *American Journalism* 34, no. 3 (2017): 262–288.
73. "Nationwide Reaction to Civil 'Wrongs' Bill Could Mean Kennedy's Blackmail Will Boomerang," *Cahaba Valley News*, November 6, 1963, 1. See also Clarence Manion, "New FCC Ruling Gags Radio, TV," *Cahaba Valley News*, November 6, 1963, 3.
74. Hal Totten, "Cahaba Valley News to Expand with New Offices, Name Change," *Cahaba Valley News*, November 13, 1963, 1, 3.
75. "When Will 'Rights' Boosters Face Facts?" *Birmingham Independent*, March 25, 1964, 1.
76. "Some in Birmingham Side with Reds?" *Cahaba Valley News*, July 17, 1973, 1.
77. "Pro-Administration Columnist Verifies Our Expose Last July," *Birmingham Independent*, April 22, 1964, 1.
78. For ads referring to *The Birmingham News* as "liberal" see page 4 of the April 22, 1964, issue, and page 2 of the April 26, 1964, issue of the *Birmingham Independent*.
79. "Welcome Shelby County Independent," *Birmingham Independent*, August 4, 1965, 1, emphasis in original.
80. "Dedicated to a Free America!" *Birmingham Independent*, January 1, 1964, 1, emphasis in original.
81. "The Birmingham Independent Has Outgrown Its Name!" *Birmingham Independent*, September 20, 1967, 1. For circulation figures, see "Statement of Ownership, Management and Circulation," *Birmingham Independent*, October 25, 1967, 3. The first issue of the *Alabama Independent* ran November 1, 1967.
82. Regular *Independent* contributor Ralph Compton described himself as a Birch "Section Leader" in private correspondence in which he coordinated distribution efforts for the paper in advance of its 1964 rebrand. Letter from Compton to Jimmy Jones, November 17, 1963, Box 3, Folder "John Birch Society (1)," Jimmy C. Jones papers, private collection of Andrea Gilbreath, Birmingham, Alabama.
83. For example, see "The Time Has Come," John Birch Society advertisement, *Birmingham Independent*, January 1, 1964, 3.
84. Jones and his wife Joyce were leaders of John Birch Society Chapter 387 in Birmingham in the early to mid-1960s. See undated correspondence from Parker Richards of the John Birch Society Home Office to Mr. Jones documenting new members and

4. BEYOND BUCKLEY 231

monthly dues receipts, Box 3, Folder "John Birch Society (1)," Jimmy C. Jones papers, private collection of Andrea Gilbreath, Birmingham, Alabama.

85. Jones contributed more than two dozen bylined articles to the *Independent* between October 1964 and February 1968. He was most prolific in 1965 and 1966.
86. In July 1965, for instance, the *Independent* serialized a pamphlet by Birch founder Robert Welch on civil rights.
87. The *Independent* regularly editorialized against Johnson and the Civil Rights Act in the spring of 1964. See "Are There 51 Loyal Americans in the Senate?" *Birmingham Independent*, February 19, 194, 1; "Spells Ruin to Small Businessmen," *Birmingham Independent*, March 4, 1964, 1; "Pledged Demos Must Back Civil 'Rights' Bill," *Birmingham Independent*, March 11, 1964, 1; "When Will 'Rights' Boosters Face Facts?"; "'Rights' Bill Ties with Communist Creed," *Birmingham Independent*, April 15, 1964, 1; and "'Rights' Bill Key to Communist Plot," *Birmingham Independent*, June 3, 1963, 1.
88. Fulton Lewis Jr., "Washington Report," *Birmingham Independent*, March 11, 1964, 3.
89. "Mainstream of Malignancy," *Birmingham Independent*, September 23, 1964, 1.
90. For more on how the 1964 Goldwater campaign fueled conservative belief in liberal media bias, see Rich Shumate, *Barry Goldwater, Distrust in Media, and Conservative Identity: The Perception of Liberal Bias in the News* (Lexington, 2021).
91. "Positive Action Supporting Goldwater," *Birmingham Independent*, June 24, 1964, 1.
92. "Goldwater Smears," *Birmingham Independent*, August 26, 1964, 2.
93. "How They Won: All the Odds Were for Them," *Birmingham Independent*, November 11, 1964, 4.
94. Transcribed by the author from archival footage featured in *Mr. Conservative: Goldwater on Goldwater*, DVD, directed by Julie Anderson (New York: Zeitgeist Films, 2006).
95. "Reflections on Elections," *Birmingham Independent*, November 11, 1964, 2.
96. A handful out of dozens of examples: "Oppose Police Review Boards," *Birmingham Independent*, December 2, 1964, 1; "American Press Failing Public," *Birmingham Independent*, April 28, 1965, 6; Betty Acton, "Demonstrations! Will They Ever Stop?" *Birmingham Independent*, January 19, 1966, 1; "Miss Knight Tells the Truth About the New York Times," *Birmingham Independent*, May 24, 1966, 6; "Did They Tell You About This?" *Birmingham Independent*, August 10, 1966, 1; William M. Butsch, "Navy Flier Takes Issue with 'New York Times' Reporter on Hanoi," *Birmingham Independent*, January 18, 1967, 1; and "CBS Sevareid Mourns Ruby and Sneers at Dallas," *Birmingham Independent*, February 22, 1967.
97. Editors called on readers to "filter" the news in "Crisis," *Birmingham Independent*, October 21, 1964, 2.
98. Subscriber solicitation, *Birmingham Independent*, August 30, 1967, 1.
99. Tom Anderson, "News Behind the News," *Birmingham Independent*, July 15, 1964, 1.
100. "Operation Smoke Screen," *Birmingham Independent*, July 29, 1964, 1.
101. Letter to Editor from Pryde Hinton, *Birmingham Independent*, May 11, 1966, 2.
102. T. J. Campbell, "Why They Hate George Wallace," *Alabama Independent*, April 10, 1968, 3.

103. Harry Stanley, "A Dissertation on Freedom of the Press," *Alabama Independent*, April 10, 1968, 3.
104. See, for instance, the hour-long CBS News documentary *Thunder on the Right*, broadcast nationwide in February 1962.
105. "Not Guilty of These," *Birmingham Independent*, January 1, 1964, 2.
106. "Smear Campaign Is On," *Birmingham Independent*, December 2, 1964, 2.
107. Some examples: "Clampdown on the Right?" *Birmingham Independent*, October 28, 1964, 2; "Reuther in Selma? Directing His Memorandum," *Birmingham Independent*, March 24, 1965, 3; "Walter Reuther Communism Twist on Churches, Political Influence in White House Exposed," *Birmingham Independent*, March 31, 1965, 5; and Grace S. Dorrah, "Red 'Sails' Still Flyin,'" *Birmingham Independent*, February 15, 1967, 4.
108. "Pennsylvania Legislature Attacks Dr. Carl McIntire," *Birmingham Independent*, February 16, 1966, 1; Harry Browne, "Ten Examples of Extremism," *Birmingham Independent*, March 9, 1966, 2; and "McIntire Invites U Thant, Gus Hall to Radio," *Birmingham Independent*, February 21, 1968, 2.
109. "Strangely Silent," *Birmingham Independent*, August 26, 1964, 2; and "General Walker Loses Again," *Birmingham Independent*, November 1, 1967, 1.
110. "Birmingham Audiences Stirred by the Courage and Dedication of Dr. Hargis," *Birmingham Independent*, July 13, 1966, 1; and P. A. Nichols, "Views on the News," *Birmingham Independent*, April 19, 1967, 6.
111. "Throw the Scoundrels Out!" *Birmingham Independent*, October 22, 1965, 4.
112. Harry Stanley, "Buckley Slaps at Robert Welch and George Wallace," *Birmingham Independent*, April 26, 1967, 1–2. See also letter to *Birmingham Independent* from Harry Stanley, February 7, 1968, 2.
113. Harry Stanley, "Buckley Rebuttal," *Alabama Independent*, December 6, 1967, 4–5.
114. "Nixon for Prez," *National Review*, November 5, 1968, 1097.
115. David Norris, "Sometimes No News Is Good News," *Alabama Independent*, October 16, 1968, 1–2.
116. "The Power of George Wallace," *National Review*, November 19, 1968, 1152–1153.

5. LIBERAL MEDIA GOES MAINSTREAM

1. "Transcript of the Address by Vice President Spiro T. Agnew Des Moines, Iowa, November 13, 1969," in Marvin Barrett, ed., *The Alfred I. Dupont-Columbia University Survey of Broadcast Journalism, 1969–1970* (Grosset & Dunlap, 1970), 137.
2. Rick Perlstein, ed., *Richard Nixon: Speeches, Writings, Documents* (Princeton University Press, 2008), 170. For full text of Nixon's entire speech, see 170–190.
3. "Transcript of the Address by Agnew, November 13, 1969," 134.
4. Christopher Lydon, "Agnew Attacks Press as Unfair; Names 2 Papers," *New York Times*, November 21, 1969, 1.
5. "Agnew Demands Equal Time," *Time*, November 21, 1969, 18.

6. See Heather Hendershot, *When the News Broke: Chicago 1968 and the Polarizing of America* (University of Chicago Press, 2022); and Todd Gitlin, *The Whole World Is Watching: Mass Media in the Making and Unmaking of the New Left* (University of California Press, 1980).
7. Marvin Barrett, ed., *The Alfred I. Dupont-Columbia University Survey of Broadcast Journalism, 1968–1969* (Grosset & Dunlap, 1969).
8. "Agnew Demands Equal Time," 19. White appeared on *Firing Line* on September 22, 1969, to discuss his latest book, *The Making of the President 1968*.
9. Barrett, *The Alfred I. Dupont-Columbia University Survey, 1969–1970*, 32–33.
10. Patrick Brogan, *Spiked: The Short Life and Death of the National News Council* (Priority Press, 1985).
11. Reed Irvine, "A Proposal," 1, 6, Carton 114, Folder "AIM 1969," Accuracy in Media Papers, BYU.
12. Letter from Arthur G. McDowell to Raymond Bareiss, March 11, 1966, Box 137, Folder 4, Philbrick Papers, LOC.
13. Letter from Arthur G. McDowell to F. J. McNamara, May 5, 1953, Box 137, Folder 5, Philbrick Papers, LOC; and Letter from Arthur G. McDowell to John G. Keenan, October 6, 1958, Box 24, Folder 43, Research Files of Counterattack, TAM. For additional evidence of McDowell's friendly rapport with American Business Consultants, see Box 22, Folders 28 and 35, Research Files of Counterattack, TAM.
14. "Arthur McDowell Dies in Auto Crash While on Union Mission," *UIU Journal*, October 1966, 1–2, Box 137, Folder 4, Philbrick Papers, LOC.
15. Letter from Reed Irvine to Mimi Jaffe, October 25, 1978, Carton 31, Folder 12, Accuracy in Media Papers, BYU.
16. Michael T. Kaufman, "Reed Irvine, 82, the Founder of a Media Criticism Group, Dies," *New York Times*, November 19, 2004.
17. For examples of Irvine's economic writings on monetary policy, see Carton 6, Folder 69, Accuracy in Media Papers, BYU.
18. Reed Irvine, "Marijuana," *Evening Star*, September 20, 1969; and Reed Irvine, "Sex Education," *Evening Star*, June 10, 1969. Both in Carton 6, Folder 73, Accuracy in Media Papers, BYU.
19. Reed Irvine, "Wiretaps and Internal Security," *Evening Star*, March 4, 1971; and Reed Irvine, "Waskow, BUF and Police Control," *Evening Star*, July 28, 1968. Both in Carton 6, Folder 73, Accuracy in Media Papers, BYU.
20. Reed Irvine, "The US and Vietnam," *Evening Star*, October 25, 1969, Carton 6, Folder 73, Accuracy in Media Papers, BYU.
21. Reed Irvine, "Civil Disobedience," *Evening Star*, December 21, 1969, Carton 6, Folder 73, Accuracy in Media Papers, BYU.
22. Irvine wrote a letter to the managing editor of the Newseum (a now-defunct journalism museum then based in Rosslyn, Virginia) protesting that its exhibit on *Red Channels* "perpetuates the notion that those who opposed communism were the enemies of freedom." In defending the blacklist, Irvine cited liberally from the rationale *Counterattack* editors used to introduce their list of supposed subversives. Letter from Reed

Irvine to Eric Newton, April 14, 1997, Carton 131, Folder "Chron—March–April, 1997," Accuracy in Media Papers, BYU.

23. Irvine acknowledged the similarities between AIM's project and that of *Red Channels* but emphasized one key difference: "*Red Channels* was concerned with persons, not program content.... We focus on the content, not on the people responsible for that content." See Letter from Reed Irvine to Jim Motavalli, December 7, 1983, Carton 19, Folder 1 (October–December 1983), Accuracy in Media Papers, BYU.

24. Reed Irvine, "Reflections on the 20th Anniversary of AIM," delivered at the National Press Club, September 22, 1988, Carton 92, Folder "AIM 20th Anniversary Symposium," Accuracy in Media Papers, BYU.

25. Reed Irvine, "A Proposal," 1, 6.

26. While there is no evidence that Irvine was familiar with or directly influenced by Hunt's writings on the press and public opinion, there is evidence that Irvine was broadly aware of Hunt's media activism. See Letter from Reed Irvine to Richard C. Wald, August 20, 1973, Carton 94, Folder "AIM 1974," Accuracy in Media Papers, BYU.

27. H. L. Hunt, "Background of Facts Forum," *Facts Forum News*, December 1954, 28.

28. H. L. Hunt, "Famous Wildcatter Finds Word to Help Bewildered World: It Is 'Constructive,'" *Shreveport Times*, December 2, 1950.

29. Sen. Barry Goldwater was also a key proponent of the notion that there existed a latent conservative majority that was somehow "forgotten" or left behind by both interest groups (such as labor unions and civil rights organizations) and the mainstream press. Barry Goldwater, "The Forgotten American: A Statement of Proposed Republican Principles, Programs, and Objectives," *Human Events*, January 27, 1961, 3.

30. "Transcript of the Address by Vice President Spiro T. Agnew Des Moines, Iowa, November 13, 1969," in Barrett, *The Alfred I. Dupont-Columbia University Survey, 1969–1970*, 135.

31. Undated press release on the topic of Vice President Agnew's speech, signed by Benjamin Ginzburg, Carton 114, Folder "AIM 1969," Accuracy in Media Papers, BYU.

32. See Letter from Reed Irvine to Anne W. Branscomb, May 23, 1978, Carton 7, Folder 104, Accuracy in Media Papers, BYU.

33. "What Is AIM?" undated, with marginalia, Carton 114, Folder "AIM 1969," Accuracy in Media Papers, BYU. While undated, the letter was clearly circulated among AIM organizers prior to or at the moment of the group's formal founding. It lists as AIM secretary Neil Albert Salonen, then president of the anticommunist Freedom Leadership Foundation. By November 1969, after which AIM materials proliferate, Salonen's name is absent, replaced by Ginzburg.

34. It is worth noting that by the 1980s, both Agnew and Nixon had made modest personal donations to support AIM. Agnew donated $500 in December 1976; see Letter from Reed Irvine to Spiro T. Agnew, December 23, 1977, Carton 71, Folder "B," Accuracy in Media Papers, BYU. Nixon donated $1,000 in 1984, during a summer in which Irvine and Nixon correspondent relatively regularly. See Letters from Reed Irvine to Richard

5. LIBERAL MEDIA GOES MAINSTREAM   235

Nixon, July 6, July 9, July 12, July 19, and September 20, 1984, Carton 19, Folder 7, Accuracy in Media Papers, BYU.

35. The Accuracy in Media Papers, archived at BYU, contain few materials from the group's first two years of existence. For clearly incomplete examples of the group's earliest efforts and correspondence, see especially Carton 6, Folders 64–68, Accuracy in Media Papers, BYU.

36. Letter from Reed J. Irvine to Mrs. Edmund D. Campbell, April 20, 1970, Carton 6, Folder 68, Accuracy in Media Papers, BYU.

37. "Spreading the Message of Accuracy in Media," *AIM Report*, June 1973, insert. Somewhat undercutting Kalish's insistence of impartiality, this section of *AIM Report* was reprinted from the June 18, 1973, issue of *The Right Report*, "a newsletter that tells you what is happening on the American right," published by Richard Viguerie in the early 1970s. I accessed the *AIM Report* in bound volumes housed at New York Public Library. I reviewed all issues spanning 1972 through 1981.

38. AIM was officially incorporated on June 17, 1971, in the District of Columbia. Its initial filing named three officers: Reed J. Irvine, John K. McLean, and Abraham H. Kalish. For a copy of Accuracy in Media's incorporation paperwork, see Letter, with attachments, from Reed Irvine to Perry Peters, March 23, 1984, Carton 19, Folder 5 (January–March 1984), Accuracy in Media Papers, BYU. John McLean worked as a political analyst for the CIA from 1956 to 1960 and became an active participant in conservative groups in Alexandria, Virginia, thereafter. See "John K. McLean, 83, Former CIA Analyst," *Washington Times*, August 29, 2005.

39. These figures come from Kalish's public remarks to *The Right Report* in the summer of 1973. See "Spreading the Message of Accuracy in Media." AIM did not implement formal accounting practices until June 17, 1971. According to the group's initial IRS filing, AIM raised $6,411.71 in 1971. See Letter and enclosures from Internal Revenue Service District Director to Accuracy in Media, November 20, 1973, Carton 7, Folder 84, Accuracy in Media Papers, BYU. In the subsequent eleven months, by November 6, 1972, contributions to AIM had already grown sixfold, to $36,601.74. See Letter and enclosures from John K. McLean to Reed J. Irvine, November 13, 1972, Carton 7, Folder 84, Accuracy in Media Papers, BYU.

40. Press release announcing the AIM National Advisory Board, August 2, 1971, Carton 71, Folder "AIM Bulletins—1971," Accuracy in Media Papers, BYU. Earlier that year Staggers had subpoenaed CBS as part of a congressional investigation into antimilitary press bias, arguably aimed at punishing news outlets reporting on the Pentagon Papers. See Corydon B. Dunham, *Fighting for the First Amendment: Stanton of CBS vs. Congress and the Nixon White House* (Praeger, 1997).

41. Letter from Morris L. Ernst to Accuracy in Media, June 9, 1971, Container 130.1, Morris Leopold Ernst Papers (hereafter, Ernst Papers), MS-1331, Harry Ransom Center, University of Texas, Austin (hereafter, HRC).

42. See Letter from Morris L. Ernst to A. H. Kalish, June 16, 1971, Ernst Papers, HRC.

43. Letter from Abraham H. Kalish to Morris Ernst, June 18, 1971, Container 130.1, Ernst Papers, HRC.

44. Ernst heeded a recommendation from Dean Acheson, with whom Ernst was friendly. See Letter from Morris L. Ernst to Reuven Frank, August 27, 1971, Container 98.5, Ernst Papers, HRC.
45. Letter from Morris Ernst to Abraham Kalish, June 22, 1971; Letter from Abraham Kalish to Morris Ernst, June 26, 1971; and Letter from Morris Ernst to Abraham Kalish, June 30, 1971; all three in Container 130.1, Ernst Papers, HRC.
46. *AIM Report*, February 1973. The Ernst profile and a reprint of the January 11, 1973, edition of Ernst's *Villager* column can be found on the last page of an unnumbered insert.
47. Ernst, *First Freedom*, xiv; also quoted in *AIM Report*, February 1973.
48. Edith Efron, *The News Twisters* (Nash, 1971), xi–xii; see also Edith Efron with Clytia Chambers, *How CBS Tried to Kill a Book* (Nash, 1972).
49. "CBS News Shows Favoritism to McGovern," *AIM Report*, October 1972, 3.
50. "CBS Radio News Shows Favoritism to McGovern," *AIM Report*, November 1972, 7.
51. Morris L. Ernst, "I Have a Concern," *Villager*, December 14, 1972, Container 130.1, Ernst Papers, HRC. As part of this research, I also reviewed every Morris Ernst column for *The Villager* published between September 1963 and January 1974, all accessed on microfilm at New York Public Library.
52. Letter from Morris L. Ernst to Abraham Kalish, January 18, 1972, Container 130.1, Ernst Papers, HRC.
53. Letter from Morris Ernst to Abraham Kalish, July 23, 1973, Container 130.1, Ernst Papers, HRC. While Ernst made the connection between AIM's work and that of the liberal media reform movement of the 1940s, Kalish did not. In response to Ernst's insistence that AIM focus on its role in preserving a marketplace of ideas, Kalish suggested that "nobody" had "developed in some depth" such a theory and invited Ernst to do so for the *AIM Report*. Ernst declined to write such an article but replied asking whether Kalish had read *The First Freedom* and offering to send him a copy. See Letter from Abraham Kalish to Morris Ernst, August 8, 1973; and Letter from Morris Ernst to Abraham Kalish, August 17, 1973, both in Container 130.1, Ernst Papers, HRC.
54. See "List of people to whom MLE has asked Kalish to send sample copies, etc.," Container 130.1, Ernst Papers, HRC.
55. Letter from Morris L. Ernst to Spiro Agnew, March 2, 1973, Container 130.1, Ernst Papers, HRC.
56. Bryce W. Rucker, *The First Freedom* (Southern Illinois University Press, 1968).
57. In addition to Kalish, Luce's audience likely included many John Birch Society members and allies. That Luce targeted such a readership is evidenced by his decision to advertise in *The Review of the News*. See Phillip Abbott Luce, "What We Conservatives Have Got to Do About George McGovern," *Review of the News*, September 6, 1972. For more on Luce's highly public defection from radical left to radical right, see Phillip Abbott Luce, "Why I Quit the Extreme Left," *Saturday Evening Post*, May 8, 1965, 32–33. Luce would go on to write for several conservative movement publications, including *National Review*. See Stephen Walter Charry, "Phillip Abbott Luce and the Pink Sheet on the Left: New Right Anti-Communism in the 1970s" (MA thesis, Washington State University, 1990).

58. Kalish wrote letters to Frank on August 11 and August 17, and to Frank's boss, Julian Goodman, on August 18. Frank took issue with Kalish's "bullying" in a lengthy reply defending the network's part-time employment of the correspondent in question. See Letter from Reuven Frank to Abraham Kalish, August 19, 1971. All correspondence referenced accessible in Container 98.5, Ernst Papers, HRC.
59. See Letter from Reuven Frank to Morris Ernst, August 25, 1971, and Letter from Morris Ernst to Reuven Frank, August 27, 1971, Container 98.5, Ernst Papers, HRC. Ernst wrote that Frank's request was "the least I can expect of any organization with a name such as Accuracy in Media, Inc."
60. Letter from Morris Ernst to Abraham Kalish, August 30, 1971, emphasis in original, Container 98.5, Ernst Papers, HRC.
61. Letter from Abraham Kalish to Morris Ernst, October 1, 1971, in response to letter from Morris Ernst to Abraham Kalish, September 27, 1971, both in Container 130.1, Ernst Papers, HRC.
62. Letter from Morris Ernst to Reuben Frank, October 6, 1971, Container 130.1, Ernst Papers, HRC.
63. For a deeply researched analysis of how press criticism (right and left) impacted professional journalistic practices during this era, see Matthew Pressman, *On Press: The Liberal Values That Shaped the News* (Harvard University Press, 2018). See also Kevin M. Lerner, "A System of Self-Correction: A. M. Rosenthal, Daniel Patrick Moynihan, Press Criticism and the Birth of the Contemporary Newspaper Correction in the *New York Times*," *Journalism History* 42, no. 4 (2017): 191–200.
64. Luther A. Huston, "Eyes and Ears of AIM Monitor All News Media," *Editor & Publisher*, August 21, 1971, 42.
65. "Helping Hand," *Columbia Journalism Review*, January/February 1972, 4–6.
66. Abraham H. Kalish, "AIM as Media Critic: A Reply," *Columbia Journalism Review*, May/June 1972.
67. See Christopher Cimaglio, "'A Tiny and Closed Fraternity of Privileged Men': The Nixon–Agnew Anti-Media Campaign and the Liberal Roots of the US Conservative 'Liberal Media' Critique," *International Journal of Communication* 10 (2016): 1–19.
68. "Transcript of Address by Agnew Extending Criticism of News Coverage to Press," *New York Times*, November 21, 1969, 22.
69. "ASNE President Charges: Nixon Seeks to Control News Media," *Editor & Publisher*, November 22, 1969, 9.
70. Luther A. Huston, "Sigma Delta Chi Welcomes Women to Full Membership," *Editor & Publisher*, November 22, 1969, 13.
71. "Dear Mr. Vice President," *Editor & Publisher*, November 22, 1969, 6.
72. "Smoke Signals?" *Editor & Publisher*, November 29, 1969, 6.
73. Alfred Balk, "Beyond Agnewism," *Columbia Journalism Review*, Winter 1969–1970, 14–19.
74. Theodore H. White, "America's Two Cultures," *Columbia Journalism Review*, Winter 1969–1970, 8–13.

75. Edwin Diamond, "Multiplying Media Voices," *Columbia Journalism Review*, Winter 1969–1970, 22–27.
76. The Twentieth Century Fund was also the financial backer of the Institute for Propaganda Analysis, a short-lived media literacy initiative that played an important role in stigmatizing right-wing radio commentary during the interwar years. See A. J. Bauer, "Glittering Generalities: Reconsidering the Institute for Propaganda Analysis." *International Journal of Communication* 18 (2024): 1976–1994.
77. Brogan, *Spiked*, 16.
78. Letter from Abraham H. Kalish to Murray J. Rossant, December 4, 1972. Box 31, Folder 5, National News Council records, SW0102, Social Welfare History Archives, University of Minnesota, Minneapolis (hereafter, NNC).
79. Myriad letters from Abraham Kalish and Reed Irvine to executives at these outlets, carbon copied to the National News Council, can be found in Box 31, Folder 5, NNC. The pace was such that AIM earned a side-eyed mention in a *Washington Post* profile of the council, which had reportedly been "hearing several times a week" from AIM but had yet to receive a legitimate complaint. See Stephen Isaacs, "Media Panel Fights Obscurity," *Washington Post*, December 2, 1973, H2.
80. Letter from Abraham H. Kalish to Murray J. Rossant, December 11, 1972, Box 31, Folder 5, NNC.
81. Memorandum from Bill Arthur to Ned Schnurman, August 21, 1973, Box 31, Folder 5, NNC.
82. Letter from Abraham H. Kalish to William B. Arthur, October 22, 1973, Box 31, Folder 5, NNC.
83. Letter from Ned Schnurman to Abraham H. Kalish, November 2, 1973; and Letter from Abraham H. Kalish to Ned Schnurman, November 7, 1973, both in Box 31, Folder 5, NNC.
84. Minutes from November 12, 1973, meeting of the National News Council, pp. 7–8, Box 3, Folder 5, NNC.
85. For a list of all complaints filed with the National News Council from 1973–1984, see Box 92, Folder 1, NNC.
86. Undated, unsigned memo distinguishing the National News Council from Accuracy in Media, Box 31, Folder 6, NNC.
87. For a helpful overview of this conflict from AIM's perspective, see *AIM Report*, February 1975; and *AIM Report*, March 1975.
88. See "Jack Anderson Column Is Found 'Inaccurate,'" *Washington Post*, February 6, 1975, A3.
89. Jack Anderson, "'Accuracy in Media' a Front," United Feature Syndicate as published in the *Miami Herald*, March 11, 1975, clipping accessed in Carton 90, Folder "Anderson File," Accuracy in Media Papers, BYU.
90. Letter from Peter J. Celliers to Morris Ernst, March 6, 1975, Container 130.1, Ernst Papers, HRC.
91. Letter from Morris Ernst to Peter Celliers, March 7, 1975, Container 130.1, Ernst Papers, HRC.

92. See especially Letters from Reed Irvine to Jack Anderson dated October 4 and December 9, 1974, Carton 92, Folder "Jack Anderson," Accuracy in Media Papers, BYU.
93. Letter from Francis G. Wilson to editors of all newspapers carrying Jack Anderson's column, March 8, 1975, Container 130.1, Ernst Papers, HRC.
94. Letter from Reed Irvine to Morris Ernst, March 9, 1975, Container 130.1, Ernst Papers, HRC.
95. See Letters from Morris Ernst to Reed Irvine dated March 13 and April 9, 1975, Container 130.1, Ernst Papers, HRC.

6. CONSERVATIVE PRESS CRITICISM AND THE NEW RIGHT

1. The issue included an interview with Accuracy in Media founder Reed Irvine, reprinted from the John Birch Society weekly magazine *Review of the News*.
2. Richard A. Viguerie, "Big Media, Big Bias," *Conservative Digest*, October 1984, 46–47.
3. Richard Viguerie, in conversation with author, Manassas, Virginia, July 8, 2014. Asked to recall where he got "access to conservative ideas" before the infrastructure of the modern conservative movement was built, Viguerie reported that he listened to radio broadcasters John T. Flynn, Dan Smoot, and Fulton Lewis Jr.
4. For a helpful history of how several key conservative media figures—most notably, Clarence Manion, Henry Regnery, and William Rusher—played in this effort, see Nicole Hemmer, *Messengers of the Right: Conservative Media and the Transformation of American Politics* (University of Pennsylvania Press, 2016).
5. John A. Andrew, *The Other Side of the Sixties: Young Americans for Freedom and the Rise of Conservative Politics* (Rutgers University Press, 1997), 225. See also Gregory L. Schneider, *Cadres for Conservatism: Young Americans for Freedom and the Rise of the Contemporary Right* (New York University Press, 1999).
6. "Opportunity For Young Man, Conservative," *National Review*, July 15, 1961, 28; and David Franke, "Tower's Victory in Texas," *National Review*, July 15, 1961, 16, 30.
7. Viguerie, in conversation with author, emphasis his; and Richard Viguerie and David Franke, *America's Right Turn: How Conservatives Used New and Alternative Media to Take Power* (Bonus Books, 2004), dedication page.
8. By Viguerie's own admission, the term *New Right* was coined by *Washington Star* reporter John Fialka, who named Viguerie the movement's "godfather" in the summer of 1975. John Fialka, "The Godfather of the 'New Right' Feels the Torch Is Passing," *Washington Star*, June 23, 1975, A1, A10. Viguerie readily embraced the label, as evidenced in Richard Viguerie, *The New Right: We're Ready to Lead* (Viguerie Company, 1981).
9. Irvine also sent the proposal to AIM's first donor, Wilson C. Lucom; its first executive secretary, Benjamin Ginzburg; and the executive secretary of CACA, Marx Lewis, among others. Reed Irvine, "A Proposal," 1, 6, Carton 114, Folder "AIM 1969," Accuracy in Media Papers, BYU.

10. George Fowler, "The Press . . . Left, Right, Or Center?" *New Guard*, March 1961, 5–6; 6.
11. Lizabeth Cohen, *A Consumers' Republic: The Politics of Mass Consumption in Postwar America* (Vintage, 2003), 292–344; 309.
12. Peter S. Fischer, "Twenty Million Negroes—A Neglected Market," *Reporter of Direct Mail Advertising*, February 1963, 16–20.
13. Milton Pierce, "Politics: The Sleeping Giant of Direct Mail," *Reporter of Direct Mail Advertising*, March 1964, 23–26, 29–30.
14. Pierce, "Politics," 23.
15. For an inside account of the efforts to draft Goldwater, see J. William Middendorf II, *A Glorious Disaster: Barry Goldwater's Presidential Campaign and the Origins of the Conservative Movement* (Basic Books, 2006).
16. See especially Rick Perlstein, *Before the Storm: Barry Goldwater and the Unmaking of the American Consensus* (Hill & Wang, 2001).
17. So central are mailing lists to the direct marketing industry that *Reporter of Direct Mail Advertising* dedicated an entire special issue to the topic in July 1963—a special issue that, given his reported heavy readership at the time, Viguerie would have most certainly consumed with interest.
18. Viguerie, in conversation with author; and Viguerie and Franke, *America's Right Turn*, 98–103. Over the years, the Viguerie Company was headquartered in McLean, Tyson's Corner, Falls Church, and Manassas. By 1975, when he launched *Conservative Digest*, Viguerie had relocated his office to Falls Church.
19. For deeper histories of the objectivity within professional journalism, see Michael Schudson, "The Objectivity Norm in American Journalism," *Journalism* 2, no. 2 (2001): 149–170; and David T. Z. Mindich, *Just the Facts: How 'Objectivity' Came to Define American Journalism* (New York University Press, 1998).
20. Daniel C. Hallin, "The Passing of the 'High Modernism' of American Journalism," *Journal of Communication* 42, no. 3 (1992): 14–25; 15.
21. See William Rusher, "To the Readers of *National Review*," *National Review*, January 16, 1960, 34. For an early account of the magazine's financial troubles, see William F. Buckley Jr., "Can a Little Magazine Break Even?" *National Review*, October 10, 1959.
22. For a history of these contentious efforts by right-wing broadcasters to circumvent the Fairness Doctrine, and the consequences, see Heather Hendershot, *What's Fair on the Air: Cold War Right-Wing Broadcasting and the Public Interest* (University of Chicago Press, 2011). See also Paul Matzko, *Radio Right: How a Band of Broadcasters Took on the Federal Government and Built the Modern Conservative Movement* (Oxford University Press, 2020).
23. Fialka, "The Godfather of the 'New Right.'"
24. See Letter from Reed Irvine to Col. Charles F. Densford, March 29, 1979, Carton 31, Folder 10 "Reed Irvine Chron File January 1979," Accuracy in Media Papers, BYU.
25. "AIM Becomes Part Owner of Top News Media," *AIM Report*, July 1973, "Economic Council Letter" insert, 3.

26. "Texas Businessman Heads Group Seeking Control of CBS Network," *Birmingham Independent*, September 8, 1965, 3. See also "Media Unlimited to Sue CBS," *Birmingham Independent*, April 6, 1966, 3.
27. Paul Harvey, "Little David and the CBS Goliath," *Birmingham Independent*, October 8, 1965, 8.
28. *AIM Bulletin* press releases, April 23, 1974, and May 7, 1974, Carton 94, Folder "AIM 1974," Accuracy in Media Papers, BYU.
29. See "Accuracy in Broadcasting," *Investor Responsibility Research Center*, Analysis no. 6, March 24, 1975, Carton 115, Folder "Accuracy in Broadcasting Investor Responsibility Research Center," Accuracy in Media Papers, BYU.
30. "AIM Seeks Shareholder Support for TV Network Reforms," *AIM Report*, January 1975, 1–2.
31. Press release charging *Washington Post* with "systematically suppressing news that would be of interest to its readers," August 3, 1971, Carton 71, Folder "AIM Bulletins—1971," Accuracy in Media Papers, BYU.
32. For an especially detailed history of the myriad social, cultural, and political dynamics that resulted in Republican and conservative soul searching by 1975, see Rick Perlstein, *Invisible Bridge: The Fall of Nixon and the Rise of Reagan* (Simon and Schuster, 2014).
33. Perlstein, *Invisible Bridge*, 321.
34. William A. Rusher, *The Making of the New Majority Party* (Sheed & Ward, 1975); and "New Books: The Making of the New Majority Party," *Review of the News*, June 11, 1975, 43–46.
35. See also Patrick J. Buchanan, *The New Majority: President Nixon at Mid-Passage* (Girard, 1973).
36. Kevin P. Phillips, *Mediacracy: American Parties and Politics in the Communications Age* (Doubleday, 1975), 33.
37. While a reviewer for the *New York Times* agreed with Phillips's premise that the postindustrial knowledge economy was causing tectonic shifts in US political culture, he rejected Phillips's description of a putatively liberal new elite: "There is no doubt that something's afoot in the land but, praise God, it is not a hydra-headed monster called 'mediacracy.'" Phil Tracy, "Mediacracy," *New York Times*, May 4, 1975.
38. Jeffrey Hart, "Who Do You Hate?" *National Review*, May 9, 1975, 517. See also "Realignment Politics," *National Review*, February 28, 1975, 201–204.
39. See Medford Evans, "Conspiracy Revealed in *New York Times*," *Review of the News*, September 17, 1975, 31–38.
40. In its second issue *Conservative Digest* published an excerpt of William Rusher's *The Making of the New Majority Party*. In the third issue it republished a Kevin Phillips *Newsweek* column that riffed off his findings in *Mediacracy*. See William A. Rusher, "The Making of the New Majority Party," *Conservative Digest*, June 1975, 40–43; and Kevin P. Phillips, "Reagan and Wallace: Shaping the Right Deal for America," *Conservative Digest*, July 1975, 30–31.

41. Viguerie, in conversation with author.
42. Circulation figures are culled from statements of ownership, management, and circulation published each December in *Conservative Digest*. By the end of December 1975 the magazine boasted a paid circulation of forty-five thousand. Circulation averaged six-figures for the first and only time in 1977, before declining by approximately ten thousand per year through the mid-1980s, when it leveled out averaging in the mid- to low twenty thousands. My analysis of *Conservative Digest* involved reviewing all issues from 1975 through 1985, accessed in bound volumes at New York Public Library.
43. Richard A. Viguerie, "From the Publisher," *Conservative Digest*, May 1975, 1.
44. Viguerie, in conversation with author.
45. Abraham Kalish, "How to Help Your Child Break the TV Habit," *Conservative Digest*, June 1975, 47.
46. "CBS and the Fall of Saigon," *Conservative Digest*, July 1975, 5. The article, which accused CBS of bias and of "turning public sentiment against" war in Vietnam, was initially printed in the April 1975 issue of *AIM Report*. AIM's presence in *Conservative Digest* was irregular but steady.
47. Herschensohn authored the book *The Gods of Antenna* (Arlington House, 1976), which doubled as a critique of liberal bias in television news and a defense of Nixon.
48. Brien Benson, "How to Fight Bias in the News," *Conservative Digest*, September 1977, 10.
49. Benson, "How to Fight Bias," 13. For more on how Nixon-era conservatives paved the way for right-wing dominance of cable news, see Kathryn Cramer Brownell, *24/7 Politics: Cable Television and the Fragmenting of America from Watergate to Fox News* (Princeton University Press, 2023).
50. Facsimile from Reed Irvine to Chip Wood, September 1, 1988, Carton 56, Folder "Irvine Chron., July–September 1988," Accuracy in Media Papers, BYU. Wood had requested that Irvine sign his name to a "generic" endorsement of *Conservative Digest*, but Irvine responded with his own personally tailored blurb emphasizing the magazine's particular role in confronting the liberal media hegemony.
51. Instances of *Conservative Digest* either explicitly promoting or reprinting AIM's media criticism, in both advertising and editorial content, are widespread. For two especially concentrated examples, see the September 1977 and October 1984 issues, both of which feature cover stories and expanded coverage on liberal media bias. Reed Irvine contributed to, and AIM featured prominently in, both issues. "How to Fight Bias in the News," *Conservative Digest*, September 1977; "The Conventions: Were the Networks Objective," *Conservative Digest*, October 1984.
52. Although geographically distant from its Northern Virginia organizers (she lived in St. Louis, Missouri), Schlafly was an especially celebrated and influential figure within the New Right and received the sort of hagiographical profiles in *Conservative Digest* typically reserved for politicians like Ronald Reagan and George Wallace. See William J. Gill, "The First Lady of American Conservatism," *Conservative Digest*, September 1975, 28–31.

6. CONSERVATIVE PRESS CRITICISM AND THE NEW RIGHT 243

53. Elaine Donnelly, *One Side Versus the Other Side: A Primer on Access to the Media* (Eagle Forum Education and Legal Defense Fund, 1981), accessed via Patrick Henry College Library, Purcellville, Virginia. See also, "Eagle Forum Is Offering New Media Primer," *Conservative Digest*, December 1981, 37.
54. For example, in July 1969—two months before AIM was informally launched—Schlafly was pejoratively referring to "liberal *Newsweek*" and lamenting that liberal candidates for office benefited from the "strong support of the press." See "Shift to the Right—Rift on the Left," *Phyllis Schlafly Report*, July 1969.
55. Solicitation letter from Phyllis Schlafly to Mrs. S. Ballentine, received November 5, 1974. This letter, as well as the issues of *The Phyllis Schlafly Report* cited in this chapter, is accessible in the Group Research Collection housed in the Rare Book & Manuscript Library at Columbia University.
56. For a helpful contemporaneous explanation of the citizens agreement phenomenon, see Preston R. Padden, "The Emerging Role of Citizens' Groups in Broadcast Regulation," *Federal Communications Bar Journal* 25 (1972): 82–110. See also Philip M. Napoli, "Public Interest Media Advocacy and Activism as a Social Movement," *Annals of the International Communication Association* 33, no. 1 (2009): 385–429.
57. "How to Cope with TV and Radio Bias," *Phyllis Schlafly Report*, April 1976, section 2.
58. "Secret TV Station Contracts with Liberal Coalitions," *Phyllis Schlafly Report*, February 1982, section 1. In addition to pressuring the FCC, Eagle Forum used the citizens' agreements issue to solicit donations. See Solicitation letter from Phyllis Schlafly to L. A. Meacham, received March 23, 1983, Carton 89, Folder "Eagle Forum," Accuracy in Media Papers, BYU.
59. Correspondence between Greg Brown and Reed Irvine, March 1983, Carton 89, Folder "Eagle Forum," Accuracy in Media Papers, BYU.
60. There was considerable collaboration between groups. For example, in 1986 AIM joined forces with Eagle Forum, American Security Council, and Conservative Caucus in condemning the ABC television thriller *Amerika*. See Reed Irvine, "ABC's 'Amerika': A Good Idea Gone Wrong," December 17, 1986, Carton 23, Folder "Irvine Chron October–December 1986," Accuracy in Media Papers, BYU.
61. Irvine also spread AIM's message through a syndicated column, run by 130 newspapers and magazines with a total circulation of two million. For a thorough assessment of AIM's reach at the end of 1977, as reported to the group's primary funder the Scaife Family Charitable Trusts, see Letter from Reed Irvine to R. Daniel McMichael, November 8, 1977, Carton 71, Folder "Reed Irvine Outgoing Chron File," Accuracy in Media Papers, BYU.
62. Richard A. Viguerie, "From the Publisher: You the Contributor Are the Real Hero of 1980 Election," *Conservative Digest*, December 1980, 40.
63. For an exception, see "The Mugging of the President," *AIM Report*, October 11, 1981.
64. AIM received six-figures-worth of annual contributions in the latter half of the 1970s and reported an annual income of more than $1 million for the first time in 1982. While formidable for a relatively small organization, the sum was insufficient to the task of

counteracting putative liberal bias in a mainstream media consisting of three major broadcast networks and dozens of major newspapers. Carton 71, Folder "AIM Financial 12/76 o 10/82," Accuracy in Media Papers, BYU.

65. For a profile elucidating Dolan's influential role in the New Right, see "NCPAC's Terry Dolan: He's Playing Key Role in New Right's Successes," *Conservative Digest*, December 1980, 2–5.

66. S. Robert Lichter and Stanley Rothman, "Media and Business Elites: Two Classes in Conflict?," *Public Opinion* 4, no. 5 (1981): 42–46, 59–60. An influential book-length version of this study was published five years later; see S. Robert Lichter, Stanley Rothman, and Linda Lichter, *The Media Elite: America's New Powerbrokers* (Adler & Adler, 1986).

67. John T. (Terry) Dolan, "Strategy to Combat the Liberal Media," April 1983, emphasis in original, Box 13, Folder "National Conservative Foundation (1 of 2)," Morton Blackwell Files, Ronald Reagan Presidential Library (hereafter, RR).

68. See Letter from Reed Irvine to Harold W. Siebens, July 29, 1983, with "Accuracy in Media Television Project" report enclosed, Carton 19, Folder "July–September 1983," Accuracy in Media Papers, BYU.

69. Media studies scholar Arthur Hayes has interpreted *Television's Vietnam* as among AIM's greatest successes as a media watchdog. See Arthur S. Hayes, *Press Critics Are the Fifth Estate: Media Watchdogs in America* (Praeger, 2008).

70. Lawrence J. Delaney Jr. and Leslie Lenkowsky, "The New Voice on Campus: 'Alternative Student Journalism,'" *Academic Questions* 1, no. 2 (1988): 32–38.

71. In his 1983 proposal Dolan had suggested establishing a tongue-in-cheek "Janet Cooke Award," named after a disgraced *Washington Post* reporter who was found to have fabricated a profile of an eight-year-old heroin addict. Dolan hoped to use the award to identify particularly egregious instances of liberal media bias. While the award never came to be, the "Janet Cooke Award" became the name of a recurring column in the Media Research Center's newsletter *MediaWatch* from the late 1980s through the 1990s.

72. Farah once approached Irvine about a partnership whereby the Western Journalism Center would serve as a sort of West Coast branch of AIM. Irvine does not seem to have responded, and the partnership never came to fruition. See Letter from Joseph Farah to Reed Irvine, November 9, 1992, Carton 133, Folder "Farah, Joseph," Accuracy in Media Papers, BYU.

73. In a letter to a senior vice president at the department store Neiman Marcus, Irvine noted his acquaintance with "many of the people who are involved with the Heritage Foundation, including Ed Feulner" and reported that the think tank was "dedicated to the cause of bringing the country around to more sensible policies in fields ranging from education to national defense." See Letter from Reed Irvine to Dudley J. Ramsden, January 28, 1980, Carton 31, Folder 11 "Irvine Chron file January, 1980," Accuracy in Media Papers, BYU. Irvine was among twelve hundred supporters to attend a March 1979 gala hosted by Eagle Forum to celebrate its successes is opposing the Equal Rights Amendment and wrote several letters complaining to news outlets for failing to report on the "eloquent address" of Schlafly, who Irvine regarded as "a woman of

tremendous achievements." See, especially, Letter from Reed Irvine to George Beveridge, April 12, 1979, Carton 31, Folder "Reed Irvine Chron File January 1979," Carton 31, Folder 11 "Irvine Chron file January, 1980," Accuracy in Media Papers, BYU.

74. Names of members and insight into the Council for National Policy's underreported activities are drawn primarily from two sources: A pamphlet containing the program for the Council for National Policy's board of governors meeting held in Dallas, Texas, on August 17–18, 1984, accessed in Box 20F, Folder "National Council for Policy," Faith Ryan Whittlesey Files, RR; and council publications and ephemera found in Box 6, Folders "Council for National Policy 1–2," Morton Blackwell Files, RR. See also Carton 1, Folder 10, Accuracy in Media Papers, BYU.
75. Letter from Reed Irvine to Louis Jenkins, April 4, 1983, Carton 19, Folder "Irvine Chron April–June, 1983," Accuracy in Media Papers, BYU. Irvine resigned in 1983 but seems to have maintained some form of affiliation or contact with the group through at least 1985.
76. Letter from Reed Irvine to Margo Carlisle, October 2, 1985, Carton 1, Folder 10, Accuracy in Media Papers, BYU.
77. Letter from Reed Irvine to Rudolph S. Rasin, June 17, 1986, Carton 22, Folder "Irvine Chron April–June 1986," Accuracy in Media Papers, BYU.
78. Letter from Reed Irvine to Richard J. Mathias, January 11, 1985, Carton 1, Folder 11, Accuracy in Media Papers, BYU.
79. For more on Irvine's work with Conservative Leadership Conference, see Carton 91, Folder "Conservative Leadership Conference," Accuracy in Media Papers, BYU.

7. THE END OF FAIRNESS

1. Rush Limbaugh, *See, I Told You So* (Pocket Books, 1993), 291–292.
2. Ken Magri, "Living Under Limbaugh," *Sacramento News & Review*, February 19, 2009.
3. Brian Rosenwald, *Talk Radio's America: How an Industry Took Over a Political Party That Took Over the United States* (Harvard University Press, 2019), 28. See also Zev Chafets, *Rush Limbaugh: An Army of One* (Sentinel, 2010).
4. James Bowman, "The Leader of the Opposition," *National Review*, September 6, 1993, 44–52; 44.
5. Limbaugh, *See, I Told You So*, 333, emphasis in original.
6. For a helpful analysis of the policy's legacy among progressives and conservatives alike, see Victor Pickard, "The Strange Life and Death of the Fairness Doctrine: Tracing the Decline of Positive Freedoms in American Policy Discourse," *International Journal of Communication* 12 (2018): 3434–3453.
7. Limbaugh, *See, I Told You So*, 323–340; 325.
8. Limbaugh, *See, I Told You So*, 336. See also *Broadcasting Yearbook 1980*, D-74; *Broadcasting & Cable Yearbook 1993*, B-524; and *Broadcasting & Cable Yearbook 1996*, B590, all available at https://www.worldradiohistory.com/Broadcasting-Yearbook.htm.
9. Limbaugh, *See, I Told You So*, 87–88.

10. For a more detailed account of this conflict, see Paul Matzko, *Radio Right: How a Band of Broadcasters Took on the Federal Government and Built the Modern Conservative Movement* (Oxford University Press, 2020).
11. Fred W. Friendly, *The Good Guys, the Bad Guys and the First Amendment: Free Speech vs. Fairness in Broadcasting* (Vintage, 1975), 32–42.
12. Nicole Hemmer, in *Messengers of the Right: Conservative Media and the Transformation of American Politics* (University of Pennsylvania Press, 2016), notes that Cook's article helped her realize the extent of right-wing broadcast activism before the 1980s. As I've argued elsewhere, partisan watchdog and oppositional research efforts on both the Left and Right are important archives of political conflict. Historians who hope to build on Hemmer's and my work while studying the 1990s onward should look for contemporaneous works published by Chip Berlet. See A. J. Bauer, "Agent and Archive: Chip Berlet and the Historicity of Right-Watchers," in *Exposing the Right and Fighting for Democracy: Celebrating Chip Berlet as Journalist and Scholar*, ed. Pam Chamberlain, Matthew Lyons, Abby Scher, and Spencer Sunshine (Routledge, 2021).
13. Fred J. Cook, "Radio Right: Hate Clubs of the Air," *Nation*, May 25, 1964, 523–527.
14. For an account of these early days of FCC Fairness Doctrine enforcement, see Friendly, *Good Guys, the Bad Guys*, 12–31. See also Federal Communications Commission, "Applicability of the Fairness Doctrine in the Handling of Controversial Issues of Public Importance," 29 Fed. Reg. 10416, *Federal Communications Commission Reports* 40 FCC (1964): 598–614.
15. Cook, "Radio Right," 526.
16. Friendly, *Good Guys, the Bad Guys*, 42.
17. Friendly, *Good Guys, the Bad Guys*, 9.
18. Friendly, *Good Guys, the Bad Guys*, 10.
19. Friendly, *Good Guys, the Bad Guys*, 43–49.
20. *Red Lion Broadcasting Co. Inc. v. FCC*, 395 US 367 (1969).
21. CBS, NBC, and PBS vigorously contested AIM's many complaints and lawsuits against each. ABC, conversely, seems to have yielded somewhat to AIM's pressure. For example, AIM praised ABC in February 1974 for engaging in prior restraint, canceling an episode of the *Dick Cavett Show* that was due to feature several leaders of the New Left. See "ABC Tells Dick Cavett to Air Both Sides of Controversial Issues," *AIM Report*, February 1974, 1–2.
22. "Statement of Accuracy in Media, Inc. in the matter of the Handling of Public Issues Under the Fairness Doctrine and the Public Interest Standards of the Communications Act Before the Federal Communications Commission," March 30, 1972, Carton 94, No Folder (loose papers), Accuracy in Media Papers, BYU.
23. See, for example, Elaine Donnelly, "Protecting the 'Marketplace of Ideas,'" *Detroit News*, January 5, 1984, clipping accessed in Box 1, Folder "FCC Fairness Doctrine 1984," Elaine Chenevert Donnelly Papers, Bentley Historical Library, University of Michigan (hereafter, UM).
24. "Accuracy in Media Sues to Compel FCC Action on Fairness Doctrine Complaints," *AIM Report*, December 1972.

25. "FCC Acts on AIM Complaint Against NBC on Pension Program," *AIM Report*, February 1973.
26. "NBC Distorts the Pension Picture, Giving Assistance to Controversial Legislation," *AIM Report*, January 1973.
27. "FCC Rules That NBC Program Violated Fairness Doctrine, Finds Program on Pension Plans Unfair as AIM Charged," *AIM Report*, May 1973.
28. "AIM Complaint Against NBC's Documentary on Private Pension Plans Upheld by Federal Communications Commission," *AIM Report*, December 1973, 1–2.
29. "AIM Upsets the Networks," *AIM Report*, July 1973, 4–5.
30. "Our Bitter Pill," *AIM Report*, March 1975, 1, 7. Irvine again challenged the FCC's "guts" in reporting the Supreme Court's decision not to take AIM's appeal. See "Taps for 'Pensions,'" *AIM Report*, March 1976, 8.
31. "AIM Hits Two FCC Nominees for Fairness Doctrine Stand," *AIM Report*, July 1974, 3–4.
32. Irvine launched his syndicated column in August 1975, and within a month fifty-seven daily and two weekly newspapers, representing a combined circulation of more than 1.4 million, had signed up to receive it. See "AIM Column Off to a Fast Start," *AIM Report*, September 1975, 7. The column launched as the NBC lawsuit reached a critical juncture, with AIM filing a last-ditch appeal to the Supreme Court. See "'Pensions' Case Rehearing Denied," *AIM Report*, August 1975, 6.
33. Reed J. Irvine, "Flunking the FCC," *AIM Report*, August 1975, 4. For additional examples of Irvine critiquing the FCC's implementation of the Fairness Doctrine in 1975, see also Reed J. Irvine, "CBS Under the Gun," *AIM Report*, September 19, 1975; Reed J. Irvine, "Fairness: The Broken Promise," *AIM Report*, October 3, 1975; Reed J. Irvine, "Son of A Gun," *AIM Report*, October 10, 1975; and Reed J. Irvine, "Irresponsibility in Public Broadcasting," *AIM Report*, November 28, 1975. All sources in this note from Carton 7, Folder 83, Accuracy in Media Papers, BYU.
34. Reed J. Irvine, "The Fairness Doctrine Is Foully Administered," April 15, 1977, Carton 6, Folder 70, Accuracy in Media Papers, BYU.
35. Eyvette Flynn, Memorandum for the Director of OMB, Subject: Fairness Doctrine, April 15, 1987, p. 3, William Ball Files, OA15332, Folder: Fairness Doctrine II, RR.
36. "Reagan Appoints a Communications Lawyer to FCC," *New York Times*, March 14, 1981; and Milton Mueller, "Interview with Mark S. Fowler," *Reason*, November 1, 1981.
37. For a detailed accounting of Reagan's 1976 primary campaign against Ford, see Rick Perlstein, *Invisible Bridge: The Fall of Nixon and the Rise of Reagan* (Simon and Schuster, 2014).
38. "FCC Outlook: Fowler Leading Contender for Chairmanship; Lee to Get the Nod in Interim," *Broadcasting*, November 19, 1981, 31.
39. Margaret Garrard Warner, "FCC Head Is Expected to Be Mark Fowler, A Nominee Sure to Please Broadcasters," *Wall Street Journal*, March 13, 1981, 8.
40. "Goldenson Goes to the Heart of the Matter," *Broadcasting*, September 22, 1980, 24. See also "The Laissez Faire Legacy of Charlie Ferris," *Broadcasting*, January 19, 1981, 37–42; 37.

41. Ernest Holsendolph, "FCC Change Promised," *New York Times*, May 19, 1981, D2.
42. "FCC Head Vows Eased TV Rules," *New York Times*, June 13, 1981, 31.
43. Mueller, "Interview with Mark S. Fowler."
44. "FCC Sets Forth Proposals for Amending Communications Act," September 17, 1981, Box 1, Folder "FCC Fairness Doctrine 1984," Elaine Chenevert Donnelly Papers, Bentley Historical Library, UM.
45. "FCC Sets Forth Proposals."
46. Mark S. Fowler, "Freedom of (Electronic) Speech," *Washington Post*, September 20, 1981, C7.
47. "Fairness Without Doctrine," *Washington Post*, September 21, 1981, A12.
48. "What's Fair on the Modern Air," *New York Times*, September 29, 1981, A26.
49. "One of Their Own in the White House," *Broadcasting*, January 26, 1981, 23–24.
50. "Remarks by President Ronald Reagan During Interview with TV Guide Writers. Oval Office." January 18, 1982, NAID: 161344568, Collection: Records of the White House Communications Agency (Reagan Administration), Series: Presidential Audio Recordings, January 20, 1981–January 20, 1989, RR.
51. Juanita Frankie Clogston, "The Repeal of the Fairness Doctrine and the Irony of Talk Radio: A Story of Political Entrepreneurship, Risk, and Cover," *Journal of Policy History* 28, no. 2 (2016): 375–396.
52. "Cronkite Warns of Growing Trend of Censorship," *Broadcasting*, April 12, 1982, 32.
53. Letter with enclosed speech script from Mark S. Fowler to T. Kenneth Cribb, March 22, 1982, Edwin Meese III Files, Box 30 (OA 9450), Folder: "Federal Communications Commission (4)," RR.
54. "Hands Crossed?" *Broadcasting*, April 12, 1982, 7; and "Reagan Supports First Amendment Rights for Broadcasters," *Broadcasting*, April 12, 1982, 31.
55. Caroline E. Mayer, "NAB Prodded by Fowler to Fight Restrictions," *Washington Post*, April 8, 1982, D11, D14.
56. General Fairness Doctrine Obligations of Broadcasters, Notice of Inquiry, 49 Fed. Reg. 20,317 (1984).
57. *FCC v. League of Women Voters*, 468 US 364 (1984).
58. Federal Communications Commission, "In the Matter of Inquiry into Section 73.1910 of the Commission's Rules and Regulations Concerning the General Fairness Doctrine Obligations of Broadcast Licensees," in Gen. Docket 84–282, FCC 85-495 (Adopted: August 7, 1985), 147.
59. See, for examples, "Reed Irvine (AIM) oral statement of February 1, 1983, on the Fairness Doctrine"; "Statement of Reed Irvine . . . in Opposition to S. 1917 Repealing the Fairness Doctrine, Before the Senate Committee on Commerce, Science and Transportation, Feb. 1, 1984"; "Statement of Reed Irvine . . . Before the Federal Communications Commission Hearing on the Fairness Doctrine, February 8, 1985," all found in Carton 116, No Folder (loose papers), Accuracy in Media Papers, BYU.
60. John T. Hemenway, "Concern of Accuracy in Media," statement before to the Federal Communications Commission in regard to the proposed modification in the

7. THE END OF FAIRNESS   249

Fairness Doctrine, the Personal Attack Rule, and Political Editorial Rules," September 6, 1983, Carton 116, No Folder (loose papers), Accuracy in Media Papers, BYU.

61. "A Joint Release From: Accuracy in Media, American Legal Foundation, American Media Business Council, Committee for a Free Press, Conservative Caucus, and Leadership Council," August 15, 1983, Carton 116, No Folder (loose papers), Accuracy in Media Papers, BYU.

62. "Statement of Reed Irvine . . . Before the Federal Communications Commission Hearing on the Fairness Doctrine, February 8, 1985," Carton 116, No Folder (loose papers), Accuracy in Media, BYU.

63. Reed Irvine, "Conservatives Should Demand the Enforcement of the Fairness Doctrine, Not Abolition," Carton 116, No Folder (loose papers), Accuracy in Media, BYU.

64. Paul Weyrich, "Some Good from Osgood," *Conservative Digest*, July 1984, 42.

65. Memorandum for the President, Subject: Enrolled Bill S 742—Fairness in Broadcasting Act of 1987 from James Miller III, June 12, 1987, David Bockorny Files, OA 17458, Folder: "Fairness Doctrine," RR.

66. Memorandum for the President, Subject: Enrolled Bill S 742.

67. Memorandum for Rhett Dawson from Gary Bauer, Subject: Fairness Doctrine Legislation, June 16, 1987, Series I, Box 2, Folder "Fairness Doctrine," Howard H. Baker Jr. Files, RR.

68. See, for example, Memorandum for the President, Subject: "Enrolled Bill S. 742—Fairness in Broadcasting Act of 1987," June 12, 1987, OA15332, Folder "Fairness Doctrine I," William Ball Files, RR.

69. Memorandum for Rhett Dawson from Gary Bauer.

70. See Letter from Phyllis Schlafly to Elaine Donnelly, January 29, 1982; and Elaine Donnelly, "Why FCC Fairness Rules Should Not Be Repealed," September 1982, both found in Box 1, Folder "FCC Fairness Doctrine 1984," Donnelly Papers, UM. See also "FCC Tries to Abolish TV Fairness & Decency Rules," *Phyllis Schlafly Report*, December 1983, section 1.

71. Statement by President Ronald Reagan addressed to the Senate of the United States, June 20, 1987, OA18016, Folder "Fairness Doctrine," Public Affairs/Records, RR.

72. "Phasing Out Fairness," *AIM Report*, July-B 1987. Irvine cited Schlafly's Stop ERA campaign as an example of the Fairness Doctrine's successful applications.

73. Michael Massing, "Who's Afraid of Reed Irvine? The Rise and Decline of Accuracy in Media," *Nation*, September 13, 1986, 200–214.

74. Edward S. Herman and Noam Chomsky, *Manufacturing Consent: The Political Economy of the Mass Media* (Pantheon, 1988), 27–28. Interestingly, Herman and Chomsky built their "propaganda model" on Ben Bagdikian's 1983 book *The Media Monopoly*. As we saw in chapter 3, Bagdikian was the reporter who exposed Facts Forum as a right-wing front in late 1953 and early 1954.

75. AIM saw the proliferation of conservative media outlets as more blessing than curse. See, for example, Cliff Kincaid, "Talk Radio: A Boon for Conservatives," *Human Events*, July 27, 1991.
76. For details of AIM's collaborations with NET, see Carton 135, Folder "NET Correspondence," Accuracy in Media Papers, BYU.
77. AIM initially announced its change of position on the Fairness Doctrine in September 1993, attributing the shift to the proliferation of conservative media outlets: "We are struck by the explosion of media outlets now available to the American public.... That strong alterative voices are gaining favor with the public galls liberals." Transcript, Joe Goulden and Cliff Kincaid, *Media Monitor*, "Media No Longer Needs Fairness Doctrine," September 16, 1993, Carton 134, Folder "Limbaugh, Rush," Accuracy in Media Papers, BYU.
78. Transcript, Reed Irvine and Cliff Kincaid, "Who's Behind the Fairness Doctrine?" *Media Monitor*, aired November 17, 1993, Carton 134, Folder "Limbaugh, Rush," Accuracy in Media Papers, BYU.
79. Lewis Grossberger, "The Rush Hours," *New York Times*, December 16, 1990, 58.
80. Transcript, *Rush Limbaugh Radio Show*, November 19, 1993 (approx. 1:40 p.m.), Folder "Limbaugh, Rush," Accuracy in Media Papers, BYU. Emphasis in original.
81. See Note with enclosures from Cliff Kincaid to Reed Irvine, December 6, 1993, Carton 134, Folder "Limbaugh, Rush," Accuracy in Media Papers, BYU. By March 1994 Kincaid had gone so far as to retain legal counsel in preparation for a defamation suit that seems never to have materialized. See Letter from Alan P. Dye to Rush Limbaugh, March 21, 1994, Carton 134, Folder "Limbaugh, Rush," Accuracy in Media Papers, BYU.
82. For more on the importance of taste in the success of right-wing media, see Reece Peck, *Fox Populism: Branding Conservatism as Working Class* (Cambridge University Press, 2019). For more on the role of humor in right-wing media, see A. J. Bauer, "Why So Serious? Studying Humor on the Right," *Media, Culture & Society* 45, no. 5 (2023): 1067–1074; Raúl Pérez, *The Souls of White Jokes: How Racist Humor Fuels White Supremacy* (Stanford University Press, 2022); and Matt Sienkiewicz and Nick Marx, *That's Not Funny: How the Right Makes Comedy Work for Them* (University of California Press, 2022).
83. Limbaugh, *See, I Told You So*, 88. See also Charlie Bertsch, "Gramsci Rush: Limbaugh on the 'Culture War,'" *International Gramsci Society Newsletter*, no. 6 (August 1996), 11–15.
84. Richard Viguerie, in conversation with author, Manassas, Virginia, July 8, 2014. Viguerie insisted that New Right leaders were, for the most part, not well versed in socialist strategy, and he denied having read Lenin or Gramsci. Limbaugh, on the other hand, name-dropped Gramsci in his 1993 book *See, I Told You So*.
85. Kathleen Hall Jamieson and Joseph Cappella, *Echo Chamber: Rush Limbaugh and the Conservative Media Establishment* (Oxford University Press, 2008).
86. Transcript, *Rush Limbaugh Radio Show*, November 19, 1993.

CONCLUSION

1. For an astute depiction of the milieu in which I cut my political teeth, see John Ganz, *When the Clock Broke: Con Men, Conspiracists, and How America Cracked Up in the Early 1990s* (Farrar, Straus and Giroux, 2024).
2. Mary Ann Baker, in conversation with author, June 27, 2018.
3. I found my copy of this sticker some thirty years later at Jim Reed Books / The Museum of Fond Memories in Birmingham, Alabama. Thanks to McDowell for including a dated copyright notification on the sticker so I could appropriately situate it.
4. For a foundational account of how journalists' status as "secondary definers" of the news can result in moral panics, see Stuart Hall, Chas Critcher, Tony Jefferson, John Clarke, and Brian Roberts, *Policing the Crisis: Mugging, the State, and Law and Order* (Macmillan, 1978), 53–77.
5. See Kathleen Hall Jamieson and Joseph, Cappella, *Echo Chamber: Rush Limbaugh and the Conservative Media Establishment* (Oxford University Press, 2008).
6. Rush Limbaugh, in conversation with Steve Kroft, *60 Minutes* (CBS News), October 6, 1991.
7. For more on Limbaugh and the conservative takeover of AM radio, see Brian Rosenwald, *Talk Radio's America: How an Industry Took Over a Political Party That Took Over the United States* (Harvard University Press, 2019).
8. Elizabeth Kolbert, "TV Channel Plans Conservative Talk, All Day, All Night," *New York Times*, November 27, 1993, 1, 9.
9. Reece Peck, *Fox Populism: Branding Conservatism as Working Class* (Cambridge University Press, 2019).
10. Jim Rutenberg, "Conservative Cable Channel Gains in Ratings War," *New York Times*, September 18, 2000, C1.
11. For a taste of this complication, see Lawrence K. Grossman, "Bullies on the Block," *Columbia Journalism Review*, January/February 1997, 19–20. Biographies of Ted Turner and Rupert Murdoch also variously narrate the complicated political and financial machinations that ultimately pushed Time Warner to carry Fox News, against Turner's opposition.
12. Gabriel Sherman, *The Loudest Voice in the Room: How the Brilliant, Bombastic Roger Ailes Built Fox News—and Divided a Country* (Random House, 2014).
13. John Lippman, "News Corp. Reports Loss of $23 Million," *Wall Street Journal*, February 8, 2001, B15.
14. Jim Rutenberg, "Cable's War Coverage Suggests a New 'Fox Effect' on Television Journalism," *New York Times*, April 16, 2003, B9.
15. David Brock, *Republican Noise Machine: Right-Wing Media and How It Corrupts Democracy* (Crown, 2004).
16. Jamieson and Cappella, *Echo Chamber*, vii.
17. I conducted a multi-sited ethnography of the Tea Party movement in the summer of 2010 and can personally attest to attending meetings organized by these and other

right-wing groups. See also Theda Skocpol and Vanessa Williamson, *The Tea Party and the Remaking of Republican Conservatism* (Oxford University Press, 2016).

18. See "The Right-Wing Media Machine," *Extra!* Special Edition, March/April 1995. *Extra!* was the magazine of the progressive media watchdog Fairness and Accuracy in Reporting (FAIR).
19. Jeremy W. Peters, "A Compass for Conservative Politics," *New York Times*, July 10, 2011.
20. Andrew Breitbart, *Righteous Indignation: Excuse Me While I Save the World!* (Grand Central Publishing, 2011), 15; 4, emphasis in original.
21. For more on the history of digital news, including *Breitbart*, see Ben Smith, *Traffic: Genius, Rivalry, and Delusion in the Billion-Dollar Race to Go Viral* (Penguin, 2023).
22. James Rainey, "Breitbart.com Sets Sights on Ruling the Conservative Conversation," *Los Angeles Times*, August 1, 2012; and Max Kutner, "Meet Robert Mercer, the Mysterious Billionaire Benefactor of Breitbart," *Newsweek*, November 21, 2016.
23. Michael Canyon Meyer, "The Daily Caller," *Columbia Journalism Review*, January 17, 2011; Michael Grynbaum, "Tucker Carlson Sells His Stake in The Daily Caller," *New York Times*, June 10, 2020; and Anthony Nadler, A. J. Bauer, and Magda Konieczna, *Conservative Newswork: A Report on the Values and Practices of Online Journalists on the Right* (Tow Center for Digital Journalism, Columbia University, 2020).
24. Ben Smith, "How to Fight Liberals: Imitate Them," *Politico*, January 5, 2012.
25. Nadler et al., *Conservative Newswork*.
26. For a helpful overview, see Taylor Lorenz, *Extremely Online: The Untold Story of Fame, Influence, and Power on the Internet* (Simon & Schuster, 2023).
27. Rebecca Lewis, "Alternative Influence: Broadcasting the Reactionary Right on YouTube," *Data & Society*, September 18, 2018. See also Eviane Leidig, *The Women of the Far Right: Social Media Influencers and Online Radicalization* (Columbia University Press, 2023).
28. David Carr, "Will the Standard Pass from Murdoch to Anschutz?" *New York Times*, June 10, 2009; and Michael Calderone, "Phil Anschutz's Conservative Agenda," *Politico*, October 16, 2009.
29. Kara Boomgarden-Smoke, "The Washington Examiner Announces a 'Shift' in Their Business Model," *New York Observer*, March 19, 2013; and Tim Arango, "New Owner for a Magazine as Political Tastes Change," *New York Times*, B1, B4.
30. Michael M. Grynbaum and Jim Rutenberg, "The Weekly Standard, Pugnacious to the End, Will Cease Publication," *New York Times*, December 14, 2018; and Jim Rutenberg, "A Conservative Magazine May Pay a Price for Being Unfriendly to Trump," *New York Times*, December 5, 2018.
31. For more on this dynamic, see Yunkang Yang, *Weapons of Mass Deception: How Right-Wing Media Wage Information Warfare and Undermine American Democracy* (Oxford University Press, 2025).
32. Yochai Benkler, Robert Faris, and Hal Roberts, *Network Propaganda: Manipulation, Disinformation, and Radicalization in American Politics* (Oxford University Press, 2018), 105–155.

33. Benkler et al., *Network Propaganda*, 13–14.
34. Quoted in Matt Carlson, Sue Robinson, and Seth C. Lewis, *News After Trump: Journalism's Crisis of Relevance in a Changed Media Culture* (Oxford University Press, 2021), 9.
35. See "American Views 2022: Part 2: Trust, Media and Democracy," a Gallup/Knight Foundation Survey, January 2023.

SELECTED BIBLIOGRAPHY

Adorno, Theodor W., Else Frenkel-Brunswik, Daniel Levinson, and Nevitt Sanford. *The Authoritarian Personality*. Harper & Brothers, 1950.

Ahearn, Lorraine, and Barbara Friedman. "A Commemorative Bind: How the *Birmingham News* Redressed Past Journalistic Failure Through Contemporary Civil Rights Memory." *Journalism History* 48, no. 4 (2022): 283–302.

Aitken, Hugh G. J. "Allocating the Spectrum: The Origins of Radio Regulation." *Technology and Culture* 35, no. 4 (1994): 686–716.

Alterman, Eric. *What Liberal Media? The Truth About Bias and the News*. Basic Books, 2003.

American Business Consultants, *Red Channels: The Report of Communist Influence in Radio and Television*. Counterattack, 1950.

Anderson, Benedict. *Imagined Communities: Reflections on the Origins and Spread of Nationalism*. Verso, 2006.

Anderson, Brian C. *South Park Conservatives: The Revolt Against Liberal Media Bias*. Regnery, 2005.

Andrew, John A. *The Other Side of the Sixties: Young Americans for Freedom and the Rise of Conservative Politics*. Rutgers University Press, 1997.

Atwood, Elizabeth. "Reaching the Pinnacle of the 'Punditocracy': James J. Kilpatrick's Journey from Segregationist Editor to National Opinion Shaper." *American Journalism* 31, no. 3 (2014): 358–377.

Bagdikian, Ben H. *The Media Monopoly*. Beacon, 1983.

Barrett, Marvin, ed. *The Alfred I. Dupont-Columbia University Survey of Broadcast Journalism, 1968–1969*. Grosset & Dunlap, 1969.

Barrett, Marvin, ed. *The Alfred I. Dupont-Columbia University Survey of Broadcast Journalism, 1969–1970*. Grosset & Dunlap, 1970.

Bauer, A. J. "Agent and Archive: Chip Berlet and the Historicity of Right-Watchers." In *Exposing the Right and Fighting for Democracy: Celebrating Chip Berlet as Journalist and Scholar*, ed. Pam Chamberlain, Matthew Lyons, Abby Scher, and Spencer Sunshine. Routledge, 2021.

Bauer, A. J. "The Alternative Historiography of the Alt-Right: Conservative Historical Subjectivity from the Tea Party to Trump." In *Far-Right Revisionism and the End of History: Alt-Histories*, ed. Louie Dean Valencia-García. Routledge, 2020.

Bauer, A. J. "Glittering Generalities: Reconsidering the Institute for Propaganda Analysis." *International Journal of Communication* 18 (2024): 1976–1994.

Bauer, A. J. "Propaganda in the Guise of News: Fulton Lewis Jr. and the Origins of the Fairness Doctrine." *Radical History Review* 141 (2021): 7–29.

Bauer, A. J. "Why So Serious? Studying Humor on the Right." *Media, Culture & Society* 45, no. 5 (2023): 1067–1074.

Bauer, A. J., and Anthony Nadler. "Competing for Cultural Authority: Journalism Studies Must Account for the Right." *Journalism Studies* 26, no. 5 (2025): 624–637. https://doi.org/10.1080/1461670X.2025.2454344.

Bayley, Edwin R. *Joe McCarthy and the Press*. University of Wisconsin Press, 1981.

Bedingfield, Sid. *Newspaper Wars: Civil Rights and White Resistance in South Carolina, 1935–1965*. University of Illinois Press, 2017.

Bedingfield, Sid. "Who Is Nicholas Stanford? The *New York Times* Music Critic and His Secret Role in the Rise of the 'Liberal Media' Claim." *American Journalism* 35, no. 4 (2018): 398–419.

Bell, Daniel, ed. *The End of Ideology: On the Exhaustion of Political Ideas in the Fifties*. Free Press, 1960.

Bell, Daniel, ed. *The Radical Right: The New American Right, Expanded and Updated*. Doubleday, 1963.

Beltrán, Cristina. *The Trouble with Unity: Latino Politics and the Creation of Identity*. Oxford University Press, 2010.

Benjamin, Walter. "Theses on the Philosophy of History." In *Illuminations*, ed. Hannah Arendt, trans. Harry Zohn. Shocken, 2007.

Benkler, Yochai, Robert Faris, and Hal Roberts, *Network Propaganda: Manipulation, Disinformation, and Radicalization in American Politics*. Oxford University Press, 2018.

Berlant, Lauren. *The Queen of America Goes to Washington City: Essays on Sex and Citizenship*. Duke University Press, 1997.

Bertsch, Charlie. "Gramsci Rush: Limbaugh on the 'Culture War.'" *International Gramsci Society Newsletter*, no. 6 (August 1996): 11–15.

Breitbart, Andrew. *Righteous Indignation: Excuse Me While I Save the World!* Grand Central, 2011.

Brock, David. *The Republican Noise Machine: Right-Wing Media and How It Corrupts Democracy*. Crown, 2004.

Brogan, Patrick. *Spiked: The Short Life and Death of the National News Council*. Priority Press, 1985.

Brownell, Kathryn Cramer. *24/7 Politics: Cable Television and the Fragmenting of America from Watergate to Fox News*. Princeton University Press, 2023.

Buchanan, Patrick J. *The New Majority: President Nixon at Mid-Passage*. Girard, 1973.
Burst, Ardis. *The Three Families of H. L. Hunt*. Weidenfeld & Nicolson, 1988.
Cadava, Geraldo L. *The Hispanic Republican: The Shaping of an American Political Identity, from Nixon to Trump*. Ecco, 2020.
Carlson, Matt, Sue Robinson, and Seth C. Lewis, *News After Trump: Journalism's Crisis of Relevance in a Changed Media Culture*. Oxford University Press, 2021.
Chafets, Zev. *Rush Limbaugh: An Army of One*. Sentinel, 2010.
Charry, Stephen Walter. "Phillip Abbott Luce and the Pink Sheet on the Left: New Right Anti-Communism in the 1970s." M.A. thesis, Washington State University, 1990.
Cimaglio, Christopher. "'A Tiny and Closed Fraternity of Privileged Men': The Nixon–Agnew Anti-Media Campaign and the Liberal Roots of the US Conservative 'Liberal Media' Critique." *International Journal of Communication* 10 (2016): 1–19.
Clark, Fred G., and Richard Stanton Rimanoczy, *How to Be Popular, Though Conservative*. D. Van Nostrand, 1948.
Clogston, Juanita Frankie. "The Repeal of the Fairness Doctrine and the Irony of Talk Radio: A Story of Political Entrepreneurship, Risk, and Cover." *Journal of Policy History* 28, no. 2 (2016): 375–396.
Cohen, Lizabeth. *A Consumers' Republic: The Politics of Mass Consumption in Postwar America*. Vintage, 2003.
Connell, Tula A. *Conservative Counterrevolution: Challenging Liberalism in 1950s Milwaukee*. University of Illinois Press, 2016.
Cox, Patrick L. *Ralph W. Yarborough, the People's Senator*. University of Texas Press, 2001.
Crespino, Joseph. *In Search of Another Country: Mississippi and the Conservative Counterrevolution*. Princeton University Press, 2007.
Critchlow, Donald T. *Phyllis Schlafly and Grassroots Conservatism: A Woman's Crusade*. Princeton University Press, 2005.
Curl, John. *For All the People: Uncovering the Hidden History of Cooperation, Cooperative Movements, and Communalism in America*. PM Press, 2012.
Cushman, Robert. *Keep Our Press Free*. Public Affairs Committee, 1946.
Dallek, Matthew. *Birchers: How the John Birch Society Radicalized the American Right*. Basic Books, 2023.
Delaney, Lawrence J., Jr., and Leslie Lenkowsky. "The New Voice on Campus: 'Alternative Student Journalism.'" *Academic Questions* 1, no. 2 (1988): 32–38.
Dillard, Angela D. *Guess Who's Coming to Dinner Now? Multicultural Conservatism in America*. New York University Press, 2002.
Dobbs, Ricky F. *Yellow Dogs and Republicans: Allan Shivers and Texas Two-Party Politics*. Texas A&M University Press, 2005.
Donnelly, Elaine. *One Side Versus the Other Side: A Primer on Access to the Media*. Eagle Forum Education and Legal Defense Fund, 1981.
Dunham, Corydon B. *Fighting for the First Amendment: Stanton of CBS vs. Congress and the Nixon White House*. Praeger, 1997.
Edwards, David, and David Cromwell. *Guardians of Power: The Myth of the Liberal Media*. Pluto, 2005.

Efron, Edith. *The News Twisters*. Nash, 1971.
Efron, Edith, with Clytia Chambers. *How CBS Tried to Kill a Book*. Nash, 1972.
Ernst, Morris L. *The First Freedom*. Macmillan, 1946.
Feldstein, Mark. *Poisoning the Press: Richard Nixon, Jack Anderson, and the Rise of Washington's Scandal Culture*. Farrar, Straus and Giroux, 2010.
Fones-Wolf, Elizabeth A. *Selling Free Enterprise: The Business Assault on Labor and Liberalism, 1945-60*. University of Illinois Press, 1994.
Forde, Kathy Roberts, and Sid Bedingfield, eds. *Journalism and Jim Crow: White Supremacy and the Black Struggle for a New America*. University of Illinois Press, 2021.
Formisano, Ronald P. *Boston Against Busing: Race, Class, and Ethnicity in the 1960s and 1970s*. University of North Carolina Press, 1991.
Freelon, Deen, Alice Marwick and Daniel Kreiss. "False Equivalencies: Online Activism from Left to Right." *Science* 369, no. 6508 (2020): 1197–1201.
Friendly, Fred W. *The Good Guys, the Bad Guys and the First Amendment: Free Speech vs. Fairness in Broadcasting*. Vintage, 1975.
Ganz, John. *When the Clock Broke: Con Men, Conspiracists, and How America Cracked Up in the Early 1990s*. Farrar, Straus and Giroux, 2024.
Gary, Brett. *Dirty Works: Obscenity on Trial in America's First Sexual Revolution*. Stanford University Press, 2021.
Gary, Brett. "Morris Ernst's Troubled Legacy." *Reconstruction: Studies in Contemporary Culture* 8, no. 1 (2008): 22–37.
Gary, Brett. *The Nervous Liberals: Propaganda Anxieties from World War I to the Cold War*. Columbia University Press, 1999.
Gaziano, Cecilie. "How Credible Is the Credibility Crisis?" *Journalism Quarterly* 65, no. 2 (1988): 267–279.
Gibson, John. *How the Left Swiftboated America: The Liberal Media Conspiracy to Make You Think George Bush Was the Worst President in History*. Harper Collins, 2009.
Gillis, William. "The Anti-Semitic Roots of the 'Liberal News Media' Critique." *American Journalism* 34, no. 3 (2017): 262–288.
Gitlin, Todd. *The Whole World Is Watching: Mass Media in the Making and Unmaking of the New Left*. University of California Press, 1980.
Goldberg, Bernard. *Bias: A CBS Insider Exposes How the Media Distort the News*. Regnery, 2001.
Goodman, Mark, and Mark Gring. "The Ideological Fight over Creation of the Federal Radio Commission in 1927." *Journalism History* 26, no. 3 (2000): 117–124.
Greenberg, David. "The Idea of 'the Liberal Media' and Its Roots in the Civil Rights Movement." *The Sixties: A Journal of History, Politics and Culture* 1, no. 2 (2008): 167–186.
Greene, Robert, II. "*National Review* and the Changing Narrative of Civil Rights Memory 1968-2016." In *News on the Right: Studying Conservative News Cultures*, ed. Anthony Nadler and A. J. Bauer. Oxford University Press, 2019.
Groseclose, Tim. *Left Turn: How Liberal Media Bias Distorts the American Mind*. St. Martin's, 2011.

Hall, Stuart, Chas Critcher, Tony Jefferson, John Clarke, and Brian Roberts. *Policing the Crisis: Mugging, the State, and Law and Order.* Macmillan, 1978.

Hallin, Daniel C. "The Passing of the 'High Modernism' of American Journalism," *Journal of Communication* 42, no. 3 (1992): 14–25.

Hayes, Arthur S. *Press Critics Are the Fifth Estate: Media Watchdogs in America.* Praeger, 2008.

Haynes, John Earl, Harvey Klehr, and Alexander Vassiliev. *Spies: The Rise and Fall of the KGB in America.* Yale University Press, 2009.

Heckman, Meg. *Political Godmother: Nackey Scripps Loeb and the Newspaper That Shook the Republican Party.* Potomac Books / University of Nebraska Press, 2020.

Hemingway, Mollie Ziegler. *Trump vs. The Media.* Encounter Books, 2017.

Hemmer, Nicole. *Messengers of the Right: Conservative Media and the Transformation of American Politics.* University of Pennsylvania Press, 2016.

Hemmer, Nicole. *Partisans: The Conservative Revolutionaries Who Remade American Politics in the 1990s.* Basic Books, 2022.

Hendershot, Heather. *Open to Debate: How William F. Buckley Put Liberal America on the Firing Line.* Broadside, 2016.

Hendershot, Heather. *What's Fair on the Air? Cold War Right-Wing Broadcasting and the Public Interest.* University of Chicago Press, 2011.

Hendershot, Heather. *When the News Broke: Chicago 1968 and the Polarizing of America.* University of Chicago Press, 2022.

Herman, Edward S., and Noam Chomsky. *Manufacturing Consent: The Political Economy of the Mass Media.* Pantheon, 1988.

Herndon, Booton. *The Story of Fulton Lewis, Jr.: Praised and Damned.* Human Events, 1958.

Herschensohn, Bruce. *The Gods of Antenna.* Arlington House, 1976.

Hofstadter, Richard. *The Paranoid Style in American Politics and Other Essays.* Knopf, 1966.

Hosang, Daniel Martinez, and Joseph E. Lowndes, *Producers, Parasites, Patriots: Race and the New Right-Wing Politics of Precarity.* University of Minnesota Press, 2019.

Hunt, H. L. *Alpaca.* Hunt Press, 1960.

Hunt, H. L. *Alpaca Revisited.* H. L. Products, 1967.

Hunt, H. L. *H. L. Hunt Early Days.* Parade Press, 1973.

Hunt, H. L. *Fabians Fight Freedom.* H. L. Hunt Press, n.d.

Hunt, H. L. "Famous Wildcatter Finds Word to Help Bewildered World: It Is 'Constructive,'" *Shreveport Times*, December 3, 1950.

Hunt, H. L. *HLH Columns.* HLH Products, n.d.

Hunt, H. L. *Hunt Heritage: The Republic and Our Families.* Parade Press, 1973.

Hunt, H. L. *Hunt for Truth.* HLH Products, 1965.

Hunt, H. L. *Why Not Speak?* H. L. Hunt Press, 1964.

Huntington, John S. *Far-Right Vanguard: The Radical Roots of Modern Conservatism.* University of Pennsylvania Press, 2021.

Hurt, Harry, III. *Texas Rich: The Hunt Dynasty from the Early Oil Days Through the Silver Crash.* Norton, 1981.

Hustwit, William P. *James J. Kilpatrick: Salesman for Segregation*. University of North Carolina Press, 2013.

Irvine, Reed. *Media Mischief and Misdeeds*. Regnery Gateway, 1984.

Jack, Caroline. *Business As Usual: How Sponsored Media Sold American Capitalism in the Twentieth Century*. University of Chicago Press, 2024.

Jamieson, Kathleen Hall, and Joseph Cappella, *Echo Chamber: Rush Limbaugh and the Conservative Media Establishment*. Oxford University Press, 2008.

Janson, Donald, and Bernard Eismann, *The Far Right*. McGraw-Hill, 1963.

Jefferson, Hakeem. "The Politics of Respectability and Black Americans' Punitive Attitudes." *American Political Science Review* 117, no. 4 (2023): 1448–1464.

Johnson, Paul Elliott. *I, The People: The Rhetoric of Conservative Populism in the United States*. University of Alabama Press, 2022.

Keeley, Joseph Charles. *The China Lobby Man: The Story of Alfred Kohlberg*. Arlington House, 1969.

Keller, William W. *The Liberals and J. Edgar Hoover: Rise and Fall of a Domestic Intelligence State*. Princeton University Press, 1989.

Kreiss, Daniel, and Shannon C. McGregor. "A Review and Provocation: On Polarization and Platforms." *New Media & Society* 26, no. 1 (2023): 556–579.

Kruse, Kevin. *White Flight: Atlanta and the Making of Modern Conservatism*. Princeton University Press, 2007.

Kurtz, Howard. *Media Madness: Donald Trump, the Press, and the War on Truth*. Regnery, 2018.

Lahey, Edwin A. "Bedside Manner in Radio." In *Molders of Opinion*, ed. David Bulman. Bruce Publishing, 1945.

Lamont, Corliss, ed., *The Trial of Elizabeth Gurley Flynn by the American Civil Liberties Union*. Horizon Press, 1968.

Lane, Julie B. "Cultivating Distrust of the Mainstream Media." In *News on the Right: Studying Conservative News Cultures*, ed. Anthony Nadler and A. J. Bauer. Oxford University Press, 2019.

Lassiter, Matthew D. *The Silent Majority: Suburban Politics in the Sunbelt South*. Princeton University Press, 2006.

Lee, Tien-Tsung. "The Liberal Media Myth Revisited: An Examination of Factors Influencing Perceptions of Media Bias." *Journal of Broadcasting & Electronic Media* 49, no. 1 (2005): 43–64.

Leidig, Eviane. *The Women of the Far Right: Social Media Influencers and Online Radicalization*. Columbia University Press, 2023.

Lerner, Kevin M. "A System of Self-Correction: A. M. Rosenthal, Daniel Patrick Moynihan, Press Criticism and the Birth of the Contemporary Newspaper Correction in the *New York Times*." *Journalism History* 42, no. 4 (2017): 191–200.

Leslie, Warren. *Dallas Public and Private: Aspects of an American City*. Grossman, 1964.

Lewis, Rebecca. "Alternative Influence: Broadcasting the Reactionary Right on YouTube," Data & Society, September 18, 2018.

Lichter, S. Robert, and Stanley Rothman. "Media and Business Elites: Two Classes in Conflict?." *Public Opinion* 4, no. 5 (1981): 42–46, 59–60.

Lichter, S. Robert, Stanley Rothman, and Linda S. Lichter. *The Media Elite: America's News Powerbrokers.* Adler & Adler, 1986.

Limbaugh, Rush. *See, I Told You So.* Pocket Books, 1993.

Lombardo, Timothy J. *Blue-Collar Conservatism: Frank Rizzo's Philadelphia and Populist Politics.* University of Pennsylvania Press, 2018.

Lora, Ronald, and William Henry Longton, eds. *The Conservative Press in Twentieth-Century America.* Greenwood, 1999.

Lorenz, Taylor. *Extremely Online: The Untold Story of Fame, Influence, and Power on the Internet.* Simon & Schuster, 2023.

Lowndes, Joseph E. *From the New Deal to the New Right: Race and the Southern Origins of Modern Conservatism.* Yale University Press, 2008.

MacLean, Nancy. *Democracy in Chains: The Deep History of the Radical Right's Stealth Plan for America.* Viking, 2017.

Major, Mark. "Objective but Not Impartial: Human Events, Barry Goldwater, and the Development of the 'Liberal Media' in the Conservative Counter-Sphere." *New Political Science: A Journal of Politics and Culture* 34, no. 4 (2012): 455–458.

Marion, George. *The 'Free Press': Portrait of a Monopoly.* New Century, 1946.

Massing, Michael. "Who's Afraid of Reed Irvine? The Rise and Decline of Accuracy in Media." *The Nation,* September 13, 1986, 200–214.

Mattson, Kevin. *Rebels All! A Short History of the Conservative Mind in Postwar America.* Rutgers University Press, 2008.

Matzko, Paul. *The Radio Right: How a Band of Broadcasters Took on the Federal Government and Built the Modern Conservative Movement.* Oxford University Press, 2020.

Mayer, Jane. *Dark Money: The Hidden History of the Billionaires Beyond the Rise of the Radical Right.* Doubleday, 2016.

McCann, Irving G. *Case History of the Smear by CBS of Conservatives.* McCann Press, 1966.

McChesney, Robert. *Telecommunications, Mass Media, and Democracy: The Battle for the Control of U.S. Broadcasting, 1928–1935.* Oxford University Press, 1988.

Middendorf, J. William, II, *A Glorious Disaster: Barry Goldwater's Presidential Campaign and the Origins of the Conservative Movement.* Basic Books, 2006.

Milkman, Paul. *PM: A New Deal in Journalism, 1940–1948.* Rutgers University Press, 1997.

Miller, Edward H. *A Conspiratorial Life: Robert Welch, the John Birch Society, and the Revolution of American Conservatism.* University of Chicago Press, 2021.

Miller, Edward H. *Nut Country: Right-Wing Dallas and the Birth of the Southern Strategy.* University of Chicago Press, 2015.

Mindich, David T. Z. *Just the Facts: How 'Objectivity' Came to Define American Journalism.* New York University Press, 1998.

Moreton, Bethany. *To Serve God and Wal-Mart.* Harvard University Press, 2009.

Morris, Aldon D. "Birmingham Confrontation Reconsidered: An Analysis of the Dynamics and Tactics of Mobilization." *American Sociological Review* 58, no. 5 (1993): 621–636.

Mulloy, D. J. *The World of the John Birch Society: Conspiracy, Conservatism, and the Cold War.* Vanderbilt University Press, 2014.

Mwakasege-Minaya, Richard M. "Cold War Bedfellows: Cuban Exiles, US Conservatives, and Media Activism in the 1960s and 1970s." *Historical Journal of Film, Radio, and Television* 41, no. 1 (2021): 114–135.

Mwakasege-Minaya, Richard M. "Exiled Counterpoint: Cuban Exile Reception, Media Activism, Conservatism, and the National Educational Television Network." *Chiricú Journal: Latina/o Literatures, Arts, and Cultures* 4, no. 2 (2020): 37–61.

Nadler, Anthony, and A. J. Bauer. "Conservative News Studies: Mapping an Unrealized Field." In *News on the Right: Studying Conservative News Cultures*, ed. Anthony Nadler and A. J. Bauer. Oxford University Press, 2019.

Nadler, Anthony, and A. J. Bauer, eds. *News on the Right: Studying Conservative News Cultures.* Oxford University Press, 2019.

Nadler, Anthony, A. J. Bauer, and Magda Konieczna, *Conservative Newswork: A Report on the Values and Practices of Online Journalists on the Right.* Tow Center for Digital Journalism, Columbia University, 2020.

Napoli, Philip M. "Public Interest Media Advocacy and Activism as a Social Movement." *Annals of the International Communication Association* 33, no. 1 (2009): 385–429.

Nash, George H. *The Conservative Intellectual Movement in America Since 1945.* Intercollegiate Studies Institute, 1998.

Nelson, Anne. *Shadow Network: Media, Money, and the Secret Hub of the Radical Right.* Bloomsbury, 2019.

Nickerson, Michelle M. *Mothers of Conservatism: Women and the Postwar Right.* Princeton University Press, 2014.

Niven, David. *Tilt? The Search for Media Bias.* Praeger, 2002.

Omi, Michael, and Howard Winant, *Racial Formation in the United States.* 3rd ed. Routledge, 2014.

Oppenheimer, Daniel. *Exit Right: The People Who Left the Left and Reshaped the American Century.* Simon & Schuster, 2016.

Padden, Preston R. "The Emerging Role of Citizens' Groups in Broadcast Regulation." *Federal Communications Bar Journal* 25 (1972): 82–110.

Peck, Reece. *Fox Populism: Branding Conservatism as Working Class.* Cambridge University Press, 2019.

Pérez, Raúl. *The Souls of White Jokes: How Racist Humor Fuels White Supremacy.* Stanford University Press, 2022.

Perlstein, Rick. *Before the Storm: Barry Goldwater and the Unmaking of the American Consensus.* Hill & Wang, 2001.

Perlstein, Rick. "I Thought I Understood the American Right. Trump Proved Me Wrong," *New York Times Magazine*, April 11, 2017.

Perlstein, Rick. *The Invisible Bridge: The Fall of Nixon and the Rise of Reagan.* Simon and Schuster, 2014.

Perlstein, Rick. *Nixonland: The Rise of a President and the Fracturing of America.* Scribner, 2008.

Perlstein, Rick. *Reaganland: America's Right Turn 1976–1980*. Simon and Schuster, 2021.

Perlstein, Rick, ed., *Richard Nixon: Speeches, Writings, Documents*. Princeton University Press, 2008.

Phillips, Kevin P. *Mediacracy: American Parties and Politics in the Communications Age*. Doubleday, 1975.

Phillips-Fein, Kim. "Conservatism: A State of the Field." *Journal of American History* 98, no. 3 (2011): 723–743.

Phillips-Fein, Kim. *Invisible Hands: The Businessmen's Crusade Against the New Deal*. Norton, 2009.

Pickard, Victor W. *America's Battle for Media Democracy: The Triumph of Corporate Libertarianism and the Future of Media Reform*. Cambridge University Press, 2014.

Pickard, Victor W. "The Strange Life and Death of the Fairness Doctrine: Tracing the Decline of Positive Freedoms in American Policy Discourse." *International Journal of Communication* 12 (2018): 3434–3453.

Pressman, Matthew. "The New York *Daily News* and the History of Conservative Media." *Modern American History* 4, no. 3 (2021): 219–238.

Pressman, Matthew. *On Press: The Liberal Values That Shaped the News*. Harvard University Press, 2018.

Reinhard, David W. *The Republican Right Since 1945*. University of Kentucky Press, 1983.

Rieder, Jonathan. *Canarsie: The Jews and Italians of Brooklyn Against Liberalism*. Harvard University Press, 1985.

Rigsby, Enrique DuBois. "A Rhetorical Clash with the Established Order: An Analysis of Protest Strategies and Perceptions of Media Responses, Birmingham, 1963." PhD diss., University of Oregon, 1990.

Rigueur, Leah Wright. *The Loneliness of the Black Republican: Pragmatic Politics and the Pursuit of Power*. Princeton University Press, 2014.

Roberts, Gene, and Hank Klibanoff, *The Race Beat: The Press, The Civil Rights Struggle, and the Awakening of a Nation*. Knopf, 2006.

Robin, Corey. *The Reactionary Mind: Conservatism from Edmund Burke to Sarah Palin*. Oxford University Press, 2011.

Rosenwald, Brian. *Talk Radio's America: How an Industry Took Over a Political Party That Took Over the United States*. Harvard University Press, 2019.

Rucker, Bryce W. *The First Freedom*. Southern Illinois University Press, 1968.

Rusher, William A. *The Making of the New Majority Party*. Sheed & Ward, 1975.

Rymph, Catherine E. *Republican Women: Feminism and Conservatism from Suffrage Through the Rise of the New Right*. University of North Carolina Press, 2006.

Schlesinger, Arthur. *The Vital Center: The Politics of Freedom*. Houghton Mifflin, 1949.

Schneider, Gregory L. *Cadres for Conservatism: Young Americans for Freedom and the Rise of the Contemporary Right*. New York University Press, 1999.

Schreiber, Ronnee. *Righting Feminism: Conservative Women and American Politics*. Oxford University Press, 2008.

Schudson, Michael. "The Objectivity Norm in American Journalism." *Journalism* 2, no. 2 (2001): 149–170.

Sedgwick, Eve Kosofsky. "Paranoid Reading and Reparative Reading, or, You're So Paranoid, You Probably Think This Essay is About You." In *Touching Feeling: Affect, Pedagogy, Performativity.* Duke University Press, 2003.

Seldes, George. *The Facts Are . . . A Guide to Falsehood and Propaganda in the Press and Radio.* In Fact, 1942.

Seldes, George. *Facts and Fascism.* In Fact, 1943.

Seldes, George. *Never Tire of Protesting.* Lyle Stuart, 1968.

Seldes, George. *Witness to a Century: Encounters with the Noted, the Notorious, and the Three SOBs.* Ballantine, 1987.

Seldes, George. *You Can't Print That! The Truth Behind the News, 1918–1928.* Payson & Clarke, 1929.

Senko, Jen. *The Brainwashing of My Dad.* Sourcebooks, 2021.

Sharp, Joanne P. *Condensing the Cold War: Readers Digest and American Identity.* University of Minnesota Press, 2000.

Sharlet, Jeff. *The Family: The Secret Fundamentalism at the Heart of American Power.* HarperCollins, 2009.

Shepherd, Lauren Lassabe. *Resistance from the Right: Conservatives and the Campus Wars in Modern America.* University of North Carolina Press, 2023.

Sherman, Gabriel. *The Loudest Voice in the Room: How the Brilliant, Bombastic Roger Ailes Built Fox News—and Divided a Country.* Random House, 2014.

Shumate, Rich. *Barry Goldwater, Distrust in Media, and Conservative Identity: The Perception of Liberal Bias in the News.* Lexington, 2021.

Sienkiewicz, Matt, and Nick Marx, *That's Not Funny: How the Right Makes Comedy Work for Them.* University of California Press, 2022.

Skocpol, Theda, and Vanessa Williamson. *The Tea Party and the Remaking of Republican Conservatism.* Oxford University Press, 2016.

Smith, Ben. *Traffic: Genius, Rivalry, and Delusion in the Billion-Dollar Race to Go Viral.* Penguin, 2023.

Smoot, Dan. *The Hope of the World.* Miller, 1958.

Smoot, Dan. *The Invisible Government.* Western Islands, 1962.

Smoot, Dan. *People Along the Way.* Tyler Press, 1993.

Sproule, J. Michael. *Propaganda and Democracy: The American Experience of Media and Mass Persuasion.* Cambridge University Press, 1997.

Steele, Richard W. *Propaganda in an Open Society: The Roosevelt Administration and the Media, 1933–1941.* Greenwood, 1985.

Svirsky, Leon, ed., *Your Newspaper: Blueprint for a Better Press.* Macmillan, 1947.

Usher, Nik. "Re-Thinking Trust in the News." *Journalism Studies* 19, no. 4 (2018): 564–578.

Viguerie, Richard. *The New Right: We're Ready to Lead.* Viguerie Company, 1981.

Viguerie, Richard, and David Franke. *America's Right Turn: How Conservatives Used New and Alternative Media to Take Power.* Bonus Books, 2004.

Villard, Oswald Garrison. *The Disappearing Daily: Chapters in American Newspaper Evolution.* Knopf, 1944.

Wallace, David. "Piercing the Paper Curtain: The Southern Editorial Response to National Civil Rights Coverage." *American Journalism* 33, no. 4 (2016): 401–423.

Walsh, David Austin. *Taking America Back: The Conservative Movement and the Far Right.* Yale University Press, 2024.

Welch, Robert. *The Blue Book of the John Birch Society.* Western Islands, 1959.

Williams, Julian. "Black Radio and Civil Rights: Birmingham, 1956–1963." *Journal of Radio Studies* 12, no. 1 (2005): 47–60.

Winfield, Betty Houchin. *FDR and the News Media.* University of Illinois Press, 1990.

Yang, Yunkang. *Weapons of Mass Deception: How Right-Wing Media Wage Information Warfare and Undermine American Democracy.* Oxford University Press, 2025.

INDEX

Accuracy in Media (AIM), 156–160, 167–170, 174–180; and ABC News, 148–149; and Abraham Kalish, 127–128, 131–132, 135; and anticommunism, 121–122, 126; and Benjamin Ginzburg, 125–126; and CBS News, 130, 136–137, 148, 158; and Central Intelligence Agency (CIA), 157–158, 235n38; and *Conservative Digest*, 154–155; and credibility, 127; and Fairness Doctrine, 168, 174, 177–179; and Federal Communications Commission, 156, 167–170, 175; and fundraising, 127, 235n39; and impartiality, 126, 132–133, 136; and Jack Anderson, 139; and liberal bias, 18, 137, 153; and Morris Ernst, 129–131, 138–140, 236n53; and NBC News, 138, 148, 168–169; and *National Review*, 150; and the New Right, 144, 148, 150, 155–157, 159, 176, 180; and *The New York Times*, 136, 148; and Reed Irvine, 124, 144, 148, 156, 158, 160; and Richard M. Nixon, 142, 234n34; and Ronald Reagan, 157–158, 177–178; and Rush Limbaugh, 179–180; and shareholder campaigns, 149–150; and Spiro T. Agnew, 125, 129, 234n34; and *The Washington Post*, 136, 148, 238n79

Acheson, Dean, 127–128, 236n44
Agnew, Spiro, 17, 44, 117, 119–121, 125, 129, 131, 133–135, 138, 234n34
Ailes, Roger, 20, 186
AIM Report, 128, 154, 157
Alabama Sovereignty Commission, 109
Amazon, 1
American Broadcasting Company (ABC News), 17, 26, 80, 112, 129–130, 141, 148–149, 154, 162, 167, 171, 175, 246n21
American Business Consultants, 13, 48, 59–63, 74, 122, 124, 218n73, 219n30, 233n13; and Accuracy in Media, 122, 124; and *Counterattack*, 61, 62, 74; and George Seldes, 59–63; and *Red Channels*, 13, 61, 63; and *Plain Talk*, 48, 59–60
American Civil Liberties Union (ACLU), 10, 37, 44–45, 127, 166, 176,
American Conservative Union, 4, 16–17, 94–95, 160, 184
American Independent Party, 116
Americans for Democratic Action, 5, 176
American Legal Foundation, 156, 175
American Mercury, 11, 53, 58, 216n51
American Newspaper Guild, 55

American Opinion, 17, 96–98, 11, 228n28
American Society of Newspaper Editors (ASNE), 18, 133
Anderson, Tom, 109, 113
Anderson, Jack, 138–140
Anschutz, Philip, 191
Answers for Americans, 68, 80, 93, 142
anti-Black racism, 3, 8, 23, 50, 105–106, 121
anticommunism, 3–4, 8, 13–14, 27, 77, 84, 138, 178, 181, 193; and Accuracy in Media (AIM), 121–122, 126; anticommunist groups, 16; and journalists, 55, 58, 73–74; and lending libraries, 16, 76
anticommunist newspapers, 17, 227n23; and Dewitt Wallace, 54; and Joseph Alsop, 110; and left-wing activists, 55; and Morris Ernst, 45–46; and Phillip Abbott Luce, 131; and press criticism, 57, 61–62; and right-wing activists, 41, 47–48, 58–62, 64–68, 76, 81–83, 86–88, 91–92, 95, 97–98, 104, 115–117, 124, 126–127, 129, 158, 163, 217n66; and Robert McCormick, 48
Associated Press, 11, 18, 50–51, 89, 112, 116
Atlantic Monthly, 12, 56
authoritarianism, 2, 4

Bagdikian, Ben H., 15, 88–89, 150, 224n101, 249n74
Balk, Alfred, 134–136
Balter, Sam, 27–28
Bannon, Steve, 189, 192
Bauer, Gary, 176–177
Beck, Glenn, 187, 190, 192
Bezos, Jeff, 1
Biden, Joseph R., 1
Birmingham (AL), 6, 104, 106–110, 118
Birmingham Independent, The, 96, 104, 110–116, 118
Black, Algernon, 32
Black Americans, 77, 83, 95, 105, 108, 119–120, 145, 204n27, 226n8
Black Freedom struggle, 17, 118, 131
Black Power, 17, 123

Blackwell, Morton, 160
Blaze, The, 190, 192
Breitbart, 189–190, 192; Andrew, 188–189; and ACORN, 188; and Donald Trump, 20, 192
Briggs Jr., John G., 105
broadcasters, 15, 26, 29, 57, 107, 112, 120–121, 142, 156, 162, 167, 169–170; evangelical, 14, 116, 165; independent, 168; liberal, 27–28; reactionary, 33–36, 39; rights of, 24, 41, 174; right-wing, 16, 24–25, 29–31, 147, 163–166, 179
broadcast industry, 10, 28, 124, 129, 167, 176; bias, 19, 64, 130, 134, 152; and Black-owned media, 135; "both sides," 14–15, 35, 37, 69, 72–73, 88, 91, 98, 125, 173; conservative, 125; and editorials, 25–27, 37–38, 44, 69, 73; and Facts Forum, 66–68, 82, 97–98; and FCC, 42, 44, 171; journalists, 19, 87; monopolies, 40, 46, 129, 131, 133–134; and radio stations, 27, 41, 66; regulation of, 24, 26, 42, 46, 155, 171–172, 174–175, 184, 194, 208n19; and television stations, 66, 83, 148–149
broadcast licensees, 11, 23, 25, 156, 177
broadcast licenses, 22, 24, 156, 169
Brock, David, 186
Brown v. Board of Education of Topeka, 82, 95
Buchanan, Pat, 3, 151
Buckley Jr., William F., 2–4, 15–17, 68–69, 91–92, 142, 147, 163; and *God and Men at Yale*, 77; and *Firing Line*, 121, 184; and *The Birmingham Independent*, 116; and John Birch Society, 96, 102–103, 117, 146; and *National Review*, 47, 64, 93–96, 105, 116, 143, 150; and Robert Welch, 103
Bulwark, The, 191
Bush, George H.W., 159, 161, 183
Bush, George W., 183–184, 186, 190

Cable News Network (CNN), 171, 186, 189, 193
Carlson, Tucker, 189
Carson, John, 38–39
CBS News, 17–18, 26–27, 41, 100–101, 112, 125–126, 129–130, 136–138, 141, 148–149, 154, 158, 167, 175–176, 185

Center for American Freedom, 189
Center for American Progress, 189
Chicago Tribune, The, 48, 127
Citizens' Councils, 3, 70, 106
Clinton, Hillary Rodham, 6, 192
Clinton, William (Bill), 161, 178, 182, 188
Columbia Broadcasting Company; *See* CBS News
Columbia Journalism Review (CJR), 132, 134, 136
Commission on Freedom of the Press, 11
Communist Party USA, 13, 49–50, 55, 58–63, 87, 90, 115, 214n16, 215n43
Conservative Digest, 141, 144, 152–155, 157, 176
conservative identity, 2, 7, 9, 21, 71–73, 86, 142, 147, 148, 151–154, 181, 183
conservative movement, 2–4, 9, 102, 153, 159, 185, 193; and Accuracy in Media (AIM), 18; and activists, 3, 7, 15, 17, 25, 45, 73, 96, 112, 115, 138, 142, 151, 155, 188–189; and anticommunism, 4, 16; and Birchers, 16; and capitalism, 8; and celebrity culture, 188; and commentators, 102, 118, 191; and community pressure groups, 156; and conservative identity, 2, 7; and ideology, 75–76, 160; and media activism, 5–6, 15, 18, 44, 94; and New Deal opposition, 12; and policy, 8; and press criticism, 5–7, 9–10, 13–17, 19, 24, 94–96, 164, 231n90; and propaganda consciousness, 11; and respectability politics, 3, 8, 14, 20, 95–96, 193, 226n8; and social welfare liberalism, 12; strategy, 2, 18, 96; and "ultra" conservatives, 14, 84
conservatism, 4, 9, 42, 68, 108, 111, 116, 142, 162, 183–184, 226n8; and Accuracy in Media (AIM), 138, 159; and anticommunism, 8; and Barry Goldwater, 16; centrist, 53; and conflict with liberalism, 5; and constructivism, 14, 67–69, 72–73, 92; critics of, 2; and Facts Forum, 84, 86; fusionist, 3, 20, 94, 143, 187, 191; histories of, 2, 7, 105, 112, 203n23; and H. L. Hunt, 72; and ideology, 157; and liberal media, 48; and media, 69; and the New Deal, 11, 95; and the New Right, 18, 144, 148; as political identity, 147; and Richard M. Nixon, 151; and Robert A. Taft, 71; and Rush Limbaugh, 163, 181; and Turning Point USA, 190; ultra, 88; and universities, 143; and William F. Buckley Jr., 15–16, 92–93, 96
conspiracism, 6–7, 29, 42, 52–55, 59, 103, 121, 129, 178–179, 188
consumer cooperative movement, 28–32, 35–41, 210n32
Cooke, Janet, 18, 244n71
Correction Please, 99, 111, 228n28
Coulter, Ann, 98
Council Against Communist Aggression (CACA), 65, 122–124, 218n73
Council for National Policy, 159, 245n74
Counterattack, 13, 59, 61–63, 65, 74, 122, 124

Daily Caller, 189
Daily Signal, 189
Daily Wire, 190, 192
Daily Worker, 49, 62, 66, 87, 90
Dallas Morning News, 71, 74, 78, 82, 182–183
Dan Smoot Report, The, 98, 219n36
Democratic National Committee, 28, 164–166
Democratic Party, 105, 129; conservatism within, 92; and Dixiecrat Revolt, 77–78
de Toledano, Ralph, 55, 58, 64, 216n52
disinformation, 193
Dolan, Terry, 158–159, 244n71
Donnelly, Elaine, 177
Downey Jr., Morton, 161
Drudge Report, 188
Durbrow, Eldridge, 127–128
Dye, David W., 148–149

Eagle Forum, 155–157, 159, 164, 168, 176–177
Echo Chamber (Jamieson and Cappella), 20, 187
Editor & Publisher, 51, 107–108, 132–133

Edwards, Lee, 18, 144, 150,
Efron, Edith, 129, 154
Eggleston, George T., 53–54
Eisenhower, Dwight D., 71, 77–78, 88, 102, 220n50
Equal Rights Amendment (ERA), 8, 18, 147, 155, 168, 177, 244n73, 249n72
Ernst, Morris L., 10, 46–48, 65, 127–133, 138–140; and Accuracy in Media, 126–132, 236n53; and American Civil Liberties Union (ACLU), 44–45; and progressive media reform movement, 10, 44–48, 56. *See also The First Freedom*
Evans, Medford, 15, 68, 98, 143, 152
Evans, M. Stanton, 98, 143

Facts Forum, 14–16, 42, 64, 66–69, 73–78, 89, 91, 94, 165–166, 178, 181; and anticommunism, 85–86; and audience, 80–81; and broadcast programming, 82; and high schools, 79; and H. L. Hunt, 92, 97, 124; and impartiality, 150; and John Birch Society, 100; and letter-writing contests, 82–83; and polling, 82–86; and the press, 96, 142; and programming, 80, 95; and race, 79; and Robert Dedman, 90; and Robert Welch, 97–98; and *Time Magazine*, 90, 102
Facts Forum News, 81–82, 89–90, 96, 125, 143, 152
Fairness Doctrine, 35, 43, 160, 162–164, 171–174, 184–185; and Accuracy in Media (AIM), 167–170, 175, 177–178; and Carl McIntire, 23–24; and Facts Forum, 66, 73, 93, 115–116; and Federal Communications Commission (FCC), 11, 15, 25, 42, 64, 66, 73, 93, 147, 162, 165–167, 169–170, 176–177; and Fox News Channel, 20; and Mark S. Fowler, 19; and neutrality, 42; and New Deal Era, 41; and Rush Limbaugh, 19; and WXUR, 23–24
Fairness in Broadcasting Act of 1987, 162–163, 176–177, 179

Fairness and Accuracy in Reporting (FAIR), 252n18
Federal Bureau of Investigation (FBI), 13, 45–46, 59–63, 65, 73–76, 97–98, 132
Federal Communications Commission (FCC), 8, 183; and Accuracy in Media (AIM), 156, 167–170, 174–176, 181; and broadcast editorials, 73; and Carl McIntire, 23–24, 41–42; and complaints, 18, 121, 148; and conservatives, 16; founding of, 10; and Fulton Lewis Jr., 29, 31, 37–38; and James Lawrence Fly, 26, 40; and John Carson, 38–39; and license renewals, 154; and Mark S. Fowler, 19, 171, 173–175; and Mayflower Doctrine, 36–40, 69; and NBC News, 168–170; and newspapers, 11; and radio stations, 25–27; and radio transmissions, 22; and right-wing propaganda, 42; and Robert McCormick, 28; and Rush Limbaugh, 163; sanctions, 147; and Voice of Freedom Committee, 32–33. *See also* Fairness Doctrine
Federal Radio Commission, 23, 207n12
Firing Line, 94–95, 116, 121, 184
First Amendment, 24–26, 44, 46, 172, 174, 177
First Freedom, The (Ernst), 10, 46, 56, 128, 131, 236n47. *See also* Ernst, Morris L.
Forbes, 51
Fortune, 57, 70
Fowler, Mark S., 19, 156, 170–175
Fox News, 7, 20, 163, 178, 180, 183, 186–187, 189–190, 192–193
Fly, James Lawrence, 26, 28, 39–40, 208n14
Flynn, Elizabeth Gurley, 45
Flynn, John T., 142
Franke, David, 143
Frank, Reuven, 131–132, 237n58
freedom of expression, 26, 33–34, 44
freedom of the press, 11, 114, 135, 141, 174; and editorial freedom, 173
freedom of speech, 26, 46

freedom of thought, 46, 128, 130
Freedom Works, 187

Gay and Lesbian Alliance Against Defamation (GLAAD), 179
Ginzburg, Benjamin, 125–127, 234n33, 239n9
Gladwell, Malcolm, 98
Goldwater, Sen. Barry, 16, 42, 106, 112, 116, 145–146, 164–166, 184, 234n29
Gramsci, Antonio, 163, 180, 188, 250n84

Hamilton Combs, George, 93
Hanighen, Frank, 58
Hannity, Sean, 187
Hargis, Rev. Billy James, 14, 42, 116, 165–166
Harris, Kamala, 2
Harvey, Paul, 109, 149
Headlines and What's Behind Them, 13, 62
Heatter, Gabriel, 32–33
Hemenway, John D., 174
Hemmer, Nicole, 4, 15, 58, 68
Heritage Foundation, 159, 244n73; and *Townhall*, 188; and *Daily Signal*, 189
Hollenbeck, Don, 32
Hoover, J. Edgar, 13, 45, 63, 75, 213n11, 219n36
Hoover, Herbert, 209n27
Human Events, 13, 42, 48, 58, 98, 101, 106, 143, 184
Hunt, H. L., 14, 66, 80–83, 124, 151, 165; and anticommunism, 86–87; and Birchers, 146; and Facts Forum, 67–69, 74, 76, 79, 92, 97; and Fairness Doctrine, 73; life of, 69–72; and *Life Line*, 125, 184; and Robert Welch, 98
Hunt, Lyda, 97, 222n63, 227n24
Hunt, Nelson Bunker, 159
Huntington, John, 3
Hutchins Commission, 11
Hutchins, Robert M., 11

Ickes, Harold, 28
Institute for Propaganda Analysis, 11, 211n49, 238n76

Indianapolis Star, The, 98
In Fact, 49–52, 54–56, 59–64, 90, 99, 133, 163, 209n29, 217n64
Irvine, Reed J., 65, 121, 123–127, 139–140, 148, 150, 154, 156, 158–160, 168–170, 175–179, 181. *See also* Accuracy in Media (AIM)
Isaacs, Norman, 133

Jim Crow, 104–107, 222n64. *See also* segregation
John Birch Society, 3, 17, 104, 106, 109, 111, 115–116, 124, 142, 152, 164–165, 184, 187; and Alfred Kohlberg, 59; and anticommunism, 95; and Barry Goldwater, 114; and Dan Smoot, 98; and Medford Evans, 15; and media criticism, 100–104; and members, 100, 110; and Robert Welch, 16, 97, 101; and William F. Buckley, 69, 96, 103
Johnson, Lyndon B., 16, 112, 115, 146, 163–166
Jones, Jimmy C., 111, 230n84, 231n85
journalism, 49, 107–108, 135, 140, 148, 173, 183–184, 186, 189, 193–195; advocacy, 149, 167; and bias, 138; broadcast, 28; conservative, 69, 98, 158; and cultural authority, 2; high modern, 46, 146; leaders, 122; mainstream, 43, 69, 194; muckraking era of, 48; and professional organizations, 133; reform of, 11, 57, 114; "trust in," 18, 137

Kalish, Abraham, 127–128, 130–133, 136–137, 150, 153, 235nn37–39, 236n53, 237n58
Kaltenborn, H. V., 32–33
Kamp, Joseph, 13
Kennedy, John F., 16, 42, 108–109, 163–165, 173
Kennedy, Robert F., 41, 115, 120, 165
Kilpatrick, James J., 102, 106, 228n38
Kincaid, Cliff, 178–179, 250n81
Kirkpatrick, Ted "T.C.," 59–60, 65, 74, 218n73
Kirk, Charlie, 190
Kohlberg, Alfred, 59–60, 129, 227n23
Ku Klux Klan, 3, 38, 50, 82, 108

Lacy, Robert B., 28
laissez-faire capitalism, 4, 8, 75
Levine, Isaac Don, 59, 65, 216n58
Lewis Jr., Fulton, 28–32, 35–36, 41, 60, 93, 112, 142, 209nn27–29; and consumer cooperative movement, 28–32, 35–41; and Mayflower Doctrine, 33, 37–39; and Facts Forum, 68, 91; and John Birch Society, 101
Lewisville Leader, 184
liberalism, 4, 6, 33, 42, 72, 96, 161; popular front, 48; social, 34; social welfare, 12
"liberal media," 2, 4–7, 9, 48, 92, 94, 138, 152, 158, 160, 163, 178; bias, 2, 4, 7, 19, 44, 47, 64, 95, 107, 114, 120, 122, 125, 133–136, 138, 142, 144, 148, 153–155, 157–159, 180, 183, 195, 231n90; claim, 16–18, 21, 96, 117, 137, 230n72; criticism, 130; elite, 19; hegemony, 24; reform, 37, 45, 128, 236n53
libertarianism, 4, 12, 36, 41, 46–47, 126, 129, 142, 159, 171
Libertarian Party, 187
Life, 56, 69, 71, 107
Life Line, 125, 184
Limbaugh, Rush, 19–20, 142, 159, 161–164, 179–183, 185–188
Loos, Karl D., 31
Los Angeles Times, 2
Luce, Phillip Abbott, 131, 236n57
Lyons, Eugene, 47–48, 54, 55, 57–58, 60, 62, 64, 65, 103, 127, 216n51–52, 217n63; and Accuracy in Media, 127; and *American Mercury*, 58, 216n51; and George Seldes, 48, 54; and *New Leader*, 47, 55, 57–58; and *Plain Talk*, 60, 62, 65; and *National Review*, 64, 103, 216n52

mainstream media, 2, 4–6, 8, 56, 58, 73, 86, 95–96, 135, 148, 178, 184–185, 193–194; and bias, 43, 102, 120, 122, 155; and civil rights movement, 17; and conservative movement, 141; critical disposition toward, 20, 64, 67–69, 90, 92, 94, 99–100, 103, 124, 138, 142, 144, 157, 176, 180, 183, 186, 191; distrust of, 10, 14, 16, 43, 104, 113, 118, 154, 187; and Facts Forum, 15, 66, 85; and Fairness Doctrine, 172; and George Seldes, 50–51, 57; and liberal bias, 18, 91, 94, 137, 151, 163; and liberal perspective, 11; and New Right, 18. *See also* journalism, "liberal media"
Manion, Clarence, 15, 68, 91, 94, 101, 109, 165, 227n23
Manufacturing Consent (Herman and Chomsky), 178
Mayflower Doctrine, 26–27, 29–39, 69, 223n74
Mayflower hearings, 29, 33, 40, 44
McCabe, Ben, 30–31
McCain, John, 187
McCarthy, Sen. Joseph, 14, 61, 75, 77, 85–87, 89; McCarthyism, 13, 40, 48, 55, 85, 88, 95. *See also* Second Red Scare
McCormick, Colonel Robert, 27–28, 48–49, 58
McDowell, Arthur G., 124, 127, 183; and Council Against Communist Aggression, 65, 122
McDowell Luncheon Group, 65, 122, 124, 127
McGill, Ralph, 104, 109, 112
McGovern, George, 129
McIntire, Carl, 14, 22–24, 26, 41–42, 116, 163–165
Media Research Center, 159, 244n71
Medias Unlimited (see David W. Dye)
Meta, 1
Meyer, Frank, 143
Miller, George E., 82
Minton, Bruce, 49–50, 214n16
misinformation, 1, 31, 103, 106
MSNBC, 2, 186, 189
Murdoch, Rupert, 20, 186, 190–191, 251n11
Murphy, Ross, 30–31, 211n43
Musk, Elon, 1
Mutual Broadcasting System, 28, 37, 209n31

Nathan, George Jean, 53
Nation, The, 5, 27, 50, 56, 165
National Association for the Advancement of Colored People (NAACP), 37, 45

National Association of Broadcasters, 25, 36, 166, 173, 176
National Association of Manufacturers (NAM), 29–30, 52–53, 122, 209n29, 210n39
National Broadcasting Company (NBC), 17, 26, 112, 126, 129–131, 148–149, 154, 167–168, 175, 246n21, 247n32
National Committee to Uphold Constitutional Government, 37
National Conservative Foundation, 158
National Conservative Political Action Committee, 176
National Council for Civic Responsibility, 164
National Council of Farmer Cooperatives, 31, 37
National Empowerment Television (NET), 178, 185–186
National Farmers Union, 37
nationalism, 4, 56, 59, 98
National Journalism Center, 98
National News Council (NNC), 18, 121, 131, 135–138, 149, 238n79
National Press Club, 171
National Review, 5, 116–117, 127, 137, 143, 147, 150–152, 154, 162, 184, 190, 192; and Birchers, 101, 103; and colorblind racism, 105; and Eugene Lyons, 64; founding of, 2, 15; and George Seldes, 57; and H. L. Hunt, 68; and Medford Evans, 98; and M. Stanton Evans, 98; as movement media, 20; and press criticism, 95; and racial politics, 106; and Ralph de Toledano, 64; and Robert Welch, 16; and William F. Buckley Jr., 47, 93–94, 102; and William Rusher, 94
National Rifle Association, 176
National Tax Equality Association (NTEA), 30–31, 35, 210nn38–39, 211n44
Nazi Germany, 53–54
Nazis, 2, 29, 45, 52, 201n2
neoliberalism, 3, 13, 52, 54
New Deal, 3–4, 10–13, 26, 28–29, 34, 41–42, 49, 52, 64, 75, 95, 141, 146, 152, 171, 207n12,

208n14; anti–New Dealers, 11, 53, 58, 77, 216n51
New Leader, The, 47–48, 55–58, 60
New Republic, 5, 27, 49–50
News and Courier, 105
Newsmax, 188; TV, 20, 190, 193
newspapers; and advertisements, 53, 83; anticommunist, 17; and bias, 10, 63, 85, 99, 132; and Birchers, 102; chains, 10; community, 96; companies, 18; conservative, 53, 110; and "crisis," 10, 56; and editors, 16, 97, 133; and industry, 10–11, 46, 48, 133–134, 194; large circulation, 104; letters to, 81–82, 101, 123; local, 68, 74–77, 81, 83, 108, 111, 115, 118, 128, 184; mainstream, 120, 154; national, 148, 157; ownership of, 26, 47, 49–52; and presidential endorsements, 134; and radio stations, 26; as reactionary media, 9; rights of, 173; segregationist, 105; Southern, 106; student, 94, 159
New Masses, 49
New Republic, 5, 27, 49–50
Newsweek, 99–100, 135, 138, 154, 165–166, 243n54
New York Herald Tribune, 53
New York Times, The, 13, 15, 41, 104–105, 112, 126, 136, 138, 148–149, 171–172, 176, 179, 186, 193
New York Times Magazine, The, 2
New York World, 53, 165
Nixon, Richard M., 17, 44–45, 116–117, 119–121, 126, 129, 138–139, 142, 144, 150–152, 154, 186, 234n34
Nock, Albert Jay, 12, 15
Norris, David, 116–117
Norris, Dwight W., 100
Norris, John M., 166

Obama, Barack, 187, 189
One America News Network, 20, 190, 193
Owens, Candace, 190

paleoconservatism, 3, 192–193
Palmer, Paul, 11, 53–54
Panama Canal, 18, 153
Paper Curtain, 104–106, 110
Parker, Dorothy, 32
Patel, Neil, 189
Perlstein, Rick, 2–3
Phillips, Kevin, 19, 151–153, 241n37
Phyllis Schlafly Report, The, 155, 243n55
Pickard, Victor, 4, 24, 37, 46, 208n19
Plain Talk, 13, 48, 58–60, 62, 65, 74, 129, 216n52, 216n58
Popular Front, 12, 14, 45, 48, 49
progressive media reform movement, 4, 6, 11, 24–28, 32–34, 45, 55–56, 58, 64–65, 122, 133, 162, 211n49
propaganda, 11–14, 32, 34, 53, 90, 111, 113; communist, 57, 60, 74, 81; counter, 164; initiatives, 52; political, 28; reactionary, 27, 33, 54, 89; right-wing, 25–26, 42, 62, 67–68, 88; wartime, 58
propaganda consciousness, 9, 11
pseudo-conservatives, 4
Public Broadcasting Act of 1967, 173
public opinion, 7, 9, 12, 18, 32, 34, 49–50, 56, 62, 67, 72–73, 80, 82, 100, 104; polling, 71, 81, 83–85, 107, 134, 153; and Richard Nixon, 119
Public Opinion, 19

Reader's Digest, 45, 54, 59–60, 62, 205n45
Reagan Revolution, 2–3, 94, 144
Reagan, Ronald, 16, 19, 47, 94, 138, 141, 146, 156–164, 170–171, 173, 175–177, 182, 184, 186–187
Reason, 171–172
Red Channels, 13, 48, 61, 63, 124, 217n61, 233n22, 234n23
Red Lion Broadcasting, 166–168, 171, 174
Regnery, Henry, 15, 68, 94
Regnery, William H., 58
Republican Noise Machine, The (Brock), 6
Republican Party, 3, 8, 15, 20, 28, 77, 92, 105, 117, 142, 146, 151, 170, 181–184, 187, 192;

and Barry Goldwater, 42, 112, 114, 164; and conservative grassroots, 125; and George Wallace, 116; and John Tower, 143; and Vietnam War, 119
respectability politics, 3, 8, 14, 20, 95–96, 193, 226n8
Reuther, Walter, 41, 115, 165; Reuther Memo, 42, 115, 163, 165, 212n70–71
Review of the News, 17, 96–99, 111
Richmond News Leader, 102, 106
Right Side Broadcasting Network, 190
Rimanoczy, Richard Stanton, 12
Roosevelt, Franklin D., 10–11, 26, 28–29, 40, 52–53, 64, 133, 208n14
Rucker, Bryce W., 131
Rusher, William, 15, 68, 94, 137, 143, 150–151

Saturday Evening Post, 51
Schlafly, Phyllis, 8, 156, 167, 242n52, 243n54, 244n73, 249n72; and citizens agreements, 155–156, 243n58; and Eagle Forum, 112, 168, 177; and New Right, 18; and Fairness Doctrine, 177; *The Phyllis Schlafly Report*, 155
Schwarz, Dr. Fred, 16, 41, 91
Scott, Vernon, 30
Scribner's Commentator, 53–54, 58
Second Red Scare, 13, 55, 64; blacklisting, 13, 48, 61, 124, 217n61, 233n22; red-baiting, 13, 35, 39–40, 47, 50, 55–58, 63, 87, 216n48; McCarthy hearings, 95, 193. *See also* McCarthyism
segregation, 18, 45, 77–79, 82, 95, 102, 104–109, 112, 117
Seldes, George, 4, 10, 14, 29, 48–50, 52–53, 64, 209n29, 214n16; *In Fact*, 51, 54, 61–63; allegations of Communist Party affiliation, 14, 59–60, 65; and Eugene Lyons, 47, 60; and *The New Leader*, 55–58
Shapiro, Ben, 190, 192
Shreveport Times, 73

Smoot, Dan, 68, 80–81, 91, 101, 142, 165, 219n36, 227n24; and Facts Forum, 74–77, 89, 97–99, 166; and John Birch Society, 101
Sokolsky, George, 53, 102
Southern Strategy, 8, 117, 151,
Staggers, Harley, 127, 235n40
Stanton, Frank, 27
State of the Nation, 80
Stormer, John, 113

Taft, Sen. Robert A., 71, 77–78, 142–143, 220n50
Tea Party movement, 187–190, 251n17
Time, 66, 84–85, 90, 93, 97, 102, 105, 112, 120, 121, 138, 154, 166
Tolbert, Frank X., 71
Tower, John, 143
Truman, Harry, 45, 77, 133
Trump, Donald J., 1–3, 20, 183, 190–193
Turning Point USA, 190
TV Guide, 129, 154, 173
Twitter, 1–2, 189–190, 192

Union Leader, 105
United States Chamber of Commerce, 73, 76, 120, 133, 219n30

Viguerie, Richard, 18, 141–148, 150, 152–153, 157–159, 163, 176, 180–181, 185, 235n37, 239n3, 240nn17–18, 250n84
Villager, The, 128
Virginia Commission on Constitutional Government, 106
Voice of Freedom Committee (VOF), 32–34, 39, 211n46–47
Voorhis, Jerry, 32, 211n44

Walker, Edwin, 116
Wallace, DeWitt, 54

Wallace, George, 109, 113–114, 116–117, 184
Wallace, Henry A., 28
Wallace, Lurleen, 113
Wall Street Journal, The, 20, 186, 191
Waring, Thomas R., 105–106
Warren, Earl, 95, 102, 111, 226n11
Washington *Evening Star*, 123, 239n8
Washington Examiner, 191
Washington Free Beacon, 189
Washington Post, The, 1–2, 18, 126, 133, 136, 148–150, 172, 176, 191
Washington Times, The, 191
Weekly Standard, 190
Welch, Robert, 3, 16, 95, 97–104, 116; and *American Opinion*, 97–98, 227n21; and conspiracism, 102–103; and John Birch Society, 97, 100–102; and *National Review*, 16, 95; and *Review of the News*, 99; and William F. Buckley Jr., 116
Western Journalism Center, 159
Westmoreland, Gen. William C., 18
Weyrich, Paul, 18, 20, 159–160, 163, 176, 178, 185
White, Byron, 166–167
White, Dana, 1
white identity politics, 17, 193
white nationalists, 192
White Power movement, 3
white Southerners, 105–108, 117; Democrats, 112
white supremacists, 3, 95, 104–105
white supremacy, 8, 17, 96
White, Theodore H., 121, 134–135
Wysor, W. G., 31, 35–37, 212n57

Young Americans for Freedom, 16, 94, 143–144, 184

Zuckerberg, Mark, 1

GPSR Authorized Representative: Easy Access System Europe, Mustamäe tee 50, 10621 Tallinn, Estonia, gpsr.requests@easproject.com

www.ingramcontent.com/pod-product-compliance
Lightning Source LLC
Chambersburg PA
CBHW022041290426
44109CB00014B/937